Revisi

WorkBook

Evidence

Second Edition

EDITOR: B.L Raisbeck, LLB

REVISED AND UPDATED BY S. McKie, LLB, Barrister

HLT Publications

HLT PUBLICATIONS
200 Greyhound Road, London W14 9RY

First Edition 1991
Second Edition 1992

ISBN 0 7510 0006-X

British Library Cataloguing-in-Publication.

A CIP Catalogue record for this book is available from the British Library.

Printed and bound in Great Britain.

CONTENTS

Acknowledgement		v
Introduction		vii
Studying Evidence		ix
Revision and Examination Technique		xi
Table of Cases		xvii
Table of Statutes		xxxi
Chapters		
1	Introduction to Evidence	1
2	Evidence Illegally or Unfairly Obtained	4
3	Burdens and Standards of Proof	12
4	Competence and Compellability	28
5	Corroboration	39
6	Hearsay - General Exclusion	59
7	Hearsay - Statutory Admissibility in Civil Cases	76
8	Hearsay - Statutory Admissibility in Criminal Cases	91
9	Character Evidence	111
10	Similar Fact Evidence	132
11	Opinion Evidence	157
12	Public Policy	169
13	Privilege	182
14	Proof without Evidence	203
15	University of London LLB (External) 1991 Questions and Suggested Solutions	233

ACKNOWLEDGEMENT

Some questions used are taken or adapted from past University of London LLB (External) Degree examination papers and our thanks are extended to the University of London for their kind permission to use and publish the questions.

Caveat

The answers given are not approved or sanctioned by the University of London and are entirely our responsibility.

They are not intended as 'Model Answers', but rather as Suggested Solutions.

The answers have two fundamental purposes, namely:

a) To provide a detailed example of a suggested solution to an examination question, and

b) To assist students with their research into the subject and to further their understanding and appreciation of the subject of Laws.

INTRODUCTION

This Revision WorkBook has been designed specifically for those studying Evidence to undergraduate level. Its coverage is not confined to any one syllabus, but embraces all the major evidence topics to be found in university or polytechnic examinations, and will be of utility to students preparing for Bar Finals as the book covers that syllabus also.

However, since it is anticipated that many students will be intending to sit the University of London LLB external examinations, the questions used are primarily from past evidence papers from that course. Each chapter contains in its first few pages, brief notes explaining the scope and overall content of the topic covered in that chapter. There follows, in each case, a list of key points which will assist the student in studying and memorising essential material with which the student should be familiar in order to fully understand the topic.

Additionally in each chapter there will be a question analysis which will list and compare past examination questions on similar topics in evidence papers. Students are reminded that in order to derive maximum benefit from this WorkBook, they should possess a full set of past examination papers issued by University of London for this subject, for the years 1983-90 inclusive. The purpose of such a question analysis is to give an appreciation of the potential range of questions possible, and some idea of variations in wording, different formats in questions and alternative modes of combining different issues in one question.

Each chapter will end with several typical examination questions, together with skeleton solutions and suggested solutions. Wherever possible, the questions are drawn from University of London external evidence papers 1983-90. However it is inevitable that, in compiling a list of questions by topic order rather than chronologically, not only do the same questions crop up over and over again in different guises, but there are gaps where questions have never been set at all. Where a topic has never been covered in an examination question, a specimen question will have been written as an example, together with skeleton answer and suggested solution.

Undoubtedly, the main feature of this Revision WorkBook is the inclusion of as many past examination questions as possible. While the use of past questions as a revision aid is certainly not new, it is hoped that the combination of actual past questions from the University of London LLB external course and specially written questions, where there are gaps in examination coverage, will be of assistance to students in achieving a thorough and systematic revision of the subject.

Careful use of the Revision WorkBook should enhance the student's understanding of Evidence and, hopefully, enable him to deal with as wide a range of subject matter as anyone might find in an Evidence law examination, while at the same time allowing him to practise examination techniques while working through the book.

INTRODUCTION

In this revised 1992 edition a new final chapter has been inserted which contains the complete June 1991 University of London LLB (External) Evidence question paper, followed by suggested solutions to each question. Thus the student will have the opportunity to review a recent examination paper in its entirety, and can, if desired, use this chapter as a mock examination - referring to the suggested solutions only after first having attempted questions.

STUDYING EVIDENCE

The study of Evidence, whether as a first degree subject or for Bar examinations, requires an awareness that topics cannot be learned in isolation. Evidence is very closely integrated, in that very few topics can be compartmentalised; in most instances material studied at any one point will impinge upon and relate to materials studied at other points. Whatever the approach taken by lecturers, or authors of textbooks, on Evidence, there will invariably be cross-referencing.

In the early stages the subject will appear disjointed and difficult to rationalise and therefore understand; only towards the end of a course of study of the subject will the pieces of the jigsaw start to interlock. A recommended approach, therefore, is to read, several times, an introductory book on Evidence *before* beginning study of the subject in depth - thus acquiring a somewhat superficial but usefully coherent and cohesive awareness which will be invaluable when examining specific areas and relating them to others. The same introductory book can also be used to good effect as part of the revision process, to reinforce the 'lateral thinking' needed in Evidence.

Evidence is never taught as a first year undergraduate subject. Whether studying for a Law Degree or Bar Finals, an Evidence student must have some knowledge of law, especially Criminal Law, and of basic procedure (both criminal and civil) to excel in this adjectival subject. However, in Evidence examinations it is not detailed knowledge of substantive law which is required, but merely a very basic knowledge of substantive law and procedure, and detailed knowledge of the evidentiary issues involved. Evidence 'problem questions' may appear to require the examinees to deal with Criminal, Company, Tort, Contract Law etc, but the examiner is testing knowledge of Evidence - using as a realistic vehicle some criminal or other scenario.

In studying Evidence, therefore, the student must be aware of the integrated nature of the subject, be basically conversant with principles of substantive law; and be wary of concentrating on a few topics - as they might well be covered in only one or two examination questions!

REVISION AND EXAMINATION TECHNIQUE

(A) REVISION TECHNIQUE

Planning a revision timetable

In planning your revision timetable make sure you don't finish the syllabus too early. You should avoid leaving revision so late that you have to 'cram' - but constant revision of the same topic leads to stagnation.

Plan ahead, however, and try to make your plans increasingly detailed as you approach the examination date.

Allocate enough time for each topic to be studied. But note that it is better to devise a realistic timetable, to which you have a reasonable chance of keeping, rather than a wildly optimistic schedule which you will probably abandon at the first opportunity!

The syllabus and its topics

One of your first tasks when you began your course was to ensure that you thoroughly understood your **syllabus**. Check now to see if you can write down the **topics** it comprises from memory. You will see that the chapters of this WorkBook are each devoted to a syllabus topic. This will help you decide which are the key chapters relative to your revision programme. Though you should allow some time for glancing through the other chapters.

The topic and its key points

Again working from memory, analyse what you consider to be the key points of any topic that you have selected for particular revision. Seeing what you can recall, unaided, will help you to understand and firmly memorise the concepts involved.

Using the WorkBook

Relevant questions are provided for each topic in this book. Naturally, as typical examples of examination questions, they do not normally relate to one topic only. But the questions in each chapter *will* relate to the subject matter of the chapter to a degree. You can choose your method of consulting the questions and solutions, but here are some suggestions (strategies 1-3). Each of them pre-supposes that you have read through the author's notes on key points and question analysis, and any other preliminary matter, at the beginning of the chapter. Once again, you now need to practise working from *memory*, for that is the challenge you are preparing yourself for. As a rule of procedure constantly test yourself once revision starts, both orally and in writing.

Strategy 1

Strategy 1 is planned for the purpose of *quick revision*. First read your chosen question carefully and then jot down in abbreviated notes what you consider to be the main points at issue. Similarly, note the cases and statutes that occur to you as being relevant for citation purposes. Allow yourself sufficient time to cover what you feel to be relevant. Then study the author's *skeleton solution* and skim-read the *suggested solution* to see how they compare with your notes. When comparing consider carefully what the author has included (and concluded) and see whether that agrees with what you have written. Consider the points of variation also. Have you recognised the key issues? How relevant have you been? It is possible, of course, that you have referred to a recent case that *is* relevant, but which had not been reported when the WorkBook was prepared.

Strategy 2

Strategy 2 requires a nucleus of *three hours* in which to practise writing a set of examination answers in a limited time-span.

Select a number of questions (as many as are normally set in your subject in the examination you are studying for), each from a different chapter in the WorkBook, without consulting the solutions. Find a place to write where you will not be disturbed and try to arrange not to be interrupted for three hours. Write your solutions in the time allowed, noting any time needed to make up if you *are* interrupted.

After a rest, compare your answers with the *suggested solutions* in the WorkBook. There will be considerable variation in style, of course, but the bare facts should not be too dissimilar. Evaluate your answer critically. Be 'searching', but develop a positive approach to deciding how you would tackle each question on another occasion.

Strategy 3

You are unlikely to be able to do more than one three hour examination, but occasionally set yourself a single question. Vary the 'time allowed' by imagining it to be one of the questions that you must answer in three hours and allow yourself a limited preparation and writing time. Try one question that you feel to be difficult and an easier question on another occasion, for example.

Mis-use of suggested solutions

Don't try to learn by rote. In particular, don't try to reproduce the *suggested solutions* by heart. Learn to express the basic concepts in your own words.

Keeping up-to-date

Keep up-to-date. While examiners do not require familiarity with changes in the law during the three months prior to the examination, it obviously creates a good impression if you can show you are acquainted with any recent changes. Make a habit of looking through one of the leading journals - *Modern Law Review, Law Quarterly Review* or the *New Law Journal*, for example - and cumulative indices to law reports, such as the *All England Law Reports* or *Weekly Law Reports*, or indeed the daily law reports in *The Times*. The *Law Society's Gazette* and the *Legal Executive Journal* are helpful sources, plus any specialist journal(s) for the subject you are studying.

(B) EXAMINATION SKILLS

Examiners are human too!

The process of answering an examination question involves a *communication* between you and the person who set it. If you were speaking face to face with the person, you would choose your verbal points and arguments carefully in your reply. When writing, it is all too easy to forget *the human being who is awaiting the reply* and simply write out what one knows in the area of the subject! Bear in mind it is a person whose question you are responding to, throughout your essay. This will help you to avoid being irrelevant or long-winded.

The essay question

Candidates are sometimes tempted to choose to answer essay questions because they 'seem' easier. But the examiner is looking for thoughtful work and will not give good marks for superficial answers.

The essay-type of question may be either purely factual, in asking you to *explain the meaning* of a certain doctrine or principle, or it may ask you to *discuss* a certain proposition, usually derived from a quotation. In either case, the approach to the answer is the same. A clear programme must be devised to give the examiner the meaning or significance of the doctrine, principle or proposition and its origin in common law, equity or statute, and cases which illustrate its application to the branch of law concerned.

The problem question

The problem-type question requires a different approach. You may well be asked to advise a client or merely discuss the problems raised in the question. In either case, the most important factor is to take great care in reading the question. By its nature, the question will be longer than the essay-type question and you will have a number of facts to digest. Time spent in analysing the question may well save time later, when you are endeavouring to impress on the examiner the considerable extent of your basic legal knowledge. The quantity of knowledge is itself a trap and you must always keep within the boundaries of the question in hand. It is very tempting to show the examiner the extent of your knowledge of your subject, but if this is outside the question, it is time lost and no marks earned. It it inevitable that some areas which you have studied and revised will not be the subject of questions, but under no circumstances attempt to adapt a question to a stronger area of knowledge at the expense of relevance.

When you are satisfied that you have grasped the full significance of the problem-type question, set out the fundamental principles involved. You may well be asked to advise one party, but there is no reason why you should not introduce your answer by:

> 'I would advise A on the following matters ...'

and then continue the answer in a normal impersonal form. This is a much better technique than answering the question as an imaginary conversation.

You will then go on to identify the fundamental problem, or problems posed by the question. This should be followed by a consideration of the law which is relevant to the problem. The source of the law, together with the cases which will be of assistance in solving the problem, must then be considered in detail.

Very good problem questions are quite likely to have alternative answers, and in advising A you should be aware that alternative arguments may be available. Each stage of your answer, in this case, will be based on the argument or arguments considered in the previous stage, forming a conditional sequence.

If, however, you only identify one fundamental problem, do not waste time worrying that you cannot think of an alternative - there may very well be only that one answer.

The examiner will then wish to see how you use your legal knowledge to formulate a case and how you apply that formula to the problem which is the subject of the question. It is this positive approach which can make answering a problem question a high mark earner for the student who has fully understood the question and clearly argued his case on the established law.

Examination checklist

1 Read the instructions at the head of the examination carefully. While last-minute changes are unlikely - such as the introduction of a *compulsory question* or *an increase in the number of questions asked* - it has been known to happen.

2 Read the questions carefully. Analyse problem questions - work out what the examiner wants.

3 Plan your answer *before* you start to write. You can divide your time as follows:

   (a) working out the question (5 per cent of time)

   (b) working out how to answer the question (5 to 10 per cent of time)

   (c) writing your answer

Do not overlook (a) and (b)

4 Check that you understand the rubric *before* you start to write. Do not 'discuss', for example, if you are specifically asked to 'compare and contrast'.

5 Answer the correct number of questions. If you fail to answer one out of four questions set you lose 25 per cent of your marks!

Style and structure

Try to be clear and concise. Basically this amounts to using paragraphs to denote the sections of your essay, and writing simple, straightforward sentences as much as possible. The sentence you have just read has 22 words - when a sentence reaches 50 words it becomes difficult for a reader to follow.

Do not be inhibited by the word 'structure' (traditionally defined as giving an essay a beginning, a middle and an end). A good structure will be the natural consequence of setting out your arguments and the supporting evidence in a logical order. Set the scene briefly in your opening paragraph. Provide a clear conclusion in your final paragraph.

TABLE OF CASES

R *v* Abadom [1983] 1 WLR 126; [1983] 1 All ER 364 CA	79, 159, 167, 179
Abrath *v* North Eastern Railway Co (1886) 11 App Cas 247; (1883) 11 QBD 440	85, 87, 224
R *v* Acton Justices, ex parte McMullen (1991) 92 Cr App R 98	97
R *v* Adams [1980] QB 575	10
A-G *v* Mulholland [1963] 2 QB 477	173
A-G of Hong Kong *v* Yip Kai-Foon [1988] 2 WLR 326; [1988] 1 All ER 153	151
R *v* Agar (1990) 90 Cr App R 318	170, 173, 175, 178, 181, 243
Agassiz *v* London Tramway Co (1872) 21 WR 199	79, 126
Air Canada *v* Secretary of State for Trade (No 2) [1983] 2 AC 394; [1983] 1 All ER 910 HL	169, 173, 174, 180, 189, 243
Ajodha *v* The State [1982] AC 204; [1981] 2 All ER 193	99, 103
Alexander *v* Rayson [1936] 1 KB 169	225
Alfred Crompton Amusement Machines Ltd *v* Customs and Excise Commissioners (No 2) [1974] AC 405	173, 175, 180, 196
R *v* Alladice [1988] Crim LR 608; (1988) 87 Cr App R 380; [1987] NLJR 141	5, 10, 74, 93, 105, 106, 148, 176, 236, 238
R *v* Anderson [1988] QB 678; [1988] 2 All ER 549	113, 133, 155, 238, 239, 241
R *v* Andrews [1987] AC 281; [1987] 1 All ER 513	63, 66, 68, 107, 140, 163, 252, 253, 254
R *v* Apicella (1985) 82 Cr App R 295	9
Ashburton (Lord) *v* Pape [1913] 2 Ch 469	184, 193, 249
R *v* Ataou [1988] QB 798; [1988] 2 All ER 321	184
R *v* B County Council, ex parte P [1991] 2 All ER 65	77
R *v* Bainbridge (1991) The Times 25 January	112
Balabel *v* Air India [1988] Ch 317; [1988] 2 All ER 246	183
R *v* Baldwin [1986] Crim LR 68130	33
R *v* Ball [1983] 1 WLR 801; [1983] 2 All ER 1089	217
Banbury Peerage Case, The (1811) 1 Sim & St 153	212, 226, 228
R *v* Barker [1941] 2 KB 381	9, 75, 104
Barkway *v* South Wales Transport Executive [1949] 1 KB 54	245
R *v* Barrett (1991) 92 Cr App R 61	92, 148
R *v* Barrington [1981] 1 WLR 419	133, 152, 256, 257
R *v* Barton [1973] 1 WLR 115	184, 193
R *v* Baskerville [1916] 2 KB 658	39, 44, 46, 57, 127, 251
R *v* Bass [1953] 1 QB 680	50

Bater *v* Bater [1951] P 35 85, 89
Bates (Thomas) & Son *v* Wyndham's Lingeries Ltd
[1981] 1 WLR 505; [1981] 1 All ER 1077 85
R *v* Bathurst [1968] 2 QB 99 50, 255
R *v* Beck [1982] 1 WLR 461 42, 152
R *v* Bedingfield (1879) 14 Cox CC 341 63, 66, 68, 107
Berryman *v* Wise (1791) 4 Term Rep 366 214
Bilbie *v* Lumley (1802) 2 East 469 220
R *v* Birtles (1911) 6 Cr App R 177 206
R *v* Bishop [1975] QB 274 114, 127, 129
Blake *v* Albion Life Assurance Society (1878) 4 CPD 94 144
R *v* Blastland [1986] AC 41; [1985] 2 All ER 1095 59, 67, 107, 153, 154, 255
Blunt *v* Park Lane Hotel [1942] 2 KB 253 192
Blyth *v* Blyth [1966] AC 643 47, 85, 209, 232
Boardman *v* Phipps [1967] 2 AC 46 87
R *v* Bond [1906] 2 KB 389 144
R *v* Boyes (1861) 30 LJ QB 301; 1 B & S 311 122, 190, 192
R *v* Boyson [1991] Crim LR 274 112
R *v* Bradford Justices, ex parte Wilkinson [1990] RTR 59 33, 37
R *v* Bradley (1980) 70 Cr App R 200 151
R *v* Bradshaw (1986) 82 Cr App R 79 167
Brandao *v* Barnett (1846) 12 Cl & Fin 787 220
Bratty *v* Attorney-General for Northern Ireland [1963] AC 386;
[1961] 3 All ER 523 47, 245
British Steel Corporation *v* Granada TV [1982] AC 1096;
[1980] 3 WLR 774; [1981] 1 All ER 417 171, 173, 174, 182, 196
R *v* Britzman; R *v* Hall [1983] 1 WLR 350;
[1983] 1 All ER 369; (1983) 76 Cr App R 134 115, 117, 120, 121, 123, 124, 127, 129, 130, 240
Broadhurst *v* R [1964] AC 441; [1964] 1 All ER 111 44
R *v* Brooks (1991) 92 Cr App R 36 133, 146
Broome *v* Broome [1955] P 190 173, 175
R *v* Brown (1991) The Times 13 December 42, 58, 152
R *v* Brown and Daley (1988) 87 Cr App R 52 170
Brown *v* Matthews [1990] 2 All ER 155 171, 175
R *v* Bryant [1979] QB 108 112, 114
R *v* Buckley (1873) 13 Cox CC 293 64, 66
Buckinghamshire County Council *v* Moran [1989] 3 WLR 152 186
R *v* Burke (1985) 82 Cr App R 156 127, 128, 129, 131
Burmah Oil *v* Bank of England [1980] AC 1090;
[1979] 3 WLR 722 HL; [1979] 3 All ER 700 169, 173, 174, 180, 189, 243
Burr *v* Ware RDC [1939] 2 All ER 688 89, 183
R *v* Butler (1987) 84 Cr App 12 133, 134, 155

R *v* Butterwasser [1948] 1 KB 4 240
Butler *v* Board of Trade [1971] Ch 680 185, 193
Buttes Gas and Oil *v* Hammer (No 3) [1981] 1 QB 223 170

Calcraft *v* Guest [1898] 1 QB 759 184, 193, 247, 249
Callis *v* Gunn [1964] 1 QB 495 9
R *v* Carr-Briant [1943] KB 607 15, 24, 26, 53, 216
R *v* Carrington [1990] Crim LR 330 134
R *v* Chance [1988] QB 932; [1988] 3 All ER 225 39, 41, 58, 251
R *v* Chandler [1976] 1 WLR 585; [1976] 3 All ER 105 45, 50, 54, 68, 95
Chandler *v* DPP [1964] AC 763 50
Chandrasekera *v* R [1937] AC 220 71, 252, 254
R *v* Chard (1971) 56 Cr App R 268 CA 158, 163, 253, 255
Chard *v* Chard [1956] P 259 206, 209, 226, 228
R *v* Charles (1976) 68 Cr App R 334 45
Chipchase *v* Chipchase [1939] P 391 209, 230
Chocoladefabriken Lindt *v* The Nestlé Co Ltd [1978] RPC 287 194
R *v* Christie [1914] AC 545 139
R *v* Chung (1991) 92 Cr App R 314 93
R *v* Cole [1990] 2 All ER 108 96, 254
Conway *v* Rimmer [1968] AC 910 169, 172, 174, 180, 196, 242, 243
R *v* Coulman (1927) 20 Cr App R 106 240
R *v* Courtnell [1990] Crim LR 115 51
R *v* Cox and Railton (1884) 14 QBD 153 183, 184, 193
R *v* Cramp (1880) 14 Cox CC 390 42, 54, 55, 68
R *v* Crampton (1991) 92 Cr App R 369 93, 105
R *v* Cresswell (1876) 1 QBD 446 214
R *v* Cross (1990) 91 Cr App R 115 18
R *v* Crown Court at Snaresbrook, ex parte DPP [1988] 1 All ER 315 183, 193
R *v* Cruttenden [1991] 3 All ER 242 31
R *v* Cullinane [1984] Crim LR 420 57
Customs and Excise Commissioners *v* Harz & Power [1967] 1 AC 760 147

D *v* NSPCC [1978] AC 171; [1977] 1 All ER 589 169, 170, 172, 173, 175, 178, 179, 180, 186, 190, 194, 196, 242, 243
D (a minor), Re [1986] 2 FLR 189 77
D (infants), Re [1970] 1 WLR 599 179
Davey *v* Harrow Corporation [1958] 1 QB 60 219
R *v* Davies [1962] 1 WLR 1111; [1962] 3 All ER 97 79, 160, 165
Davies *v* DPP [1954] AC 378 41, 50, 52, 57, 100, 150, 153
R *v* Deacon [1973] 1 WLR 696 188
R *v* Deacon [1987] Crim LR 404 8

Derby & Co Ltd *v* Weldon (No 8) [1990] 3 All ER 762 184, 185, 193
R *v* Donovan [1934] 2 KB 498 20
R *v* Dowley [1983] Crim LR 168 42, 46
DPP *v* A and BC Chewing Gum [1968] 1 QB 159 159, 167
DPP *v* Blake (1989) 89 Cr App R 179 93
DPP *v* Boardman [1975] AC 421 HL; [1974] 3 All ER 887 102, 118, 120, 121, 132, 133, 136, 142, 143, 144, 145, 146, 148, 152, 155, 166, 168, 249, 256
DPP *v* Kilbourne [1973] AC 296 44
DPP *v* Marshall [1988] 3 All ER 683 8, 176
DPP *v* Ping Lin [1976] AC 574 147
DPP *v* Smith [1961] AC 290 217
DPP *v* United Telecasters Ltd (1990) 91 ALR 1 16
Duff Development Co *v* Government of Kelantan [1924] AC 797 219, 221
R *v* Dunbar [1958] 1 QB 1 53
Duncan *v* Cammell Laird [1942] AC 624 169, 172, 180, 196, 242, 243
R *v* Dunkley [1927] 1 KB 323 240

R *v* Edwards [1975] QB 27 13, 14, 15, 16, 17, 21, 23, 24, 26, 216, 225
R *v* Edwards [1991] NLJ 91 112
Ellis *v* Home Office [1953] 2 QB 135 173, 175
Emmanuel *v* Emmanuel [1946] P 115 218
R *v* Evans [1965] 2 QB 295 42

Fay *v* Prentice (1845) 14 LJ CP 298 219, 221
Folkes *v* Chadd & Ors (1782) 3 Doug 157 163
Ford *v* Lewis [1971] 2 All ER 983 198
R *v* Foster [1984] 3 WLR 401 160-1
R *v* Fowler (1988) 86 Cr App R 219 151
Fox *v* Chief Constable of Gwent [1985] 3 All ER 392 10
Francis & Francis *v* Central Criminal Court [1988] 3 All ER 775 183
R *v* Fulling [1987] QB 426; [1987] 2 All ER 65 73, 92, 93, 105, 108, 147
R *v* Funderburk [1990] 2 All ER 482 84

Gain *v* Gain [1961] 1 WLR 1469 173
R *v* Galbraith [1981] 1 WLR 103; [1981] 2 All ER 1060 18, 47, 120, 225
R *v* Gallagher [1974] 1 WLR 1204; [1974] 3 All ER 118 50
R *v* Garbett (1847) 1 Den CC 236 192
Gaskin *v* Liverpool City Council [1980] 1 WLR 1549 179
Gatty & Gatty *v* Attorney-General [1951] P 444 209
R *v* Gaynor [1988] Crim LR 242 5, 10
R *v* Geering (1849) 18 LJMC 215 137

Gibson *v* Wales [1983] 1 WLR 393	204
Gilbey *v* GWR Co (1910) 102 LT 202	88
R *v* Gilbert (1977) 66 Cr App R 237	54
R *v* Gill [1963] 1 WLR 841	236, 237, 245
R *v* Gill and Ranuana [1989] Crim LR 358	6, 8
Goddard *v* Nationwide Building Society [1986] 3 WLR 734	194, 249
R *v* Goldenberg (1989) 88 Cr App R 285	93
R *v* Golder [1960] 1 WLR 1169; [1960] 3 All ER 457	84
R *v* Goodwin (1989) The Independent 23 November	244
R *v* Governor of Pentonville Prison, ex parte Osman [1989] 3 All ER 701	184
R *v* Graham [1973] Crim LR 628	50
R *v* Grannel (1989) Times 16 August CA	94, 105
R *v* Grant [1960] Crim LR 424	20
Gray *v* Barr [1970] 2 QB 626	85
Great Atlantic Insurance Co *v* Home Insurance Co [1981] 1 WLR 529; [1981] 2 All ER 485	189
Guiness Peat Properties *v* Fitzroy Robinson [1987] 1 WLR 1027; [1987] 2 All ER 716	184, 201, 249
H *v* Schering Chemicals Ltd [1983] 1 WLR 143; [1983] 1 All ER 849 QBD	77, 80, 81, 86, 197, 248
R *v* Hagan (1873) 12 Cox CC 357	126
Halford *v* Brookes (1991) The Times 1 October	25, 26, 82, 89, 199
Hall *v* R [1971] 1 WLR 298; [1971] 1 All ER 322	45, 54, 55, 68, 95, 110
R *v* Hallett [1986] Crim LR 462	178
R *v* Hampshire County Council, ex parte Ellerton [1985] 1 WLR 749	85, 199
R *v* Hardy (1794) 24 State Trials 199	170
Hargreave *v* Spink [1892] 1 QB 25	220
Harmony Shipping Co *v* Saudi Europe Line [1979] 1 WLR 1380	158, 168
R *v* Harris (1986) 84 Cr App R 75	54
Harris *v* DPP [1952] AC 694 HL	137
R *v* Harry (1988) 86 Cr App R 105	60, 70, 71, 254
Hart *v* Lancs & Yorks Rail Co (1869) 21 LT 261	89
R *v* Harvey [1988] Crim LR 241	93, 105
R *v* Harwood [1989] Crim LR 285	8, 236, 237
R *v* Hayes [1977] 1 WLR 234; [1977] 2 All ER 288	29
Hehir *v* Commissioner of Police for the Metropolis [1982] 1 WLR 715	175
Helliwell *v* Piggott-Sims [1980] FSR 582	4, 236, 249
R *v* Hennessey (1978) 68 Cr App R 419	178
R *v* Hepworth & Fearnley [1955] 2 QB 600	151, 217
R *v* Hill (1851) 2 Den 254	166
R *v* Hills (1988) 86 Cr App R 26	57
Hill *v* Baxter [1958] 1 QB 277	24, 207

Hollington *v* Hewthorn [1943] KB 587	160
Home Office *v* Harman [1983] AC 280; [1982] 1 All ER 532	196
R *v* Horn (1912) 7 Cr App R 200	20
Hornal *v* Neuberger Products Ltd [1957] 1 QB 247; [1956] 3 All ER 970	25, 26, 82, 85, 87, 89, 199, 247, 250
R *v* Horne [1990] Crim LR 188	42
Hoskyn *v* Metropolitan Police Commissioner [1979] AC 474	33, 34, 36
Howe *v* Malkin (1878) 40 LT 196	63
R *v* Hubbard (1991) The Times 15 January	30
R *v* Hughes (1949) 33 Cr App R 59	73
R *v* Hunt [1987] AC 352; [1987] 1 All ER 1	12, 13, 14, 15, 16, 17, 18, 19, 20, 21, 22, 23, 24, 25, 26
Hunter *v* Chief Constable of the West Midlands Police [1982] AC 529; [1981] 3 All ER 727	161
Hurst *v* Evans [1917] 1 KB 352	85
R *v* Hutchinson (1822) 2 B & C 608 n	162
Huyton-with-Roby UDC *v* Hunter [1955] 1 WLR 603, 609	218
R *v* Inch (1990) 91 Cr App R 51	158
R *v* Inder (1977) 67 Cr App R 143	152
Ingram *v* Percival [1969] 1 QB 548	205, 223
Inquiry under the Company Securities (Insider Dealing) Act 1985, Re [1988] 1 All ER 203	186
R *v* Ismail [1990] Crim LR 109	92
ITC Film Distributors *v* Video Exchange [1982] Ch 431	4, 7, 184, 193
R *v* Jackson [1953] 1 WLR 591	53, 54, 155, 252
James *v* R (1970) 55 Cr App R 299	44, 55
R *v* Jarvis and Jarvis [1991] Crim LR 374	49
Jayesena *v* R [1970] AC 618	47
Jeffrey *v* Black [1978] QB 490	7, 9
R *v* Jenkins (1945) 31 Cr App R 1	129
R *v* Johanssen (1977) 65 Cr App R 101	133, 136, 152, 256
R *v* John [1973] Crim LR 113	140
John *v* Humphreys [1955] 1 WLR 325; [1955] 1 All ER 793	21, 25
R *v* Johnson [1961] 1 WLR 1478	50, 245
R *v* Johnson [1989] 1 All ER 121	170, 181
Jones *v* DPP [1962] AC 635; [1962] 1 All ER 569	113, 117, 130, 238, 239
Jones *v* Livox Quarries [1952] 2 QB 608	198-9
Jones *v* Metcalfe [1967] 1 WLR 1286	110
Jones *v* South Eastern Railway (1918) 87 LJKB	127
Joseph Hargreaves Ltd, Re [1900] 1 Ch 347	175

Kajala *v* Noble (1982) 75 Cr App R 749	87
R *v* Kearley [1991] Crim LR 282	60, 70
R *v* Keeling [1942] 1 All ER 507	54, 110
R *v* Keenan [1990] 2 QB 54; [1989] Crim LR 720	6, 10, 73, 74, 236, 238
R *v* Kelly (1985) Times 27 July	33, 37
R *v* Kempster (1990) 90 Cr App R 14	161
R *v* Khan (1987) 84 Cr App R 44	34
R *v* Khan [1991] Crim LR 51	130
King *v* R [1969] 1 AC 304	9
R *v* King [1967] 2 QB 338; [1967] 1 All ER 379	46, 144
Kinsella *v* Marshall (1988) The Times 19 April	237
Kite, The [1933] P 154	245
R *v* Knight (1960) 50 Cr App R 122	55
Konigsberg, Re [1989] 3 All ER 289	184
Kuruma *v* R [1955] AC 197	141, 236
R *v* Lake (1977) 64 Cr App R 172	96
R *v* Lamb (1980) 71 Cr App R 198	51
R *v* Lanfear [1968] 2 QB 77	158
Langham *v* Governors of Wellingborough School [1932] LJ KB 513	245
R *v* Lasseur [1991] Crim LR 53	114, 240
La Roche *v* Armstrong [1922] 1 KB 485	194
R *v* Leatham (1861) 8 Cox CC 498	4, 7, 9
R *v* Lee [1976] 1 WLR 71	114, 130
R *v* Levy [1987] Crim LR 48	112
R *v* Lewes JJ [1973] AC 388	172, 173
R *v* Lewis (1982) 76 Cr App R 33	146
R *v* Lewis [1989] Crim LR 61	203
R *v* Lillyman [1896] 2 QB 167	49, 251
R *v* List [1966] 1 WLR 9; [1965] 3 All ER 710	144
R *v* Lobell [1957] 1 QB 547	15, 245
R *v* Lovell [1990] Crim LR 111	42
Lowery *v* R [1974] AC 85	158, 159, 163, 168, 253, 255
R *v* Lucas [1981] QB 720	42, 47, 52, 66-7, 100, 251, 252
R *v* Lumley (1869) LR 1 CCR 196	214
R *v* Lunt (1987) 85 Cr App R 241	133, 155
R *v* Lydon (1987) Crim LR 407	164
R *v* McCay [1990] Crim LR 338	64, 141, 163, 252
R *v* McGranaghan (1991) The Times 1 November	134, 142
R *v* McGovern (1991) 92 Cr App R 228	93
R *v* McIvor [1987] Crim LR 409	106
R *v* McLean (1968) 52 Cr App R 80	110
McQuaker *v* Goddard [1940] 1 KB 687	204
M'Naghten's Case (1843) 10 Cl & Fin 200	14, 20, 26, 165, 216, 225
Mahadervan *v* Mahadervan [1964] P 233	208-9, 209

Makin *v* Attorney General for New South Wales
[1894] AC 57 PC 132, 136, 239, 256
Malindi *v* R [1967] AC 439 122, 123
Mancini *v* DPP [1942] AC 1 15, 16, 51, 245
R *v* Manji [1990] Crim LR 512 94
Marks *v* Beyfus (1890) 25 QBD 494 102, 173, 174, 175, 181, 242, 243
R *v* Marr (1990) 90 Cr App R 154 112
R *v* Marshall [1977] Crim LR 106 153
R *v* Masih [1986] Crim LR 395 255
R *v* Mason (1911) 7 Cr App R 67 179
R *v* Mason [1988] 1 WLR 139;
[1987] 3 All ER 481 5, 7, 8, 10, 72, 73, 94,
104, 142, 148, 176, 236, 237
R *v* Mathias (1989) 139 NLJ 1417 31
R *v* Mattison [1990] Crim LR 117 161
Matto *v* Crown Court at Wolverhampton [1987] RTR 337 5, 10
Maxwell *v* DPP [1935] AC 309 114, 240
Miller *v* Minister of Pensions [1947] 2 All ER 372 26
R *v* Mitchell (1892) 17 Cox CC 503 252
Mole *v* Mole [1951] P 21 186
Monckton *v* Tarr (1930) 23 BWCC 504 207
Monroe *v* Twistleton (1802) Peak Add Cas 30
Mood Music Publishing Co Ltd *v* De Wolfe Publishing Ltd
[1976] 1 Ch 119; [1976] 1 All ER 463 81, 135, 201
Morris *v* Davies (1837) 5 Cl & Fin 163 27, 246
Morris *v* Stratford-on-Avon RDC [1973] 1 WLR 1059;
[1973] 3 All ER 263 89, 198
Munro Brice & Co *v* War Risks Association [1918] 2 KB 78 85
Murdoch *v* Taylor [1965] AC 574;
[1965] 1 All ER 406 74, 115, 117, 119, 128,
130, 156, 168, 239, 241
R *v* Murphy [1965] NI 138 8
R *v* Mutch [1973] 1 All ER 178 30, 33, 53, 156
Myers *v* DPP [1965] AC 1001 49, 61, 66, 68, 69, 70, 71, 109, 139

R *v* Nagy [1990] Crim LR 187 44
Nance *v* British Columbia Electric Railway Co
[1951] AC 601; [1951] 2 All ER 448 198
Naylor *v* Preston Area Health Authority [1987] 1 WLR 958 160
Neilson *v* Laugharne [1981] 1 QB 736 175, 201
R *v* Nelson (1978) 68 Cr App R 12 114, 121, 123
Nembhard *v* R [1982] 1 All ER 183 66
R *v* Newton & Carpenter (1859) 1 F & F 641 162
Ng Chun Pui *v* Lee Chuen Tat (1988) The Times 25 May 245
Nimmo *v* Alexander Cowan & Sons Ltd [1968] AC 107 15, 21
Noor Mohamed *v* R [1949] AC 182; [1949] 1 All ER 365 152, 188

Normanshaw *v* Normanshaw (1894) 69 LT 468	190
R *v* Norton [1910] 2 KB 496	139
R *v* Novac (1976) 65 Cr App R 107	133, 136, 152, 257
R *v* Nye & Loan (1977) 66 Cr App R 252	140
R *v* Oakwell [1978] 3 All ER 1233	117
R *v* O'Donnell (1917) 12 Cr App R 219	44
R *v* Ollis [1900] 2 QB 758	144
R *v* Osborne [1905] 1 KB 551	46, 127, 251
R *v* Osbourne; R *v* Virtue [1973] 1 QB 678	71, 140, 141, 163, 251, 252
R *v* Owen (1986) 83 Cr App R 100	115
R *v* Oyesiku (1971) 56 Cr App R 240	127
R *v* P (1991) 93 Cr App R 267	134, 136, 146, 149, 166, 249
Paddock *v* Forrester (1842) 3 Man & G 903	191
Parkes *v* R [1976] 1 WLR 1251; [1976] 3 All ER 380	45, 54, 68, 95
R *v* Parris (1988) Times 2 November	5
R *v* Payne [1963] 1 All ER 848	237
Peach v Commissioner of Police for the Metropolis [1986] QB 1064; [1986] 2 All ER 129	175, 185
R *v* Peach [1990] 2 All ER 966	40
R *v* Pearce (1979) 69 Cr App R 365	118, 138, 139
Peete, Re, Peete *v* Crompton [1952] 2 All ER 599	206
R *v* Perry [1909] 2 KB 697	68, 107
R *v* Perry [1984] Crim LR 680	135, 151, 155
Phene's Trusts, Re (1870) 5 Ch App 139	230
Piermay Shipping Co *v* Chester [1978] 1 WLR 411	90
Piers *v* Piers (1849) 2 HL Cas 331	206, 208, 228, 246
R *v* Pike (1829) 3 C & P 598	66, 107
R *v* Podola [1960] 1 QB 325	20
R *v* Powell [1986] 1 All ER 193; [1985] 1 WLR 1364	121, 124, 127, 129, 131, 239, 240
R *v* Prager [1972] 1 WLR 260	73
R *v* Prater [1960] 2 QB 464	41, 156
Preston-Jones *v* Preston-Jones [1951] AC 391	27
Prudential Assurance Co *v* Edmonds (1877) 2 AC 487	209, 246
R *v* Putland [1946] 1 All ER 85	22
R *v* Quinn [1990] Crim LR 581	5, 6, 10, 176
R *v* Rance; R *v* Herron (1975) 62 Cr App R 118	137
R *v* Rankine [1986] QB 861; [1986] 2 All ER 566	170, 178, 181, 243
Rasool *v* West Midlands Passenger Transport Executive [1974] 3 All ER 638	81
Ratten *v* R [1972] AC 378	60, 65, 69, 70, 107, 140, 163, 252, 253, 254

R *v* Redd [1923] 1 KB 104 113, 238, 239
R *v* Redgrave (1981) 74 Cr App R 10 168
R *v* Redpath (1962) 46 Cr App R 139 55, 251
R *v* Reid (1990) 90 Cr App R 121 51
Reynolds *v* Llanelly Associated Tinplate Co [1948] 1 All ER 140 222
R *v* Reynolds [1989] Crim LR 220 255
R *v* Rhodes [1899] 1 QB 77 53
R *v* Rice [1963] 1 QB 857 69, 70, 71, 164
R *v* Rimmer & Beech [1983] Crim LR 250 158
Rio Tinto Zinc Corporation *v* Westinghouse Electric Corporation [1978] AC 547; [1978] 1 All ER 434 182, 190, 192
R *v* Roberts [1942] 1 All ER 187 126
R *v* Robertson [1968] 1 WLR 1767 20
R *v* Robertson; R *v* Golder [1987] QB 920; [1987] 3 All ER 231 161
Rogers *v* Home Secretary [1973] AC 388 170, 196
R *v* Rouse [1904] 1 KB 184 129, 240
R *v* Rowson [1985] 2 All ER 539 74
R *v* Rowton (1865) 34 LJMC 57; Le and Car 520 117, 154, 168, 238, 239, 240, 241, 256, 258
R *v* Rudd (1948) 32 Cr App R 138 74
Rush & Tompkins *v* GLC [1988] 3 WLR 939 194

R *v* Samuel (1956) 40 Cr App R 8 114
R *v* Samuel [1988] 2 WLR 920; [1988] 2 All ER 135 5, 10, 94, 102, 106, 148, 176, 236, 237
R *v* Sanders (1991) 93 Cr App R 245 167
R *v* Sang [1980] AC 402 5, 6, 7, 9, 102, 142, 147, 236
Sastry Velaider Aronegary *v* Sambecutty Vailalie (1881) 6 App Cas 364 228, 246
R *v* Sat-Bhambra [1988] Crim LR 453 93, 105
Savings & Investment Bank *v* Gasco Investments [1984] 1 WLR 271; [1984] 1 All ER 296 Ch D 81, 86, 197
R *v* Scarrott [1978] QB 1016 CA 39, 133, 136, 152, 249, 256
Science Research Council *v* Nassé [1980] AC 1028; [1979] 3 WLR 762 171, 173, 196
R *v* Secretary of State for the Home Department, ex parte Khajawa [1984] AC 74 85
Secretary of State for Defence *v* Guardian Newspapers [1984] 3 WLR 986; [1984] 3 All ER 601 181, 186, 196
R *v* Seaman (1978) 67 Cr App R 234 133
R *v* Seighley (1911) 6 Cr App R106 156
Selvey *v* DPP [1970] AC 304; [1968] 2 All ER 497 114, 115, 117, 119, 124, 129, 178, 240
Sharples *v* Halford (1991) The Times 9 October 170
Shenton *v* Tyler [1939] Ch 620 30
R *v* Shepherd [1904] 1 Ch 456 232

R *v* Shone (1983) 76 Cr App R 72 71
R *v* Silcott [1987] Crim LR 765 96
R *v* Silverlock [1894] 2 QB 766 CCR 102
R *v* Simbodyal (1991) The Times 10 October 160
R *v* Simmons [1987] Crim LR 630 40
R *v* Simpson [1983] 1 WLR 1494 204
R *v* Sims [1946] 1 KB 531; [1946] 1 All ER 697 137, 144
R *v* Smith (1915) 11 Cr App R 229 136
R *v* Smith [1979] 1 WLR 1445 158, 167
R *v* Smith (Robert William) (1985) 81 Cr App R 286 43
Sodastream *v* Thorn Cascade [1982] RPC 459 157
Sodeman *v* R [1936] 2 All ER 1138 51
South Shropshire District Council *v* Amos [1987] 1 All ER 340 186, 194
Sparks *v* R [1964] AC 964; [1964] 1 All ER 727 60, 84, 163
R *v* Sparrow [1973] 1 WLR 488 53, 156, 255
R *v* Spence [1990] Crim LR 341 30
R *v* Spencer; R *v* Smails [1987] AC 128 152
R *v* Spilby (1990) 91 Cr App R 186 61
R *v* Spinks [1982] 1 All ER 587 160
Stapley *v* Gypsum Mines Ltd [1953] AC 663;
[1953] 2 All ER 478 199
Statue of Liberty, The [1968] 1 WLR 739 250
R v Steane [1947] KB 997 217
R *v* Stewart (1986) 83 Cr App R 327 153
Stirland *v* DPP [1944] AC 315 114
R *v* Storey (1968) 52 Cr App R 334 138, 251, 252
Stotesbury *v* Turner [1943] KB 370 191
R *v* Straffen [1952] 2 QB 911; [1952] 2 All ER 657 146
Subramaniam *v* Public Prosecutor [1956] 1 WLR 965 126
R *v* Summers (1952) 36 Cr App R 14 26
Sussex Peerage Case, The (1844) 11 Cl & Fin 85 62, 67
R *v* Sutton (1816) 4 M & S 532 222

R *v* Tanner (1977) 66 Cr App R 66 114, 123
Taylor dec'd, Re [1961] 1 WLR 9 206
Taylor *v* Chief Constable of Cheshire [1986] 1 WLR 1479;
[1987] 1 All ER 225 61
Taylor *v* Taylor [1967] P 25; [1965] 2 WLR 779;
[1965] 1 All ER 872 207, 209
Teper *v* R [1952] AC 480 64, 69, 70, 84
Theodoropoulas *v* Theodoropoulas [1964] P 311 186
Thompson *v* R [1918] AC 221 144
R *v* Thompson (1976) 64 Cr App R 96 33
R *v* Thomson [1912] 3 KB 19 66
R *v* Tomkins (1977) 67 Cr App R 181 7, 184
R *v* Toner (1991) 93 Cr App R 382 158, 163

Toohey v MPC [1965] AC 595 — 158, 255
R *v* Tooke (1989) The Times 29 October — 251, 252
R *v* Tricoglus (1976) 65 Cr App R 16 — 133, 152, 257
R *v* Trigg [1963] 1 WLR 305 — 44, 46
Tunbridge Wells Borough Council *v* Quietlynn [1985] Crim LR 594 — 10
R *v* Turnbull [1977] QB 224; [1976] 3 All ER 549 — 42, 51, 56, 58, 110, 117, 177, 251, 254
R *v* Turnbull (1984) 80 Cr App R 104; [1984] Crim LR 620 — 107, 140
R *v* Turner [1944] 1 KB 463 — 114
R *v* Turner (1975) 61 Cr App R 67 — 165
R *v* Turner [1975] QB 834; [1975] 1 All ER 70 — 158, 159, 163, 168, 178
Tweny *v* Tweny [1946] 1 All ER 564 — 246
R *v* Tyrer (1990) 90 Cr App R 446 — 93

R *v* Varley (1982) 75 Cr App R 242; [1982] 2 All ER 519 CA — 115, 117, 119, 120, 123, 128, 239, 241
Ventouris *v* Mountain (1991) The Independent 4 March — 183, 201, 249
R *v* Vickers [1972] Crim LR 101 — 240
R *v* Vincent (1840) 9 C & P 275 — 126
R *v* Virgo (1978) 67 Cr App R 323 — 50

W *v* Edgell [1990] 2 WLR 471 — 171, 190
R *v* Wainwright (1875) 13 Cox CC 171 — 64, 66, 69
R *v* Waite [1892] 2 QB 600 — 215
R *v* Wallwork (1958) 42 Cr App R 153 — 29, 32, 46, 49, 55, 83, 126, 127
R *v* Walsh [1989] Crim LR 822 — 6, 10
R *v* Warwickshall (1783) 1 Leach 263 — 75
R *v* Watts [1983] 3 All ER 101 — 121, 124, 127, 129, 131, 241
Waugh *v* R [1950] AC 203 — 50, 66
Waugh *v* British Railways Board [1981] 1 QB 736; [1980] AC 521; [1979] 2 All ER 1169 — 185, 189, 190, 193, 201, 249
Webster *v* James Chapman [1989] 3 All ER 939 — 184, 185, 190
R *v* Weightman (1991) 92 Cr App R 291 — 158, 163, 165, 168
Wentworth *v* Lloyd (1864) 10 HL Cas 589 — 192
R *v* Westfall (1912) 7 Cr App R 176 — 130
Wetherall *v* Harrison [1976] QB 773 — 223, 224
Wheeler *v* Le Marchant (1881) 17 Ch D 675 — 189
R *v* Whitehead [1929] 1 KB 99 — 43, 54, 55, 68, 110,127
R v Wickham (1971) 55 Cr App R 199 — 30
Williams *v* Home Office [1981] 1 All ER 1151 — 173
R *v* Willshire (1881) 6 QBD 366 — 207
R *v* Wiltshire CCR (1881) 6 QBD 366 — 210
R *v* Winfield [1939] 4 All ER 164 — 113, 114

R *v* Wink (1834) 8 C&P 397 127
Wong Kam Ming *v* R [1980] AC 247 74
R *v* Wood [1987] 1 WLR 779 151
R *v* Wood & Parker (1841) 5 Jur 225 154
R *v* Woodcock (1789) 1 Leach 500 162
Woodhouse *v* Hall [1980] Crim LR 645; (1981) 72 Cr App R 39 70, 71, 254
Woolmington *v* DPP [1935] AC 462 14, 15, 16, 17, 20, 23, 24, 25, 26, 27, 47, 224, 244, 246
Wright *v* Tatham (1837) 7 Ad & E 313 71, 84

X *v* Y [1988] 2 All ER 648 186
X Ltd *v* Morgan-Grampian Ltd [1990] 2 WLR 1000 186

R *v* Yacoob (1981) 72 Cr App R 313 34
Ymnos, The [1981] 1 Lloyd's Rep 550 200

TABLE OF STATUTES

Children and Young Persons Act 1933	77, 97
s1	176
s38	251
s38(1)	41, 126, 251
s42	97, 109
s43	97, 109
s50	211
Children and Young Persons Act 1963	
s16(1)	211
Children Act 1989	77
s96	29
Civil Evidence Act 1968	2, 27, 76, 78, 80, 85, 86, 88, 195, 197, 247, 248
s1	76
s2	76, 80, 81, 89, 197, 198, 200, 220, 248, 249, 250
s2(1)	88, 200
s2(2)	79, 89
s4	62, 76, 77, 80, 81, 85, 86, 88, 89, 96, 197, 220, 248, 249, 250
s4(1)	89
s4(3)	86
s5	76, 77, 81, 200, 201, 250
s6	88, 89, 97, 201, 248, 250
s6(1)	82, 89
s6(3)	78
s8	76, 88, 198, 248
s9	61, 62, 84, 87, 89, 157, 190, 247, 248
s10	76
s11	27, 160, 161
s12	161
s14	190
s16	190
Civil Evidence Act 1972	76, 78, 159, 247, 248
s1	76, 77, 80, 200
s2	79, 159
s3	159, 167
s3(1)	179
s3(2)	160
s3(3)	159

Company Securities (Insider Dealing) Act 1985	
s1	18
s1(1)	18
s3	18
Contempt of Court Act	
s10	171, 179, 181, 186, 242, 244
Criminal Appeals Act 1968	
s2(1)	51
Criminal Evidence Act 1898	36, 115, 121, 129, 131, 132, 135, 154, 233, 238, 239
s1	29, 116
s1(a)	29, 121, 190
s1(b)	30, 33, 48, 50, 122, 155
s1(d)	35
s1(e)	113, 122, 130, 189
s1(f)	113, 119, 122, 124, 130, 155, 233, 238, 239
s1(f)(i)	113, 115, 121, 122, 238, 239
s1(f)(ii)	113, 114, 115, 116, 119, 120, 121, 122, 125, 127, 128, 129, 130, 131, 138, 139, 154, 155, 167, 168, 177, 178, 238, 239, 240, 241
s1(f)(iii)	74, 115, 116, 117, 119, 120, 121, 123, 124, 125, 128, 130, 150, 153, 154, 156, 166, 168, 239, 241
Criminal Evidence Act 1979	
s1	153
Criminal Justice Act 1933	
s25	110
Criminal Justice Act 1967	
s9	97, 102, 109
s10	203
s10(2)	203
s11	118
Criminal Justice Act 1988	96, 97, 125
ss23-28	96
s23	96, 109, 110, 164, 165, 178, 253, 254, 256, 257
s23(1)	109, 178
s23(1)(ii)	109
s23(2)	165
s23(2)(a)	109
s23(2)(a)-(c)	178
s23(3)	97, 178
s23(3)(b)	109
s24	62, 96, 97, 100, 110
s24(1)	110
s24(4)	96, 110
s25	96, 97, 165, 254
s25(1)	178

Criminal Justice Act 1988 (continued)	
s25(2)	96
s25(2)(d)	178
s26	96, 97
s30	159
s30(3)	165, 167
s32	97, 98, 110, 126
s32(1)(b)	97
s32(2)	97
s32(1A)	97
s32A	98, 110, 126
s33A	29, 32
s33A(2)	29
s34	39, 57, 58, 126, 177, 251
s34(1)	29, 41
s34(2)	83, 110, 179
s34(3)	110
Schedule 2	96
para 3	97
Criminal Justice Act 1991	32, 55, 77, 97, 110, 126
s52	28, 83, 125, 126, 179
s52(1)	29
s52(2)	29, 32, 41
s54	97
s55	97
Criminal Law Act 1967	
s6	107
Criminal Law Amendment Act 1867	
s6	109
Criminal Procedure Act 1865	
s5	84
s8	253
Criminal Procedure (Attendance of Witnesses) Act 1965	33, 56
Criminal Procedure (Insanity) Act 1964	
s6	20
Criminal Procedure (Insanity and Unfitness to Plead) Act 1991	20
European Communities Act 1972	
s4(2)	220
Evidence Amendment Act 1853	
s1	30
Evidence Further Amendment Act 1869	30
Factories Act 1961	
s29(1)	21

Family Law Reform Act 1969	
s26	206, 212
Financial Services Act 1986	
s27	16, 17, 18, 19
s58	16, 18
s207(3)	16, 18
Homicide Act 1957	
s2	15, 53
s2(2)	13, 167
Interpretation Act 1978, s3	220
Law Reform (Contributory Negligence) Act 1945	198
Magistrates' Courts Act 1952	
s81	15, 21
Magistrates' Courts Act 1980	
s101	13, 14, 15, 21, 23, 24, 26
s102	97
s103	97
s105	97, 109
Matrimonial Causes Act 1965	
s43(1)	35
Misuse of Drugs Act 1971	
s5	22
s28(2)	21
Offences Against the Person Act 1861	
s18	125
s20	125
s47	125
Official Secrets Act 1911	
s1(2)	135
Perjury Act 1911	
s13	40
Police and Criminal Evidence Act 1984	29, 33, 34, 36, 64, 91, 92, 96, 99, 104, 141, 155
s10(2)	184
s56	106
s58	105
s62(10)	43
s65(3)	43
s66	5, 7, 94, 103, 140, 238
s67(11)	10, 73, 94, 104

Police and Criminal Evidence Act 1984 (continued)
s68 96
s69 96, 100
s74 151, 161
s74(1) 161
s74(2) 161
s76 4, 61, 72, 73, 74, 75, 91, 92, 94, 95, 99, 103, 104, 105, 107, 108, 147, 148, 237, 255
s76(1) 255
s76(2) 92, 255
s76(2)(a) 94, 105, 108
s76(2)(b) 92, 93, 94, 104, 105, 108, 148
s76(3) 92, 99
s76(4) 75
s76(5) 95, 105, 108
s76(6) 95, 105, 108
s76(8) 92, 94, 103, 108, 147
s77 91, 147
s77(1) 105
s77(3) 105
s78 3, 5, 6, 7, 8, 9, 10, 11, 61, 72, 73, 74, 75, 94, 95, 101, 102, 104, 105, 106, 131, 138, 141, 142, 147, 174, 176, 236, 237, 238
s78(1) 5, 94, 140
s80 28, 30, 31, 32, 33, 34, 36, 37, 66, 83, 188
s80(1) 34, 255
s80(1)(a) 32, 56, 69, 107, 188
s80(1)(b) 37
s80(2) 37
s80(3) 32, 35, 69, 255
s80(3)(a) 32, 35, 37
s80(3)(b) 37, 56
s80(4) 34, 35
s80(5) 30, 37
s80(9) 35
s81 159, 167
s82 255
s82(1) 72, 91, 95
s82(3) 91, 95, 137, 236
Schedule 3
para 8 100
para 11 100
para 12 100
Prevention of Corruption Act 1916
s2 15, 21

Prevention of Crime Act 1953	
s1(1)	21, 24
Rehabilitation of Offenders Act 1974	257
Road Traffic Regulations Act 1967	
s78A	216, 217, 218
Road Traffic Regulations Act 1984	40
s89	40
Sexual Offences Act 1956	40, 56, 97, 109
s9	164
s32	21
Summary Jurisdiction Act 1848	
s14	21
Summary Jurisdiction Act 1879	
s39(2)	15
Theft Act 1968	
s22	151
s27(3)	135, 150, 151
s27(3)(a)	152
s27(3)(b)	151, 152
s30(2)	83
Treason Act 1895	40
Witnesses Act 1806	190

1 INTRODUCTION TO EVIDENCE

1.1 General

1.2 Types of evidence

1.3 Cogency of evidence

1.1 General

Rules of evidence are mainly exclusionary, because many of them developed at a time when trial by jury was the rule rather than the exception, and it was thought that jurors would be unduly influenced by knowledge of previous convictions of the accused; by hearsay evidence; by character evidence; by opinion evidence of a non-expert etc. Despite many recent reforms, it is still generally true to state that the courts in England are not apprised of all the facts, not even of all the relevant facts, but only of those facts which the laws of evidence allow - and even some of these facts may be excluded in the discretion of the judge.

To be capable of admissibility, evidence must be *legally* relevant, ie must have reached a sufficiently high point on the scale of relevance. For example, if D is charged with theft, it is not legally relevant (although it may be logically relevant) that he has several previous convictions for theft. It *is* legally relevant that he was seen in the store at the time and that he had the goods - alleged by the prosecution to have been stolen by him - in his possession.

However, although his being seen in the store is legally relevant, the fact of his being seen is not necessarily admissible - eg the prosecution may wish to inform the court that a customer, or a store detective, not available to give evidence at the trial, saw D in the store. Such evidence would be *hearsay* if it is to be related by a person other than said customer or store detective, and may therefore not be admissible. Thus, the hearsay rule may exclude relevant evidence. Further, relevant evidence may be excluded by other exclusionary rules, such as that giving protection against a person's incriminating himself (self-incrimination privilege); evidence may be in a communication between a person and his legal adviser and therefore protected by legal professional privilege; evidence may be excluded as a matter of public policy on the grounds that disclosure would be injurious to state security or some other protected public interest (public interest immunity). Therefore, it is vital that at the outset one realises that in evidence relevance and admissibility are *not synonymous*. To be admitted in court, evidence *must* be legally relevant - but legally relevant evidence will not necessarily be admitted in court, because of one or more of the exclusionary rules which comprise most of the law of evidence.

1.2 Types of evidence

Admissible evidence may take one of several forms, for example:

a) *Testimony*

This is the oral evidence of a witness. It may be evidence of what that witness perceived, ie 'direct testimony', or alternatively it may be what another person perceived and the witness is reporting that to the court as evidence of its truth, ie 'hearsay'. In civil trials hearsay is now generally admissible, since the passing of the Civil Evidence Act 1968; in criminal trials hearsay is inadmissible unless it falls into one of the recognised categories of admissible hearsay, eg *res gestae* statements, freely made confessions, dying declarations.

b) *Documentary evidence*

Here, a document is adduced in evidence. For the purposes of evidence, there is no all embracing definition of 'document'. It includes not only a document in writing but also photographs, maps, plans, drawings, blue-prints, cassettes, micro-dots etc. The document may be admitted because its content, or its existence, is relevant. As regards content of a document, the 'best evidence' rule would dictate production of the original, but increasingly the law of evidence provides for admissibility of copies of documents. The original document is 'primary' evidence, the copy is 'secondary' evidence.

c) *Real evidence*

Real evidence comprises objects produced for inspection by the court in order that the court may draw inferences from the condition, existence etc of the object. Real evidence would therefore include a document produced purely as evidence of its condition or existence rather than of its contents. In the case of both documentary and real evidence there must be some testimony as to, for example, the authenticity of the documents, the location where the real evidence was discovered, otherwise the documentary or real evidence will have little if any cogency in itself.

d) *Circumstantial evidence*

Circumstantial evidence may be contrasted with 'direct' evidence, in that the latter relates to some fact in issue of which the witness has 'direct' or first-hand knowledge, whereas the former comprises evidence of facts from which an inference may, or may not, be drawn as to the fact in issue. For example, in a murder trial a witness may give testimony which is 'direct' evidence of his seeing the accused stab the victim, or may give circumstantial evidence of the accused's motive, eg that on several occasions he had heard the accused voice his violent disposition toward, hatred of, and/or intention to kill the victim. Circumstantial evidence may be in the form of testimony, documentary or real evidence; examples are evidence of motive, opportunity, identity (eg finger prints of the accused at scene of crime).

1.3 Cogency of evidence

Evidence may be admissible, but mere admissibility does not further the cause of the party adducing the evidence. What must be assessed, and what will be crucial in deciding the case, is the cogency, ie the probative value, or the weight of the admissible evidence. Cogency is a matter of degree, from technical admissibility with little or no probative value at one end of the spectrum to cogency so strong as to be probative to the extent of being conclusive at the other end.

Admissibility of evidence is a question of law to be determined by the judge, often in a *voir dire* ('trial within a trial') in the absence of the jury. Cogency of such admissible evidence is a question of fact, to be determined by the jury; for example, in a criminal trial the jury will evaluate the cogency of prosecution and defence evidence which they have been allowed to hear (ie which the judge has ruled admissible) in deciding whether the prosecution has proved the guilt of the accused beyond reasonable doubt.

However, in deciding on the admissibility of an item of evidence, the judge will be influenced by the degree of relevance of that evidence and thus to some extent by its cogency. Also a judge may withdraw an issue from the jury where a party has failed to discharge an evidential burden, eg if the defence in a criminal trial attempts to run a defence of sane automatism in an effort to secure an acquittal, the judge will withdraw that defence from the jury unless the defence adduce sufficient evidence in support of the alleged automatism. So, although the jury, as the tribunal of fact, is not concerned with the admissibility of evidence, the judge, when deciding the legal question of admissibility, cannot divorce this completely from the cogency, or weight, of the evidence under scrutiny.

Finally, to add to the uncertainty in evidence, the judge in a criminal trial has a discretion to exclude admissible evidence where its probative value is outweighed by its prejudicial effect on the defence; here again the judge is concerned with the cogency of evidence. This overriding discretion is, apparently, in addition to the statutory discretion given by s78, Police and Criminal Evidence Act 1984, to exclude 'unfair evidence'.

All these concepts, all these issues, will be examined in depth in the ensuing chapters, and constitute the major part of the law of evidence.

2 EVIDENCE ILLEGALLY OR UNFAIRLY OBTAINED

2.1 Introduction

2.2 Key points

2.3 Analysis of questions

2.4 Questions

2.1 Introduction

If evidence has been obtained by some criminal or tortious or other unlawful act (eg in breach of contract) or by some unfair or improper means which is not in breach of the law (eg trickery, bribery), then at common law such evidence would usually be admissible if it was relevant to the facts in issue before the court.

2.2 Key points

The first question to be asked is whether the evidence is admissible as a matter of *law*; if that is answered in the affirmative, the question is then whether the judge ought, in his discretion, to exclude it.

a) *Admissibility in law*

The common law position prevails, ie 'It matters not how you get it; if you steal it even, it would be admissible in evidence' (per Crompton J in *R* v *Leatham* (1861) 8 Cox CC 498, 501). There are two exceptions to this:

i) If evidence consists of a confession which has been obtained in consequence of some inducement, or by oppression (s76 Police and Criminal Evidence Act 1984)

ii) If the evidence of one party is filched in court by the other party - as this would probably amount to a contempt of court (*ITC Film Distributors* v *Video Exchange* [1982] Ch 431).

b) *Discretion to exclude*

i) Civil cases

There is a paucity of authority, but it would seem that in civil cases there is no discretion to exclude admissible evidence (*Helliwell* v *Piggott-Sims* [1980] FSR 582).

ii) Criminal cases

- Common law discretion

In criminal cases there has been evidence of ambivalence by the courts in the exercise, and control, of discretion to exclude. The conflict is between admitting all relevant, admissible evidence to ensure that those who are guilty of crime are convicted, and the view that to admit such improperly obtained evidence condones and even encourages the improprieties of (usually) the police. This conflict was discussed at length in the House of Lords in *R* v *Sang* [1980] AC 402, but there was still a substantial amount of uncertainty. *R* v *Sang* was authority for the overriding discretion to exclude evidence which is more prejudicial than probative, but apart from that denied the existence of any exclusionary discretion (confessions apart) unless, apparently, the evidence was obtained by oppression, or improperly obtained from the suspect after the commission of the offence.

This uncertainty remained until an attempt was made by Parliament to clarify matters.

- Statutory discretion

Section 78(1) Police and Criminal Evidence Act 1984 provides:

'In any proceedings the court may refuse to allow evidence on which the prosecution proposes to rely to be given if it appears to the court that, having regard to all the circumstances, including the circumstances in which the evidence was obtained, the admission of the evidence would have such an adverse effect on the fairness of the proceedings that the court ought not to admit it.'

It has been held that s78 applies to all evidence including evidence of identification (*R* v *Quinn* [1990] Crim LR 581) and confessions (*R* v *Mason* [1987] 3 All ER 481). The courts have been much more prepared to exercise their exclusionary discretion since s78 became operative in 1986, and have given due weight to breaches by the police of the Codes of Practice issued under s66 of the Act.

Although the discretion to exclude is being more widely exercised, it is not clear for what reason evidence is being excluded under s78 - some cases imply that the rationale is that of discouraging police misconduct (eg *R* v *Mason*, supra; *Matto* v *Crown Court at Wolverhampton* [1987] RTR 337; *R* v *Alladice* [1987] NLJR 141), others that it is protecting the civil rights of the suspect in police custody (eg *R* v *Samuel* [1988] 2 WLR 920; *R* v *Gaynor* [1988] Crim LR 242; *R* v *Parris* (1988) The Times 2 November). There is, however, some doubt whether s78 affects the so-called defence of entrapment. In *R* v *Sang*, the House of Lords said entrapment is no defence, and that cannot be changed by any evidential discretion. But the case of *Gill and Ranuana* [1989] Crim LR 358 suggests otherwise (see suggested solution to Question 1, below).

If the exclusion is to discipline the police, then only where they wilfully abuse their powers should the discretion be exercised; if the exclusion is to protect the suspects' rights then the *bona fides* of the police are irrelevant. In the case of *R* v *Quinn* [1990] Crim LR 581, the cases of *Walsh* [1989] Crim LR 822 and *Keenan* [1989] Crim LR 720 were approved to suggest that where there is a significant and substantial breach of a Code of Practice, this could result in the exclusion of the evidence obtained, even in absence of bad faith.

2.3 Analysis of questions

Questions on evidence illegally, or especially unfairly, obtained, have tended to concentrate on confessions made by suspects after some physical or psychological pressure, or some breach of the Codes of Practice (formerly some breach of the Judges' Rules). However, since s78 Police and Criminal Evidence Act 1984 became law in 1986, the tendency has been more to set questions on judicial discretion to exclude. Although confessions will be dealt with in Chapter 8, it is at this stage useful to examine the discretion given to the courts to exclude evidence which is otherwise in all respects admissible.

2.4 Questions

Question 1

Sykes is charged with unlawful possession of drugs, and with offering to supply controlled drugs. The prosecution case includes a statement by PC Plod to the effect that he posed as a member of the 'Acidhouse Club' and having thus obtained entry asked Sykes to get him some amphetamine tablets as he 'needed a lift'. After some persuasion from Plod, Sykes stated that he could obtain some by the following evening and they would cost £1 each. Plod then arrested Sykes.

At the police station Sykes was told, untruthfully, that his fingerprints were required to eliminate him from a murder enquiry and would be used for no other purpose. With Sykes still in custody, Inspector Knab called at Sykes's home and told Mrs Sykes that her husband was being held as a murder suspect. Mrs Sykes immediately fainted; Knab stepped over her, entered the house and found in Mrs Sykes's wardrobe a tin containing cannabis resin. The fingerprints on the tin included some which matched those taken from Sykes.

Discuss the evidentiary aspects.

Written by editor

Skeleton solution

- Introduction; admissibility of improperly obtained evidence and discretion to exclude.

- Discretion per *R* v *Sang* - prejudice and cogency.

- Section 78 Police and Criminal Evidence Act 1984 and interpretative case law. Rationale of exclusionary discretion.

Suggested solution

The question is concerned with the admissibility of improperly or unfairly obtained evidence and with the discretion to exclude such evidence despite its admissibility. Although generally in criminal cases the courts, in deciding on admissibility of evidence other than confessions, are not concerned with how the evidence was obtained but only with its relevance to the fact in issue, ie the guilt of the accused (*R* v *Leatham* (1861); *Jeffrey* v *Black* (1978)); there are exceptional situations when the illegal obtaining of evidence will render it inadmissible (*ITC Film Distributors* v *Video Exchange* (1982); *R* v *Tompkins* (1977)); but such limited exceptions have no bearing on this problem.

In the case of *R* v *Sang* (1980) the House of Lords confirmed the existence of an inherent discretion in criminal courts to exclude otherwise admissible evidence if its probative value is outweighed by its prejudicial effect on a fair trial of the accused. This balancing act would not have to be performed in the case of Sykes's, since all the evidence is strongly probative of his guilt and no more prejudicial than any cogent prosecution evidence would be. However, in *R* v *Sang* their Lordships appeared to recognise the existence of a discretion to exclude evidence improperly obtained after the commission of the offence (which seemed to be restricted to evidence obtained from the accused) and evidence obtained by oppression.

On the authority of *R* v *Sang*, therefore, the fingerprints obtained from Sykes could be excluded, but not those obtained from his house despite the (unorthodox) improper means of entry. As regards Sykes's offering to supply the amphetamine, he would not be permitted to raise a defence of entrapment, ie the offer would never have been made but for the coercion or persuasion of PC Plod, because in *R* v *Sang* the House of Lords stated emphatically that there is no such defence in English law.

Section 78 Police and Criminal Evidence Act 1984 became law in 1986, and gives the criminal courts a discretion to exclude otherwise admissible evidence it if *appears* to the court, having regard to *all* circumstances, that the evidence would have such an adverse effect on the *fairness* of the proceedings that the court ought not to admit it.

Although in the cases interpreting and applying s78, there is some conflict as to whether the decision to exercise the exclusionary discretion should depend on whether the police have *wilfully* flouted the law and/or the Codes of Practice issued under s66 of the Act, there is no doubt that, given the way in which Sykes was tricked into giving his fingerprints, those prints albeit legally admissible would be excluded. With regard to the method of entry into Sykes's home, it would appear that Inspector Knab was aware that what he said to Mrs Sykes was a lie - to obtain the desired effect, no doubt (ie told in the knowledge that Mrs Sykes was likely to faint) - in which case the prints on the box ought to be excluded (*R* v *Mason* (1987)).

Even if Knab satisfied the court that he was genuinely mistaken as to the reason for Sykes's detention, the method of entry is improper, as is therefore his search of the bedroom; it would certainly seem to be more than a trivial breach of the Codes of Practice (*R* v *Deacon* (1987)), and therefore would not merely be taken into account by the court in deciding whether to invoke the s78 exclusion, but would most probably lead to the box of cannabis resin, with Sykes's fingerprints on it, being excluded from the prosecution's evidence.

Although 'fairness' to the accused in a criminal trial is something which the courts have found very difficult to define with scientific precision (*R* v *Murphy* (1965)), it is accepted that 'fairness of the proceedings' in s78 is not restricted to the proceedings in the courtroom but includes the activities of the police in entering premises, interviewing suspects etc (*R* v *Mason*).

With regard to the second charge, that of offering to supply controlled drugs, it would seem that the courts cannot concern themselves with the fairness or otherwise of police entrapment of suspects. In substantive criminal law, as was stated categorically in *R* v *Sang*, there is no such defence as entrapment, therefore it should not be allowed into the law through the 'evidentiary' back door. Since s78 became law, there is one reported case where plain clothes police officers, without identifying themselves, bought intoxicating liquor; the seller was charged with selling the liquor without a licence and it was held on appeal that the evidence of the police officers was *not* to be excluded under s78 (*DPP* v *Marshall* (1988)). The case of *R* v *Gill and Ranuana* (1989) however, suggests that entrapment is something which could be taken into account under s78 even though no such defence exists in English law. Although in the case of *Harwood* (1989) it was said, obiter, that the rule that entrapment was not a defence could not be evaded by a procedural device of preventing prosecution adducing evidence of the commission of the offence, the trial court in *R* v *Gill* (above) had reservations about this. See the commentary to the *Gill* case, which suggests *Harwood* and *DPP* v *Marshall* are wrong if they suggest s78 is incapable of excluding evidence obtained by entrapment.

The views of the House of Lords in *Sang*, it is submitted, cannot necessarily hold fast since the statutory enactment of s78 by dishonest police activity results in the exclusion of a confession (eg *Mason* (1987)), and if it would result in the exclusion of Syke's fingerprints essentially because of police misconduct, it could be argued that there is no difference between Knab lying to Sykes about the murder charge, and lying to him about his identity when in the nightclub - each could result in the exclusion on the evidence under s78, on the basis that s78 is concerned to some degree, it seems, in disciplining the police.

The answer which *Gill* seems to suggest is that s78 does not automatically lead to the exclusion of evidence obtained by entrapment, but it leaves the door open for the trial judge to look at all the circumstances of the individual case to see if the admission of the evidence would have an adverse effect upon the fairness of the proceedings.

Entrapment apart, therefore, s78 has led to a shift in judicial attitudes to police improprieties and denial of suspects' rights; this greater control of the police by exclusion of evidence so obtained will be of benefit to Sykes on the first charge, but will not avail him on the second charge.

Question 2

'It is no part of a judge's function to exercise disciplinary powers over the police or prosecution as respects the way in which evidence to be used at the trial is obtained by them', per Lord Diplock in *R* v *Sang* [1980] AC 402 at p436.

Discuss.

Written by editor

Skeleton solution

- Introduction; reason for inclusion of illegally or unfairly obtained evidence.
- Common law position; contrast US approach.
- Discretion to exclude under s78 Police and Criminal Evidence Act 1984.

Suggested solution

In English law the judiciary adhered to the statement of Crompton J in *R* v *Leatham* (1861): 'It matters not how you get it; if you steal it even, it would be admissible in evidence'. The attitude of the judges, reflected in the Common Law rules of evidence in criminal trials, was that the manner in which evidence was obtained by the police had no bearing on its admissibility; the sole factor governing admissibility was relevance to the guilt or innocence of the accused. As recently as 1978, Lord Widgery CJ stated in the case of *Jeffrey* v *Black* (1978): 'I have not the least doubt that an irregularity in obtaining evidence does not render the evidence inadmissible. Whether or not the evidence is admissible depends on whether or not it is relevant to the issues in respect of which it is called'. This attitude to admissibility is reflected again in the statement of Lord Diplock cited in the question.

The approach of the Common Law was that if there were any impropriety on the part of the police this did not 'taint' probative evidence; if the accused was aggrieved by the misconduct of the police, then his remedy was to bring an action in the appropriate court, or, if the misconduct was not unlawful, to invoke the procedure available for complaints against the police - but that was an issue which was ancillary to the cogency of the evidence obtained and therefore had no bearing on the admissibility of the evidence at the trial of the accused.

In *R* v *Sang* the House of Lords recognised the existence of a *discretion* in the criminal courts to exclude such admissible evidence. The discretion certainly extended to excluding evidence which was more prejudicial to a fair trial of the accused than it was probative of his guilt; but how wider than that, if at all, it extended, is unclear from the speeches in *R* v *Sang*. It *appeared* to extend to excluding otherwise admissible (documentary) evidence improperly obtained from the accused after the commission of the offence, for example, (see *R* v *Barker* (1941)) and to evidence obtained by police conduct which was unfair, oppressive or morally reprehensible (*R* v *Sang* (1980); see also *Jeffrey* v *Black*; *Callis* v *Gunn* (1964); *King* v *R* (1969)), but the ambit of the exclusionary discretion was unclear, given the conflicting speeches in *R* v *Sang*, and the lack of any clear guidance in subsequent cases (*R* v *Apicella*

(1985); *R* v *Adams* (1980); *Fox* v *Chief Constable of Gwent* (1985); *Tunbridge Wells BC* v *Quietlynn* (1985)).

The reason for the lack of clarity was the ambivalence of the criminal judiciary as to whether their role was to discipline the police by excluding evidence obtained by their misconduct, or alternatively to include all relevant, cogent evidence, however obtained, to ensure that the guilty did not avoid conviction even though this might necessitate apparent condonation of police impropriety. In the USA, the courts are always aware of the constitutional rights of the individual, and therefore are not prepared to condone unconstitutional behaviour on the part of the police which infringes those rights - the sanction imposed is to exclude evidence so obtained even though this might result in an acquittal of an apparently guilty defendant. In English common law the view is, generally, that to admit improperly obtained evidence is not a condonation, far less an encouragement, of police misconduct, and that relevance of the evidence is the overriding factor.

In 1986, s78 Police and Criminal Evidence Act 1984 came into force, giving the courts a statutory discretion to exclude 'unfair evidence'; in addition to this, the Codes of Practice issued under s66 to regulate police conduct in the investigation of crime (replacing the Judges' Rules) were given full legal status (s67(11) Police and Criminal Evidence Act 1984). From 1986, the way in which evidence is obtained is one of the factors to be taken into consideration in deciding whether to exclude otherwise admissible material.

Since s78, and the Codes of Practice, became law, the judges have been freed of the shackles put on them by the Law Lords in *R* v *Sang*, and in general their approach has been to exclude evidence which would have an adverse effect on the fairness of the proceedings. Although their exclusion of evidence improperly obtained seems to be indicative of the 'disciplinary' approach which is denied by Lord Diplock in the quotation, there is now some ambivalence in the reported cases between disciplining the police for deliberately flouting the law or the Codes of Practice and the protecting the rights of the suspect by excluding evidence obtained after a denial (whether deliberate or mistakenly innocent) of those rights by the police (see *Matto* v *Crown Court at Wolverhampton* (1987); *R* v *Alladice* (1987); *R* v *Mason* (1987); and of *R* v *Gaynor* (1988) and *R* v *Samuel* (1988)). In *R* v *Quinn* (1990) Lord Lane CJ says the function of the judge under s78 is to protect the fairness of the proceedings, and usually proceedings are fair if a jury hears all relevant evidence from each side. But proceedings may become unfair if, eg, one side is allowed to adduce evidence which, for one reason or another, the other side cannot properly challenge, or where there has been an abuse of process, eg because evidence has been obtained in deliberate breach of procedures laid down in an official Code of Practice.

But the court also approved the cases of *Walsh* (1989) and *Keenan* (1989), citing them as authority for the general proposition that a significant and substantial breach of a Code of Practice may well result in the exclusion of evidence obtained in consequence, even in the absence of bad faith.

Although there is now a new conflict, the judges are much more prone to exclude evidence in their newly-written discretion under s78, despite the continuance of the strict legal admissibility from pre-1986. Whether protecting suspects' rights, or insisting on compliance with the general law or the specific Codes of Practice by police investigators, the judges can now be said to be exercising, whether directly or indirectly, disciplinary powers over the police. From the low constitutional point reached in *R* v *Sang*, and evinced in the quotation, the judges appear to have seized the opportunity given to them by Parliament by the Police and Criminal Evidence Act to temper the inclusionary, draconian, common law, with a liberal interpretation of their exclusionary discretionary powers under s78.

3 BURDENS AND STANDARDS OF PROOF

3.1 Introduction

3.2 Key points

3.3 Analysis of questions

3.4 Questions

3.1 Introduction

The most important distinction is that between the legal burden - the burden of *proof* - and the evidential burden - the burden of adducing evidence. Only when this distinction is clearly understood can a student do justice to the express and implied exceptions in criminal cases where the legal, as opposed to evidential burden, is on the accused. The recent House of Lords decision in *R* v *Hunt* [1987] AC 352 has made this a popular area for examiners.

3.2 Key points

It is vital that students understand the following concepts and issues:

a) Legal burden is the obligation placed on a party to prove a fact in issue, eg on the prosecution to prove the guilt of the accused and to prove all other issues they raise during the trial.

b) Evidential burden is the obligation placed on a party to adduce enough evidence about an asserted fact for that fact to become a justiciable issue, eg the prosecution must adduce enough evidence of the guilt of the accused for the court to be satisfied that there is a case for the defence to answer.

c) Evidential burden is considered at only two points in a trial:

   i) at the beginning, to decide which party begins;

   ii) at any time during the trial in deciding whether enough evidence has been adduced in support of an asserted fact for it to become a justiciable issue, ie require the opposing party to adduce evidence in rebuttal.

d) Which party must prove the issue in dispute, and other issues raised during the trial, ie which party must discharge the legal burden, is decided by rules of law, either statute or case law.

e) The rule in civil cases is, generally, that the party who asserts must prove, ie he must discharge the legal burden of proof. For example, in a suit in negligence, the plaintiff (as well as having to discharge the evidential burden) has the legal burden of proving duty, breach and consequential damage. The defendant, if the defence is a simple denial, bears no legal burden, *but* if some defence is raised which goes beyond that, eg an assertion that the plaintiff was contributorily negligent, then the defendant has the legal burden of proving that assertion. Thus, generally, the party asserting an affirmative bears the legal burden; there are exceptions to this, where a negative assertion is an essential element of a party's case, eg in a suit in malicious prosecution the plaintiff must prove the absence of reasonable cause for the defendant's institution of proceedings.

f) The rule in criminal cases is, generally, that where a burden is borne by the accused it is an evidential burden only. There are three types of defences which, exceptionally, will require the accused to discharge a legal burden of proof if they are to succeed:

   i) insanity and unfitness to plead;

   ii) express statutory exceptions - ie where a statute expressly stipulates that the accused must prove an issue (eg a defence of diminished responsibility to a charge of murder, per s2(2) Homicide Act 1957);

   iii) implied statutory exceptions - s101 Magistrates' Courts Act 1980 in summary trials and *R* v *Edwards* [1975] QB 27 in jury trials provide that if the accused relies for his defence on any 'exception, exemption, proviso, excuse or qualification', then he has the legal burden of proving that defence. In this area of the incidence of the legal burden in criminal trials, the House of Lords decision in *R* v *Hunt* (1987) is important.

g) The *standard* of proof, which determines how much evidence a party must adduce to discharge a legal burden of proof, varies depending on whether it is a civil or a criminal trial. In civil trials the standard is on balance of probabilities; the more serious the allegation made by a party the more evidence the court will require to be satisfied, but even where the allegation by a party is of the commission of a crime by his opponent the standard remains the civil one, ie he must prove that what he alleges is more likely than not the truth. In criminal trials the prosecution must prove the guilt of the accused to the criminal standard, ie beyond reasonable doubt; additionally, whenever the prosecution bears a legal burden of proving any issues during the course of the trial it must prove beyond reasonable doubt. In the exceptional situations where the accused bears a legal, as opposed to merely evidential, burden (see (f)(i)(ii)(iii) above) the *standard* of proof is always the civil standard.

3.3 Analysis of questions

Burdens (and standards) had tended to form only part of a question, often merged with presumptions, judicial notice etc, until *R* v *Hunt* was reported in 1987, since when examiners have considered that there is now sufficient controversy for this area to merit a self-contained question. Doubtless until there is further clarification, and resolution of some of the uncertainty created by *R* v *Hunt*, this topic will be well worth the time spent by the student in mastering the not over-complex details.

3.4 Questions

Question 1

'Throughout the web of the English Criminal Law one golden thread is always seen, that it is the duty of the prosecution to prove the prisoner's guilt ...' (Viscount Sankey LC in *Woolmington* v *DPP*). Is there anything to be seen of the golden thread after *R* v *Edwards* and *R* v *Hunt*?

University of London LLB Examination
(for External Students) Evidence June 1987 Q1)

General comment

There is no trick to this question except that it is important to remember to answer the question set, namely whether there is anything left of the golden thread following *R* v *Edwards* and *R* v *Hunt*. This is a question which should be within the competence of all students.

Skeleton solution

- Rule in *Woolmington* v *DPP* - exceptions in case.
- Evidential burden - does *Woolmington* affect it?
- Section 101 Magistrates' Courts Act 1980 - exception, exemption, proviso, excuse or qualification.
- *R* v *Edwards* - application to Crown Courts.
- *R* v *Hunt* - legal burden on defendant by implication.
- Erosion of golden thread.

Suggested solution

In *Woolmington* v *DPP* (1935) the House of Lords laid down that a person accused of murder who puts forward the defence of accident does not have to prove this defence; it is for the prosecution to prove that death was caused deliberately or recklessly not for the defendant to prove that it was an accident. The House took the opportunity to lay down the general rule, known as the golden thread, that it is always for the prosecution to prove the accused's guilt beyond reasonable doubt.

The House did accept that in certain special cases the accused will bear a burden of proof, but that they are limited to two: (a) the defence of insanity; and (b) cases where statute places the burden on him. The first of these exceptional rules had been established since *M'Naghten's Case* (1843) and the House was in no doubt that it was correct. The second is an inevitable product of the supremacy of Parliament - if a statute clearly says that the accused must prove his defence in a particular case then the courts are not able to ignore this.

There are several examples of statutes expressly stating that the defendant has to prove his defence, for example s2 of the Homicide Act 1957 (diminished responsibility) and s2 of the Prevention of Corruption Act 1916 (non-corruption). In these cases there can be no doubt of the position because the statute says that something must be 'proved'. But, even where the defendant has to prove something, he is still protected in that the standard of proof required of him is only to prove his defence on balance of probabilities (*R* v *Carr-Briant* (1943)) and not to prove his case beyond reasonable doubt which is the standard when the burden is on the prosecution.

Nothing in *Woolmington* v *DPP* affects what has become known as the evidential burden. This is the duty to raise an issue by evidence before the judge is obliged to direct the jury to consider it. There are many instances of the defendant having the duty to raise a particular line of defence, for example, self-defence (*R* v *Lobell* (1957)) and provocation (*Mancini* v *DPP* (1942)), but once he has done this then it is for the prosecution to prove beyond reasonable doubt that the defence in question is not available.

In summary proceedings (ie magistrates' court trials) s101 of the Magistrates' Courts Act 1980 lays down that the defendant must prove his defence if he is relying on 'any exception, exemption, proviso, excuse or qualification' to a statutory offence. For example, if he is charged with supplying intoxicating liquor without having a licence; or with driving without a licence. Section 101 is a re-enactment of earlier statutory provisions (s39(2) Summary Jurisdiction Act 1879, s81 Magistrates' Court Act 1952) and, like them, expressly applies only to summary trials and not to trials on indictment.

The absence of any statutory rule applicable to the Crown Court was held to be irrelevant in *R* v *Edwards* (1975). In that case the Court of Appeal held that s101 is a restatement of the common law and, therefore, sets out the rule to be applied in the Crown Court. The decision in *R* v *Edwards* was criticised strongly by Zuckerman in the *Law Quarterly Review* ((1976) 92 LQR 401) where it was pointed out that the result of *R* v *Edwards* was to place the legal burden of proof on the defendant in many more cases than the House of Lords seemed to consider appropriate in *Woolmington* v *DPP*. Whether *R* v *Edwards* can properly be reconciled with *Woolmington* v *DPP* depends upon whether dicta in *Woolmington* v *DPP* that the defendant bears a burden of proof where statute places such a burden on him were intended to cover only cases where statute expressly said that the accused must 'prove' something, or whether it extended to cases where the statute only impliedly placed the burden on the accused.

Certainly in relation in s101 it appears that 'any exception, exemption, proviso, excuse or qualification' was interpreted to place a legal burden on the accused both where statute expressly so provided and where such a result was implied from the Act (*Nimmo* v *Alexander Cowan & Sons* (1968)). *R* v *Edwards* decided that by statute a legal burden could be placed on the accused either expressly or impliedly.

In *R* v *Hunt* (1987) the House of Lords accepted that there was great force in Zuckerman's criticisms of *R* v *Edwards*, but held that by statute a legal burden could, nonetheless, be placed on the accused by implication. An ambiguous dictum of Lord

Simon in *Mancini* v *DPP* which could be read to say that the defendant only has to prove his defence if statute expressly places that burden on him was said to be properly construed as allowing the burden to be imposed by implication. On the construction of the particular statute in question in *R* v *Hunt* the House of Lords held that the burden was not on the accused. The House approved *R* v *Edwards* in its result.

The result of *R* v *Edwards* and *R* v *Hunt* has been to make clear that statute can place a legal burden on the accused either expressly or impliedly. It had been argued that *Woolmington* v *DPP* laid down a rule that this could only be done expressly, but such arguments are now in vain. This does not mean that the golden thread has been destroyed, because it must still be clear from the Act concerned that it was intended by Parliament that the accused should bear a legal burden. If there is doubt then it will still be resolved in his favour. The formulation in *Hunt* has been accepted by the High Court of Australia in *DPP* v *United Telecasters Ltd* (1990) - seemingly on the basis that it will result in more imprecise formulation in statutory law, and therefore policy will have greater control over the imposition of the legal burden.

Question 2

Section 27 of the Financial Services Act 1986 provides that 'subject to s58 below, no person other than an authorised person shall issue ... an investment advertisement in the United Kingdom, unless its contents have been approved by an authorised person'.

Section 58 provides that 'Section 27 does not apply to ... any advertisement which ... consists of ... any document permitted to be published by listing rules ...' of the International Stock Exchange in London.

Section 207(3) provides that 'for the purposes of this Act an advertisement issued outside the United Kingdom, shall be treated as issued in the United Kingdom if it is directed to persons in the United Kingdom ...'

Suppose that Makeabuck is charged with contravening s27 in that he had issued such an advertisement in the UK inviting investors to buy shares of Hong Kong companies without obtaining approval of its contents from an authorised person. Suppose that Makeabuck's position is that though some of his advertisements did appear on video screens in the UK, they were issued in Hong Kong and were not directed at persons in the UK; that all documents which were issued in the UK were permitted by the International Stock Exchange's listing rules; and that in any case his advertisements were approved by the Bang-On Bank which was an 'authorised person' under the Act.

Consider the burden and standard of proof in the case under English Law in the context of the following items of evidence:

a) a document produced by a computer containing a register of all persons authorised to carry on investment business in the UK kept under the Financial Services Act, but which does not contain the Bang-On Bank's name;

b) a copy of an authorisation issued to Bang-On Bank under the Act which is in Makeabuck's possession.

Adapted from University of London LLB Examination
(for External Students) Evidence June 1988 Q1

General comment

No difficulty should be caused by the requirement to state the standard of proof placed on the prosecution and defence in a criminal case. But the placing of the burden is more difficult. There is no authority on the Financial Services Act provisions in question, so general principles must be applied. Necessarily the examiner may disagree with the candidate in his application of the rule in *Hunt*, but provided the principles are stated clearly full credit will be given.

Skeleton solution

- Elements of the offence - burden and standard in general.
- Burden and standard on each element.

Suggested solution

In general it is for the prosecution to prove every element of a criminal charge, both actus reus and mens rea, beyond reasonable doubt (*Woolmington* v *DPP* (1935)). But this general principle is subject to exceptions and, in particular, to an exception that where statute expressly or by implication places a burden on the defendant then that is where the burden lies (*R* v *Hunt* (1987)).

The offence under s27 of the Financial Services Act 1986 has five elements: (a) the publication of an investment advertisement; (b) which is not permitted to be published by listing rules of the International Stock Exchange in London; (c) in the UK; (d) by an unauthorised person; and (e) without the approval of an authorised person.

Whether, as regards any element the burden of proof is on the prosecution or defence is a matter of the proper construction of the Act. In *R* v *Hunt* the House of Lords held that the presumption must be that it is for the prosecution to prove everything which needs to be proved. Where an offence is committed by someone who does an act without first obtaining a licence or some other permission from an official body this presumption will be rebutted provided it is simple for the defendant to prove that he had the necessary permission, but very difficult for the prosecution to prove that he did not. Lord Griffiths recognised in his speech that the vast majority of cases in which a burden is placed on the defendant will be cases where he is accused of doing something without the necessary permission. But he also recognised that a careful definition must be made of the act which is prohibited so that it is known whether the defendant really is asserting a defence. For example, in *R* v *Hunt* itself the offence charged was the possession of a certain type of morphine. The Court of Appeal held that once it was established that the defendant had possession of morphine it was for him to prove that it was not of the type alleged, but the House of Lords disagreed. In other words the defendant was not putting forward the defence that the substance was not as alleged, rather it was a necessary ingredient of the prosecution case for the prosecution to prove that it was of the alleged type.

The prosecution will have to call its evidence first and if at the close of its case it has failed to call evidence which could amount to proof beyond reasonable doubt on those issues on which it bears a legal burden, the judge will have no option but to accede to a submission from Makeabuck that there is no case to answer (*R* v *Galbraith* (1981)).

In Makeabuck's case the five elements of the offence must be considered separately because the burden may not be on the same party on each. Undoubtedly it will be for the prosecution to prove that the advertisements about which complaint is made are investment advertisements. This is a matter on which the prosecution is certainly competent as the defence to call evidence. Makeabuck does not raise as his defence that the advertisements were not investment advertisements, but that does not preclude the prosecution from having to prove that they were.

Section 58 of the 1986 Act provides that s27 does not apply to any document permitted to be published by listing rules of the International Stock Exchange in London. The effect of this section depends upon whether it means: (a) it is an offence to publish an investment advertisement unless it is permitted by the rules; or (b) only those advertisements which are not permitted by the rules should not be published. The difference between these meanings is one of substance and not just emphasis in that the first construction means that Makeabuck is putting forward a defence when he says the advertisements are permitted by the rules, whereas the second makes it a necessary part of the prosecution case that the advertisements are not permitted. The case of *Cross* (1990) involved similar wording to the present statute. It concerned s1 of the Company Securities (Insider Dealing) Act 1985 s1(1) which creates the offence and is said to be subject to s3, which allows the dealing where it is not done by the individual for profit, or avoidance of loss. The Court of Appeal held that the burden to prove the applicability of s3 lay with the defendant. However, the court seemed to place emphasis on the fact that the matters in s3 were peculiarly within the defendant's own knowledge. Here, we are concerned with a document permitted to be published by listing rules, and the absence of permission in the rules is something which can be proved just as simply by the prosecution as by the defence. In effect this element of the offence is in the same position as the requirement in *R* v *Hunt* that the morphine was of the prohibited type. Naturally Makeabuck should call what evidence he has if he wishes to allege that the advertisements were authorised by the listings rules, but there would not formally be a burden on him to do so.

The need for the advertisement to be issued in the UK raises a different point. Section 207(3) extends the definition of issuing in the UK from its obvious starting point of advertisements which are issued in the UK for use in the UK to cover also advertisements issued outside the UK but directed to persons in the UK. In the same way the prosecution would have to prove that any advertisement was an investment advertisement so it would be necessary for it to call evidence of the origin of the advertisement. There is no reason in principle why the prosecution should not have to prove that the advertisement was of the prohibited type. It is submitted that the origin of the advertisement is just as much a vital element of the prosecution case as is whether or not it is an investment advertisement. It may be that all the prosecution has to do is prove that the advertisement was received in the UK and then it will be for the defence to bring forward evidence that it was issued outside the UK. But the burden on the defence may be no more than an evidential burden so that it would then be for the prosecution to prove that although it was issued outside the UK it was directed to persons in the UK.

Whether or not Makeabuck is an authorised person is a matter on which he is likely to bear a legal burden, that is a burden to prove authorisation on a balance of probabilities. The position is effectively the same as where someone charged with selling alcohol without a licence claims that he has a licence, in which case the burden is on the defence to establish that a licence has been granted (*R* v *Edwards* (1975)). It appears, in any event, that Makeabuck does not claim that he has is authorised. It if is correct that the burden is on the defence, the prosecution will not have to call evidence with a view to establishing that Makeabuck is not authorised because it will be presumed that he is not unless he raises the issue.

Makeabuck does argue that the Bang-On Bank is authorised and that he issued the advertisements with its approval. It would, it is submitted, be unreasonable to expect the defence to have access to information from which it could prove whether someone who approved an advertisement was authorised to do so. We are told that Makeabuck may be in a position to do so in this case, but where the burden lies under s27 must be the same in every case and not all defendants can expect to be in Makeabuck's position. The prosecution may not know that Makeabuck is going to raise the defence that his advertisement was approved by the Bang-On Bank. Therefore it will be for Makeabuck to raise the issue. He will bear an evidential burden, in other words he must raise some credible evidence that the Bang-On Bank gave approval. But it will then be for the prosecution to prove beyond reasonable doubt that the Bang-On Bank is not authorised.

Question 3

The decision in *Hunt* [1987] AC 352 'fashions some workable guidelines out of unpromising material and encourages courts to seek out and apply the intentions of Parliament in a consistent way.'

Discuss.

University of London LLB Examination
(for External Students) Evidence June 1989 Q5

General comment

A mere narrative on the express and implied reversal of the burden of proof in some criminal statutes leading to the decision in *R* v *Hunt* would not be sufficient to achieve high marks. A critical analysis of the law pre-*Hunt* and discussion of the guidelines in that case is imperative for a comprehensive answer.

Skeleton solution

- Incidence of the legal burden of proof generally in criminal cases - *Woolmington* v *DPP*.
- Exceptions, where defence bears the burden:
    i) at common law;
    ii) examples of express statutory exceptions;
    iii) implied statutory exceptions.
- Discussion, and criticism of *R* v *Hunt*.

Suggested solution

The general rule in criminal cases is that the prosecution bears the legal burden of proving every element of its case; whether the prosecution assertions be positive or negative is immaterial, thus once the defence discharges the evidential burden in respect of any defence that defence, even if affirmative in its nature, must be disproved beyond reasonable doubt by the prosecution if the accused is to be convicted. Thus, for example the prosecution has the burden of proving absence of consent if that is raised as a defence to a charge of assault (*R* v *Donovan* (1934)) or of rape (*R* v *Horn* (1912)).

This general rule was enunciated by Lord Sankey LC in the celebrated case of *Woolmington* v *DPP* (1935). From his now famous speech, the following passage is notorious:

'Throughout the web of the English criminal law one golden thread is always to be seen, that it is the duty of the prosecution to prove the prisoner's guilt subject to what I have already said as to the defence of insanity and subject also to any statutory exception. No matter what the charge ... the principle that the prosecution must prove the guilt of the prisoner is part of the common law of England and no attempt to whittle it down can be entertained.'

Implicit in Lord Sankey's classic statement are exceptions to the 'golden thread', ie, where the defence of insanity is raised, and where the legal burden is placed by statute on the defence.

In the case of insanity the legal burden is affected by the presumption of sanity - therefore the accused pleading insanity (*M'Naghten's Case* (1843)) or unfitness to plead because of defective intellect (*R* v *Podola* (1960)) bears the burden of proving that assertion; the standard of proof in such cases is merely the civil standard of balance of probabilities (*R* v *Podola*). (Where the prosecution raises the issue of unfitness to plead, or alleges insanity or diminished responsibility under the provisions of s6 Criminal Procedure (Insanity) Act 1964 (which is not changed by the provisions of the Criminal Procedure (Insanity and Unfitness to Plead) Act 1991), then the prosecution bears the burden of proof but to the criminal standard of beyond reasonable doubt: *R* v *Grant* (1960); *R* v *Robertson* (1968)).

Evidentially, insanity causes few problems, and was recognised as a loose strand of the 'golden thread', as were statutory exceptions. Again, in the case of express statutory provisions, Parliament has in those situations decreed that on some issue the defence shall exceptionally bear a burden of proof, although obviously the prosecution still bears the legal burden of proof to the criminal standard on all other issues. For example, s32 Sexual Offences Act 1956 provides that regarding the offence of knowingly living on the earnings of prostitution, a man who lives with a prostitute 'shall be presumed to be knowingly living on the earnings of prostitution, unless he proves the contrary.' Another example is provided by s1(1) Prevention of Crime Act 1953, whereby it is an offence for a person to have an offensive weapon in a public place 'without lawful authority or reasonable excuse, the proof whereof shall lie on him.' (There are other express provisions in s2 Prevention of Corruption Act 1916; s2(2) Homicide Act 1957; s28(2) Misuse of Drugs Act 1971.) The reasons for the reversal of the burden of proof on these specific issues are mainly of public policy, and although purists disagree with these exceptions there is no scope for inconsistency in the courts' applying Parliament's intentions.

The 'unpromising material' where inconsistency abounded was in the area of implied, as opposed to express, statutory provisions. Section 101 Magistrates' Courts Act 1980 (formerly s81 Magistrates' Courts Act 1952 which revised s14 Summary Jurisdiction Act 1848) provides in essence that where a defendant in a summary trial relies for his defence on 'any exception, exemption, proviso, excuse or qualification', the burden of proof shall be on the defence, 'notwithstanding that the information or complaint contains an allegation negativing the exception, exemption, proviso, excuse or qualification.' This provision applies to summary trials, but in 1975 it was held that similar principles applied to trials on indictment (*R* v *Edwards* (1975)); and this was confirmed by the House of Lords in *R* v *Hunt* (1987).

A clear-cut example of a provision to which s101 applies is the offence of driving a motor vehicle on a road without being the holder of a current driving licence. Once the prosecution prove that the defendant was driving a motor vehicle on a road, the defendant will be convicted of the offence unless he proves the qualification on which he must rely for his defence, ie proves that at the relevant time he held a current driving licence for that class of motor vehicle (*John* v *Humphreys* (1955)). Although whether a driver is qualified or not is easily checked by the prosecution, s101 has been held to apply to this, and other 'licence' cases; the reason for the application of s101 is not that the court is dealing with facts peculiarly within the knowledge of the defendant (and thus easier for him to prove the affirmative than the prosecution prove the negative) but that s101 is undoubtedly applicable so the burden of proving the qualification is on the defendant.

A case giving rise to some difficulty was that of *Nimmo* v *Alexander Cowan* (1968). Under s29(1) Factories Act 1961: 'every place at which any person has at any time to work ... shall, so far as is reasonably practicable, be made and kept safe for any person working therein.' An employee alleged that his place of work had not been made and kept safe, and although the case was a civil one, it has substantial relevance in the present context. In the House of Lords it was made clear that where the burden of proof lay would be the same whether the proceedings were criminal or civil. The House of Lords, on their interpretation of the statute, decided that the employee did not have to show that it was reasonably practicable to keep the place safe, but rather the defendant (the employers) had to discharge the legal burden of proving that it was *not* reasonably practicable to keep the place safe. The decision was by a bare majority, which is indicative of the problems of construing statutory provisions which may by implication reverse the burden of proof.

An earlier, and difficult, case concerned a prosecution for the offence of acquiring rationed goods without surrendering the appropriate ration coupons (*R* v *Putland* (1946)). The Court of Criminal Appeal held that the prosecution bore the burden of proving the acquisition of the goods *and* the failure to surrender the coupons.

It was against this background of apparent inconsistency in interpretation that the case of *R* v *Hunt* reached the House of Lords in 1987. Hunt was charged with the unlawful possession of a controlled drug (morphine), contrary to s5 Misuse of Drugs Act 1971. The Misuse of Drugs Regulations 1973 provide that s5 does not apply to any morphine preparation containing no more than 0.2 per cent morphine. The prosecution adduced no evidence of the percentage of morphine in the substance found in Hunt's possession and the defence therefore submitted there was no case to answer. The judge refused to accept the submission and Hunt was convicted, having then changed his plea to guilty. The Court of Appeal dismissed his appeal, holding that the facts were covered by the implication in the statute and regulation that the burden of proving the substance's morphine content was on Hunt.

On appeal to the House of Lords, the decision of the Court of Appeal was reversed. Their Lordships stated that every case must depend on the construction of the particular legislation, and further stated that if there is, on construction, no clear indication as to where the burden of proof should lie, then the court may consider policy, including considerations of practicality such as the ease with which one party or the other could discharge the burden of proof (whether affirmative or negative). They further stated that it can never be readily assumed that Parliament intended a defendant to prove his innocence, so the courts should be reluctant to make such an inference from the wording of any but the clearest of statutory provisions. Especially where the statutory offence was a serious one (as in the case of Hunt's alleged unlawful possession of morphine) any ambiguity must be resolved in favour of the accused person.

The 'guidelines' of their Lordships in *R* v *Hunt* may be workable; if the guidelines are followed then, apart from unambiguous wording in a statute, there is virtually a presumption that the accused shall not bear a burden of proving the issue(s) referred to in the statute, and the more serious the offence charged the stronger the presumption. However, this may be in conflict with the 'policy' guideline, and in any case it presupposes that the courts cannot construe the statute to discover a clear indication of where the burden shall lie. Although the courts may have been encouraged to seek out and apply the intentions of Parliament in a consistent way, the courts are prone to overlooking the intention of Parliament in their fervour to construe statutes linguistically. More important was the failure of the House of Lords to adopt the proposal of the 11th Report of the Criminal Law Revision Committee ([1972] Cmnd 4991) that burdens on the defence should be evidential only, both on general principles of criminal law and for the sake of clarity - clarity which will probably become increasingly elusive as conflicting guidelines in *R* v *Hunt* are bent by the courts.

Question 4

Isaac had been charged with fishing in the River Isis, at a place where fishing is unlawful unless a licence is held. The offence of fishing without a licence is triable either way, with a maximum sentence of a fine of £2,000 on summary conviction and on conviction on indictment of a fine and/or two years imprisonment.

Explain and discuss the incidence of the burdens and standards of proof.

Written by editor

Skeleton solution

- Introduction re evidential and legal burdens and standards of proof in criminal cases.
- *Woolmington* v *DPP*, and exceptions to general rule in criminal cases.
- Summary trials - s101 Magistrates' Courts Act 1980.
- Trials on indictment - the 'Rule in *R* v *Edwards*'.
- Examination of, and discussion of, *R* v *Hunt*, and application to problem question.

Suggested solution

The general rule in criminal trials is that the prosecution bears the burden of proving every element of the offence charged to the criminal standard of proof, ie beyond reasonable doubt, and that when there is a burden placed on the defence it is merely an evidential burden, ie a burden of adducing enough evidence to make the issue triable (*Woolmington* v *DPP* (1935)). At the outset the prosecution also bears an evidential burden regarding the offence charged, ie if insufficient evidence is adduced by the prosecution to support a *prima facie* case, then a submission by the defence of 'no case to answer' will be successful, and the accused will be acquitted without the need for rebutting defence evidence to be called.

So, generally, in respect of every element of both *actus reus* and *mens rea*, the prosecution must discharge first the evidential and then the legal burden, to the criminal standard, to secure a conviction. Again, generally, a simple denial by the accused does not result in his having to discharge *any* burden; but if the defence case goes beyond a mere denial of the prosecution's allegation, eg a defence of duress is raised, then the defence bears a burden, but the usual situation is that the burden the defence must discharge is only an evidential burden, ie adduce enough evidence for the defence to be left to the jury unless the prosecution lead evidence which is sufficient to refute that defence beyond reasonable doubt. If the defence does not discharge that evidential burden, then the defence will be withdrawn from the jury, ie it never becomes an issue for the court (*Hill* v *Baxter* (1958)).

In *Woolmington* v *DPP* Lord Sankey LC stated that it is the duty of the prosecution 'to prove the prisoner's guilt subject to ... the defence of insanity and subject also to any statutory exception'. It was not clear whether Lord Sankey was referring to *express* statutory exceptions only, or whether the was including *implied* statutory exceptions to the general rule ('the golden thread') that all burdens of proof are on the prosecution. What was, and remains, clear, is that in summary trials s101 Magistrates' Courts Act 1980 provides that where the defence relies on 'any exception, exemption, proviso, excuse or qualification' in answer to an information charging a statutory offence, then the legal burden of proof must be discharged by the defence.

In trials on indictment it has been decided that the same statutory exceptions to the general rule apply (*R* v *Edwards* (1975)). Had this not been so, then in the case of offences triable either way the incidence of the legal burden of proof regarding any exception, exemption etc would have depended on the trial venue - which would have been sheer nonsense!

A small handful of statutes state *expressly* that the accused must prove some issue, or some defence, albeit always to the civil standard of proof only (*R* v *Carr-Briant* (1943)). A prime example is s1 Prevention of Crime Act 1953 which makes it an offence for a person to have with him in a public place an offensive weapon 'without lawful authority or reasonable excuse, the proof whereof shall lie on him'. In this small number of statutes there is no uncertainty - the defence *must prove*, not merely adduce enough evidence to raise a reasonable doubt or enough evidence to make the defence assertion an issue for the court, ie the defence must discharge a legal, not merely evidential, burden.

However, in the case of the imposition of a legal burden on the defence by implication the case of *R* v *Hunt* (1987) reviewed *Woolmington* v *DPP* and *R* v *Edwards*, and laid down guidelines for the construction of statutes which create an offence by prohibiting the doing of some act save in specified circumstances or by specified classes of persons etc. The most important statements in *R* v *Hunt* were firstly that Lord Sankey's statement referred to both express *and implied* statutory exceptions to the 'golden thread'; secondly, that in the final resort each case will depend on the construction and interpretation of the particular statute and that where there is insoluble ambiguity the court may take into account matters of policy, including the ease a party would have in discharging the legal burden and the seriousness of the offence. In the case of *R* v *Hunt* the offence charged was unlawful possession of morphine; their Lordships stated that the 1973 Misuse of Drugs Regulations created problems of construction and interpretation, thus, given the gravity of the offence, the resultant ambiguity had to be resolved in Hunt's favour and his conviction had to be quashed.

Addressing Isaac's problem, it would be for the prosecution to discharge the legal burden of proving that Isaac was fishing in a stretch of the River Isis where to fish without the requisite licence was prohibited by a penal statute. Given the discharge of the legal burden to the criminal standard on those issues, the question is then whether the prosecution must further prove beyond reasonable doubt that Isaac did not have the required licence; or whether Isaac would have to discharge an evidential burden regarding the licence, ie adduce enough evidence of his possession of a licence for that to become an issue for the court and to result in an acquittal if not then refuted by the prosecution; or finally whether, given the proof by the prosecution of the fishing, the location, and the need for a licence, Isaac then bears a legal burden of proving his 'qualification'.

Prior to *R* v *Hunt* there was no doubt that in cases involving licensed activities it was for the accused 'actor' to prove that he was licensed (see, for example, *John* v *Humphreys* (1955)), but since the pronouncements in *R* v *Hunt*, it would be for the courts now to construe the statute under which Isaac is charged and if there is ambiguity in its wording as to the incidence of the burden,then matters of policy must be taken into consideration, eg how easily can Isaac prove, or the prosecution disprove, Isaac's possession of the appropriate licence? The seriousness of the offence may be a relevant, or deciding, factor if the statute is incapable of construction - in which event it should be irrelevant whether Isaac is tried summarily or on indictment; but given the different maximum penalties stipulated, the mode of trial in this case *could* possibly be the determinant, which cannot be what was intended by the House of Lords in *R* v *Hunt*, but evinces the uncertainty which that case has introduced into this area of evidence.

Question 5

'To import the criminal standard of proof into a civil proceeding is to confuse the respective functions and needs of the criminal and civil processes.'

Discuss.

University of London LLB Examination
(for External Students) Evidence June 1990 Q3

Skeleton solution

- General rule in criminal proceedings - exceptions.
- Express statutory exceptions - implied statutory exceptions.
- Civil proceedings - general rule in *Hornal* - exceptions - matrimonial cases and cases of extreme seriousness - *Halford* v *Brookes*.

Suggested solution

In order to answer this question it is necessary to establish the distribution of the standard of proof in criminal proceedings. By this means it is possible to evaluate the extent to which the approach applied in such proceedings can be translated to civil proceedings.

The general rule in criminal proceedings is that the prosecution bears the legal burden in accordance with the *Woolmington* (1935) principle. The standard of proof on which the jury is directed is that the facts in issue must be proved beyond reasonable doubt (*Miller* v *Minister of Pensions* (1947)) or so that the jury are satisfied so that they are sure of the accused's guilt (*R* v *Summers* (1952)). To this general rule there are notable exceptions. The accused bears the legal burden in respect of the defence of insanity (*M'Naghten's Case* (1843)) and any statutory exception (*Woolmington*). This latter phrase incorporates both express statutory exceptions and where the exception is implied (*R* v *Hunt* (1987), confirming the assumption of what was said in *Woolmington*).

It is relatively easy to establish express statutory exceptions from the wording of the statute but implied exceptions can be more problematical and are governed by the criteria of *R* v *Edwards* (1975) and *R* v *Hunt*. They are where an offence is subject to exceptions, exemptions, provisos, excuses or qualification, which is the wording of s101 of the Magistrates' Court Act 1980 and declaratory of the common law (*R* v *Edwards*).

Where an exception to the *Woolmington* principle does apply, the standard of proof is the balance of probabilities (*R* v *Carr-Briant* (1943)). In other words, the jury is directed that the accused discharges the burden on him if they are satisfied that his version is more probable than not.

In translating this approach to the civil forum, the first and perhaps obvious point is that since very few civil actions are now tried with a jury, the form of the direction on the standard of proof could not appropriately be incorporated into the civil jurisdiction. In fact the tribunal in civil actions is usually the judge.

The next and more substantial point is whether there is any justification for importing a standard of proof beyond reasonable doubt as a general requirement for civil proceedings whilst at the same time leaving the current civil standard in place relative to the same matters which may be raised by one or other of the parties coinciding with the exceptions to the *Woolmington* principle which exist in civil cases.

It is submitted that to provide a standard of proof beyond reasonable doubt in civil proceedings would ignore the fact that in criminal proceedings the trial is for the liberty of the individual in which the State is a party, whereas in civil proceedings the trial is of 'equals' and the stakes do not amount to a threat to liberty of either party. The development of the criminal standard of proof very much reflects these features. Moreover, it would also conflict with existing authority, in particular with *Hornal* v *Neuberger Products* (1957), which establishes that the allegation of a crime in civil proceedings attracts the civil standard of proof. If the criminal standard were applied, application of a lower standard to coincide with the exceptions to *Woolmington* would have to be justified. Such justification is hard to see. Since a civil action is in a legal sense between equals for the settlement of a private dispute, it also follows that there can be no justification jurisprudentially for a lower standard of proof for insanity (if raised by the defendant) or for statutory exceptions on which the defendant seeks to rely. Yet a good deal of fuss was caused at the end of 1991 by a case decided by the High Court (QBD) - *Halford* v *Brookes & Another* (1991) - a civil action alleging battery was brought by the mother of a murder victim, against the alleged killers. The court decided that the criminal standard of proof should be adopted. Because of the serious nature of the allegations, the judge decided that the case should be conducted as if the defendants were being tried for murder in a criminal court. But the case causes problems - as a civil court it was allowed to draw adverse inferences when the defendant refused to testify, unlike in criminal cases. Also, hearsay evidence was allowed in under the Civil Evidence Act 1968 which would not have been at a criminal trial. Also, similar fact evidence would be more admissible. And, of course, there would be the usual problems of a trial within a trial when there is no jury. However, it is unlikely that this case would be followed in future for these very reasons.

There is, it is true, some other case law, particularly in the field presumptions and matrimonial proceedings, in which the criminal standard has been indicated. Examples are to be found in the old case of *Morris* v *Davies* (1837) (presumption of validity of marriage) and the relatively recent authorities such as *Preston-Jones* v *Preston-Jones* (1951) (proof of grounds for divorce). It is doubtful, however, how far these cases represent the present law, a view reinforced by the fact that that they have been largely overtaken by statutory intervention which has provided for a standard of proof on the balance of probabilities. To the extent that the degree of proof varies in civil proceedings, it is attributable to the fact that the courts require a greater weight of evidence before being satisfied on the balance of probabilities. In those cases in which the legal burden in civil cases is reversed, such as arises under s11 of the Civil Evidence Act 1968, the standard of proof is the usual civil standard and wholly consistent with the fact that civil proceedings are concerned with the settlement of disputes between private parties standing on equal terms in court.

Thus the only circumstances in which the proposition in the question would not be sound is, it is submitted, if the legal burden referred to in the question were the burden on an accused in cases where an exception to the *Woolmington* principle applies. That standard is a balance of probabilities - in other words, the present civil standard.

4 COMPETENCE AND COMPELLABILITY

4.1 Introduction

4.2 Key points

4.3 Analysis of questions

4.4 Questions

4.1 Introduction

Following the enactment of s80 Police and Criminal Evidence Act 1984 the competence and compellability of the spouse of an accused person has been simplified, and drastically changed. The compellability of the accused may well become an issue for the courts and Parliament if proposed changes to the right of silence become law.

4.2 Key points

a) *Distinguish competence and compellability*

i) Competence

general rule is that all persons are competent as witnesses, ie they may give evidence. Exceptions to the general rule include children; persons of defective intellect; the accused as a prosecution witness.

ii) Compellability

general rule is that all competent witnesses are compellable, ie they can be compelled (under threat of punishment for contempt of court as a last resort) to give evidence. This does not mean that the witness will always have to answer every question put to him (he may claim that his answer will tend to incriminate him, for example, or the matter may be the subject of legal professional privilege). Exceptions to the general rule of compellability are only two - the accused and his spouse.

b) *Children*

The law used to be that a child's competence was tested by inquiring into his or her understanding of the oath. According to the result of that test, the child could give sworn or unsworn evidence in criminal proceedings, but could only give sworn evidence in civil proceedings. Now s52 of the Criminal Justice Act 1991 has changed this as far as criminal proceedings are concerned. Now all children's evidence in such proceedings is given unsworn, whether they understand the oath or not - s52(1) inserts this as s33A into the Criminal Justice Act 1988. A 'child' is defined for these purposes as someone under the age of 14 - s33A(2). Therefore, in criminal proceedings those aged 14 or over give sworn evidence, but each group's competence is tested like any adult's - s52(2) - with s34(1) Criminal Justice Act 1988 ceasing to have effect.

As for civil proceedings, s96 of the Children Act 1989 (which came into force at the end of 1991) allows a child to give unsworn evidence in certain circumstances, for the first time.

Section 96 applies to any civil proceedings, and any child witness (which is defined in the Act as someone under the age of 18). If, in the opinion of the court, the child does not understand the nature of the oath, the child's evidence can be heard by the court if, in its opinion:

i) he understands that it is his duty to speak the truth; and

ii) he has sufficient understanding to justify his evidence being heard.

In civil cases there is no fixed age, obviously, at which a child becomes competent to give sworn evidence, though it has been suggested that this will normally be between the ages of eight and ten: *R* v *Hayes* (1977). It has also been stated that it would be most undesirable to call as a witness to give unsworn evidence in a criminal trial a child aged five: *R* v *Wallwork* (1958). However, s52(2) of Criminal Justice Act 1991 seems to suggest that child witnesses should now be presumed to be competent like any other witness until the contrary is shown, when that child gives evidence in criminal proceedings.

c) *Persons of defective intellect*

If a proposed witness appears to suffer from some impairment of intellect - which could be the result of mental illness or handicap, or drink or drugs, then his competence to give sworn evidence must be tested by the judge; if he does not understand the nature and solemnity of the oath, he is incompetent; if of defective intellect but nevertheless adjudged competent, the jury must decide how much weight, if any, to attach to the evidence of the witness. If the defect appears to be caused by drink or drugs there will be an adjournment before competence is tested.

d) *The accused*

The accused is incompetent as a witness for the prosecution. A co-accused is similarly incompetent unless he has already been acquitted or convicted or unless he has otherwise ceased to be a co-accused, eg a successful application for separate trials has been made. Once the co-accused becomes competent for the prosecution he is also compellable.

Section 1 Criminal Evidence Act 1898 (as amended by the Police and Criminal Evidence Act 1984) states: 'Every person charged with an offence shall be a competent witness for the defence at every stage of the proceedings, whether the person is charged solely, or jointly with any other person. Provided as follows: (a) A person so charged shall not be called as a witness in pursuance of this Act except upon his own application ...' Therefore the accused may given evidence for the defence, but is not compellable either as a witness in his own defence or that of a co-accused.

Section 1(b) of the 1898 Act provides that 'the failure of any person charged with an offence to give evidence shall not be made the subject of any comment by the prosecution'. Comment *may* be made, therefore, on the silence of the accused, by the judge and by a co-accused: *R* v *Mutch* (1973); *R* v *Wickham* (1971); comment not being obligatory - *R* v *Spence* (1990). A defendant who does refuse to answer the questions of the police after his arrest, and also remains silent at trial, does not thereby add weight to the evidence of a co-defendant or other prosecution witnesses who choose to speak - *R* v *Hubbard* (1991).

e) *Spouse of the accused*

Section 80 Police and Criminal Evidence Act 1984 has drastically changed the competence and compellability of the accused's spouse:

i) spouse is always competent for the prosecution unless husband and wife are jointly charged with an offence, and is always competent for co-accused of other spouse;

ii) spouse is compellable as witness for the prosecution or for co-accused of other spouse only if the offence charged involves assault on, or injury or threat of injury to the spouse of the accused or a person under 16, or if the offence charged is a sexual offence in respect of a person under 16;

iii) spouse is always competent to give evidence on behalf of the accused (even if both spouses jointly charged) and is always compellable *unless* both spouses are jointly charged;

iv) prosecution cannot comment on failure of spouse to testify.

f) *Ex -spouses*

i) Civil cases

The effect of s1 Evidence Amendment Act 1853 and the Evidence Further Amendment Act 1869 is to make the spouse of a party in a civil trial competent and compellable. The 1853 Act has been construed strictly: *Shenton* v *Tyler* (1939), and therefore the decision in *Monroe* v *Twistleton* (1802) appears to remain binding, ie that an ex-spouse is incompetent to give evidence about events which occurred during the subsistence of the marriage.

ii) Criminal cases

Section 80(5) Police and Criminal Evidence Act 1984 states:

'In any proceedings a person who has been but is no longer married to the accused shall be competent and compellable to give evidence as if that person and the accused had never been married.'

The wording is unambiguous, and the effect is that an ex-spouse is competent and compellable whether for prosecution or defence, and whether or not the evidence relates to occurrences during the subsistence of the marriage: *R* v *Mathias* (1989). The case of *R* v *Cruttenden* [1991] 3 All ER 242 made it clear that the divorced spouse is competent and compellable in any proceedings which take place after s80(5) came into effect even if the events about which he or she was to give evidence occurred before it came into effect.

4.3 Analysis of questions

Competence and compellability of witnesses will very rarely constitute a self-contained question; it will often comprise a part of a problem question embracing other areas such as corroboration etc. Occasionally, since s80 Police and Criminal Evidence Act 1984 was enacted there have been essay questions especially on spouses' competence and compellability. Therefore the problem question which follows is NOT a typical degree or Bar Final question - but competence and compellability will appear again in later chapters as *part* of problem questions.

4.4 Questions

Question 1

Albert Jones was driving the family car with his wife Bertha in the front passenger seat and their 15-year-old son Charles and seven-year-old daughter Diane in the rear seats. The car was knocked off the road by an oncoming lorry which failed to stop. Charles was killed instantly, and Bertha and Albert both sustained cuts and bruises. Immediately before the incident Diane shrieked: 'Look out, Daddy!'; she was very shocked, but sustained no physical injury.

Albert has been charged with causing death by reckless driving. Bertha made a statement to the police to the effect that Albert was driving far too fast, could not negotiate a bend in the road and thus hit the lorry and was swept off the road; she now does not wish to testify for the prosecution. Diane made a statement: 'Daddy was on the proper side of the road - Mummy's side was near the fence - I shouted very hard when I saw a great big lorry slide across the road towards Daddy's car.'

Discuss the evidentiary problems.

Written by editor

Skeleton solution

- Competence and compellability generally.
- Compellability of spouses - s80 Police and Criminal Evidence Act 1984 and its interpretation.
- Competence of children in criminal trials.

Suggested solution

The prosecution will have to prove beyond reasonable doubt that:

- Albert was driving the car recklessly; and
- that reckless driving was a cause of the death of Charles; it is not necessary to prove that it was the only cause, so long as it was a cause of the death. (On causation in criminal cases, see textbooks on Criminal Law, and consider *R* v *Hennigan* (1971).)

Bertha, as the spouse of Albert, the accused, is now a competent witness for the prosecution (as she is not charged jointly with them - see Police and Criminal Evidence Act 1984 s80(1)(a)), but whether she is compellable depends on the interpretation of s80(3) Police and Criminal Evidence Act 1984.

Diane, aged seven, being a 'child' for the purposes of s33A of Criminal Justice Act 1988 (as amended by Criminal Justice Act 1991), shall be presumed to be competent unless the contrary is shown - s52(2) Criminal Justice Act 1991. She can give unsworn evidence, and there is now no need to test her understanding of the oath. The case law before the 1991 Act suggested a child of the age of five should not be called to give evidence in a criminal case - *R* v *Wallwork* (1958), but above that age it was more likely that he or she would be called. However, being only seven, it could be argued that it would be fairly easy for the prosecution to rebut the presumption that Diane is competent. Yet it all depends not on age but on the individual child.

If Diane gives evidence in Albert's defence her evidence does not need to be corroborated - s52(2) Criminal Justice Act 1991, and the judge is not required to warn the jury of the dangers of convicting without corroborative evidence, but the jury themselves may attach little or no weight to Diane's evidence, dependent on how she gives her evidence and withstands cross-examination by prosecuting counsel.

Section 80 Police and Criminal Evidence Act 1984 makes the spouse of an accused person a competent witness for the prosecution whatever the charge, unless the spouse is a co-accused. However, competence means that the spouse *may* give evidence if she wishes; Bertha can be compelled to give evidence against Albert only in the limited class of cases stipulated in s80(3), of which the relevant paragraph is s80(3)(a) which makes the spouse of the accused a compellable prosecution witness if:

'the offence charged involves an assault on, or injury or a threat of injury to, the wife or husband of the accused or a person who was at the material time under the age of 16.'

Section 80(3)(a) is not very clear, but in the situation in the question the offence charged involves injury to a person under 16, Charles, who was allegedly killed by Albert's reckless driving. If Charles had not died, but had suffered some non-fatal injury, the charge against Albert would have been reckless driving - therefore arguably it would not have been covered by s80(3)(a) as it would not have been in issue that Charles (and Bertha) had been injured, nor that Diane had feared immediate injury to herself. However, since Charles, under 16 years of age, has been fatally injured, and that injury must be part of the prosecution's case against Albert, then Bertha is a compellable witness for the prosecution against her spouse. Her attendance would probably be secured by a witness order or summons (Criminal Procedure (Attendance of Witnesses) Act 1965): if she does not attend when ordered or summoned to do so, a warrant may be issued for her arrest - *R* v *Bradford Justices, ex parte Wilkinson* (1990); if, having been sworn, she refused to testify, she would be in contempt of court. If she gave evidence, but contradicted her previous statement, and showed enmity to the prosecuting counsel, then with leave of the judge she could be treated as a hostile witness, and her examination by prosecuting counsel would resemble a cross-examination, with questions being put to her on her previous statement as to her husband's driving (see, for example, *R* v *Baldwin* (1986) and *R* v *Thompson* (1976)).

Albert cannot be compelled to testify in his own defence; if he does so testify then he can (and probably will) be subjected to rigorous cross-examination. If he elects not to testify, the prosecution cannot comment on his silence (s1(b) Criminal Evidence Act 1898, as amended by Police and Criminal Evidence Act 1984), although the judge may comment - but the tenor of the judge's comment (if any) is restricted by case law (*R* v *Mutch* (1973)) and Albert's election not to testify has no evidential value.

Given the unwillingness of Bertha to testify for the prosecution, her evidence if she is compelled is unlikely to carry much weight, therefore it could be that a plea by Albert's counsel of 'no case to answer' would be successful at the conclusion of the prosecution's case, ie the prosecution have not even discharged the evidential burden, therefore there is not even a *prima facie* case. If such a plea is unsuccessful, or is not made, then Albert would be well advised to testify in his own defence if the only other defence witness is a child of tender years who may be adjudged incompetent as a witness; and if allowed to testify, she is *not* an independent, disinterested witness. Bertha, once she has been called as a prosecution witness, is not permitted to give evidence for the defence (*R* v *Kelly* (1985)). Albert's counsel should also bear this in mind when deciding whether or not to call Albert (who must be called, if he is going to testify, before other defence witnesses).

Question 2

'Recent legislative changes prove that Parliament cares little for the sanctity of marriage, whereas the Common Law had always considered the natural repugnance of the public at the prospect of a wife's giving evidence, or especially being forced to give evidence, against her husband.'

Discuss — Written by editor

Skeleton solution

- Introduction - position before 1986 summarised.
- The case of *Hoskyn* v *MPC* (1979).
- Section 80 Police and Criminal Evidence Act 1984.

- Interpretation of s80 and critical examination of its implications.

Suggested solution

Before the Police and Criminal Evidence Act 1984 the spouse of an accused was, as a general rule, incompetent as a prosecution witness. The spouse was competent as a witness for the accused, but as a witness for a co-accused was competent only if the accused spouse consented. The reason for these restrictions on the competence of a spouse as a witness for the prosecution, and even as a witness for a co-accused, was above all the respect of the Common Law for the sanctity of marriage and therefore to the unity between man and wife. Hence, no such restrictions applied to co-habitees - even where, unbeknown to one of the parties to a wedding ceremony the other was already married and therefore the marriage was bigamous, or for any other reason the marriage was void, there was no question of unity and therefore the parties were competent and compellable against each other (*R* v *Yacoob* (1981); *R* v *Khan* (1987) which was decided before the 1984 Act was law). In conflict with this policy decision to uphold the institution of marriage was, on occasions, the need to ensure that the criminal spouse was convicted, and therefore there were Common Law and Statutory exceptions to the general rule, eg violence by one spouse against another, child destruction, bigamy, sexual offences against children. In these exceptional situations, there was often some doubt as to whether the spouse was merely a competent prosecution witness or was compellable. the conflict was resolved in the House of Lords in *Hoskyn* v *Metropolitan Police Commissioner* (1979) where it was stressed that generally the spouse of the accused is incompetent as a prosecution witness and that in the exceptional situations the spouse was *never* compellable, merely competent. The decision was not universally welcomed; specifically it was thought that the police would be further deterred from intervening in 'domestic disputes' when their prospective key witness could reconsider and decide not to testify and given the lack of compellability the case would therefore be abandoned for lack of prosecution evidence.

In the case of *Hoskyn* the facts were that Hoskyn had wounded Ms Janis Grimshaw with intent to do her grievous bodily harm. Three days before he was to appear for trial in the crown court he and Ms Grimshaw married. She did not want to testify against him but the trial judge ruled that she was compellable (as a hostile witness) and Hoskyn was convicted. Their Lordships quashed his conviction, ruling that Mrs Hoskyn was competent but not compellable as a prosecution witness and therefore the judge was wrong in compelling her to testify - and without her testimony the case against Hoskyn was not proved beyond reasonable doubt. The fact that she was giving evidence about an event which occurred before her marriage to Hoskyn did not affect her compellability; what was relevant was that she was a spouse forced to testify against her accused husband.

Section 80 Police and Criminal Evidence Act 1984 became law in 1986, overruling the decision in *Hoskyn*; it provides that a spouse is always competent to testify for the prosecution against the other, accused, spouse, whatever the charge, unless the two spouses are charged jointly with an offence (s80(1) and (4)).

Section 80(3) further provides that the spouse of the accused is compellable for the prosecution if:

a) 'the offence charged involves an assault on, or injury or a threat of injury to, the wife or husband of the accused or a person who was at the material time under the age of sixteen; or

b) the offence charged is a sexual offence alleged to have been committed in respect of a person who was at the material time under that age.'

Where the spouses are jointly charged with an offence, then s80(3), obviously, does not apply (s80(4)). Section 80(9) of the Act repeals the pre-existing law regarding marital confidences:

'Section 1(d) of the Criminal Evidence Act 1898 (communications between husband and wife) and s43(1) of the Matrimonial Causes Act 1965 (evidence as to marital intercourse) shall cease to have effect.'

The effect of s80(9) is that the compellable spouse of the accused, or the competent spouse having chosen to testify, cannot refuse to disclose the content of marital communications made by the accused spouse albeit they were confidential, nor can the testifying spouse refuse to answer relevant questions as to when sexual intercourse took place with the accused spouse.

It is therefore true to state that s80 supports the administration of criminal justice at the expense of the sanctity of marriage where the two are in conflict, but s80 has gone further than the Criminal Law Revision Committee advocated in its Eleventh Report (1972) Cmnd 4991. Firstly, violence towards or a sexual offence against a person under 16 is not restricted, as was proposed, to persons in the household of the spouses, and therefore this area of compellability is more difficult to justify. Secondly, in s80(3)(a) the phrase 'an assault on, or injury or a threat of injury to' (the other spouse or any person under 16) is both broader in scope than proposed, and is far from clear. It is certain that the phrase covers criminal assaults on the other spouse or any person under 16, but it is not clear what 'injury or threat of injury' means apart from an assault, yet those words cannot be superfluous; ***presumably***, therefore, a spouse would be compelled to testify against the accused spouse if the charge was causing death by reckless driving of a person under 16, or arson where the life of such a person or persons was endangered. It will be left for the judges to interpret s80(3)(a), and thereby to determine to what extent there exists any regard in this area of compellability for the institution of marriage.

Question 3

Bill and Denis are charged with indecent assault on Freda, aged 17, and with raping Gertie, aged 15. Agnes, Bill's wife, made a statement to the police in which she stated that she had witnessed both incidents, but she is now unwilling to give evidence. Bill and Dennis assert that they have never touched the girls.

Consider whether Agnes is a competent, or compellable, witness for:

a) the prosecution;

b) Denis;

c) Bill.

Written by editor

Skeleton solution

- Introduction; spouses as witnesses.
- Agnes - competent/compellable for:
    a) prosecution;
    b) Denis;
    c) Bill.
- Brief discussion of problems raised by s80 Police and Criminal Evidence Act 1984.

Suggested solution

The general rule at common law was that a spouse of an accused person was incompetent as a witness for the prosecution; by virtue of the Criminal Evidence Act 1898 the spouse was competent as a witness for the accused and competent, provided the accused consented, as a witness for a person charged jointly with the accused. The rationale of this general rule was that the law respected the sanctity of marriage and, recognising the unity of husband and wife, considered it undesirable (even abhorrent) that one spouse testify against the other, whether as a witness for the prosecution or as a witness for a person jointly charged with the other spouse as that evidence could be unfavourable to the other spouse's defence.

Even prior to the Police and Criminal Evidence Act 1984 there were numerous statutes which created exceptions to the general rule governing the spouse as a prosecution witness, but in 1979 the House of Lords held that, in all these exceptional situations, the spouse of the accused was competent as a witness for the prosecution, but *never* compellable (*Hoskyn* v *MPC* (1979)). Pre-1984, therefore, the law in this area was very complex; as a prosecution witness the spouse of the accused was generally incompetent, but was competent by virtue of numerous statutory exceptions; as a witness for the accused she was competent but not compellable; as a witness for a person charged jointly with the accused spouse the other spouse was competent with the consent of the accused spouse but not compellable. So, pre-1984 a spouse was either incompetent, competent with consent of the other, accused, spouse, exceptionally, competent - but *never* compellable as a witness.

Section 80 of the Police and Criminal Evidence Act 1984 swept aside these, presumably archaic, restrictions on competence, and, further made the spouse compellable in specified circumstances. The spouse is now competent in every situation, unless charged jointly with the other spouse, and is compellable as a prosecution witness if the offence is a sexual offence against a person under 16, or is an offence involving injury to that spouse or a person under 16.

Applying s80 to the given facts, Agnes is compellable as a prosecution witness to the rape of Gertie, as the offence with which Bill, her spouse, is charged is 'a sexual offence alleged to have been committed in respect of a person who was at the material time under 16' (s80(3)(a) and (b)). Whether she is compellable as a prosecution witness to the indecent assault on Freda depends on the age of Freda 'at the the material time', ie if, at the time of the alleged indecent assault Freda was under 16, then Agnes is a compellable prosecution witness; if Freda was 16, then Agnes is merely competent. Despite her reluctance, if Agnes is compellable then her attendance can be secured by a witness order or witness summons (Criminal Procedure (Attendance of Witnesses) Act 1965). If she still refuses to attend a warrant can be issued for her arrest - *R* v *Bradford Justices, ex parte Wilkinson* (1990) If, having attended, she refuses to testify, she may be punished for contempt of court; if she shows enmity towards the prosecutor in giving her evidence and contradicts her previous statement, then, with leave of the judge, she may be treated as a hostile witness - in which case her examination-in-chief will take the form of a cross-examination, and consequently her evidence will lack the cogency it might otherwise have had. The prosecutor, therefore, may be reluctant to call Agnes if she shows hostility and is adamant that she does not intend to testify against her husband. (Regarding the competence and compellability of Agnes, it is irrelevant that they were not married at the time of the alleged incidents giving rise to the charges - s80 is concerned with the marital status of the accused and the potential witness at the time of the trial. Conversely, if Agnes and Bill had divorced by the time of the trial, then Agnes will be competent and compellable as if she had never been Bill's wife (s80(5)).)

Agnes is now competent as a witness for Denis whether or not Bill consents to her giving evidence for his co-accused at their joint trial (s80(1)(b)). However, her compellability as a witness for Denis is subject to the same restrictions as outlined above regarding her compellability as a prosecution witness. Whether competent or compellable as a witness to testify for Denis, the competence or compellability of Agnes is not subject to the consent of Bill - since s80 became law the wishes of the accused spouse in this context are irrelevant.

Agnes is a compellable witness for Bill, despite her previous apparent willingness to give evidence against him (s80(2)). However, if Agnes is compelled to give prosecution evidence in respect of the rape charge (and, subject to Freda's age at the time of the incident, the indecent assault charge), then she is no longer available as a witness for the defence, whether for her spouse, Bill, or his co-accused, Denis (*R* v *Kelly* (1985)).

Several problems are caused by s80, not all of them by some ambiguities in its wording, and not all of them relevant to this problem. Those which are relevant are:

a) If a successful defence application is made for separate trials of Bill and Denis, then Agnes is compellable as a witness for the prosecution, or defence, at Denis's trial, and her marital status is irrelevant.

b) Whether or not Bill and Denis are jointly tried, if the counts of rape and indecent assault are severed, and therefore tried separately, then Agnes may be compellable as a prosecution witness at the trial for rape, but not at the trial for indecent assault, but at both trials she would be compellable as a witness for Bill, but not Denis.

c) If there are separate trials of Bill and Denis, or if they are tried jointly, and Agnes gives prosecution evidence under compulsion, she may have to be treated as a hostile witness, But if the compulsion is permissible only in respect of the alleged rape, not the indecent assault, it may be difficult to the point of impossibility to put her previous statement to her in her examination-in-chief without referring to both alleged incidents as they may be inextricably linked in her statement.

5 CORROBORATION

5.1 Introduction

5.2 Key points

5.3 Analysis of questions

5.4 Questions

5.1 Introduction

The requirement for evidence to be corroborated is exceptional in English law, and the exceptional circumstances where the court will concern itself with corroboration have been whittled away by s34 Criminal Justice Act 1988, but also rendered more complex by decisions such as that in *R* v *Chance* (1988). In law degree and Bar Final examinations it is unusual to be faced with a question dealing solely with corroboration; as happens so often in Evidence papers questions about the area dealt with in this chapter will include a test of the students' knowledge of other, overlapping, areas such as burdens of proof, right of silence etc. Nevertheless, corroboration is an important issue in the laws of evidence in criminal trials.

5.2 Key points

The following should be understood by the student who wishes to be conversant with corroboration:

a) *Definition of corroboration*

The best definition is a combination of that given in *R* v *Baskerville* (1916) and *R* v *Scarrott* (1978), ie 'relevant, admissible and credible evidence, originating from a source independent of the witness requiring corroboration, and implicating the accused in a material particular.'

b) *Functions of judge and jury*

It is the function of the judge to decide whether evidence (either in itself, or aggregated with other evidence) is capable of amounting to corroboration. If the judge decides this in the affirmative, he must then leave it to the jury to decide whether the evidence *is* corroborative. If the judge decides this in the negative, he must direct the jury to disregard that evidence because, for example, it is not credible, not independent etc.

c) *Corroboration a pre-requisite to conviction*

Four statutes stipulate that an accused person cannot be convicted of the offences stipulated on the evidence of only one witness:

i) Offences of procuration - for sexual intercourse or prostitution - of women contrary to the Sexual Offences Act 1956.

ii) The offence of driving a motor vehicle on a road at an excessive speed, contrary to the Road Traffic Regulations Act 1984. Section 89 provides that a driver cannot be convicted of exceeding the speed limit on the uncorroborated opinion evidence of one witness as to the speed of the vehicle. There are two caveats:

- the corroboration requirement arises only when the charge is exceeding the speed limit - so if the charge were driving at a speed or in a manner which was reckless, the corroboration requirement would not have to be met;
- corroboration is required of the *opinion* evidence of one witness, therefore if the evidence is of fact, eg a police officer's reading of a radar speed device, corroboration is *not* required.

iii) The Treason Act 1895 requires the evidence of two or more witnesses for a conviction of high treason.

iv) Section 13 Perjury Act 1911 provides that a person cannot be convicted of perjury on the uncorroborated testimony of only one witness as to the *falsity* of any statement made by the accused which is alleged to be false. Therefore, if the statement was believed to be false, but unbeknown to the maker happened to be true, then there is no corroboration requirement. Where corroboration as to the *falsity* is required, it does not matter if two witnesses give evidence as to the falsity of the defendant's statement, and each heard him admit its falsity together, on the same occasion: *R* v *Peach* [1990] 2 All ER 966.

d) *Corroboration warning required as a matter of law*

There are two situations where the judge must warn the jury of the danger of convicting on the uncorroborated testimony of a prosecution witness. The judge must in these cases give the 'full' corroboration warning, ie must direct the jury that it would be dangerous to convict on the uncorroborated evidence, but if they are satisfied beyond reasonable doubt of the accused's guilt on the basis of the uncorroborated evidence, then a conviction will not be quashed by an appeal court on the grounds that the jury was misdirected:

i) Sexual offences

The evidence of the complainant should be corroborated, or a full warning given of the danger of convicting on her uncorroborated testimony. The offence charged must be a sexual offence; if some other offence, eg false imprisonment, is charged and the prosecution allege that the commission of the offence was accompanied by some sexual misconduct or activity by the accused which does not constitute the offence with which he is charged, then the full corroboration warning is not required: *R* v *Simmons* [1987] Crim LR 630. Again, if the commission of the sexual offence by someone is not disputed, but the accused merely denies that he was the perpetrator, then the sexual offence corroboration warning is not appropriate: *R* v *Chance* [1988] 3 All ER 225.

A complaint made by the alleged victim at the first reasonable opportunity, ie a 'recent complaint' is admissible to show consistency, but is not corroborative because it clearly lacks the independence which is vital in corroboration. However, in exceptional situations evidence of the distressed condition of the complainant may be independent and may implicate the accused, in which event it can amount to corroboration.

ii) Accomplices testifying for the prosecution

Where an accomplice gives evidence for the prosecution, this evidence is suspect, and the judge must give the jury a 'full' warning of the danger of convicting the accused on such evidence without corroboration. An 'accomplice' was defined by Lord Simons LC in *Davies* v *DPP* [1954] AC 378, who also stated that whether a witness *is* an accomplice may be determined by the witness's own admission, his plea of guilty or his conviction. If there is no such 'proof', then the judge must leave it to the jury to decide whether on the evidence they decide the witness is an accomplice, and if so they must avert their minds to the danger of convicting on his uncorroborated testimony. Provided this warning is given, the jury may convict despite the lack of corroborative evidence. One accomplice cannot corroborate the evidence of another accomplice to the offence with which the accused is charged, no doubt because the element of credibility necessary for corroboration is lacking.

e) *Corroboration warning required as a matter of practice*

i) The evidence of children - always now to be given unsworn - does not require corroboration nor a corroboration warning - s52(2) of the Criminal Justice Act 1991 abolishing s38(1) of the Children and Young Persons Act 1933, and s34(1) Criminal Justice Act 1988. However, judges may continue as a matter of practice, rather than law, to give a corroboration warning.

ii) Accomplices testifying for the defence

An accomplice giving evidence in his own defence obviously has his own axe to grind, and will often give evidence which is unfavourable to his co-accused. Therefore, as a matter of practice, it is desirable that the jury be alerted to the dangers of convicting on that evidence if it is not corroborated. Every case must be treated according to its own particular circumstances, and the omission of a warning will not always lead to a conviction's being quashed on appeal: *R* v *Prater* [1960] 2 QB 464. Where there is no evidence pointing to the involvement of the witness in the crime of which the accused is charged, but nevertheless the witness may have some ulterior motive in testifying for the defence or for the prosecution, then the judge may direct the jury to treat that evidence with some scepticism, but a failure to do so will not necessarily result in the quashing of the conviction of the accused: *R* v *Beck* [1982] 1 WLR 461; *R* v *Lovell* [1990] Crim LR 111. The recent case of *R* v *Brown* (1991) The Times 13 December in the Court of Appeal, also makes it clear that even if the witness is not an accomplice, but his evidence might be suspect, the judge should not give a corroboration warning, but warn the jury of danger of relying on that evidence.

Similarly, where the spouse of an accomplice gives evidence which is supportive of the accomplice's evidence, the judge may give a warning to the jury to treat the spouse's testimony with caution: *R* v *Evans* [1965] 2 QB 295

f) *Identification of accused*

Evidence of identification does not need to be corroborated, and a warning against convicting on such uncorroborated evidence is not mandatory. However, because a witness identifying the accused can often be mistaken, albeit genuine, guidelines were laid down by the Court of Appeal (Criminal Division) in *R* v *Turnbull* [1977] QB 224, and any student of evidence should be conversant with the gist of what the court said, and of subsequent appellate decisions which qualify or amplify the *Turnbull* guidelines.

g) *Corroboration provided by the accused*

The accused may provide the necessary or desirable, corroboration of the evidence of prosecution witnesses:

i) If the accused tells a material lie (usually by making one statement, then retracting some, or all, of it and making another, contradictory, statement) then this *may* amount to corroborative evidence. Whether it will or not was exemplified in *R* v *Lucas* [1981] QB 720; briefly, to be corroborative the lie must be material, deliberate, and told because of fear of the truth because of a realisation of guilt. So, if the accused can give an explanation of his lies which is consistent with innocence, the lies will not amount to corroboration: *R* v *Dowley* [1983] Crim LR 168.

   Similarly, lies told by the accused when testifying in his own defence *may* corroborate other evidence, but do not necessarily, and the same criteria apply as those for lies told pre-court.

ii) The silence of the accused in court, ie the fact that he elects not to testify, can never amount to corroboration. But if the accused is accused of an offence by a person or equal terms with him, and he remains silent where it would be reasonable to expect some reply (such as a denial, an indignant retort etc), then his silence is capable of corroborating other evidence of prosecution witnesses: *R* v *Cramp* (1880) 14 Cox CC 390. Whether or not the defendant and his accuser are on equal terms is a question for the jury: *R* v *Horne* [1990] Crim LR 188.

Where the accuser is a person in authority, eg a police officer, then the silence of the accused, as the law stands at present, cannot be corroboration: *R* v *Whitehead* [1929] 1 KB 99.

iii) If the accused refuses, without any reasonable explanation, to provide samples or specimens when he is told the purpose for which they are required, then his refusal is capable of amounting to corroboration: *R* v *Smith (Robert William)* (1985) 81 Cr App R 286. This decision has been adopted in s62(10) Police and Criminal Evidence Act 1984, in respect of refusal by suspects to give intimate body samples, the phrase used being 'without good cause' rather than 'without reasonable explanation' as in *Smith*. (With regard to non-intimate samples, s65(3) of the 1984 Act provides for these to be taken without consent.)

5.3 Analysis of questions

Recent questions have tended to concentrate on evidence in sexual offence cases and evidence of identification. Corroboration in problem questions tends, still, to be combined with other evidential issues, but essay questions on the incidence and rationale of corroboration do appear, and may become more common when the erosion of the right of silence starts in the near future.

5.4 Questions

Question 1

Discuss the following extracts from the directions of a judge to a jury:

a) 'The story told by the accused in this court was in my view hardly credible compared with the accuracy of evidence of Crown witnesses. However this is a matter for you, and you members of the jury must decide whose story you prefer.'

b) 'It was pointed out by the defence that the fact that the prosecutrix did not consent to sex with the defendant rests entirely on her uncorroborated evidence. This does not matter as long as you are prepared to accept her testimony on this point, since her testimony is corroborated with regard to the fact that it was the defendant who had sexual relations with her on the day in question.'

c) 'The defendant said nothing when questioned by the questioned by the police. That is his privilege, but you would think that if he was innocent he would have denied his guilt; his silence is therefore capable of corroborating the evidence of the prosecutrix.'

Adapted from University of London LLB Examination (for External Students) Evidence June 1984 Q3

Skeleton solution

a)
- Commentary by judge - own opinion.
- Left it to jury to decide.

b) • Sexual case - corroboration warning.
- No special form of words required.
- *R* v *Baskerville* - confirms story in a material particular.
- Judge must say which evidence can be corroboration and which cannot.

c) • Right to remain silent when accused not on equal terms.
- Right of judge to comment on silence.
- Can silence be corroborative?

Suggested solution

a) The functions of judge and jury must be reflected in the summing-up. The judge must direct the jury that it is for them to consider the weight of evidence and not for him. The judge is entitled to comment on the evidence and express his opinion, but he must leave the issues to the jury (see *R* v *O'Donnell* (1917)). In *Broadhurst* v *R* (1964) it was said, obiter, by the Privy Council that the judge must say clearly that the jury is not bound by his expressions of opinion. In the present case the judge has said that the issue is for the jury, and has made it clear that they must decide who is to be believed. The direction is a proper one.

b) The evidence of the complainant must, as a matter of practice, be corroborated in a sex offence case. This means that the judge must warn the jury of the danger of convicting on her uncorroborated evidence, but that they are free to convict if they believe her even if there is no corroboration. However, the case of *R* v *Nagy* (1990) suggests the use of words such as 'it can be dangerous to convict upon that evidence alone' is not always clear enough to convey that there is no corroboration and that the jury should examine very carefully the complainant's evidence before acting on it. The Court of Appeal in *R* v *Trigg* (1963) held that such a warning must be given and a conviction is likely to be quashed if it is omitted. In the present case the warning has been given in sufficiently clear terms - no special form of words is required (see *DPP* v *Kilbourne* (1973)).

The trial judge directed the jury that the evidence of the complainant was corroborated with regard to the fact that the accused did have sex with her on the day in question and that this meant there was no need for them to look for other corroboration. In the *R* v *Baskerville* case (1916), the Court of Criminal Appeal held that corroboration, in law, means independent evidence which confirms the story told by the complainant in a material particular and implicates the accused. The corroborative evidence does not have to implicate the accused in every aspect of the offence. In *James* v *R* (1970) there was evidence other than that of the complainant which established that she had had sexual intercourse at about the time in question. This did not implicate the accused though. In the present case the corroborative evidence has implicated the accused in one material particular, and that is sufficient.

The judge was in error in directing the jury that certain evidence was corroborative on the question of whether intercourse took place. It is for the judge to say what evidence there is which could be corroboration, it is for the jury to decide whether it is in fact corroboration (*R* v *Charles* (1976)). This is an error which, it seems, is too small to lead to an appeal against conviction being upheld.

c) That there is a right to remain silent when accused of a criminal offence has been affirmed recently by the Privy Council in *Hall* v *R* (1971) and *Parkes* v *R* (1976). The right does not apply if the accuser and the accused are on equal terms, but (save with the possible, but not unreasonable exception where the accused's solicitor is present, recognised in *R* v *Chandler* (1976), the parties are not on equal terms where the accuser is a police officer. This right to silence means that silence in the face of the allegation is not regarded as an admission of guilt. For the judge to direct the jury that if he were guilty the accused would have denied his guilt is to confuse the respective roles of judge and jury and to fail to make a vital distinction. It is for the jury to decide whether the defendant is innocent or guilty. For the judge to say that an innocent man would deny guilt when accused is to substitute his opinion for that of the jury on a matter which is for them. Furthermore, since the law recognises a right to stay silent when accused of an offence, the judge is under a duty to direct the jury of this, to ensure that they do not consider his silence to bc an admission (see *Hall* v *R*). In *R* v *Chandler* it was held that the proper direction in this sort of case is for the judge to leave to the jury the question of whether the silence of the defendant when accused by the police was due to an acceptance by him of guilt, and the principle stated in the last sentence from *Hall* v *R* was disapproved. Whether *Hall* v *R* or *R* v *Chandler* displays the correct approach to this question, the result is that the trial judge's direction was wrong. The direction is also wrong in respect of the corroborative nature of the defendant's silence. Although the judge is correct in not attempting to usurp the function of the jury, ie he talks of the silence being 'capable of corroborating', he does not direct the jury that it *does* corroborate, nevertheless provided the defendant was questioned by the police without his solicitor present, then without doubt that exercise of a right given to all suspects cannot be capable of corroborating other evidence against the defendant: *Hall* v *R*. Even if a solicitor were present at the time of the police questioning, it is submitted that, despite what was said in *R* v *Chandler*, the judge is wrong in leaving it to the jury to decide whether that silence may be corroborative of other evidence; *R* v *Chandler* has never been followed and has been the subject of strong criticism albeit never expressly overruled.

Question 2

Advise, on appeal, on the following directions to juries:

a) 'Defence counsel has said a lot about the absence of corroboration. You may find corroboration of the girl's story in any evidence that supports her story as long as the evidence does not come from her mouth. You may, for instance, find corroboration if you disbelieve the defendant's story that he had not spoken to the girl on the evening of the rape.'

b) 'If the accused says he acted in a state of automatism then he must establish that fact by leading evidence.'

Adapted from University of London LLB Examination
(for External Students) Evidence June 1985 Q9

Skeleton solution

- Corroboration - definition - *Baskerville* - independence - lies as corroboration.
- Burden of proof - automatism - evidential burden on accused.

Suggested solution

a) Two points are raised in this direction, firstly the general rule on what can amount to corroboration and secondly the rule on when lies of the accused can corroborate the evidence of a prosecution witness.

The general definition of corroboration was laid down in *Baskerville* (1916), and is that corroboration must be independent evidence which implicates the accused in a material particular. The complainant in a rape case must be corroborated as a matter of practice (*R* v *Trigg* (1963)). That means that the judge must direct the jury to look for corroboration, but that they may convict in the absence of corroboration if they are satisfied of the truth of the evidence of the complainant. The element of corroboration which is often difficult in such cases is to find evidence which is independent of the complainant. The direction in this case that corroboration can come from any source except from the mouth of the complainant herself does not make the independence requirement clear enough. There may be cases where the corroboration does not come from the mouth of the complainant, but is still not independent. For example, if the complainant made a complaint of rape to her mother shortly after the alleged offence, the mother will be allowed to repeat this in evidence (*R* v *Osborne* (1905)). Such a complaint when repeated in court does not amount to corroboration even though it comes from the mouth of the mother and not that of the complainant (*R* v *Wallwork* (1958)). The independence requirement has been reduced in importance in cases where it is the distressed condition of the victim which is relied on as corroboration (*R* v *Dowley* (1983) and Oughton, 'The Distressing Nature of Corroboration' [1984] Crim LR 265), but there has been no relaxation of the principle as regards other types of corroborative evidence.

Therefore the general definition of corroboration given by the trial judge was not correct. Nonetheless, such an error could have been corrected by the trial judge correctly identifying the evidence given which could and which could not amount to corroboration. This he failed to do.

The judge directed the jury that they could find corroboration in the inconsistency of the accused's story with that of the complainant. The rule relating to when lies told in court can amount to corroboration has recently been aligned with the long-standing rule about lies told out of court. In *R* v *King* (1967) a four-part test was laid down for when lies told out of court, by the accused, could corroborate; the lies must (a) have been deliberate, (b) relate to a material issue, (c) be told because of a knowledge of guilt and a fear of the truth, and (d) must clearly be shown to be lies by evidence other than that of the person who needs to be corroborated. These same four provisions were applied to the question of lies told in court in *R* v *Lucas* (1981). The error made by the trial judge, in the question, was the failure to direct the jury that the defendant's evidence must have been shown to be lies by evidence other than that of the girl who needed to be corroborated.

This error was an error of law which, when added to the incorrect general direction, must be a good ground of appeal.

b) The general rule in all criminal cases is that it is for the prosecution to prove every element of the offence charged beyond reasonable doubt (*Woolmington* v *DPP* (1935)). In some cases the accused has to proved his defence, but these are exceptional. In other cases the accused does not have to prove his case, but he bears the burden of laying the foundation before the jury has to consider his defence. The burden on the accused in such a case being an evidential burden. Clearly in any case an accused may raise many different defences. To expect the prosecution to adduce evidence negativing any possible defence would be both confusing for the jury and an unreasonable waste of time. Therefore if the accused wishes to put forward a defence which is in some way out of the ordinary, it is for him to put before the jury some credible evidence that the defence may be available and it is then for the prosecution to prove, beyond reasonable doubt, that the defence is not open. The standard of the evidential burden has never been clearly formulated, the courts being content to use vague phrases like 'positive evidence' and 'some evidence' (*Bratty* v *Attorney-General for Northern Ireland* (1961)), 'evidence of a reasonable possibility of the existence of the defence' (*Jaysena* v *R* (1970)). It is submitted that, in line with general principles of standard of proof, the standard of the evidential burden is that if the accused wishes the jury to consider a particular defence he must raise such evidence which, if left unchallenged, could leave the jury in a reasonable doubt as to the non-existence of the defence. This definition of the standard follows the definition in *Galbraith* (1981) of the standard of the evidential burden on the prosecution.

The trial judge directed the jury that if the accused wishes to avail himself of the defence of automatism he must do so by establishing that fact by leading evidence. This direction puts too high a burden on the accused. The accused must lead evidence of automatism (see *Bratty*'s case), but he is under no obligation to establish the defence. Establish is an ambiguous word, and could be taken to mean prove. Indeed it means prove if it arises in a statute (*Blyth* v *Blyth* (1966)). Therefore, because the direction did not make it clear that the accused does not have to prove automatism, it was wrong (this answer assumes that 'automatism' means non-insane automatism).

Question 3

Consider whether there is a ground of appeal in each of the following extracts from trial judges' directions to juries:

a) 'When a victim of an alleged sexual assault has said soon afterwards that she has not consented to sexual intimacy, considerable weight may be attached to her statement by you.'

b) 'Isn't it odd that the wife of the accused did not give evidence in this case, even though the accused said in evidence that she was willing to do so; after all she could have confirmed whether the accused spent the evening watching a video film.'

c) 'I have already cautioned you about acting on the uncorroborated testimony of Biggs, since he was an accomplice, but you have heard his evidence, and further, his diary from which he refreshed his memory may show you that he is a credible and consistent witness.'

d) 'Even though Mr Colby was stabbed from behind, he said he saw the face of the man clearly reflected on the windscreen of his car. If you believe this evidence you can act upon it, even though there was no other evidence to incriminate Carrington as the assailant.'

e) 'Defence counsel cross examined the Crown's witnesses on the basis that the accused acted in self-defence. I agree with Crown counsel that it is not enough for the accused to make the allegation of self-defence, he must lead evidence to make you believe that he probably did act in self-defence.'

University of London LLB Examination
(for External Students) Evidence June 1986 Q5

General comment

It is common for the examiner to set a question on various aspects of the contents of directions to juries. This question is fairly typical of the type. It covers a wide range of topics but concentrates on corroboration and rules akin to the corroboration rules. There are no particular devious tricks in this question, though from the facts given about the case, part (d) could be construed as the kind of case where a submission of no case should have been upheld. For the purposes of the answer below, it is assumed that the judge has acted correctly in leaving the case to the jury.

Skeleton solution

a)
- Hearsay if used to prove whether or not she consented - not, if for consistency.
- Judge not allowed to tell jury how much weight to give to evidence.

b)
- Section 1(b) of the Criminal Evidence Act 1898.
- Silence is not an admission of guilt.

c) • Accomplice - corroboration warning necessary.
   • Memory - refreshing document - merely evidence of credibility.

d) • *Turnbull* direction.
   • No requirement for corroboration warning.

e) • Evidential burden only.
   • Burden on prosecution - beyond reasonable doubt.

Suggested solution

a) The rule against hearsay prevents evidence being given in criminal cases where the truth of assertions made is not within the personal knowledge of the witness giving it (*Myers* v *DPP* (1965)).

There are certain common law and statutory exceptions, but they do not concern us here. The direction of the trial judge in this case is to the effect that the jury may give considerable weight to the evidence of a witness who says that the complainant had said she had not consented. This evidence would be hearsay if tendered to prove that the complainant did not consent, because it would involve the witness giving evidence that the complainant told him that she had not consented, in order to try to prove whether or not she had consented (*R* v *Wallwork* (1958)). The witness would not know that the girl did not consent, all he could say is 'she told me that she did not consent'. That is hearsay and is inadmissible.

But, the evidence may be tendered not to prove that the girl did not consent, but to prove that she has been consistent in her story of events (*R* v *Lillyman* (1896)). This is one exception to the rule against using previous consistent statements, and this exception is confined to sexual cases - *R* v *Jarvis and Jarvis* (1991). The principle here is that if the jury has heard evidence from the complainant, it will have to decide whether she should be believed and one matter which would be relevant to that issue would be whether she had been consistent. Clearly a complainant who has changed her story is less credible than one who has stuck to her guns, and the law recognises this by allowing evidence of the complaint to be given in order to show that the girl is worthy of belief when she says in court that she did not consent.

The fact that evidence of the complaint is only relevant to the credibility of the complainant means that if she did not give evidence then the evidence of the complaint is irrelevant and inadmissible (*R* v *Wallwork*). Therefore, if the girl had not herself given evidence of lack of consent, then the trial judge would have been wrong to allow evidence of the complaint to be given and equally wrong to tell the jury that they may give it considerable weight. But, assuming the complainant did give evidence, then the only ground for complaint in relation to the summing up is that it may tend to suggest that the judge is in a position to tell the jury how much weight they should give any particular piece of evidence. It is well established that the judge is not allowed to tell the jury how much weight they should give to the evidence (*Chandler* v *DPP* (1964)). The direction here says that the jury 'may' give the evidence considerable weight. Much depends on how the judge said this, his tone of voice and phrasing could have given the impression that the jury should give that evidence considerable weight, but on the other hand he could have made it clear that the decision was for them. The written word cannot disclose the way in which things were said, and the Court of Appeal will only overturn a judge's direction where the words appear on paper to be inappropriate. The words used are equally consistent with the judge leaving the matter to the jury as they are with him telling them what to do with it, and in those circumstances the Court of Appeal is unlikely to take issue with the direction, unless the judge did not make clear that the complaint was relevant to credibility only.

b) Section 1(b) of the Criminal Evidence Act 1898 provides that the prosecution shall not comment on the failure of the accused or his wife to give evidence. That prohibition does not, however, extend to the judge making such comment. The Court of Appeal laid down in *R* v *Bathurst* (1968) that if the judge is to comment on the failure of the accused to give evidence, then his comment should make clear to the jury that the accused has a right not to give evidence and that failure to give evidence is not an admission of guilt; and in *R* v *Gallagher* (1974) the court said that comment by the judge on the failure to call a witness should be equally careful. Any comment passed by the judge should be balanced by a clear statement that it is not for the accused to prove his defence (*Waugh* v *R* (1950)) and there is clear authority to the effect that the accused does not have to prove his alibi (*R* v *Johnson* (1961)).

   The direction in this case fails to point out the necessary matters, and so is incorrect in law. It is not possible to say whether the jury would still have convicted even without the comment from the judge, therefore there is a good ground of appeal.

c) An accomplice's evidence should be corroborated as a matter of practice; in other words it is mandatory that the judge warns the jury to treat the evidence with caution but, if they are satisfied by the prosecution's case so that they feel sure of guilt, they may convict even in the absence of corroboration of what the accomplice has said (*Davies* v *DPP* (1954)). A document used to refresh a witness' memory cannot, of itself, corroborate his evidence because it is not independent of him (*R* v *Virgo* (1978)). The jury will not be allowed to see a memory-refreshing document unless it is made an exhibit, in which case they may take it with them into the jury room and may read it (*R* v *Bass* (1953)). The document is not evidence of the truth of statements made in it, however, it is merely evidence of the credibility of the witness. The judge must direct the jury that the document is not evidence against the accused (*R* v *Graham* (1973)). The direction here says that the diary may show the jury that Biggs is a credible and consistent witness, but it does not stress that the diary is not itself corroborating evidence. The failure to stress this matter is an irregularity and would be a ground of appeal, but without knowing the strength of the other evidence against the accused it is not possible to say whether it would lead to the conviction being quashed, it may be possible to apply the proviso (s2(1) Criminal Appeals Act 1968).

d) When directing a jury how to treat identification evidence the judge must follow the guidelines laid down in *R* v *Turnbull* (1977). In that case the Court of Appeal held that there is a special need for caution when the prosecution case rests wholly or mainly on evidence of one or more identifications. However, the later case of *R* v *Courtnell* (1990) suggested that the *Turnbull* warning need only be given where there is a substantial issue as to the *accuracy* of the identification . If in this case, the sole issue is the *honesty* of Mr Colby (ie he is not mistaken but is in fact lying), then *Courtnell* suggests a *Turnbull* warning is unnecessary. If the defence allege Mr Colby was mistaken, then the trial judge should warn the jury of the need for caution and should also point out the circumstances of the identification. This is not a requirement that a corroboration warning should be given, but there is a requirement that the judge explains to the jury that a witness who is sure of the correctness of the identification may nonetheless be mistaken. The direction in this case is too brief and fails to emphasise the unreliability of identifications. Failure to give the *Turnbull* direction is a reason for a conviction to be quashed because it makes the conviction unsafe or unsatisfactory (*R* v *Lamb* (1980); *R* v *Reid* (1990)).

e) The prosecution is not expected to anticipate every possible defence which may be put forward and so is not expected to lead evidence about, for example, self-defence. Instead it is for the accused to lay a foundation in order to make the question whether he acted in self-defence a live issue. The burden on the accused is evidential only; in other words the accused must put forward some credible evidence of self-defence and it is then for the prosecution to prove that the accused did not act in self-defence (*Mancini* v *DPP* (1942)). There is no clear authority as to the standard which the accused must meet in order to satisfy his evidential burden, but the nature of this burden can be explained by reference to a presumption. It will be presumed that the accused did not act in self-defence and since the burden on the prosecution is to prove the case beyond reasonable doubt this presumption amounts to a finding that the prosecution has proved lack of self-defence beyond reasonable doubt. In order for the accused to be acquitted it is necessary that the prosecution fails to prove its case beyond reasonable doubt, therefore if there is a presumption on the issue of self-defence that the prosecution has proved its case beyond reasonable doubt, so the burden on the accused must be to put forward evidence which could raise a reasonable doubt in the mind of a reasonable jury as to whether or not he acted in self-defence. It is certainly not for the accused to prove that he acted in self-defence. The direction in this case is to the effect that the accused must prove self-defence on balance of probabilities. If the accused did bear a legal burden then the balance of probabilities is the standard required of him before he has satisfied that burden (*Sodeman* v *R* (1936)), but on the issue of self-defence the accused does not bear such a burden. This is a material error of law and will lead to the conviction being quashed unless the proviso can be applied (s2(1) Criminal Appeals Act 1968), which is unlikely.

Question 4

Consider whether there is any ground of appeal in each of the following directions to juries:

a) 'I have already warned you of the dangers of convicting on the uncorroborated testimony of the woman Cynthia, since she is an accomplice, but if you come to the conclusion that the accused was lying in court, because you believe Cynthia's evidence, then that lie will be evidence which you may regard as corroboration.'

b) 'The accused pleaded diminished responsibility in this case. Now, the law is that it is up to him to satisfy you of that fact in the same way that the Crown must convince you as to his guilt. It is not enough that you think that it is probable that he was acting in a state of diminished responsibility.'

Adapted from University of London LLB Examination
(for External Students) Evidence June 1987 Q5

Skeleton solution

a)
- Accomplice - corroboration warning needed.
- What it involves.
- Lies in court - *R* v *Lucas*.

b)
- Legal burden on defendant - standard required.

Suggested solution

a) *Corroboration*

The evidence of an accomplice requires corroboration as a matter of practice (*Davies* v *DPP* (1954)). This means that the judge must warn the jury to treat the evidence with caution and to look for corroboration of it, but the warning should also say that the jury may convict notwithstanding the absence of corroboration if they are satisfied that the accomplice was telling the truth.

Lies told by the defendant in court may be corroboration of the evidence of an accomplice provided four criteria are satisfied: (a) it must be a deliberate lie; (b) relating to a material particular; (c) which was told out of a realisation of guilt and a fear of the truth; and (d) it must be shown to be a lie by evidence other than the evidence which needs to be corroborated (*R* v *Lucas* (1981)).

The jury in this case has been directed, as was the jury in *R* v *Lucas,* that if they come to the conclusion that the defendant was lying because the accomplice was telling the truth then they may treat her evidence as having been corroborated. This is a misdirection in that the jury is being told to look at the accomplice's evidence in order to decide whether the defendant is lying, and this fails the fourth criterion.

b) *Diminished responsibility*

If the defendant argues diminished responsibility in his defence to a murder charge then it is for him to prove diminished responsibility (s2 Homicide Act 1957). The standard required, however, is proof on balance of probabilities. There is no case which specifically says that the accused bears a standard of proof lower than that on the prosecution, but in *R* v *Dunbar* (1958) it was held that he does bear a legal burden of proof.

The rule is universal that whenever the defendant in a criminal case has to prove anything, the burden on him is the civil burden of balance of probabilities and not the prosecution's criminal burden of beyond reasonable doubt (*R* v *Carr-Briant* (1943)). The direction is clearly wrong.

Question 5

'Although the silence of the accused person may strengthen the inferences to be drawn from the other evidence against him, it is not capable of corroborating other evidence.'

Discuss critically.

Written by editor

Skeleton solution

- Introduction; silence in court; out of court.
- Silence in court; comment and effect.
- Silence out of court; relationship of accused.

Suggested solution

Although the question refers to 'the accused', an answer which omits reference to a suspect who later becomes 'the accused' would be incomplete. The quotation is virtually correct if it is restricted to the accused person who elects not to testify, but it has a basic flaw even then - the expression '*other* evidence' means that the speaker accepts that silence in court amounts to evidence against the accused; that is not law yet although it may be that the right of silence will be eroded in the near future (see section 5.2(g)(ii) above). Therefore, discussion of the quotation demands examination not only of silence of the accused or his trial, which can never amount to corroboration (*R* v *Jackson* (1953)), and silence when he is accused of committing an offence in a pre-trial situation.

Although the accused is a competent witness in his own defence he is not compellable (s1 Criminal Evidence Act 1898), and the prosecution is not permitted to comment on his silence. The judge may comment on the silence, as was laid down shortly after the 1898 Act was passed (*R* v *Rhodes* (1899)), but must be careful how he words such comment to the jury; in the case of *R* v *Mutch* (1973); the Court of Appeal held that the trial judge was wrong to advise the jury that they could draw adverse inferences from the failure of the accused to give an explanation consistent with his innocence. In *R* v *Sparrow* (1973) guidelines were laid down concerning judicial comment, of which the major ones are: (a) the accused's failure to give evidence has no evidential value, and may not therefore be treated as corroboration; (b) comment depends on the circumstances in every case; if the prosecution case is particularly strong, then the comment may be strong; (c) the judge must never state that silence may be equated to guilt, nor must the jury be advised, therefore, expressly or impliedly that unless the accused testifies his defence cannot succeed. It has recently been held that whether the judge comments at all is a matter for his discretion (*R* v *Harris* (1986)), but, most importantly, silence of the accused is not capable of amounting to corroboration (*R* v *Jackson*) and the judge may consider it desirable to emphasise this to the jury.

When a person is suspected of committing a crime and is accused of this out of court, then the evidential effect of his silence depends on who is his accuser. If the accuser is a person on even terms, and in the circumstances it would be reasonable to expect a reply, then silence can amount to a confession of guilt (*Parkes* v *R* (1976)) and is capable of amounting to corroboration (*R* v *Cramp* (1880)).

However, if the accuser is not on even terms with the accused, ie is a person in authority, such as a police officer, then the accused has a right of silence of which he ought to be reminded at the time; his silence therefore cannot be used as evidence against him (*Hall* v *R* (1971)), and consequently is incapable of amounting to corroboration (*R* v *Whitehead* (1929); *R* v *Keeling* (1942)). For so long as the caution remains, to remind suspects of their right of silence, then it is a contradiction in terms to give that silence any evidential value. In *R* v *Chandler* (1976) it was held that, as Chandler was accompanied by his solicitor when interviewed by the police, he and the police officers were on even terms, therefore his silence could be used as evidence against him. The case has been criticised and has not been followed; a solicitor would very probably remind his client of his right to silence, whether the police had or not, and the reasoning in *Chandler* seems illogical.

Finally, it was held in *R* v *Gilbert* (1977) that when the accused remains silent after being cautioned by the police and does not reveal his defence until the trial, the judge must not invite the jury to draw adverse inferences from the accused person's silence and subsequent 'ambush defence'.

Question 6

Albert is charged with indecent assault on Bertha, aged seven. Bertha's brother, Charles, aged 14, reported to the police that on the day in question Bertha came home in a distressed state and with her clothing disarranged and told him that Albert, the caretaker at her school, had kissed her, put his hand up her dress and when she screamed he first tried to pull her dress off but then ran away when two of her friends appeared.

That night, when Bertha's father, Fred, arrived home he was informed of the incident, he went to Albert's house and accused him of the assault and attempted to enter the house as he swore at Albert. Albert said nothing, but slammed the door and refused to open it. Fred informed the police, and Albert was interviewed at the police station the next day; he refused to answer the questions of the police officers and remained silent throughout the interview. Albert's wife, Gertrude, made a statement to the police to the effect that Albert had admitted to her that he had indecently assaulted a pupil, but Gertrude does not now wish to testify.

Discuss the evidentiary aspects.

Written by editor

Skeleton solution

- Evidence of children; corroboration; sexual offences.
- Recent complaints in sexual offences.
- Silence as evidence of guilt; as corroboration; parties on even, and uneven terms.
- Competence and compellability of spouses.

Suggested solution

If Bertha gives evidence, then as a matter of law a corroboration warning should be given, not because of her tender years, but because the offence alleged is a sexual offence. Therefore the jury must be warned of the danger of convicting on her uncorroborated evidence. She will automatically give unsworn evidence, and will be treated like other witnesses as regards her competence since the CJA 1991.

Provided Bertha gives evidence, Charles will be permitted to testify as to her 'recent complaint' which shows consistency in Bertha's evidence, but is not corroborative of her evidence, because crucially it lacks the independence which is necessary for corroboration (*R* v *Whitehead* (1929)). If Bertha does not give evidence because the prosecution feel she should not be subjected to such trauma, Charles will not be permitted to relate to the court what Bertha told him because there will be no issue of consistency (*R* v *Wallwork* (1958)).

However, whether Bertha gives evidence or not, Charles will be allowed to give evidence of what he perceived, ie Bertha's distressed state and disarranged clothing. However, that will have little, if any, weight, and if Bertha gives evidence the distress and disarray is not capable of corroborating Bertha's evidence because it does not implicate Albert, the alleged offender (*R* v *Knight* (1960) and cf *R* v *Redpath* (1962)).

When Fred accuses Albert of the offence, they are on even terms and therefore Albert's silence in the face of an accusation could amount to corroboration, provided a reply could reasonably be expected (*R* v *Cramp* (1880)). However, on the given facts, the judge may well decide that, given the belligerence of Fred coinciding with the accusation, it was a natural reaction by Albert to slam the door, rather than make some denial, retort etc and be subjected to verbal and probably physical abuse. So, if in the opinion of the judge it would not have been natural in the circumstances for Albert to reply, he will direct the jury that Albert's silence does not imply guilt and they should not consider it corroborative of Bertha's complaint.

Albert, when interviewed by the police, has a right to remain silent (*Hall* v *R* (1971)), therefore his silence cannot be evidence of his guilt, and is not capable of corroborating Bertha's evidence (*R* v *Whitehead*).

With regard to Gertrude's statement to the police, spouses are now competent as witnesses for the prosecution of the other, accused, spouse (Police and Criminal Evidence Act 1984 s80(1)(a)). As the offence with which Albert is charged is a sexual offence against a person under 16, Gertrude is not merely competent for the prosecution, she is compellable (Police and Criminal Evidence Act 1984 s80(3)(b)). If Gertrude insists, despite being informed of her compellability, that she will not testify, she may be compelled to attend by witness order or summons (Criminal Procedure (Attendance of Witnesses) Act 1965), and with leave of the court may be treated as a hostile witness. The value of her evidence in such circumstances is debatable, however.

In conclusion, given the circumstances in which Fred accused Albert and the unwillingness of Gertrude to testify for the prosecution, then, unless there is other evidence implicating Fred, it is unlikely that the case would be pursued by the Crown Prosecutor if Bertha was incompetent or psychologically incapable as a witness.

Question 7

'It is submitted that, subject to the precautions required by *R* v *Turnbull* in cases of disputed identification, the unfettered discretion approach is the best answer that English law can give to the questions whether, when and to what extent corroboration should be required.' (Cross)

Discuss.

University of London LLB Examination
(for External Students) Evidence June 1990 Q4

Skeleton solution

- General rules - corroboration as a necessity, corroboration warning as a necessity, corroboration warning in practice.
- Final category of 'suspect' witnesses.
- Desirability of corroboration in these categories.
- Confusion of jury.
- Alternatives - discretion in judge.

Suggested solution

In order to test the correctness of the proposition cited in the question, it is necessary to consider what the present rules are and the nature of their defects, and then to evaluate whether the solution proposed would resolve matters.

There is no general requirement for corroboration in English law. Corroboration therefore addresses situations which are the exception rather than the rule. They fall within recognised categories.

First, there are some statutory provisions which make corroboration a prerequisite for conviction. Perjury and procuration offences under the Sexual Offences Act 1956 are notable examples of such provisions. Second are the cases at common law where corroboration is looked for as a matter of practice. This is established, but rather misleading, terminology because the requirement is really for the judge to warn the jury of the danger of convicting on evidence which is uncorroborated. The evidence of accomplices (as defined in *Davies* v *DPP* (1954) referred to further below) and of victims in sexual cases fall within this category. Finally, there are situations where there is no corroboration (or corroboration warning) requirement as such, but where the courts recognise witnesses as being potentially unreliable and thus the judges warn juries, depending on the facts, of the special need for caution before acting on the evidence if unsupported. This category includes witnesses who may have their own interests to serve, the mentally impaired, children of tender years and also evidence of identification.

Looking first at the statutory provisions requiring corroboration as a matter of law, it could be said that if Parliament has seen fit to enact legislation requiring corroboration, the answer is that to leave the question of corroboration to the judge is clearly not an appropriate course. That said, situations change over time and the facts which influenced Parliament in imposing the requirements might not be influential today. An obvious defect is that an across-the-board requirement is inflexible and allows the judge no leeway in directing the jury, having regard to the facts of the particular case. Whether corroboration seems desirable or necessary in any given situation, the judge must direct the jury to acquit in the absence of corroboration. Perhaps a more serious defect, and one which is common to all the circumstances in which corroboration arises, lies in the nature of corroboration itself, and the way in which the judge is required the direct the jury. To be corroborative, the evidence must satisfy the test in *R* v *Baskerville* (1916) (independent from but supporting the evidence to be corroborated and implicating the accused). The judge is required to explain this to the jury together with the fact that the test may be satisfied cumulatively (*R* v *Hills* (1988)). He must identify the evidence capable of being corroborative (*R* v *Cullinane* (1984)) whilst leaving them to decide whether it is in fact so.

It is questionable how far the average jury understands the refinements or evaluates the evidence in accordance with the directions. This problem would not be cured by leaving the question of corroboration to the discretion of the judge. Rather, it requires the discontinuance of the concept of corroboration in its technical sense and its replacement with the concept of supporting evidence. Once that is done, a separate question arises of whether the requirement of supporting evidence should be left solely to the judge's discretion. Given that there has already been parliamentary intervention to impose a corroboration requirement, it would seem that some form of general requirement for supporting evidence should be made, rather than leaving matters at large wholly to the discretion of the judge. That said, Parliament has seen fit by s34 of the Criminal Justice Act 1988 to abolish the corroboration requirement for the unsworn evidence of children, so the position is not clear cut.

Moving now to the cases requiring a mandatory warning, the position is still more complicated and unsatisfactory. An accomplice, as defined in *Davies* v *DPP* is a prosecution witness who is a party to the crime, or a receiver giving evidence against the thief from whom he received stolen goods, or a party to a crime admissible under the 'similar fact' principle. Sexual cases are not defined as such but seemingly do not extend to non-sexual offences in which there has been a sexual element.

In all accomplice cases and all sexual cases except where identity is the only issue, the judge must warn the jury of the danger of convicting on uncorroborated evidence. He must go through the same routine as previously described for the statutory requirements and, having done that, must tell the jury that they may still convict even if they find no corroboration, if they are satisfied beyond reasonable doubt that the evidence is truthful. The difficulties for the average jury in relation to the statutory provisions are thus compounded for this category. It is doubtful whether many juries even understand the directions. Moreover, there is no compelling reason why the mandatory corroboration warning should apply to these cases exclusively while the situations referred to in the third category (unreliable witnesses) are not within the requirement. In the recent case of *R* v *Brown* (1991) the Court of Appeal made it clear that where a witness was not an accomplice but, nevertheless, his evidence was suspect, it was not necessary that a full corroboration warning be given; it was sufficient for the judge to warn the jury of the danger of relying on such evidence. But again, the issue is perhaps less that the warning is mandatory than that it is a warning tied to corroboration. Whilst the fact that it is mandatory is undesirable because of inflexibility, the situation is made much worse by the fact that it is linked to corroboration which results in a judge's directions probably being incomprehensible to the average jury. Thus, although the removal of the mandatory requirement for the warning and its replacement with pure judicial discretion as proposed in the question would improve matters, what is really required is the abolition of the corroboration element in its technical sense and its replacement with the requirement for supporting evidence along the lines already mentioned under the statutory provisions above.

The final question which arises from the proposition is whether it is in fact legitimate to leave matters entirely with the judge in those cases subject to the mandatory warning. Support for the affirmative answer is to be found in s34 of the Criminal Justice Act 1988 which abolishes the mandatory corroboration warning for children of tender years outright. On the other hand as with the mandatory corroboration requirements already referred to, there is an argument that, having had such requirement in the past, some ground rules on the exercise of the judge's discretion should be imposed. Some support for this view can be obtained from *R* v *Chance* (1988) which has established that for sexual cases where identity is the issue, a *Turnbull* (1977) type direction is adequate. *Turnbull* itself imposes constraints on the judge's approach to the evidence and identification cases and it can be said with some justification that accomplices and sexual cases in general should at least impose as high a requirement on the judge.

6 HEARSAY - GENERAL EXCLUSION

6.1 Introduction

6.2 Key points

6.3 Analysis of questions

6.4 Questions

6.1 Introduction

Hearsay is one of the most important areas of the laws of evidence; the rule against hearsay is complex, but the rule and the many exceptions to it will always form the basis of at least one question (and frequently several) in any Evidence examination.

In this chapter the scope and application of the exclusionary rule against hearsay will be examined, together with the important common law rules which exceptionally allowed hearsay to be adduced.

In the next two chapters, admissibility by statute in civil and criminal cases respectively will be examined - only then will the full complexity of the hearsay rule emerge.

6.2 Key points

a) Definitions of hearsay abound; to determine whether evidence is or is not hearsay (and therefore whether it is necessary to go any further and consider exceptions to the exclusionary rule) one should consider the purpose for which an out of court statement is tendered in evidence. If the statement is tendered as evidence of any fact (or opinion) expressed therein, then it is hearsay, ie if any out of court statement is tendered in order to invite the court to accept the truth of its content, that is hearsay. The statement may take various forms, ie it may be spoken, written, or in the form of a gesture:

   i) Spoken, or oral hearsay

   A good example of this is contained in the House of Lords decision in *R* v *Blastland* [1985] 2 All ER 1095, where their Lordships upheld the decision of the trial judge to exclude as inadmissible hearsay evidence of the content of a confession made by a person other than the accused. Blastland's counsel wanted this confession statement reported to the court as evidence of its truth, ie to further Blastland's defence. It was hearsay, and because it was not covered by any recognised exception to the hearsay rule, was therefore inadmissible.

Again, in *Sparks* v *R* [1964] AC 964, a white man was charged with indecent assault on a girl aged three. Sparks's counsel wanted to call as a defence witness the girl's mother to inform the court that shortly after the incident the girl had said that a coloured boy was the assailant. This evidence was being tendered to invite the court to believe the truth of the out of court statement by the girl (who did not give direct evidence herself), and was therefore hearsay, and, again, inadmissible because not covered by a recognised exception to the rule against hearsay.

ii) Written, or documentary hearsay

The same principles apply at common law as for spoken, or oral hearsay, so again the vital issue is the purpose for which the written, or printed etc, evidence is tendered.

iii) Gestures as hearsay

An affirmative nod or negative shake of the head may be hearsay just as the spoken or written affirmative or negative would be if tendered as an out of court 'statement'.

b) *The ambit of the hearsay rule*

If an out of court statement is tendered for a purpose *other* than to invite the court to accept the contents as true, then it is not hearsay. Therefore, if the fact rather than the content of the statement is what the person tendering it seeks to prove, it is not hearsay. For example, in *Ratten* v *R* [1972] AC 378 a telephone operator was permitted to give evidence that the wife of the accused had made an emergency telephone call in which she hysterically demanded the police a couple of minutes before she was fatally shot. The *fact* of the call contradicted Ratten's statement that his wife had made no telephone call; also the wife's hysteria tended to refute Ratten's defence that his gun went off as he was cleaning it and his wife was thus accidentally shot and died immediately. Therefore the evidence of the telephone operator was not hearsay. The case emphasises the point that the purpose for which the statement was tendered determines whether or not it is hearsay.

However, sometimes it is extremely difficult to know what that purpose is. In the case of *R* v *Kearley* [1991] Crim LR 282, there was the evidence of some police officers, who searched the defendant's house, that a number of people rang there to enquire about drugs. The court held the evidence to be admissible to prove that the defendant was the supplier of drugs. It was argued that the truth of the statements was irrelevant - what was important was the fact that the phone calls were made. However, it could be argued that the prosecution here was relying on the truth of the words said during those phone calls.

The case of *R* v *Harry* (1988) 86 Cr App R 105 concerned similar evidence which was held to be *inadmissible*, but the distinguishing point perhaps in this case was that the evidence was being used by one co-defendant against another. Both co-defendants were found at the same flat, but D1 wanted to use the words of the phone calls to show that it was D2 who was being asked for - hence D1 was certainly relying on the truth of the words, not just the fact that the phone calls were made.

c) *Implied assertions*

The hearsay rule applies undoubtedly to express assertions; there is some doubt as to whether implied assertions are covered by the hearsay rule. It would seem that most of the authorities (of which there is a paucity!) would support the view expressed by Lord Reid in *Myers* v *DPP* [1965] AC 1001 that implied assertions are admissible hearsay only if they come within a recognised exception to the hearsay rule.

d) *Statements on tapes, films etc*

In *Taylor* v *Chief Constable of Cheshire* [1987] 1 All ER 225 a security camera in a shop made a video recording of Taylor stealing from the shop. Police officers watched the recording and identified Taylor; the recording was returned to the shopkeeper and was accidentally erased. The police officers were allowed to testify as to what they had seen on the video recording; it was *not* hearsay, in essence it was the same as if they had been in the shop and witnessed the incident, and then gave evidence as percipient witnesses. Similarly, a police officer may give evidence as to the reading on a radar speed meter, or the speedometer of his pursuing police vehicle, or a witness may state that an incident in issue occurred on a certain date because he looked at the newspaper he had bought or at his digital watch which displayed the date; throughout there is no element of hearsay in the evidence. In *R* v *Spilby* (1990) 91 Cr App R 186, the print-out from a machine used to monitor telephone call numbers and the length of the calls was not hearsay but real evidence because, like a speedometer, it is merely an instrument which can't contribute its own knowledge.

e) *Admissibility of hearsay at common law*

When examining hearsay admissible at common law it must be borne in mind throughout that in many instances there has been statutory intervention. Some hearsay admissible at common law in both civil and criminal cases may now be admissible by statute in either civil cases, or alternatively in criminal cases.

i) Informal admissions

A statement made by a party out of court, which is adverse to his interests in the case, is an informal admission and is admissible as evidence of the truth of its contents as an exception to the hearsay rule. In civil cases informal admissions may now be related to the court by virtue of s9 Civil Evidence Act 1968 which preserves the common law exception. In criminal cases informal admissions by the accused - confessions - are governed by s76 Police and Criminal Evidence Act 1984, with judicial discretion to exclude such admissible hearsay evidence being put on a statutory basis by s78 of the same Act.

ii) Statements in public documents

Statements in most public documents are admissible at common law as evidence of the truth of their contents. The evidence was admissible as an exception to the hearsay rule because it was considered reliable and very often the official who compiled the document will have no recollection of the facts, or will have died or be unavailable, unfit etc. However, a lot of statutes now provide for the admissibility of particular classes of public documents, eg certified copies of birth certificates as evidence of a person's date of birth. In addition many statements in public documents may now be admissible in criminal cases by virtue of s24 Criminal Justice Act 1988 and in civil cases by virtue of s4 Civil Evidence Act 1968.

Nevertheless the common law admissibility is still of some importance in criminal cases; in civil cases the common law admissibility is now preserved by s9 Civil Evidence Act 1968.

iii) Statements by persons since deceased

Statements by persons who have died by the time of the trial may be admissible at common law as evidence of the truth of their contents, the most common examples of which are:

- Declarations against interest

  The rationale is the same as that for admissibility of informal admissions. The declaration must be against the pecuniary or proprietary interest of the declarant; a declaration against *penal* interest is not admissible under this head: *Sussex Peerage Case* (1844) 11 Cl & Fin 85.

- Declarations in the course of duty

  These are admissible in criminal proceedings - the declaration must have been made by a person acting under a duty to record some activity; the activity must have been undertaken and the declaration made sufficiently contemporaneously with the activity and with no motive to misrepresent the facts.

- Dying declarations

  These may be admissible at the trial for the murder or manslaughter of the declarant. The statement of the victim, oral or written, as to the cause of his injuries (usually who the assailant was) must have been made when he was under a settled, hopeless, expectation of death, and had he survived he would have been a competent witness. The rationale of this exception, that the knowledge of impending death will make the declaration as reliable as a statement given in evidence under oath, is questionable. That the judge must warn the jury to treat the declaration with some caution, and should point out that the declarant was not exposed to cross-examination is indicative of the modern approach, which accepts the admissibility but is more sceptical about the weight to be attached to such declarations.

iv) Res gestae statements

The main, and most important element of the res gestae concept is that of the admissibility of hearsay which consists of statements made with spontaneity and sufficiently contemporaneous to some relevant occurrence or some state of affairs. Though attempts are made by textbook authors to compartmentalise the different situations where *res gestae* statements are admissible, the categories adopted are merely sets of situations where the principle has been applied. In *Howe* v *Malkin* (1878) 40 LT 196 Grove J explained the rationale succinctly:

'Though you cannot give in evidence a declaration per se, yet when there is an act accompanied by a statement which is so mixed up with it as to become part of the *res gestae*, evidence of such a statement may be given.' To some extent 'so mixed up' begs the question, but the following main types of statement are those which examiners favour, with the most frequently recurring one first, for example:

- Spontaneous and contemporaneous statements

  At common law it was accepted that an occurrence could be explained by some spontaneous statement made in the heat of the moment by either a participant or a witness to the occurrence. The old cases, such as *R* v *Bedingfield* (1879) 14 Cox CC 341, evince the insistence of the common law on strict spontaneity and complete contemporaneity. The leading case is now *R* v *Andrews* [1987] AC 281 in which the House of Lords overruled *Bedingfield* as being far too strict and set out the modern criteria for admissibility:

  distortion or concoction must be safe to disregard;

  to ascertain that, it may be concluded that statements made because of involvement in, or the pressure of, the event will not be distorted or concocted, if they are made in conditions of *approximate* contemporaneity;

  to be sufficiently spontaneous for admissibility, the statement must have been so closely associated with the event which excited it that it can be safely inferred that the mind of the maker of the statement was still dominated by that event;

  other factors which bear on the possibility of concoction or distortion must be considered by the judge, eg malice of the declarant, his sobriety at the time.

  R v *Andrews* has relaxed the contemporaneity and spontaneity requirement, but they will still play a major role in assessing the reliability (and therefore admissibility) of such res gestae statements.

- Declarations as to physical or mental condition

  Statements about the contemporaneous physical or mental condition of the speaker, including his emotions, are admissible under the *res gestae* doctrine with the necessary inference of spontaneity. Statements as to sensations, symptoms etc are capable of admissibility under this head, but *not* statements as to the reason for them (but they might be admissible under another exception to the hearsay rule, eg dying declarations).

- Statements of intention

  A statement as to what the speaker intended to do is admissible as evidence of that intention on his part, but whether it is admissible as evidence of his carrying out that intention is uncertain. In *R* v *Wainwright* (1875) 13 Cox CC 171 a statement by a subsequent murder victim that she was going to visit the accused was inadmissible as evidence that she did so. *R* v *Buckley* (1873) 13 Cox CC 293 is in conflict, but the speaker was a police officer informing his superior officer of his intention to perform an act in the course of his duty, so the evidence of his intention may have been admitted as a declaration in the course of duty (supra).

- Statements explaining actions

  The statement of the perpetrator of some act may sometimes be that of the best person to explain the proper significance of that act. Provided such a statement is made contemporaneously with the act, and by the actor as opposed to an observer, then it can be admitted as hearsay under the res gestae doctrine.

  The case of *R* v *McCay* [1990] Crim LR 338 causes problems here. The Court of Appeal in this case held as admissible evidence given by a police officer as to the number chosen in an identification parade by the witness. The court appeared to use two possible grounds for the admissibility. First, that any identification carried out in accordance with Code D of Police and Criminal Evidence Act 1984 is admissible, whether hearsay or not. This can hardly be right. Secondly, it fell within an exception to the hearsay rule, res gestae. However, this goes against authorities which suggest that it does not, eg *Teper* v *R* [1952] AC 480.

6.3 Analysis of questions

Hearsay is a favourite topic of examiners, and in the case of the criminal rules excluding hearsay and the many exceptions to them it is quite common to find questions exclusively in that area - which is a fairly rare occurrence in Evidence examinations! The following questions are not, therefore, typical examination questions on hearsay, but do incorporate material referred to in previous chapters.

6.4 Questions

Question 1

Albert is charged with the murder of Betty by stabbing. Discuss the admissibility of the following:

a) Charles, walking past Albert's house, heard a woman scream: 'Don't do it to me, Albert; put that knife down!' He knocked at the door as the screams continued, got no reply, so reported to the police.

b) When the police arrived at the house, Betty staggered down the path and collapsed. Shortly before her death in hospital she recovered consciousness and said: 'Albert's done for me, but I forgive him.'

c) Betty told her mother on the day of the stabbing that she intended to visit Albert.

d) When interviewed by the police, Albert stated that he was not at home on the day of the stabbing. Subsequently he retracted that statement, said he was at home but that after an argument with Betty he went out to the pub and when he returned the ambulance was departing, with the police following.

e) David, dying of cancer a month after the murder, confessed that he was the person who had stabbed Betty at Albert's house.

Written by editor

Skeleton solution

- Examination of implied assertions and res gestae statements.
- Exceptions to hearsay rule - dying declarations and res gestae statements.
- Hearsay - statement of intention.
- Corroboration - lies told by the accused.
- Inadmissible hearsay and irrelevance.

Suggested solution

If Charles is to relate to the court what he overheard at Albert's house, it must be relevant to the fact in issue at the trial - the murder of Betty - and must not infringe any exclusionary rule of evidence. The fact that he heard screams emanating from the house, and that they seemed to be those of a female, would be admissible if relevant, for example to prove that a female was present, and was in fear, or hysterical (*Ratten* v *R* (1972)). However, that may not be relevant if Albert is not denying the presence of a female, but rather is stating only that he was not present.

If Charles tenders in evidence the content of what was screamed, as opposed to the mere fact of the scream, then the utterance implies that Albert was holding a knife and was threatening or terrorising the female with it; it is an implied assertion that Albert was present, was wielding a knife, and was threatening a female in the house.

Therefore, Charles' evidence would be hearsay to the same extent as if the statement/utterance had been an express assertion of those facts, and thus would be inadmissible unless it came within a recognised exception to the hearsay rule (*Myers* v *DPP* (1965)). The only exception would seem to be that of res gestae statements; if the time of the stabbing is established, and the screamed statement was sufficiently contemporaneous, and the other criteria as to spontaneity, concoction and distortion, and any relevant factors which may be given to the court have been taken into account, then Charles may report to the court not only the fact of the utterance, but its content (*R* v *Andrews* (1987)); and, of course, the fact of the continued screaming as he knocked at the door.

Betty's statement to the police may be admissible as a dying declaration, provided she was in settled hopeless expectation of death and if alive would have been a competent witness (*R* v *Pike* (1829)). (It is assumed that she is neither a child of tender years nor a person of defective intellect who would have been adjudged incompetent.) If she is Albert's wife, then she would now be both competent and compellable (Police and Criminal Evidence Act 1984 s80).) If she lost consciousness almost immediately after the last thrust of the knife and remained unconscious until she made her statement, then it could be argued by the defence counsel that she had not had enough time to reflect on her situation and thus could not make a dying declaration (*R* v *Bedingfield* (1879) has not been overruled on that point, although the rest of its reasoning has been overruled by *R* v *Andrews* (above)). However, the content of her statement would seem to suggest that she is aware of her impending death and is resigned to it. If her statement is admitted as a dying declaration, the judge must warn the jury to treat its significance with caution, and must point out to them that Betty was not subjected to cross-examination on her declaration (*Nembhard* v *R* (1982); *Waugh* v *R* (1950)).

If Betty's statement is not admissible as a dying declaration, it may possibly be admissible as a res gestae statement dependent on the spontaneity, contemporaneity etc as stipulated in *R* v *Andrews*. If it does not meet the criteria for either a dying declaration or a res gestae statement, then it will be inadmissible hearsay.

Betty's statement to her mother is a statement of her intention. Her mother may relate this to the court as evidence of Betty's intention to visit Albert, but that is not as relevant as is whether or not she *did* visit him. As to the latter, it would seem that the mother's evidence would be excluded as inadmissible hearsay, as the weight of authority is against the admission of such hearsay to prove the intended act was performed (*R* v *Wainwright* (1875); *R* v *Thomson* (1912); cf *R* v *Buckley* (1873)). There is conflict in the cases, and it could therefore be argued that if the interval between Betty's statement to her mother and her being stabbed at Albert's house was short, then her mother should be allowed to report the statement to the court.

Albert's retraction of his first statement and contradiction of it in his second could amount to evidence capable of corroborating prosecution evidence against him. Although in this case there is no necessity for corroboration, or a corroboration warning, nevertheless Albert's lie could be supportive of prosecution evidence unless there is some explanation for it other than one consistent with his guilt (*R* v *Lucas*

(1981)). The contradictory statements about a material issue, ie his presence at the scene and time of the crime, mean that if there is a case to answer then Albert will have to elect to testify and give an innocent explanation for his lying to the police.

If David is resigned to his death and has died by the time of the trial, his statement cannot amount to a dying declaration (he is not the homicide victim!). Again, if he survives, unless in the light of his statement a decision is taken to drop the charge against Albert and instead prosecute David, David's statement cannot be reported to the court at Albert's trial as it is not a confession statement of the accused, and is therefore inadmissible hearsay (*R* v *Blastland* (1985)). If he dies before Albert's trial, his statement is not admissible as a declaration against interest, as the declaration is not against David's proprietary or pecuniary interest, but rather against his penal interest, which does not bring it within that exception to the hearsay rule in English law (*Sussex Peerage Case* (1844)). In any event, as it is Albert, not David, who is charged with Betty's murder, an admission made by David, adverse to his interests, is not relevant to the guilt of Albert (*R* v *Blastland*).

Question 2

Green staggers out of his house, bleeding profusely from the chest and stomach, falls into the arms of a passer-by and collapses. Within minutes an ambulance and a police patrol car arrive; as Green is being transported to hospital he whispers to the ambulanceman: 'Pink has murdered me.' He dies shortly afterwards.

Meanwhile, the police officers have entered Green's house, where Mrs Green, standing next to Pink, sobs: 'It's my fault, my husband came home early and found us in bed. He was going to shoot me, but Pink struggled with him and the gun went off.'

Pink is arrested, and is interviewed by the police with his solicitor present; the police officers accuse him of murdering Green but he makes no reply.

Mrs Pink makes a statement to the police, saying Pink had told her the day before the incident that he was leaving her to live with Mrs Green, and that he and Mrs Green intended to kill Green as he would not divorce his wife. Mrs Pink and Mrs Green are now reluctant to testify.

Pink has been charged with Green's murder and intends to plead not guilty.

Advise the prosecution.

Written by editor

Skeleton solution

- Hearsay - res gestae statements.
- Silence when accused - evidential value.
- Inadmissible hearsay; statements of intention; circumstantial evidence; credibility of witnesses.
- Competence and compellability of potential witnesses.

Suggested solution

The ambulanceman's tendering of Green's statement in evidence is hearsay, and therefore will be inadmissible unless it falls into an existing, recognised, exception to the hearsay rule in criminal cases (*Myers* v *DPP* (1965)). The only applicable exceptions are dying declarations and res gestae statements. Green is the victim of homicide; the charge Pink is facing is murder; Green's statement is as to the cause of his injuries; presumably he would have been a competent witness, but, crucially, there is nothing in his statement to suggest that when he made the statement he was in settled hopeless expectation of death (*R* v *Perry* (1909)). Arguably, from the severity of his injuries it could be inferred that he was aware of his imminent death, this inference being strengthened by his reference to Pink's having murdered him, but awareness is not enough - settled, hopeless, expectation of death is imperative for admissibility (*R* v *Bedingfield* (1879)).

Green's statement may, however, be admissible as a res gestae statement. It would appear to have sufficient contemporaneity and spontaneity for the court to be satisfied that his mind was still in the control of the event, and therefore the possibility of concoction or distortion can be disregarded. Other relevant factors would be whether Green was drunk, whether there was ill-will between himself and Pink or any other reason for concoction or cause of distortion. Provided the judge averts his mind to any such known factors, and is satisfied as to the apparent reliability of Green's statement, then it will be admissible under the res gestae doctrine (*R* v *Andrews* (1987)).

Mrs Green's statement could be admissible under the res gestae doctrine, subject to the conditions just outlined, as the doctrine allows in an 'excited utterance' not only of the participants in the event but also of observers. Mrs Green's statement seems to be more akin to a narration of events than to an excited utterance forced from her by the drama of the event she witnessed. However, discussion may be otiose if Mrs Green gives direct, oral, testimony. It is stated that Mrs Green is reluctant to testify; she is not the spouse of the accused but the spouse of the victim and therefore as competent and compellable as any witness. Hence only if, under threat of punishment for contempt, she still refuses to testify will it be appropriate to consider whether the police officer who hears her statement can report it under the res gestae exception to the hearsay rule.

When a suspect is accused of a crime by a person on even terms and it would be reasonable to expect a reply, then silence can corroborate evidence implicating that suspect, and inferences can be drawn from it (*R* v *Cramp* (1880); *Parkes* v *R* (1976)). However, when the accuser is a person in authority such as a police officer, then the accuser and accused are not on even terms, and as the suspect has a right to remain silent his silence cannot amount to corroboration (*R* v *Whitehead* (1929)) and cannot give rise to inferences of guilt (*Hall* v *R* (1971)). In one case it was held that when the suspect is accompanied by his solicitor he is deemed to be on even terms with the accusing police officer (*R* v *Chandler* (1976)); the case has been strongly criticised, albeit not yet overruled.

Mrs Pink's statement would be hearsay if tendered in evidence by the police officer to whom it was made. It does not come within any exception to the hearsay rule - the statement of intention by Pink is not a statement by a person since deceased, and even if it were it would be inadmissible to tender it as evidence that Pink carried out his intended act (*R* v *Wainwright* (1875)). Mrs Pink, as the spouse of the accused, is a competent witness for the prosecution (s80(1)(a) Police and Criminal Evidence Act 1984), but where her spouse is charged with the murder of a person who is over 16, she is not compellable (s80(3) Police and Criminal Evidence Act 1984).

If neither Mrs Pink nor Mrs Green testify, then, unless there is evidence other than that outlined in the question, the prosecution will have no witnesses who can give direct testimony; there will be no percipient witness except Pink, who is not available to the prosecution. If the ambulanceman, and the police officer, are allowed to give hearsay evidence of the statements of Green and Mrs Green respectively, and especially if the presence of Pink's solicitor is held to put him on even terms with the interviewing police officer, then the prosecution may be able to discharge the legal burden of proof to the criminal standard.

Question 3

What is the problem of 'implied hearsay'? Can a definition of 'hearsay evidence' be provided which satisfactorily explains the cases?

University of London LLB Examination
(for External Students) Evidence June 1990 Q1

Skeleton solution

- Definition of hearsay - problem of implied hearsay.
- Oral evidence - indirect assertions - *Teper* versus *Ratten.*
- Documentary evidence - unintentional - *Myers* versus *Rice.*
- Conduct - rule applied to gestures.
- Conclusion - no specific definition available.

Suggested solution

The common law rule against hearsay prohibits the giving of evidence in court by any person other than someone having personal knowledge of the matters about which he speaks, where the purpose is to rely on the facts stated by him.

The rule applies irrespective of the form in which the evidence is given. Thus, A is not allowed to tell the court what B (who is not a witness) said to him when the purpose is to rely on the facts stated by B. Equally, A is not allowed to produce a letter from B to him in which those facts are stated. Nor is A allowed to give evidence of gestures he saw B give to convey the same facts.

The rule is subject to numerous exceptions but one of the most difficult problems is deciding the scope of the rule itself. In this, the problem of implied assertions (or implied hearsay) is central. The cases do not however give a clear answer. This is illustrated by examples in the three categories of oral evidence, documentary evidence and gestures.

Oral evidence:

The application of the rule is straightforward in cases where the evidence given is to rely on facts which have been relayed by someone else to the person giving the evidence. If A says in court that B told him that C hit D, the evidence is clearly hearsay of that fact. Difficulty arises however where reliance is indirect; that is the hearsay is implied. If A says in court that he heard B say 'Hello X', is this hearsay evidence of X's presence? Certainly, A has not personal knowledge of the presence of X but equally the facts which the evidence is tendered to prove arise only by inference from what B said. B did not make an assertion 'X is here', and it is questionable how far the hearsay rule should be applied. In *Teper* v *R* (1952), evidence of a witness that a bystander at the scene of a fire had been heard to utter an exclamation from which the presence of the accused at the scene of the crime could be inferred was disallowed as hearsay. In *Ratten* v *R* (1972) by contrast, the Privy Council considered that evidence from a telephone operator of hysterical utterances by the victim of a murder was not hearsay even if it was used to infer that she was being attacked by the accused. In *Woodhouse* v *Hall* (1981), evidence from policemen of offers to them by women of sexual services was held not to be hearsay in a charge of using premises for immoral purposes. The outcome in this case is consistent with a number of Australian cases where evidence of the placing of bets by telephone was tendered by policemen who heard the conversations. Yet in *R* v *Harry* (1988), evidence of telephone callers asking for an accused (as opposed to his co-accused who said he was not involved) in a drug dealing case overheard by the police was excluded as hearsay evidence of that accused as the dealer.

One case which is difficult to reconcile with *R* v *Harry* is *R* v *Kearley* (1991) - the facts were virtually the same - where police officers raided the appellant's house and whilst they were there a number of phone calls arrived, enquiring about drugs. The Court of Appeal criticised *Harry*, and so allowed in this evidence, as being original and not hearsay - the case being indistinguishable from *Woodhouse*. The point of distinction between the two cases appears to be that in *Harry* there were two co-accused involved, and the calls were relied upon to prove that only one of them was being asked for. Whereas in *Kearley*, the fact that the phone calls were made to this one place was enough. But the position is hardly clear.

Documentary evidence:

An obvious example of the operation of the rule can be seen from the decision of the House of Lords in *Myers* (1965). Documentary evidence of the serial numbers impressed in car engines compiled by workmen not called as witnesses were ruled inadmissible as hearsay. The decision in this case was reversed by statute, but is hard to reconcile with the earlier case of *R* v *Rice* (1963) in which a used airline ticket bearing the accused's name was accepted as evidence that the accused took the flight in question. The ticket did not in terms assert that he took the flight, yet that is the logical inference to be drawn from the ticket and it was tendered in evidence for that purpose. It is hard to escape the conclusion that the court was acting on implied hearsay in the form of the record of the airline employee who filled out the ticket stating the name of the passenger. It is possible to explain this and similar cases on the basis that the evidence was received as real evidence (ie a material object) but since the reason for tendering the evidence was to rely on the terms of the inscription, this rather appears to be a mechanism for sidestepping the application of the rule. Another example of uncertainty of the scope of the rule in documentary evidence arises in the so called negative hearsay cases such as *R* v *Shone* (1983). In that case, the absence of the marking of record cards to show that material had been validly withdrawn from stores was tendered as evidence of theft of the material in question.

Conduct:

Chandrasekera v *R* (1937) is a clear case in which the hearsay rule applies to gestures. The gesture in that case was direct and comparable with an oral assertion identifying the accused as the victim's assailant but according to Parke B, in *Wright* v *Tatham* (1837) the rule is applicable to any sort of conduct from which facts may be inferred. If, however, all such implied hearsay were within the rule, a great deal of cogent evidence would be rendered inadmissible and a large number of new exceptions to the hearsay rule would require recognition. The reluctance of the courts to adopt such a stringent approach can be seen in a decision in *R* v *Osbourne and Virtue* (1973). This case, decided after *Myers* (1965) (which held that only Parliament should create new hearsay exceptions) was to the effect that a policeman who has been present at an identification parade may give evidence of the identification of an accused by a witness where that witness is subsequently unable to recall making the identification when giving evidence in court. This approach leans in the oppositive direction to *Wright* v *Tatham* (1837) and indeed seems to go rather too far, it being difficult to see a great deal of distinction between the circumstances and those in *Chandrasekera*.

It is not easy to reconcile the authorities or to define the scope as a rule as the above discussion indicates. Professor Cross sought a rationale by proposing that the scope of the hearsay rule was limited to circumstances where the original maker of the statement on which reliance is placed intended to assert some fact. There is some merit in this proposition and if applied would go some way to explain cases such as *R* v *Rice* (1963) (where the booking clerk no doubt simply wrote out the name he was given mechanically) and *Woodhouse* v *Hall* (1981). Even taking this approach, however, the boundary remains blurred, as *R* v *Harry* (1988) and *R* v *Osbourne and Virtue* (1973) demonstrate. Professor Cross's approach is a reasonable attempt at securing some common basis to the approach of the courts. On the present state of the authorities, however, it must be conceded that the rule is probably incapable of precise definition.

Question 4

P, a police inspector, is investigating a theft and explosion at a factory. Knowing that O has a previous conviction for causing an explosion, P requests him one morning to come to the police station. P questions O for most of the next twelve hours without result. Eventually at about midnight, P says 'Look, I'm happy to go on all night. Why don't you do yourself a favour? Tell me who the other villains are and where the stuff is you nicked.' O, who is by now totally exhausted, says 'OK, you win, Q and I took the stuff. You'll find it in the old shed by the allotments. But I didn't want anything to do with the dynamite. Q threatened to kill me if I didn't help him.' P goes to the shed and finds the goods stolen from the factory, but, apart from O's statement, there is nothing to connect them with either O or Q. P then arrests Q, telling him that if he will produce any remaining dynamite he will not be charged with an explosives offence. Q hands over some sticks of dynamite, saying that it is all he has left.

O and Q are charged jointly with theft and causing an explosion. At the trial within a trial O admits that his statement to P was true.

Advise O and Q.

University of London LLB Examination
(for External Students) Evidence June 1990 Q8

Skeleton solution

- Evidence of O - hearsay - exception needed - s76 Police and Criminal Evidence Act 1984.
- Oppression under s76 - definition - breach of Codes of Practice.
- Reliability under s76 - definition.
- Use of s78 instead.
- Advice to Q - hearsay - cross-examination of accused on his character - s76 Police and Criminal Evidence Act 1984.

Suggested solution

Advice to O:

The police do not have first hand knowledge and can give evidence only of what they were told by O. The evidence will therefore be hearsay and inadmissible unless an exception to the hearsay rule applies. O is not compelled to give evidence and is unlikely to oblige the prosecution by giving the evidence they wish in chief at trial.

The only relevant exception appears to be s76 of the Police and Criminal Evidence Act 1984. O should, however, contend the application of s76. This will then require the prosecution to prove beyond reasonable doubt (as required by s76) that the confession (defined in s82(1) as including any statement wholly or partly adverse to the accused) was not obtained by oppression or anything said or done by P (or anyone else) which in the circumstances existing at the time was likely to make any confession by him unreliable. Further, even if s76 is satisfied, O can contend that the judge should exclude the confession under s78 which enables evidence to be excluded if in all the circumstances, including the circumstances in which the evidence was obtained, it would be unfair to allow it in. Sections 76 and 78 are not mutually exclusive: *R* v *Mason* (1987). The basis of the submissions are suggested as follows:

Section 76. Oppression is partly defined in s76 as including torture, inhuman or degrading treatment. A working definition has been proffered in *R* v *Fulling* (1987) as exercise of authority in a burdensome, harsh or wrongful manner. Though O's treatment at the hands of P could hardly be regarded as torture, O can readily argue that P's conduct falls within the *Fulling* definition. O's questioning should have been punctuated by rest periods at about two-hourly intervals in accordance with the Code of Practice on questioning unless exceptional reasons applied; for example that people would be harmed or the outcome of the investigation prejudiced. Those grounds do not necessarily follow from the facts given. Moreover, it seems that questioning went on into the late evening, not finishing until midnight. Nor, it seems, was O cautioned, or even arrested, although it may be that up to that time P did not have the requisite grounds because he had got nowhere with O. Even if that were the case, the Code of Practice on questioning issued under the Police and Criminal Evidence Act would apply in the same way as it is applied to detained persons. Failure to comply with the Code is a matter to be taken into account by the court in deciding any question, including therefore the question of exclusion on the ground of oppression (s67(11)).

Not all breaches of the Code of Practice will render a confession inadmissible but where, as appears to be the case here, the breach is significant and substantial, O is entitled to submit exclusion with some force (*R* v *Keenan* (1990)).

In relation to oppression, it is unclear from the authorities whether there is a requirement that the action occasioning the oppression should be deliberate. Indications are that this is required (*R* v *Hughes* (1949) and *R* v *Fulling*) and therefore O's case for exclusion on this ground will be enhanced if the court takes the view that P deliberately flouted the rules.

There is no requirement to show that the confession was unreliable but causation must be established. O's utterance after a long detention is indicative of this, but in making the assessment O's ability to withstand harsh questioning will be considered (compare *R* v *Prager* (1972) decided under the common law) and O does apparently have a criminal background. He may therefore be more resistant than many, though other characteristics such as his age and health will also be relevant.

Additionally, and in the alternative, O can submit that the confession falls at the reliability hurdle. His contention would be that conditions of questioning made him 'say anything'. It must however be said that the terms in which O gave a confession and the fact that the goods were found where he had said rather point away from unreliability and towards the supposition that O simply decided to 'spill the beans'.

O can call upon s78 if he is unsuccessful under s76 (*Mason*). The courts have not taken the same restrictive attitude to the exclusion under s78 as they took for exclusion under the common law. The submission would be that putting aside whether the police conduct was technically oppressive or provoked unreliability, or issues such as causation, in all the circumstances, including the circumstances in which the evidence from O was obtained, that evidence should be excluded on grounds of fairness. All the breaches of the Code of Practice are significant and substantial

(*R* v *Keenan*), which gives O a lever. Moreover, if O successfully submits that P acted in bad faith, it is likely that the evidence will be excluded (*R* v *Alladice* (1988) in which the Lord Chief Justice said that the courts will have little difficulty in excluding such evidence under this section). *Alladice* itself concerned access to legal advice, but indications are that the dictum is to be broadly construed.

Arguments about admissibility under ss76 and 78 will be taken on the voir dire. O will be free to give evidence without its being used against him at the main trial, save that if the confession is admitted, he may be cross-examined as to inconsistent statements made on the voir dire (*Wong Kam Ming* v *R* (1980)). It has been suggested that the position may be different with the subsequent enactment of s76, which makes confessions admissible, subject to the conditions of the section, in criminal proceedings quite generally. Whilst that may be the case in a technical legal sense, it is likely that the courts will exercise the s78 discretion to exclude so that the voir dire evidence is in general kept from the main trial in the same way as envisaged by *Wong Kam Ming*.

Advice to Q:

If admitted, the confession by O to P in which Q is implicated will be no evidence against Q. It will be hearsay at common law: *R* v *Rudd* (1948). Nothing in s76 allows in such evidence because under that section the confession by an accused may be given in evidence against *him* as an exception to the hearsay rule.

If O goes into the witness box and then gives testimony along the lines of his confession, then that will be evidence against Q because no hearsay element is involved. If that happens, Q will be able to submit that O has given evidence against him because, manifestly, it will undermine Q's case. We are told that O has a previous conviction and if O gives evidence at trial, Q will be able, as an exception to the general embargo on the putting of evidence of bad character to an accused by the prosecution, to cross-examine him about it under s1(f)(iii) of the Criminal Evidence Act 1898 (*Murdoch* v *Taylor* (1965)). The leave of the judge for this cross-examination will not be needed and such evidence will go to O's credibility (*Murdoch* v *Taylor*).

It may also be possible for Q to cross-examine O about his confession even if that confession is ruled inadmissible in the main trial (*R* v *Rowson* (1985)). The basis of such cross-examination is the entitlement of a party to put to an opposing witness previous inconsistent statements, evidence of which goes to that witness's credibility. It follows that Q can only proceed to cross-examine O if O changes his story at the main trial. Whether Q would actually want to cross examine O rather depends on what O changed his story to. If at the main trial O did not refer to Q's complicity, then it would obviously not be in Q's interest for such cross-examination to be pursued.

Q's statement to P is against his interest and therefore a confession within the meaning of s76. P will accordingly be able to state what Q said unless the oppression or reliability hurdles are not satisfied, or there is exclusion of the evidence under s78. The criteria have been dealt with in the advice to O. The breach of the

Code of Practice is the inducement by P that he will not be charged if he owns up. This breach Q can argue as significant and substantial.

The evidence of Q's handing over the dynamite is unlikely to be regarded as a confession, even though a confession is defined in s76 as any statement, whether in words or otherwise. To assume the hearsay rule applies to all conduct from which facts can be inferred would be to extend the scope of the rule unduly. The prosecution are likely to say that the acquisition of the dynamite by P is admissible whether or not Q's statement is excluded under s76, on the authority of s76(4) (facts discovered as a result of an inadmissible confession admissible). Q's best course then is to submit that the evidence of the handing over of the dynamite is confession-type material which should be excluded, citing *R* v *Barker* (1941) in support. This case has been criticised, and was decided under the common law, both features which the prosecution will doubtless point out. The defence can, however, refer to the fact that s76(4) merely puts the common law of *R* v *Warwickshall* (1783) on a statutory basis, and further submit that even if *Barker* is unsatisfactory, it points towards exclusion of the evidence as a matter of discretion under s78.

7 HEARSAY - STATUTORY ADMISSIBILITY IN CIVIL CASES

7.1 Introduction

7.2 Key points

7.3 Analysis of questions

7.4 Questions

7.1 Introduction

The Civil Evidence Act 1968 has virtually abolished the exclusionary hearsay rule in civil proceedings in all courts except magistrates courts exercising their civil jurisdiction. Further, the Civil Evidence Act 1972 provides generally for the admissibility of hearsay statements of opinion where such statements of fact are admissible under the 1968 Act. In civil cases it is therefore necessary to have a sound knowledge of the 1968 and 1972 Acts and of the main procedural rules governing admissibility.

7.2 Key points

a) *Admissibility - s1 of the 1968 Act*

Hearsay statements admissible under the Act, or under any other statutory provision, or by agreement of the parties:

i) 'statement' may be in words, oral or written or otherwise (s10); and may be of, or including, opinion (s1 1972 Act);

ii) 'any other statutory provision' - this examined earlier in 6.2(e)(ii).

b) *Notice procedure*

i) Generally

Section 8 of the 1968 Act makes provision for rules of court to be followed and other conditions to be met before a statement can be admitted in evidence by virtue of ss2, 4 or 5 of the Act. In High Court proceedings, RSC Ord 38 rr 20-34 apply; in county court CCR Ord 20 rr14-26 apply.

Section 2 applies to first-hand hearsay statements made orally, in a document or otherwise; these are capable of admissibility only if the statement would have been admissible had it been given as direct testimony (ie s2 does not make evidence admissible as hearsay which would be excluded if tendered as direct testimony).

Section 4 applies to second-hand hearsay statements contained in records ('second-hand' because the record is compiled by one person from information supplied by another) as well as to such statements which may be first-hand (ie the compiler of the record and the supplier of the information may be the same person). Under s4 'record' has been interpreted strictly: see *H* v *Schering Chemicals Ltd* [1983] 1 All ER 849; and *Re D (a minor)* [1986] 2 FLR 189.

Section 5 provides for the generally admissibility of statements contained in a document produced by a computer. These are restricted to statements of fact (s1 1972 Act expressly excludes s5 1968 Act from its provisions relating to opinion). The Children (Admissibility of Hearsay Evidence) Order 1990 (made under the Children Act 1989) says that in any civil proceedings before a juvenile court (what is now to be called a 'Youth Court' since the Criminal Justice Act 1991), a statement made by a child; or a statement made by a person concerned with or having control of a child that he has assaulted, neglected or ill-treated the child; or a statement included in any report by a guardian ad litem (under the Magistrates' Courts Rules 1988) or by a local authority under the Children and Young Persons Act 1969, shall all be admissible as evidence in connection with the upbringing, maintenance or welfare of a child notwithstanding any rule of hearsay. The Order also states that in High Court or County Court, evidence given in connection with the upbringing, maintenance, or welfare of a child shall be admissible notwithstanding any rule of hearsay.

The Children (Admissibility of Hearsay Evidence) Order 1991 extends this partial abolition of the hearsay rule to all 'family proceedings' in the magistrates' courts.

So it seems now that first, second, third-hand hearsay is admissible in these limited circumstances. The case of *R* v *B County Council, ex parte P* [1991] 2 All ER 65 makes it clear that as a result of these orders, a court should be very cautious in requiring the attendance of the child in these types of cases.

ii) Serving notice

Order 38 r21 provides in the case of statements under ss2, 4 or 5 that generally notice of intention to adduce such statements must be served on the other party, usually within 21 days after the matter has been set down for trial. The notice must be in the form prescribed by Ord 38 rr22 to 24, and the reason for not calling the witness to give evidence must be specified, and must be one of the reasons contained in Ord 38 r25: 'The person is dead, or beyond the seas, or unfit by reason of his bodily or mental condition to attend as a witness, or that despite the exercise of reasonable diligence it has not been possible to identify or find him, or that he cannot reasonably be expected to have any recollection of matters relevant to the accuracy or otherwise of the statement to which the notice relates.'

So there are *five* reasons, any one of which may be stated in the notice; ie death; absence from jurisdiction; unfitness to attend; impossibility to trace; lack of recollection - usually as a result of passage of time.

iii) Serving counternotice

Order 38 r26 governs the service of counternotice. Obviously, if any of the five reasons stipulated in r25 (above) applies, then counternotice cannot be served unless the reason given for not calling the person as a witness is contested. In the event of dispute, Ord 38 r27 provides for determination of that dispute pre-trial.

Where a statement has been received in prior proceedings, under either s2 or s4, then Ord 38 r28 provides that if notice has been served to tender that statement as hearsay in the instant proceedings, then application may be made to the court for specific directions as to admissibility, and mode of proof, of the statement; the court therefore has discretion to exclude such a statement even though r21 has been complied with in regard to notice. The court also has an inclusionary discretion, given to it by Ord 38 r29:

- rule 29(1) allows hearsay statements to be adduced despite the fact that notice was served out of time, or no notice was served. The discretion will be exercised in the light of fairness to the parties;
- rule 29(2) allows hearsay statements to be adduced, if otherwise the party wishing to adduce such a statement would have to call as a witness the agent, or servant, of an opposite party, or the opposite party himself. Again, this is discretionary, and the discretion only applies where none of the reasons stipulated in r25 applies, and is given to the court to cover situations where counternotice under r26 has been served - the party serving notice would otherwise have the choice of calling as a witness a person favourable to his opponent or having the evidence ruled inadmissible.

c) *Cogency of evidence*

Where evidence is admissible as hearsay under the 1968 Act, its cogency is governed by s6(3) of the Act which states that the judge must take into account all the relevant circumstances which may have any bearing on the accuracy of the hearsay statement.

7.3 Analysis of questions

Admissibility under the 1968 (and 1972) Act is a favourite topic of examiners, usually in the form of multi-part questions which include other issues such as privilege, previous convictions etc, although the other issues constitute a minor part of the total question. Occasionally there are essay questions, and rarely, problem questions, which require a knowledge of civil hearsay only, but again these are not restricted to statutory exceptions but also test knowledge of civil hearsay admissible at common law.

7.4 Questions

Question 1

Travis was killed in an accident involving an experimental train, which British Rail was developing. His widow is suing British Rail for damages. Advise as to:

a) The evidence of Noseyface that she had heard a passenger say, 'Oh no, it's not Mad Max driving the train; he's drunk again!'

b) The opinion of Muggins, an electronics engineer, that from various experiments done by his colleagues in France it was clear to him that the system in this train was defective.

Adapted from University of London LLB Examination
(for External Students) Evidence June 1983 Q1

Skeleton solution

a) Hearsay, civil case, s2 of Civil Evidence Act 1968 - RSC Ord 38 rr21-27.

b)
- Expert opinion evidence - admissibility.
- Primary fact upon which expert opinion is based - work of others - hearsay rule.

Suggested solution

a) This evidence is prima facie inadmissible hearsay as evidence that Mad Max was drunk at the relevant time. However, the widow should make use of s2 Civil Evidence Act 1968. Under s2(2) the leave of the court will be required if the passenger who was overhead is available to give evidence. However, in this eventuality, the passenger may give direct evidence of the drunkenness she perceived. In *R* v *Davies* (1962) it was held that a lay witness could give evidence that a person had been drinking, but could not give evidence that the person was unfit to drive through drink, a matter for expert medical evidence. If the passenger is unavailable to give evidence, notice should be served (Ord 38 r21) setting out the relevant particulars and the r25 reason. A counternotice will not be served unless the r25 reason is challenged. (See r26(2) and 27). So far as the statement refers to former occasions of drunkenness on the part of Mad Max the evidence could be rejected as giving rise to collateral issues (see Kelly CB in *Agassiz* v *London Tramway Co* (1872)).

b) Where a matter requires special knowledge or expertise, evidence is admissible on that matter from suitably qualified expert witnesses. In civil cases, expert evidence is invariably required to be disclosed to the other party or parties before trial (see s2 Civil Evidence Act 1972 and Ord38, rr21-31). However, it is clear from *R* v *Abadom* (1983) that where an expert expresses his opinion, the primary facts on which that opinion is based must be proved by admissible evidence given either by the expert himself or another competent witness. If such facts are proved, which does not seem to be the case here, the expert may then draw on the work of others in the same field as part of the process of arriving at his conclusion provided that he refers to that material in his evidence; in this sense, reliance on the work of others and reference to it in evidence, does not offend the hearsay rule. If the documents detailing the French experiments are accordingly hearsay, the widow should employ the Civil Evidence Act 1968. For the difficulties which can arise under the Act in relation to documents containing the results of research, and published articles concerning the same, see *H* v *Schering Chemicals* (1983).

Question 2

Pamela is suing Ewing Jewellers Ltd for the loss of a number of diamonds from a tiara which she handed in to them for repairs. Ewing are relying on an exemption clause contained in the contract exempting them for loss and are claiming that the loss occurred accidentally. Consider the admissibility of the following items of evidence:

a) A valuation certificate by Wentworth made some years ago, stating that the jewels were worth £100,000; he can no longer be traced.

b) Afton's evidence that she had handed jewellery for repairs over a year ago to Ewing and that when it was returned a number of diamonds were missing from a necklace.

c) A copy of an entry in the books of a pawnbroker, Barnes, showing that Sue Ellen, an employee at Ewing, had pledged some diamonds as security for a loan. The entries also showed the carat weight and refractive index of the diamonds as determined by the firm's computer which tally with the weight and index of Pamela's jewels.

Also advise on what standard of proof is applicable to Pamela's assertion that Sue Ellen stole the diamonds.

Adapted from University of London LLB Examination
(for External Students) Evidence June 1984 Q6

Skeleton solution

a)
- First-hand hearsay - s1 Civil Evidence Act 1972 - s2 Civil Evidence Act 1968.
- Service of notice; possible use of s4 of 1968 Act.

b)
- Relevance - similar fact evidence.

c)
- Admissibility of first statement subject to second statement - computer print-outs.
- Notice procedure.
- Exclusion clause.

Suggested solution

a) The valuation certificate would be hearsay of Wentworth's opinion of the value of the jewels. By virtue of s1 Civil Evidence Act 1972, hearsay evidence of opinion is admissible in all cases where hearsay evidence of assertions of fact is admissible. So, whether or not the certificate is admissible depends on the general rules of admissibility of hearsay evidence in civil cases.

When made by Wentworth the certificate contained information known to him. Therefore the certificate would be first-hand hearsay evidence admissible under s2 Civil Evidence Act 1968. Before the certificate would be admissible, the party relying on it, in this case Pamela, is obliged to serve notice on the other party in accordance with RSC O38 r21. The form of the notice would have to comply with O38 r22. Since Wentworth can no longer be traced Pamela should state this fact in the notice (as allowed by O38 r25). This would mean that there would be no possibility of Ewing Jewellers serving a counternotice under r26, requiring Wentworth to give evidence in person. It would not be necessary for Pamela to prove that Wentworth is overseas, ill or dead; just that he cannot be traced is sufficient (*Rasool* v *W Midlands PTE* (1974)).

It is also possible that the certificate would be admissible under s4 of the 1968 Act, if Wentworth had been acting under a duty and the certificate was a record (a document which a historian would consider to be an original source of the information recorded in it: *H* v *Schering Chemicals* (1983); *Savings and Investment Bank* v *Gasco Investments* (1984)). This would be the case if, for example, Wentworth had been making a valuation for insurance purposes. Since we are not told the circumstances in which the certificate was compiled, it would be easier to put in the certificate under s2.

That the value recorded is the value the jewels had some years ago is no obstacle to its admissibility. The court would be entitled to hear other expert evidence on the appreciation of such jewels in order to establish their value at the time of the loss.

b) All evidence is only admissible if it is relevant, that is if it tends to prove an issue in the case. For Afton to say that she had handed jewellery to Ewing over a year ago and that it was returned with diamonds missing would not prove one way or another whether the loss alleged by Pamela occurred. Although similar fact evidence is more readily admissible in civil than criminal cases (*Mood Music* v *De Wolfe* (1976)), such evidence is still only admissible if it is relevant. It is not unexpected that jewellers will occasionally lose jewels from items handed in for repair, and to prove that this happened once does not indicate whether it happened over a year later.

c) There are two aspects to the admissibility of the entry in the pawnbroker's books. There are two statements in the books, first that Sue Ellen pledged diamonds and secondly that they corresponded with the diamonds lost from Pamela's tiara. The first statement is only relevant if the second is proved, so it is the admissibility of the second statement that must be considered first.

The entries in the book contained statements recorded from the pawnbroker's computer. The admissibility of a computer print-out is governed by s5 Civil Evidence Act 1968. Section 5 contains numerous conditions of admissibility. In brief, these amount to it being necessary to prove that the computer had been operated regularly and properly at the time the print-out was obtained. If it can be proved that this was the case then the print-out would be admissible as evidence of the truth of the statement made in it. The evidence here is not the original print-out, but this does not affect its admissibility because s6(1) Civil Evidence Act 1968 allows copies of print-outs to be used if the original would have been admissible.

Before Pamela could use the document in court she would, again, have to serve notice on Ewing that she intended to do so. The form of the required notice in this case is prescribed by RSC O38 r24.

For completeness, it should, perhaps, be added that the evidence will not be admissible at all unless it shows that Sue Ellen made the pledge after the date of Pamela's loss, otherwise it would be irrelevant.

Ewing are relying on the exclusion clause in the contract to avoid liability for the loss. The operation of the *contra proferentem* rule means that the clause would be strictly construed against Ewing so that it would only exempt them for accidental loss, not deliberate or negligent loss; this would be so whether the claim is framed in contract or negligence. Therefore it is clearly relevant that Pamela should try to establish that the loss was not accidental.

When Pamela asserts theft, she is asserting the commission of a criminal offence in a civil action. This does not mean that she must prove theft to the criminal standard of beyond reasonable doubt. Her burden is to prove the allegation on balance of probabilities (*Hornal* v *Neuberger Products* (1956)). However, in the recent case of *Halford* v *Brookes* (1991) a civil action in battery was brought by a mother after the murder of her daughter - against the alleged murderers. The court held that the criminal standard of proof would be adopted despite it being a civil action, principally, it seems, because the serious nature of the allegations meant the trial should be conducted as if the defendants were being tried for murder in a criminal court.

Question 3

Choo has instituted divorce proceedings against her husband, Randy, and is living with her boyfriend, Andy, and her four year-old-child, Meggy.

Randy in the meantime has been charged with causing criminal damage to a window in Andy's flat by throwing a brick at it.

Advise as to:

a) The competence and compellability of Choo and Meggy in the criminal proceedings and the need for corroboration, if any.

b) The admissibility of Andy's evidence in the criminal proceedings that a few minutes prior to the brick hitting the window, he heard someone say on the street outside, 'Randy, what are you doing down here?'

c) What use may be made in the civil and criminal proceedings by Randy's counsel of a statement made by Choo to the insurance company that 'some drunken louts had smashed the window.'

Adapted from University of London LLB Examination
(for External Students) Evidence June 1984 Q8

Skeleton solution

a)
- Wife of accused - competent and compellable.
- Meggy - s52 Criminal Justice Act 1991 - *Wallwork.*

b) Hearsay - purpose for which evidence is being adduced.

c)
- Civil - admission - exception to hearsay rule.
- Criminal - hearsay - no exception - previous inconsistent statement.

Suggested solution

a) Choo is Randy's wife and as such is a competent witness for the prosecution against him (see s80 Police and Criminal Evidence Act 1984). If Choo had instituted the prosecution herself then she would be competent under s30(2) of the 1968 Theft Act, even though the offence is not a Theft Act offence. She is not compellable, merely competent (see s80, supra). The fact that divorce proceedings have been instituted does not affect this position, they are still married.

Choo is fully competent and compellable as a witness for her husband under s80 Police and Criminal Evidence Act 1984.

There is no rule requiring corroboration of the evidence of a wife when given either for or against her husband.

Meggy is only four years old. In *R* v *Wallwork* (1958), it was said, obiter, that a child of five should not be called as a witness. This was a statement of a rule of practice, though, and not of a legal rule making such a young child incompetent. The competence of a child is governed by common law and statute, now s52 Criminal Justice Act 1991.

According to s52 all children under 14 give unsworn evidence so there is no longer any need for trial court judges to consider a child's understanding of the oath. They are to be treated like any other witness, so one assumes children will now be presumed competent unless the contrary is shown. Unless Meggy is shown to be incompetent in some way, the trial judge should allow her to give evidence. Having done so, there is no requirement of corroboration - s34(2) Criminal Justice Act 1988. Yet the judge may still warn the jury of a need for caution as a matter of practice.

b) The evidence to be given by Andy amounts to the repetition of an assertion made by someone who is not giving evidence. There is some dispute about whether this evidence would be caught by the hearsay rule. The purpose of this evidence being introduced is to establish that Randy was at the scene of the crime at about the time at which it was committed. As such, the prosecution will wish to rely on the implied assertion in the statement heard by Andy that Randy was present. What authority there is suggests that if an implied assertion of the sort here is caught by the hearsay rule, so the evidence of Andy is hearsay (see Parke B in *Wright* v *Tatham* (1837)). In *Teper* v *R* (1952) the Privy Council held that evidence that someone had said to a passer-by 'Your place burning and you going away from the fire' was inadmissible. It was held that this evidence was hearsay. This case seems very close to the present, and it is submitted that the evidence of Andy is just as much hearsay as was that of the witness in *Teper*.

In *Teper's* case the passer-by had made her identification some 26 minutes after the fire started and more than one-eighth of a mile from the scene of the fire. The Privy Council held that it was not connected closely enough to the fire to be part of the res gestae and so admissible as an exception to the hearsay rule. In the present case the identification was made at the scene of the offence and only 'a few' minutes before the brick hit the window. It is submitted that the evidence is admissible as part of the res gestae. It does not, of course, establish that Randy committed the offence, but it indicates that he had the opportunity and that is certainly a relevant matter.

c) In the civil proceedings for divorce it seems that the statement is of dubious relevance. All it could establish is that Choo was in Andy's flat at the time, which could be relevant if Randy wishes to prove adultery by Choo. In such a case the statement would be admissible as an implied assertion. There is an implied statement that Choo was present at the time the window was broken. To put in the statement, therefore, would be to introduce hearsay evidence (given that the application of the hearsay rule to implied assertions is as stated above). Evidence of admissions may be given as an exception to the hearsay rule (see Civil Evidence Act 1968 s9).

In the criminal case Randy would want to introduce evidence of what Choo said as evidence that he did not commit the offence. The evidence is hearsay and does not come within any exception to the rule, and Randy would not be able to use it as evidence of its truth. The hearsay rule applies equally for and against the accused (*Sparks* v *R* (1964)). There is no question of the statement being an admission admissible against the prosecutor. It is, though, possible for Randy to use it. If Choo were to give evidence at trial and she implicated Randy, then he could use the statement as evidence of her inconsistency under s5 Criminal Procedure Act 1865 - as long as it can be said that the inconsistent statement is relevant to the facts in issue and is not just relevant to credit: *R* v *Funderburk* (1990). Here, the statement of Choo is relevant to the facts in issue, and so there would be no difficulty. The statement made out of court would not be evidence of its truth, though, just evidence that Choo had told a different story on a previous occasion and therefore may be entitled to less credibility as a witness (*R* v *Golder* (1960)).

Question 4

Mutchinson is suing Sardine & Co on a policy of insurance in respect of a ferry which had caught fire and which was insured by Sardine & Co. Sardine's defence is that Mutchinson had committed arson to claim the insurance money.

Advise on:

a) the burden and standard of proof in the case;

b) the admissibility of a memorandum of Mr Long, an official of the Port Authority, in which he says that he was informed by a Mr Lee, a ferry engineer, of Lee & Co, who had examined the ferry a few months prior to the incident, that the ferry was prone to fire damage due to the materials used. Mr Long is no longer with the Port Authority. Mr Lee has moved his business to Hong Kong.

Adapted from University of London LLB Examination
(for External Students) Evidence June 1986 Q6

Skeleton solution

a)
- Civil case - usual rule - he who asserts must prove.
- Alleging criminal conduct - standard of proof.

b) Second-hand hearsay - Civil Evidence Act 1968 - conditions of s4 - notice procedure.

Suggested solution

a) The normal rule in civil cases is that the plaintiff bears the legal burden of proof on all issues (*Abrath* v *North Eastern Railway Co* (1883)). In insurance claims this would mean that the claimant has to prove that he made a contract of insurance, that an event has occurred which is one of the risks insured and that that event has caused him a loss. On the facts given we are not told what risks were covered, but it will be assumed that fire was an insured peril and that fire caused by the arson of the insured, Mutchinson (M), was excluded either expressly or impliedly (*Gray* v *Barr* (1970)). The authorities on this point are not finally settled, but on the authority of *Munro, Brice & Co* v *War Risks Association* (1918) (but see *Hurst* v *Evans* (1917)) the position is that M will have to prove the policy and that there was loss by fire and then the burden as regards the proof of arson will lie on Sardine & Co (S). Even though arson is a criminal offence, in a civil action S will only have to prove arson on balance of probabilities (*Bater* v *Bater* (1951)). There are many cases which suggest that the standard of proof will be high, despite being covered by the phrase 'balance of probabilities' and perhaps it is correct to say that the task facing S is to prove on balance of probabilities that there is a high probability of M having committed arson (*Bater* v *Bater*; *Hornal* v *Neuberger* (1957); *Blyth* v *Blyth* (1966); *Thomas Bates & Son* v *Wyndham's Lingeries Ltd* (1981); *R* v *Secretary of State for the Home Department, ex parte Khajawa* (1984); *R* v *Hampshire County Council, ex parte Ellerton* (1985)).

b) The admissibility of the memorandum depends upon the rules in the Civil Evidence Act 1968. The memorandum is 'second-hand' hearsay because it contains a statement made by Mr Long which is itself hearsay - in other words if Mr Long were available to give evidence all he could say about the ferry is that Mr Lee told him it was prone to fire damage, he could not say of his own knowledge that this was the case. If Mr Long had personal knowledge of the ferry's liability to fire damage then his memorandum would be first-hand hearsay. Since he only has hearsay knowledge of that matter so his memorandum is second-hand hearsay. Second-hand hearsay evidence is only admissible if it satisfies the requirements of s4 of the 1968 Act. Section 4 requires the document to be a record, which has been defined by the courts as a requirement that it should be the sort of document to which a historian would look as an original source of the information given in it (*H* v *Schering Chemicals* (1983); *Savings and Investment Bank* v *Gasco* (1984)). It seems likely that Mr Lee's report, if he made one, was the best source of the information about the ferry, but if he made no written report then this memorandum would be the best documentary source.

On the assumption that this memorandum is the only written source of the information, then s4 sets out two further requirements which must be satisfied before the document can be used in court. Firstly, it must be proved that the person who compiled the record acted under a duty when he did so, and secondly, the information must have been supplied by a person with knowledge of the matters stated. There is no doubt that Mr Lee had actual knowledge of the information which he supplied to Mr Long, so the second requirement is met. Section 4(3) defines what is a duty for the purposes of the s4, and includes cases where records are compiled in the course of employment, so it would seem to include the making of the memorandum by Mr Long.

Before documentary hearsay evidence can be admitted under s4 it is necessary to serve notice on the other parties to the proceedings (by virtue of RSC Ord 38 which is provided for by Civil Evidence Act 1968 s8). RSC Ord 38 r21 requires notice to be given and r23 states the required contents of that notice. The notice in this case would have to set out the name of the maker of the document (Mr Long), the name of the person who originally supplied the information (Mr Lee), the nature of the record and the time place and circumstances in which it was compiled. It should also state why Mr Long and Mr Lee are not being called to give evidence. There are good grounds for not calling Mr Lee as a witness, namely that he is abroad. Reasonable steps should be taken to trace Mr Long and once these have been taken without success the record is admissible provided notice has been served (RSC Ord 38 r25).

Question 5

Yuppy is sued by his former employers Megablimps Corporation for the recovery of profits which he had made through share dealings using confidential information about Megablimps which he had obtained as a director of the company.

a) Consider the burden and standard of proof.

b) Would a tape recording of a conversation between Rough and Crude, two share traders, in which Rough tells Crude that he was sure that Megablimp shares would go up in price due to the information given him by Yuppy, be admissible in evidence? Rough and Crude are now somewhere in Acapulco.

Adapted from University of London LLB Examination
(for External Students) Evidence June 1988 Q2

Skeleton solution

- Burden and standard of proof in civil proceedings - general rules - elements to be proved - whether general rules apply.
- Tape recording - original/hearsay - notice requirement.

Suggested solution

a) In the civil action Megablimps Corporation is the plaintiff and Yuppy the defendant. The general rule is that it is for the plaintiff to prove each element of his accusation against the defendant (*Abrath* v *NE Railway* (1983)). Prima facie, this involves Megablimps Corporation in proving on a balance of probabilities that (a) Yuppy made a profit; (b) in share dealings; (c) using inside information.

Without doubt, elements (a) and (b) will have to be proved by Megablimps Corporation. It is also without doubt that the appropriate standard of proof is proof on the balance of probabilities (also known as the preponderance of probabilities) even though the allegation is that Yuppy has committed a criminal offence (*Hornal* v *Neuberger Products Ltd* (1957)).

But, once it is proved that an agent has come by a profit in the course of his employment it is presumed that he has come by it wrongly (*Boardman* v *Phipps* (1967)). This presumption places a legal burden on the agent to rebut the inference of wrongdoing. Therefore it would be for Yuppy to prove on the balance of probabilities that he did not come by the profit by use of confidential information.

b) The tape recording is original evidence of the conversation, which means that the court when hearing the tape recording will treat it as though Rough were in court giving evidence of the things said in the conversation (*Kajala* v *Noble* (1982)). The evidence is, therefore, non-hearsay in so far as Rough could give non-hearsay evidence.

But Rough's statement to Crude contained an implied assertion that Yuppy had told him something. It would therefore, be hearsay evidence of the truth of what Yuppy said. It is not clear whether the court would be entitled to draw any particular inference about what Yuppy said to Rough, but if it felt able to do so Rough's evidence would be admissible in that it would be of an admission to Yuppy.

No notice would have to be served for evidence of an admission to be given (s9 Civil Evidence Act 1968), and therefore it does not matter whether Rough and

Crude are within the jurisdiction. But it would be necessary for Megablimps to prove the authenticity of the tape recording.

Question 6

Joe arrives home one evening after work. His wife, Mary, observes a large bruise on his head; Joe complains of severe head pains, which he states were caused by Ted (a fellow employee) carelessly dropping a metal casting from the floor above, sits in his armchair and loses consciousness. He dies almost immediately.

Mary wishes to sue Joe's employers in negligence. Advise her generally as to the burdens and standards of proof, and as to the admissibility of the following:

a) a statement by the foreman to the effect that the dropping of the casting was his fault, as he had not ensured that the guard rails were fixed;

b) a circular issued by the employers shortly after Joe's death altering the safety procedures in Joe's department;

c) an accident book maintained in the factory with an entry regarding Joe's injury made by Scribe, one of the firm's clerks, but not countersigned by the foreman, Scribe since having emigrated to Russia.

Written by editor

Skeleton solution

- Hearsay - statements by persons since deceased etc.
- Civil proceedings; burdens and standards of proof.
- Foreman's statement; hearsay; admissions against interest; Civil Evidence Act 1968.
- Circular; relevance and admissibility.
- Hearsay - records - 1968 Act ss4 and 6.

Suggested solution

In her action in negligence Mary may testify as to what she directly observed; ie that Joe had a large bruise on his head; that he sat in his chair and died. She may also relate to the court Joe's complaint of severe head pains, but at common law would not be allowed to repeat his statement as to the cause of the pains as this would be inadmissible hearsay (*Gilbey* v *GWR Co* (1910)). It would not be a dying declaration, admissible at common law, because the employers are not facing a charge of homicide. However, had Joe survived, he would have been competent to testify not only as to his head pains but also as to their cause, ie Ted dropping a casting on his head (omitting 'carelessly' which is inadmissible opinion evidence). Therefore Joe's entire statement, with the omission of his opinion, would be capable of admissibility under s2(1) Civil Evidence Act 1968. Mary would have to serve notice on the employers of her intention to adduce this hearsay statement (s8 Civil Evidence Act 1968, and Ord 38 rr21-24), and in that notice would have to state the reason for the unavailability of Joe as a witness, ie he is dead (Ord 38 r25). As regards the weight to be given to Joe's statement, that is a matter for the judge, and will depend on facts such as its contemporaneity with the alleged incident and whether Joe had any motive to misrepresent the facts (s6 Civil Evidence Act 1968).

Mary, without the aid of the testimony of Joe and others, eg Scribe, must nevertheless prove, on balance of probabilities, that the employers were negligent (or vicariously liable for another employee's negligence) and that negligence caused Joe's death. Despite the fact that she is alleging misconduct by the employers which could amount to the crime of manslaughter, nevertheless the standard of proof required is the civil one (*Hornal* v *Neuberger Products Ltd* (1957)). However, the recent case of *Halford* v *Brookes* (1991), said in a civil action in battery against the alleged murderers, the standard of proof should be the criminal one. But perhaps *Hornal* would apply here because it is manslaughter which is alleged. However, given the nature of Mary's assertion the court may look for more weighty evidence than if the case concerned a simple breach of contract (*Bater* v *Bater* (1951)). If the employers should merely deny negligence, than the burden of proof remains throughout on Mary as the plaintiff; if the employers, however, should allege contributory negligence by Joe then on that issue they have a legal burden of proof to discharge.

At common law the foreman's statement would be inadmissible hearsay if reported by someone who overheard it, or to whom it was made, because the statement is an admission against his employer's interests, not against his own, and the foreman as an employee has no authority to make such an admission (s2(2) Civil Evidence Act 1968; and see *Morris* v *Stratford-on-Avon RDC* (1973)). The statement, therefore is not admissible under the common law provisions preserved by s9 of the 1968 Act (where no notice procedure needs to be followed), but *would* be admissible under s2. If Mary intends to call the foreman as a witness, then leave of the court is required before his statement can be given in evidence (*Burr* v *Ware RDC* (1939)).

A copy of the circular, although strictly offending against the 'best evidence' rule, is admissible in evidence by virtue of s6(1) Civil Evidence Act 1968; this is obviously on the assumption that the original would have been admissible. The admissibility of the circular will depend on its content, in that there may be nothing in it which is in law *relevant* to the issue of negligence. If the circular merely alters the procedures in Joe's department, then in itself it does not go to prove negligence (*Hart* v *Lancs and Yorks Rail Co* (1869)). If, however, there is legal relevance in the circular to the instant negligence issue, and the circular was issued by an agent of the employers, it could amount to an admission against their interests and be admissible without notice under s9; if issued by some servant of the employers, then Mary will have to serve notice on the employers, the circular being treated as a s2 (or possibly s4) statement.

The entry in the accident book may have evidential value, dependent on its content, in which case Mary will want to have the book (or an extract, copy etc) produced in evidence. If it was part of Scribe's duties to maintain the accident book, and if the entry was made by him from information supplied by someone with personal knowledge (or who may reasonably be supposed to have had such knowledge) of the accident involving Joe, then the requirements of s4(1) of the 1968 Act are met, and the second-hand hearsay statement contained in the record becomes admissible -

subject to the notice procedure dealt with when discussing the foreman's statement. The notice served on the employers must state that Scribe is 'beyond the seas', ie in Russia; it is not necessary for Mary to state that all reasonable steps have been taken to find him and make him available (*Piermay Shipping Co* v *Chester* (1978)). Similar provisions apply to the supplier to Scribe of the information, if his identity is known. With regard to the weight to be attached to the statement in the accident book, the provisions of s6 are again applicable; the lack of a counter-signature by the foreman could reduce the weight considerably, dependent on the extent to which this is an abnormality.

8 HEARSAY - STATUTORY ADMISSIBILITY IN CRIMINAL CASES

8.1 Introduction

8.2 Key points

8.3 Analysis of questions

8.4 Questions

8.1 Introduction

The major statutory exceptions concern confessions (with quite recent legislation on which there has been a plethora of interpretative cases) and documentary hearsay, on which there has been very recent statutory activity. In criminal cases confessions constitute an important exception to the hearsay rule, and one which will remain topical for some years and always controversial.

8.2 Key points

Common law on admissibility of confessions was altered drastically by the Police and Criminal Evidence Act 1984.

a) *Definition*

Section 82(1): '... "confession" includes any statement wholly or partly adverse to the person who made it, whether made to a person in authority or not and whether made in words or otherwise.'

Therefore a confession may be oral, written or by a gesture such as a nod of the head, and may be made to any person, not just a person in authority such as a police officer. Silence in the face of an accusation may amount, in some circumstances, to a confession.

b) *Admissibility*

As a matter of law is governed by s76 (s77 in the case of mentally handicapped persons). If a confession is unfairly obtained yet nevertheless strictly admissible, there is a statutory discretion to exclude it given by s78, over and above the general exclusionary discretion preserved in all cases by s82(3).

Confessions are treated as inadmissible hearsay unless the prosecution proves (beyond reasonable doubt) that they were not obtained by oppression, or that they were not obtained in consequence of anything said or done which was likely to render them unreliable (s76(2)). If the defence raises the question of admissibility, that in itself is enough to put the prosecution to proof (ie the defence does not have to discharge an evidential burden). Without any representation being made by the defence the court may, of its own motion, put the prosecution to proof of reliability or absence of oppression (s76(3)). When the admissibility of a confession is challenged, by the defence or the court itself, then the issue will be decided on a voir dire - ie in the absence of the jury who, if the confession is ruled inadmissible, will hear nothing of it.

i) Oppression

Oppression is not defined fully in the 1984 Act. Section 76(8) gives a partial definition:

'includes torture, inhuman or degrading treatment, and the use or threat of violence ...'

In *R* v *Fulling* [1987] 2 All ER 65, oppression was an issue in respect of Miss Fulling's confession: in the Court of Appeal Lord Lane CJ preferred the OED definition of 'oppression' to the partial definition in s76(8) or to any common law definition; thus, oppression in this confession context is 'the exercise of authority or power in a burdensome, harsh or wrongful manner; unjust or cruel treatment of subjects, inferiors etc; the imposition of unreasonable or unjust burdens'. So, when conduct falls short of the extreme oppression in s76(8), it would appear that there must be deliberate misconduct by the police, and that there is some subjectivity in the test for oppression, ie the strengths and weaknesses of the suspect are relevant to the issue of whether the treatment was harsh, cruel or burdensome. The fact that a suspect finds detention in a police station oppressive, however, is not sufficient for any subsequent confession to be excluded on the grounds of 'oppression' under s76 - something (much) more than that is needed.

In the recent case of *R* v *Ismail* [1990] Crim LR 109, the Court of Appeal made it clear that breaches of the Police and Criminal Evidence Act 1984 and the Codes of Practice during one interview could not be cured by a later properly conducted interview, when the confession was made. To allow such evidence would be to condone the flouting of the statute and the Codes of Practice. However, in the case of *R* v *Barrett* (1991) 92 Cr App R 61, the court distinguished *Ismail* in similar circumstances saying that it depended on the individual concerned and Barrett had not been affected by the breaches the way Ismail had.

ii) Unreliability

Even the *likelihood* of unreliability in consequence of something said or done is enough for a confession to be inadmissible (s76(2)(b)). The laws of evidence are concerned with the reliability, but not the truth, of the confession - which seems to be a contradiction in terms, unless s76 is to be used to discipline the police or safeguard the rights of the suspect, irrespective of the guilt of the accused. However, in the case of *R* v *Tyrer* (1990) 90 Cr App R 446, the appellant claimed she was worried about her children and wanted to get home whilst being interviewed and that is why she confessed. She also claimed that the trial judge took into account evidence given against her which was not evidence given during the voir dire. The Court of Appeal ruled that although, strictly, s76(2)(b) does not allow the court to consider the truth of the confession, nevertheless, the issue of admissibility could not be tried in complete isolation from the background of the case, and so the confession was admitted. The cases are in conflict, presumably because of the ambivalence of the judiciary in the appellate courts, eg in *R* v *Alladice* [1988] NLJR 141, although the suspect was denied his right to a solicitor, his confession was allowed in evidence because by his own admission he knew his rights and understood the cautions administered to him, therefore his confession statement was reliable despite impropriety on the part of the police. In the latter case of *R* v *McGovern* (1991) 92 Cr App R 228, the appellant was wrongfully denied access to a solicitor, and the Court of Appeal held that it was right to exclude her confession even though she later admitted its truth. See also *R* v *Chung* (1991) 92 Cr App R 314. In *R* v *Sat-Bhambra* [1988] Crim LR 453, the suspect was given a tranquilliser by the police doctor to steady his nerves, and therefore his subsequent confession was held unreliable despite the fact that there was no improper conduct by the police to induce the confession. In *R* v *Harvey* [1988] Crim LR 241, a confession was excluded as unreliable where there was no impropriety at all by the police, but the suspect, a psychopath with a low IQ, may have confessed in order to protect her lover; any unreliability was occasioned not by the words or conduct of the police but by the suspect's own mental condition. However, in the case of *R* v *Crampton* (1991) 92 Cr App R 369, the defendant was a heroin addict and was suffering from withdrawal symptoms when he was interviewed about the crime and confessed to it. The trial judge admitted the confession. On appeal, the Court of Appeal said the trial judge had been correct - because it was doubtful whether the mere holding of an interview when the appellant was withdrawing from the symptoms of heroin addiction was something 'done' within the meaning of s76(2)(b) of the Police and Criminal Evidence Act 1984. The court considered and agreed with the case of *Goldenberg* (1989) 88 Cr App R 285, where the defendant again was suffering from the withdrawal from drug addiction. The court there also held that this was not something 'done' within s76(2)(b) - ie the stimulus must be external to the suspect. It could therefore be argued that the decision in *Harvey* is correct because the stimulus did not come from the suspect but from a third party, ie the lover. But the case of *DPP* v *Blake* (1989) 89 Cr App R 179 makes it clear that the test in s76(2)(b) is objective in the sense that it is irrelevant that the police acted in perfect good faith. In *R* v *Fulling* (supra), however, there was impropriety on the part of the police but the suspect's confession was held *not* to be unreliable despite the emotional upheaval caused within her by the police statements - the conduct of the police was considered by the Court of Appeal to be merely 'unsporting'.

So inadmissibility on the grounds of potential unreliability (s76(2)(b)), or on the grounds of oppression falling short of s76(8) as provided for in s76(2)(a), as a matter of law is the subject of a mass of, often contradictory, case law. However, even though adjudged admissible a confession may nevertheless be excluded as a matter of discretion.

c) *Exclusionary discretion*

If a confession is ruled admissible under s76, above, it may nevertheless be excluded in the discretion of the judge if it appears that in all the circumstances its admission would have such an adverse effect on the fairness of the proceedings that the court ought not to admit it (s78(1)). The case of *R* v *Manji* [1990] Crim LR 512 stated that a voir dire should have been used by the trial court judge to decide if a caution had been given to the defendant, and so if he should use his s78 discretion to exclude the confession.

Where a suspect was wrongly denied access to legal advice, his confession, irrespective of its admissibility under the criteria in s76, was excluded under s78 on the grounds of unfairness: *R* v *Samuel* [1988] 2 All ER 135. Where lies were told to a suspect and to his solicitor in order to induce a confession, it was held that the confession, despite its reliability ought to be excluded under s78 because of the unfairness of the proceedings: *R* v *Mason* [1987] 3 All ER 481.

If the police are in breach of the Codes of Practice issued under s66 of the Act (these Codes replacing the old Judges' Rules), then that is a matter which must be taken into account by the court (s67(11)). Breaches of the Code on the Questioning of Suspects may be sufficiently serious to constitute oppression or render the consequent confession potentially unreliable, and therefore in either situation inadmissible under the provisions of s76. If breaches of the Code are not so serious, it is then a matter of judicial discretion, under s78, as to whether a consequent confession, albeit legally admissible, is excluded. After a series of reported Crown Court decisions in 1988 and 1989, all concerning the exercise of the discretion (or its non-exercise) to exclude confessions, the Court of Appeal held that a breach of a Code of Practice which did not lead to inadmissibility under s76 might result in unfairness - but the Court of Appeal would not interfere with the judge's exercise of his discretion under s78 unless it was apparent that he was wrong, and each case would depend on the particular circumstances involved: *R* v *Grannell* (1989) The Times 16 August CA. So it is for the judge in any particular case to decide whether there is unfairness justifying his exercise of his discretion to exclude; only if he is obviously wrong will the Court of Appeal interfere.

At common law there was throughout the criminal laws of evidence a judicial discretion to exclude evidence where its prejudicial effect outweighed its probative value, ie an exclusionary discretion which would make for a fair trial. That general discretion has been preserved by s82(3) of the 1984 Act, but to what extent that exclusionary discretion and the s78 exclusionary discretion overlap has yet to be decided by the courts, ie given there is no unfairness justifying the exclusion of a confession (s78), is it conceivable that the confession could still be excluded under s82(3)?

d) *Facts discovered in consequence of confessions*

If a confession statement is allowed in evidence, then, as regards facts discovered in consequence there is no evidentiary problem. But where the confession statement is excluded, under (s76) then, unless the defence give evidence as to how the other facts were discovered, no reference can be made to the content, or the fact, of the inadmissible confession (s76(5) and (6)).

So, although the subsequently and consequentially discovered evidence can be adduced, it cannot be linked to the accused by any reference to the inadmissible confession. But, s76(5) and (6) prohibit reference to any confession excluded under s76 - therefore if a confession is excluded under s78 in the discretion of the judge, then presumably the common law still applies and it would be acceptable for the prosecution witness to say: 'In consequence of what the accused said, I discovered X at location Y ...'

e) *Silence as a confession*

When a person is accused of having committed a crime and remains silent, then in certain circumstances that silence is capable of amounting to corroboration of other evidence against him, as has been discussed above.

Similarly, silence in the face of an out of court accusation can amount in some circumstances to adoption of the accusation as a confession. If the accused and accuser are on even terms, and it would be reasonable to expect a response, eg an indignant retort, a refutation, then silence can be left to the jury as something from which they *may*, in that situation, infer that the accused adopted the content of the accusation as his confession, ie tacitly accepted what was said as true: *Parkes* v *R* [1976] 1 WLR 1251. But where the accuser is a person in authority such as a police officer, then the silence of the suspect - whether cautioned or not - cannot amount to acceptance of the truth of the accusation, ie by exercising in that situation his right to silence the suspect cannot be providing evidence of guilt: *Hall* v *R* [1971] 1 WLR 298. In one case it was stated that when a suspect is questioned by a police officer in the presence of his solicitor, then his silence can amount to evidence of guilt since the parties are on even terms: *R* v *Chandler* [1976] 1 WLR 585. However, the reasoning in that case has, rightly, been criticised.

f) *Editing confessions*

A confession may be only partly adverse to the person who made it (s82(1) Police and Criminal Evidence Act 1984) and therefore may contain exculpatory as well as incriminatory material; in that case the whole confession statement must be reported - but the jury informed of the lack of evidential value of the exculpatory (ie 'self-serving') material. But if the confession includes references to the accused's previous convictions, bad character or other prejudicial matters, then that material *must* be excised by editing of the statement. If such editing leaves an incoherent statement, then the judge may exclude the whole statement.

If a confession statement implicates a co-accused, then the jury must be instructed that the confession is *not* evidence against that co-accused (that part of it is inadmissible hearsay). Alternatively, the confession statement may be edited so that the co-accused is not identified: *R* v *Silcott* [1987] Crim LR 765; or in exceptional cases separate trials may be ordered to avoid serious prejudice to the co-accused: *R* v *Lake* (1977) 64 Cr App R 172.

g) *Documentary hearsay*

Several statutes make provision for the admissibility of documentary hearsay in criminal proceedings, the most important now being the Criminal Justice Act 1988. Sections 23-28 and Schedule 2 of the CJA 1988 replace the provisions in the Police and Criminal Evidence Act 1984 except those in s69 relating to documents produced by computers. The overall effect is to make documentary hearsay in criminal proceedings more widely admissible.

i) Trade, business etc documents

Section 24 CJA 1988 is similar to s4 Civil Evidence Act 1968 regarding the pre-requisites for admissibility of documentary hearsay, but the conditions such as death, unavailability etc of the maker of the statement in the document do *not* apply unless the statement was prepared for the purpose of criminal proceedings or criminal investigations (s24(4)). In any event, s25 gives the criminal court a discretion to exclude such statements in the interests of justice, with mandatory considerations spelled out in s25(2). Where a statement seems to have been prepared for the purpose of criminal proceedings or investigations, then s26 stipulates that leave of the court is required before it can be adduced as hearsay evidence.

The case of *R* v *Cole* [1990] 2 All ER 108 explained the difference between ss25 and 26. Under s25 the court should admit the statement when the conditions laid down in ss23 and 24 are satisfied, unless it considers (looking at s25(2)) that it should be excluded. But under s26, the court should not allow the statement which satisfies the conditions in ss23 and 24 to be admitted, unless it concludes (looking at the wording of s26) that it should be admitted.

ii) Other documentary hearsay

Whereas s24, above, obviously covers second-hand hearsay in respect of trade or business documents (and liberalises s68 Police and Criminal Evidence Act 1984), s23 provides for the general admissibility in criminal proceedings of all first-hand hearsay in documentary form. The prerequisite for admissibility is that the maker of the statement is dead, unfit, unavailable etc (similar again to s4 Civil Evidence Act 1968), or that where the statement was made to a police officer the maker (in addition to the above disjunctive reasons), does not give evidence through fear or because he is kept out of the way (s23(3)), explained in *R* v *Acton Justices, ex parte McMullen* (1991) 92 Cr App R 98 as meaning a statement will be admissible in circumstances where someone was sought to place its maker in fear of attending court or has physically prevented him from doing so. Again, discretion to exclude (s25) and leave of the court to admit (s26) apply as in the case of s24 statements. Also, as in the case of s24 statements, Schedule 2, para 3 CJA 1988 makes provision for the weight, if any, to be attached to such hearsay statements, the court having regard to all the circumstances from which any inference can reasonably be drawn as to accuracy - similar again to the provisions in the 1968 Civil Evidence Act (s6).

iii) Depositions and witness statements

Several statutes provide for the general admissibility (subject to restrictions and usually subject to the overriding judicial discretion to exclude) of hearsay documents, for example:

- Section 102 MCA 1980 - written statements in committal proceedings.
- Section 9 CJA 1967 - written statements in criminal proceedings other than committals.
- Section 105 MCA 1980 - deposition of dangerously ill person, unavailable through illness or subsequent death to testify at trial.
- Sections 42 and 43 Children and Young Persons Act 1933, and s103 MCA 1980 - provision made for the admissibility of depositions of children or young persons as victims of certain crimes, and witness statements of children. These sections are no longer as important as they used to be. We now have s32 of the Criminal Justice Act 1988 which allows for children to give evidence via a live television link during the court proceedings. The conditions are that the crime is one of a particular group - ie assault, or cruelty to persons under the age of 16 (CYPA 1933); and indecency or sexual offences under the Sexual Offences Act 1956 - s32(1)(b) and s32(2) of Criminal Justice Act 1988. The trial must be a trial on indictment or an appeal to the Criminal Division of the Court of Appeal arising out of such proceedings. The section also applies to proceedings in Juvenile Courts ('Youth Courts' after the Criminal Justice Act 1991), and appeals to Crown Courts from there - s32(1A) of the 1988 Act, as inserted by the 1991 Act.

  The age of the child is also relevant. He or she must be under 14 if the charge is cruelty; or under 17 if a sexual offence - s55 Criminal Justice Act 1991.

  The Criminal Justice Act 1991 also extends the 1988 Act by allowing video recordings of children to be shown in court - s54 of the 1991 Act inserting s32A into the 1988 Act. It applies in the same circumstances as s32 does (above). The video recording must be of an interview between an adult and the child and must relate to any matter in issue in the proceedings. However, the child must still be called to be cross-examined in court.

8.3 Analysis of questions

Hearsay in criminal cases, and statutory exceptions to the hearsay rule, will always figure in LLB and Bar Final examinations in a variety of guises. Although sometimes questions will test knowledge of exceptions to the general, exclusionary, hearsay rule in both criminal and civil cases, it is quite common for there to be 'self-contained' criminal questions on hearsay, often concentrating on admissibility of confessions and quite commonly requiring also some knowledge of the rules relating to evidence of bad character (dealt with in Chapter 9).

8.4 Questions

Question 1

Dempsey is charged with stealing a quantity of tyres from Lorimar Ltd, a tyre manufacturer.

Makepiece, who disposed of the tyres after receiving them from Dempsey, will give evidence against Dempsey at the trial, though Makepiece will not be charged with any offence. The police will put in evidence a confession made by Dempsey while in police custody. Dempsey says he had never made a confession although he had been interrogated a very long time after his wrist watch had been removed from him in a police cell, where it was not possible for him to know the time of day or night.

Dempsey says he got the tyres from Malaysia and has an invoice addressed to him from a Malaysian company for the exact number and make of tyres which Makepiece says he received from Dempsey. Dempsey says Makepiece has 'framed' him.

The Crown, however, have subjected the tyres to chemical analysis, at Lorimar's laboratories, and have a computerised analysis that the rubber used in the tyres is not made from Malaysian sheet rubber of any kind, but is of South American origin, which is the source of rubber for the tyres which Lorimar manufactures. The computer had analysed data fed into it by scientists who had examined the chemical properties of the tyres found in Dempsey's possession.

Consider in relation to the issues in the law of evidence, how defence counsel should conduct Dempsey's defence at the trial in relation to the evidence of the confession and the cross examination of Crown witnesses. Consider also any other issues arising in the law of evidence for consideration by the trial judge.

University of London LLB Examination
(for External Students) Evidence June 1987 Q8

Skeleton solution

- Denial of confession - issue for jury.

- Issue of admissibility - s76 Police and Criminal Evidence Act 1984 - oppression - unreliability.
- Accomplice - corroboration - lies as corroboration.
- Computer print-outs - hearsay or not.

Suggested solution

The alleged confession raises two issues, firstly what procedure should be adopted when challenging it and secondly what is the law determining its admissibility. Also two things are clear about the confession, firstly that if Dempsey says that he never made a confession at all then that is a question for the jury and not for the judge; and secondly that if the prosecution argues that it was made then the jury should be directed to enquire whether it was true.

In *Ajodha* v *The State* (1981) the Privy Council held that where the defence alleges that the confession was never made then there is no issue on which to hold a trial-within-a-trial but there are two jury questions, namely whether or not it was made and whether or not it was true. Clearly there is the risk for the accused that if he is disbelieved when he says he did not make it then the jury is unlikely to consider the statement to be untrue.

There is an added difficulty here, namely that on Dempsey's expected evidence the issue of admissibility will arise, because being deprived of his watch could be considered oppressive. Although the law is unclear, it may be that s76 of the 1984 Act will be applicable because defence counsel could argue that if the jury finds that the confession was made then it would be the case that it may have been obtained improperly. Under the common law of *Ajodha* v *The State* this problem could not have arisen, but the 1984 Act allows for a test of admissibility wherever it is represented that the confession may have been obtained improperly and it must be legitimate for counsel to argue that he is entitled to a ruling on admissibility in the event that his client is not believed. It should be remembered that the prosecution will want to adduce evidence of the confession before Dempsey has given evidence, so the court will not have before it evidence that the confession was never made. It is submitted that Dempsey's counsel would be entitled to require the judge to rule on admissibility.

The test of admissibility is whether the confession was obtained by oppression or in such circumstances that any confession made by the accused would be likely to be unreliable. Oppression seems to indicate some form of physical or mental maltreatment. Depriving someone of his watch when he was unable to tell whether it was night or day may give rise to confusion and it is submitted that this could be either oppression or something which makes the confession unreliable. It is not possible to say more than that without more evidence of the circumstances in which Dempsey was held, the number of times he was questioned and the length of time for which he was questioned. The court may require the prosecution to prove admissibility even if the defence does not raise the point (s76(3) Police and Criminal

Evidence Act 1984), although it is submitted that Dempsey's counsel should act himself and not hope that the judge will intervene.

If the judge rules the confession inadmissible then no question arises whether it was made, save that as a matter of tactics the defence may wish to show the jury that the prosecution based its case around a purported confession which the judge would not allow to go before them.

It is alleged by Dempsey that Makepiece has framed him. Makepiece could be questioned about his own involvement in receiving the tyres. But because Dempsey says that it was all perfectly innocent so there would be little advantage in attacking Makepiece as being someone who is giving evidence in order to save his own skin - after all to attack Makepiece in that way would to be to admit that there was something illegal in Makepiece's reception of the tyres.

On the case as presented by the prosecution Makepiece is an accomplice and as such needs corroborating as a matter of practice (*Davies* v *DPP* (1954)). If the jury disbelieves Dempsey's evidence about the Malaysian origin of the tyres and, therefore, thinks that the invoice is a fraud, then Dempsey's lies may corroborate Makepiece's evidence, because they clearly would be deliberate lies on a material issue and were told because of a realisation of guilt and a fear of the truth. Whether the fourth criterion for the use of lies as corroboration is made out, namely that they are proved to be lies by evidence other than that which needs corroborating (*R* v *Lucas* (1981)) depends upon the admissibility of the evidence of the analysis.

It will be assumed that the tyres analysed were those disposed of by Makepiece. As the question stands this is not clear because it may suggest that other tyres found in Dempsey's possession were analysed - if that is the case then the evidence will be inadmissible because it is wholly irrelevant.

Computer print-outs are admissible under s69 of the Police and Criminal Evidence Act 1984. The conditions of admissibility in that section are additional to those which allow documentary evidence to be given. Therefore it is necessary firstly to consider whether the print-out is admissible as a document and then whether it also satisfies the computer print-out criteria. It is submitted that the computer print-out is not hearsay evidence in this case. It seems that what the computer is doing is merely comparing the data fed in by the scientists with banks of data already stored in it. In other words, it is looking at the chemical properties and comparing them with a list of properties which it has been told are possessed by South American rubber. It appears that the computer is only doing what could be done by the scientists themselves albeit probably in a longer time. Such non-hearsay evidence is admissible at common law and does not have to satisfy the requirements of s24 Criminal Justice Act 1988. But, it does have to satisfy the requirements of s69. It must be proved by the prosecution that the computer was operating properly. This can be proved by a certificate signed by a person occupying a responsible position in relation to the computer (Schedule 3, para 8, Police and Criminal Evidence Act 1984. See also paras 11 and 12 as to the weight to be attached to the print-out).

On the information in the question it is not possible to say whether the computer print-out is admissible, although if it is then it may require an expert to give evidence interpreting the print-out.

The evidence of the print-out would not necessarily disprove the genuineness of the invoice, however, because it seems to say that the tyres came from Malaysia, not that they were necessarily made of Malaysian rubber. More information about the invoice would therefore be needed before it could be said for certain whether the computer print-out shows the invoice and Dempsey's evidence to be lies. If, though, the jury is satisfied by the analysis evidence that the invoice and Dempsey's evidence are deliberate lies then that would mean that Makepiece's evidence is corroborated.

It is quite possible, of course, that Dempsey innocently bought the tyres, thinking them to be Malaysian and was himself the victim of a fraud. It would not be for Dempsey to prove that he bought them in good faith, but once he has called evidence of the circumstances of his purchase then the prosecution would have to prove that it was not all above board. The facts given are quite consistent with Dempsey having bought the goods from a rogue.

Question 2

Snort and Hype, two natives of Humberside in England have recently returned to Humberside from Colombia and are charged with importing a large quantity of a prohibited drug, cocaine, into the UK. The cocaine is a new variety which comes only from Colombia. Snort and Hype had both been in Colombia for some time and the police have evidence that Snort had served two years in a Colombian jail for three offences of dealing in this particular variety of cocaine. Police records on computer also show that until the date on which Snort and Hype had returned to Humberside, prohibited drugs seized by customs and the police had not included this particular brand of cocaine. The consignment of drugs had been found on a fishing vessel owned by Snort and Hype by police officers acting without a search warrant on a 'tip off'. Snort had been questioned by the police on two consecutive days, and had, according to the police, admitted to the offence. Snort says that during those two days he had been kept in solitary confinement and questioned without a break in a cell which had little lighting or ventilation, and that the police had threatened to hand him over to local drug barons who detested him. Snort denies making any such confession.

Is there any reason why any of the above evidence may not be admitted?

Adapted from University of London LLB Examination
(for External Students) Evidence June 1988 Q4

Skeleton solution

- Snort's convictions - relevance; prejudice.
- Absence of search warrant - effect on admissibility of evidence found - s78 Police and Criminal Evidence Act 1984 - privilege for name of informant.

- Snort's confession - challenge to making thereof - admissibility of - breaches of code of conduct.

Suggested solution

Evidence that the drug seized comes only from Columbia is admissible provided someone with relevant expertise can give oral evidence of that fact. In theory, written hearsay would be admissible, but the issue requires expert evidence and in the absence of agreement from the defence (which would allow a statement to be read (s9 Criminal Justice Act 1967)) oral evidence would be appropriate. The witness giving the evidence could be a policeman or any other person with sufficient expertise, even if he has no paper qualifications in the subject (*R* v *Silverlock* (1894)).

That Snort and Hype have been in Columbia, is also relevant, although it does not really take matters much further than to show that they had the opportunity to acquire this type of cocaine.

Snort's convictions for dealing in the type of cocaine in question could only be admitted in evidence if the fact that he dealt in the drug is probative on the question whether he imported it into the UK. In order to assess the admissibility of the evidence it is necessary to know to what issue it is alleged to be relevant. The drugs were on a fishing vessel owned by Snort and Hype, but it is not known whether either of them was on the vessel. If the defence asserts that the drug was on the vessel but that it was nothing to do with Snort, it is submitted that evidence of his previous convictions in Columbia does nothing more than invite the jury to conclude that because he has been involved with this drug in the past so he must have been involved with it on the occasion in question. Although there may be a degree of probative force in the evidence, it is submitted that it is not so probative that the inevitable prejudice is outweighed. It is submitted therefore that it is not admissible (*DPP* v *Boardman* (1975)). In any event, it cannot be evidence against Hype.

Evidence that the drugs were found by police officers acting without a search warrant may be given. At common law, that the search was illegal does not mean that evidence cannot be given about both the way the search was carried out or what was found (*R* v *Sang* (1980)). Section 78 of the Police and Criminal Evidence Act 1984 gives the judge the power to exclude evidence if its admission would have an adverse effect on the fairness of the proceedings. The judge may consider the way in which the evidence was obtained when exercising his discretion. In *R* v *Samuel* (1988) the Court of Appeal held that if evidence is obtained improperly the judge should ask whether it would have been obtained had the police acted properly throughout. In this case, if the police obtained a search warrant first there can be little doubt that the same evidence would have been found, so the discretion is not likely to be exercised to exclude the evidence.

Further, the judge would have no discretion to exclude the evidence on the ground that it was obtained by a 'tip-off' although the officers concerned would be entitled to refuse to name their informant (*Marks* v *Beyfus* (1890)).

Snort's alleged confession raises two issues. Firstly, is the admissibility of it in issue, and secondly, if it is, is it admissible? Because Snort alleges that the confession was never made, the issue raised by the defence is the factual one of whether or not it was made. That issue is for the jury and does not raise any point of law (*Ajodha* v *The State* (1982)). But, if the jury decides that he did make the alleged confession, it is submitted that the jury would not be entitled to consider that confession unless it is admissible evidence. *Ajodha* v *The State* contains a dictum from Lord Bridge to the contrary, ie that if the defence says a confession was never made the issue of voluntariness (which was the admissibility test at that time) can never arise. It is submitted that that is still correct today in many cases, but not in all.

It is for the prosecution to prove the admissibility of all evidence it tenders and if, as a matter of tactics, the defence alleges that the confession was never made, that of itself cannot render admissible a confession which in law is inadmissible.

By s76 of the Police and Criminal Evidence Act 1984, the confession would only be admissible if it is proved by the prosecution not to have been made by oppression or in circumstances likely to render any statement made by the accused unreliable. In order to raise the issue of admissibility it must be represented to the court that it was or may have been obtained by oppression or in consequence of anything said or done which was likely to render any confession unreliable.

If any police officer gives evidence of the circumstances in which Snort was detained, it is submitted that the defence would be entitled to say that notwithstanding that the making of the confession is denied, the facts alleged by the prosecution raise the issue of inadmissibility. If this is correct, then it is submitted further that the confession is likely to be inadmissible. It is clear that there were breaches of the Code of Practice issued under s66 of the 1984 Act. The breaches are that: (a) Snort was questioned in a cell rather than an interview room (Code C para 12.4); (b) the cell was not adequately lit or ventilated (Code C para 12.4); and (c) he was questioned without proper breaks in questioning (Code C para 12.7); it was not a breach that he was kept in solitary confinement (Code C para 8.1). The fact that these matters are breaches of the code is not of itself enough to render his confession inadmissible, but they will do so if they amount to oppression or render the confession potentially unreliable (*R* v *Alladice* (1988)).

Threats of violence amount to oppression (s76(8) Police and Criminal Evidence Act 1984) and it is submitted that threats to hand the accused over to others who may do him harm also amount to oppression. Oppression automatically renders a confession inadmissible, whether or not it also renders it unreliable.

The breaches outlined above may render the confession unreliable, although evidence will be needed about Snort's ability to withstand the sort of treatment he received before any conclusive view can be expressed on that matter.

Question 3

Tom is interviewed at his office by Detective Inspector Cyd. Cyd tells him that the policy of the local police is not to prosecute users of controlled drugs if they give information which results in the conviction of others. Tom states that he is not a drug user and has no useful knowledge. When Cyd states that he will guarantee Tom's immunity from prosecution if he confesses, Tom produces a number of forged prescriptions for morphine, some bearing his typed name and address and others the typed names and addresses of Dick and Harry respectively. Dick and Harry are arrested and detained in separate police cells for six hours and questioned continuously by police officers; eventually both admit to using morphine but no drugs are found by the police.

Tom, Dick and Harry are all charged with drugs offences and Tom is charged with forgery. There is medical evidence that Dick suffers from severe anxiety neurosis and that Harry has a mental age of eight.

Discuss the evidentiary aspects.

Written by editor

Skeleton solution

- Introduction - police questioning; Police and Criminal Evidence Act 1984 and Codes of Practice.
- Confessions and evidence tantamount to confessions; admissibility; discretion to exclude.
- Police impropriety; mental disorders; questioning of mentally handicapped persons.

Suggested solution

The questioning of suspects is governed by the Codes of Practice issued under s66 Police and Criminal Evidence Act 1984; although not all breaches of Codes will result in a subsequent confession being inadmissible under s76 or excluded under s78, nevertheless the Codes must be taken into account by the courts where relevant to any issue in the proceedings (s67(11)).

Cyd's statements to Tom may be innocent misrepresentations or deliberate lies; in either case, the first question which must arise is whether Cyd's statements, or one of them, caused Tom to confess. Given there was no oppression of Tom by Cyd, the crucial issue is whether any confession was, or may have been, obtained '*in consequence* of anything said or done ...' (s76(2)(b) Police and Criminal Evidence Act 1984). Tom appears to produce the forged prescriptions in consequence of Cyd's guarantee of immunity, therefore the causative link is present; however, s76(2)(b) is concerned with the reliability of any induced confession, and there would seem to be no doubt as to the reliability of the forged prescriptions. Although they are documents, their production is 'tantamount to a confession' (*R* v *Barker* (1941)), and has been induced by Cyd's words; confessions made in consequence of police lies have been excluded despite their reliability (eg *R* v *Mason* (1987)), but the exclusion has been, not because the confession was inadmissible under s76, but in the discretion of the judge under s78 because its admission would have such an adverse effect on the fairness of the proceedings.

The Court of Appeal has stated recently that not all breaches of the Codes of Practice will give rise to the exclusionary discretion under s78, and that it will not be prepared to interfere with a judge's refusal to exercise his discretion in favour of the defence unless there has been, clearly, unfairness (*R* v *Grannell* (1989)). So, on the charge of forgery, whether the prescriptions will be excluded under s78 may well depend on whether the judge adopts a stance against police impropriety or against acquittal of the guilty. Somewhat incongruously, if Tom had confessed to forging prescriptions, and had then told Cyd where the prescriptions could be discovered, then his confession might have been excluded under s76, in which case, although the prescriptions could be produced in evidence, no reference could be made to the content, or even the fact of Tom's confession to link him to the prescriptions (s76(5) and (6) Police and Criminal Evidence Act 1984).

The detention of Dick and Harry in policy custody may seem oppressive to them, but does not in itself amount to 'oppression' for the purpose of s76(2)(a) (see *R* v *Fulling* (1987)). Therefore, the court may be concerned with unreliability of their confessions under s76(2)(b), and in this context there may be a degree of subjectivity, ie the court may have regard to the likely effect of police words or conduct on the minds of Dick and Harry respectively, *not* on the notional 'reasonable man'. For example, where a suspect asserted that he was aware of his rights, and fully understood the cautions administered to him, it was held that the wrongful denial of access to a solicitor did not render his confession unreliable (*R* v *Alladice* (1988)). Further evidence of this subjectivity is seen in another case where the suspect was a psychopath with a low IQ and there was medical evidence that she could have confessed to protect her lover; her confession was held inadmissible under s76(2)(b), the unreliability being caused by her own mental state at the time (*R* v *Harvey* (1988)). If there is any evidence to show that Dick could have confessed because of his anxiety neurosis which had compelled him to make a statement to obtain his release from custody, then his confession might be held unreliable and thus inadmissible under s76(2)(b). However the recent case of *R* v *Crampton* (1991) makes it clear that to fall within s76(2)(b), the unreliability must be the result of an external stimulus, not the defendant's own psychological problems. In Harry's case, apart from any similar considerations, he is mentally handicapped as defined by s77(3), and therefore if there was no independent person present when he was interviewed and confessed, then, even if the confession is allowed in evidence, the judge must warn the jury of the special need for caution before they convict if the prosecution case depends wholly or substantially on that confession (s77(1)). This unreliability of the confessions of Dick and Harry does not require any impropriety on the part of the police (*R* v *Harvey* (above) and see also *R* v *Sat Bhambra* (1988)).

If at any time during the six hours, (apart from any breaches of the Code of Practice as regards breaks for refreshment etc) Dick or Harry were wrongly (whether deliberately or mistakenly) denied their rights of access to a solicitor (s58 Police and

Criminal Evidence Act 1984) or to have some person informed of their arrest and place of detention (s56 Police and Criminal Evidence Act 1984), then irrespective of the reliability or otherwise of their confessions the judge may exclude them in his discretion under s78 (*R* v *Samuel* (1988); *R* v *McIvor* (1987); cf *R* v *Alladice*).

A final point is that if the prescriptions are treated as 'tantamount to a confession', it could be argued, at the joint trial of Tom, Dick and Harry, that if admissible as incriminating 'confessory' evidence, their admissibility is restricted to Tom as the confessor, and as regards Dick and Harry they have no evidential value as they do not form part of any confession they have made.

Question 4

Sykes is charged with the murder of Nancy by stabbing. Oliver is prepared to testify that Nancy telephoned him and shouted: 'Come quickly, Sykes is threatening to kill me ...', the phone then going dead. Oliver raced to Nancy's house and found her lying in a pool of blood. She whispered: 'You're too late, he's done for me' and lapsed into unconsciousness. A doctor arrived, briefly examined Nancy, covered her with a blanket and accompanied her in an ambulance. The ambulance collided with a lorry and the totally charred bodies of the ambulance's occupants were recovered from the burnt out wreckage.

Oliver finds Sykes and tells him he will kill him unless he comes to the police station. Sykes is dragged to the station by Oliver; as Oliver lunges at him and punches him in the face Sykes shouts to the police officers who are present: 'Get him off me for God's sake! I killed her; the knife's down the drain outside her house.' A knife is found there, wiped clean of blood and prints.

Advise the prosecution on the evidentiary problems, given that Sykes refused to write out or sign any subsequent statement.

Written by editor

Skeleton solution

- Res gestae statement; dying declaration - competence.
- Statement by conduct.
- Causation in murder; alternative verdicts.
- Confessions; reliability; oppression; admissibility - voir dire.
- Facts discovered in consequence of confessions.

Suggested solution

Oliver may be allowed to report not only the fact but also the content of the phoned statement as a res gestae statement. If it was contemporaneous, approximately, with the stabbing and was sufficiently spontaneous to enable the court safely to ignore the possibility of concoction or distortion, and any other factors such as malice on Nancy's part are taken into account, then the judge can admit the content of the call as a res gestae statement (*R* v *Andrews* (1987)). Its admissibility is determined by the judge, who will advise the jury on factors affecting the weight they may attach to it.

The fact that Nancy was shouting or was hysterical can be stated by Oliver (*Ratten* v *R* (1972)) and is relevant to the spontaneity issue. As regards contemporaneity, this depends on how much time elapsed between the phone call and Oliver's reaching Nancy's side, since there will be no medical evidence available to pinpoint the time of the stabbing, nor very probably its severity. Given that the stabbing and the phone call were *approximately* contemporaneous, that is sufficient to satisfy the court as to that element of admissibility of the res gestae statement. Given also that Oliver found Nancy within a short time (say ten minutes) of the phone call, then her second statement could also be admissible. Such a lapse of time, coupled with questions to elicit the res gestae statement, has been accepted by the court (*R* v *Andrews*; *R* v *Turnbull* (1984)). The other major issue for the court is whether Nancy's second statement is mere narration or whether her mind is still dominated by the drama of the event - the prosecution must persuade the court of the latter for the statement to be admitted.

If the second statement is not admissible under the res gestae doctrine, it may be admissible as a dying declaration. Nancy's statement certainly implies that she entertains no hope of survival, but she must be in *settled* hopeless expectation of death (*R* v *Perry* (1909)) and therefore must have had sufficient time for reflection (*R* v *Bedingfield* (1879)). In addition, had she survived she must have been a competent witness (*R* v *Pike* (1829)); even if she is Sykes' wife she would nevertheless be competent (s80(1)(a) Police and Criminal Evidence Act 1984). Nancy's declaration does not in itself state expressly the cause of her injuries, but in conjunction with her earlier exclamation it is very relevant to their cause.

The prosecution will want Oliver to testify as to what he saw the doctor do, arguing that he would be giving evidence, as a percipient witness, of an act performed by the doctor. The defence contention would be that the doctor's covering Nancy is an implied assertion by him that Nancy is already dead, and that implied assertions, just like express assertions, constitute inadmissible hearsay unless they come within a recognised exception to the hearsay rule.

There is a paucity of authorities on implied assertions (see Lord Bridge in *R* v *Blastland* (1985) and *Cross on Evidence* (7th edition, 1990, pp529-533)), but the reason for the law's suspicion of them is the danger of concoction by the observed doctor. There seems to be little doubt that the doctor would have no motive to fabricate evidence for the observers, therefore Oliver should be allowed to state what he perceived and the jury draw their own inferences. In the unlikely event that Oliver cannot give this evidence, there may be no acceptable evidence of causation and therefore Sykes could not be convicted of murder; he could nevertheless, if the prosecution can prove his specific intent to kill Nancy when he stabbed her, be found guilty of attempted murder as an alternative verdict (s6 Criminal Law Act 1967).

Sykes' confession is damning if it is admissible. However, it may well be excluded under s76 Police and Criminal Evidence Act 1984, given the likelihood of its unreliability in consequence of Oliver's conduct (s76(2)(b) Police and Criminal Evidence Act 1984). An alternative or additional reason for the confession's inadmissibility is oppression by Oliver, which would lead to exclusion of the confession (s76(2)(a) Police and Criminal Evidence Act 1984). Lord Lane CJ, giving the judgment of the Court of Appeal in *R* v *Fulling* (1987) defined 'oppression' in this context, and his definition implies that the conduct must be that of a person in authority such as a police officer. However, he was dealing with conduct falling short of violence or threats of violence, and a partial definition of violence in the Police and Criminal Evidence Act has not been affected. Section 76(8) states that 'oppression' includes torture, inhuman or degrading treatment, and the use or threat of violence', and there is no requirement that this sort of conduct must be that of a person in authority. So, unless the prosecution can prove beyond reasonable doubt that, despite Oliver's words and conduct the confession was not made in consequence of oppression and is not likely to be unreliable, the judge (on a voir dire) will rule Sykes' confession statement inadmissible, and the jury will therefore be unaware that it was made.

If the confession is excluded under s76, then no reference can be made to it by the prosecution in order to link Sykes to the knife found in the drain, ie a police officer will not be permitted to testify: 'In consequence of what the accused said I went to the drain outside the house of the deceased and found a knife ...' (s76(5) and (6) Police and Criminal Evidence Act 1984). Therefore, unless the knife is Sykes's or unless there is some other admissible evidence to link it to Sykes it is inadmissible real evidence because it has no apparent relevance; relevance cannot be given to it by any reference to the *fact* of, let alone the content of, a confession statement excluded under s76.

Question 5

Able was taking his daughters, Baker aged 7 and Charlie aged 11, for a walk when a car horn sounded behind them. Able looked behind him and saw that a green Mercedes car had left the road and was approaching them at high speed across the wide grass verge. He pushed his daughters to one side and was run down by the car; although conscious he could not get to his feet. He saw the car stop, a man alight and chase Baker (Charlie had jumped behind a hedge); the man indecently assaulted Baker, got back in the car and drove off.

A police patrol car arrived at the scene, and both Baker and Able gave the registration number of the car as C454 VKV; Charles said the car was green. From this information Douglas was traced as the car owner, was interviewed by the police but refused to comment. He has been charged with indecent assault and reckless driving. Able, Baker and Charlie have made written statements, but Able is paralysed as a result of the incident and cannot attend court; Baker is still in shock and having to give evidence could damage her mental health.

Advise the prosecution.

Written by editor

Skeleton solution

- Hearsay; exceptions to exclusionary rule.
- Applicability of statutory exceptions; action pre-trial.
- Corroboration; sexual offences; identification; children of tender years; competence of children.
- Silence of accused; evidential value.

Suggested solution

If the police officer(s) in the patrol car are to repeat what A, B and C said to them, the only purpose is to invite the court to believe the truth of what is repeated, therefore that is hearsay and will be inadmissible unless it falls within a recognised exception to the hearsay rule (*Myers* v *DPP* (1965)). If A and B do not testify, then the same applies if a witness wishes to read their statements to the court. Therefore, unless there are common law or statutory provisions which permit this hearsay evidence in criminal proceedings it cannot be adduced.

If a doctor certifies that A is dangerously ill and is unlikely to recover, then a magistrate may take A's deposition out of court, and provided Douglas's lawyer was given notice of this and the opportunity to cross-examine A, then if A is, by the time of the trial, dead or so ill that it is unlikely that he will ever be able to travel to court or give evidence, his written statement can be read to the court (s105 Magistrates' Courts Act 1980 and s6 Criminal Law Amendment Act 1867 (an offence is indictable even though it may be tried summarily)). If any of these conditions do not obtain, eg A is not certified as dangerously ill, then his written statement may still be given in evidence if 'by reason of his bodily or mental condition' he is 'unfit to attend as a witness' (s23(1) and 2(a) Criminal Justice Act 1988). If A's condition does not come within either of these categories, then his statement, as a 's9 statement' is unlikely to be admitted, since the defence must be served with a copy and will doubtless give written notice of objection (s9 Criminal Justice Act 1967).

In the case of B's statement, if a doctor certifies that her attendance in court would involve serious danger to her life or health (including mental health), then a magistrate may take her deposition out of court, since she is under 17 and indecent assault is an offence contrary to the Sexual Offences Act 1956 (s42 Children and Young Persons Act 1933). But Douglas's lawyer must be given notice of the taking of the deposition and the opportunity to cross-examine (s43 Children and Young Persons Act 1933). If there is no such 'serious danger' to her mental health, but rather in her shocked state she has an abject fear of a court appearance, then it is conceivable, subject to how s23 Criminal Justice Act 1988 is construed, her statement would still be admissible in evidence as would the deposition. Section 23(1)(ii) and (3)(b) provide for the admissibility of such written statements if 'the person who made it does not give oral evidence through fear ...' This was inserted in the 1988 Act to cater for witnesses to terrorist activities who might fear for their lives, but on a literal construction could cover our situation.

One drawback, if in the case of A's and/or B's statement resort has to be made to s23 CJA 1988, is that leave of the court is required before the statement can be admitted, and the court must have regard to all relevant circumstances, including in particular any risk of unfairness to the accused (s25 Criminal Justice Act 1933). Alternatively a video recording of an interview with Baker could be used, under s32A of the Criminal Justice Act 1988 (as inserted by the Criminal Justice Act 1991), which could be played back to the court to replace Baker's testimony. However, she would still need to appear in court for cross-examination. Alternatively, a live TV link could be used under s32 as she is under 14. However, there may be problems with the fact that only one of the offences Douglas is charged with (indecent assault) allows for s32 and s32A to come into play.

If A and B could not recollect the car number by the time they gave their written statements and therefore the number does not appear in those statements, then a police officer tendering in evidence their oral statements would be attempting to give hearsay evidence. If he wrote down the number at the time in his notebook, and A and B verified the entry as correct, then the officer could refresh his memory from the notebook and so could A and/or B if giving evidence (*Jones* v *Metcalfe* (1967); *R* v *McLean* (1968)). If A and B do not give direct evidence, the officer could nevertheless, with leave of the court, give the particulars in his notebook as a 'statement in a document' under s24 CJA 1988 if A and B are unfit to attend or given the lapse of time cannot be expected to have any recollection of the number (s24(1) and (4)).

Charlie (C) may have relevant evidence to offer as to the identity of the assailant etc, and the fact that she is aged only 11 does not in itself necessitate corroboration or a corroboration warning (s34(2) CJA 1988). However, as one of the offences charged is indecent assault, the evidence of B, or A, of the assault will require corroboration as a matter of practice; there can be a conviction without corroboration provided a warning is given; also B, unsworn, can now corroborate A, unsworn or sworn (s34(3) CJA 1988, as amended by Criminal Justice Act 1991). If A saw not only the assailant but also the incident, there is more corroborative evidence. As regards the identity of the assailant, the evidence of one witness *may* be sufficient for the court to be satisfied, but supportive evidence (even though it does not amount to 'corroboration' as defined in evidence) is highly desirable where the accused was not previously known, sighting not very good etc - per the guidelines in *R* v *Turnbull* (1977). Even though A, B and C identify Douglas, the judge should still caution the jury, where the identification is disputed by the defence, on the general unreliability of visual identification evidence of this sort.

Douglas's refusal to comment when interviewed will amount to a Road Traffic offence if he refuses to state who was driving the car at the time, given that, presumably, he is the registered owner. But his silence when accused of committing the offences cannot amount to corroboration when his accuser is a police officer (*R* v *Whitehead* (1929); *R* v *Keeling* (1942)) nor can it in those circumstances amount to an adoption by him of the accusation as his confession, because he has a right to remain silent of which he should have been reminded (*Hall* v *R* (1971)).

9 CHARACTER EVIDENCE

9.1 Introduction

9.2 Key points

9.3 Analysis of questions

9.4 Questions

9.1 Introduction

Character evidence, especially that of the accused and its admissibility in the course of the trial, is one of the most difficult areas of evidence, but one with which all students must be conversant as it will appear in almost every examination paper on Evidence. For example, there is often, in problem questions, a statement that a person has previous convictions; that should immediately alert the examinee to the fact that the bad character of that person (usually the accused) will require discussion. Any witness in criminal or civil proceedings is liable to be cross-examined as to character, including previous convictions, to destroy or damage his credibility as a witness; the one exception is the accused who elects to testify - that witness is given protection from such gratuitous cross-examination, except where he has discarded that protection or where evidence of his previous bad character has become relevant to his guilt on the charge he faces.

Although, therefore, evidence of the bad character of the accused is the major area of concern, something must be said, briefly, of character of parties in civil cases and of character of witnesses in civil and criminal cases.

9.2 Key points

a) *Parties to a civil action*

Dependent on what issues are raised in the pleadings in civil cases, the character of a party may be in issue - 'character' here referring to general reputation, disposition *and* particular conduct. A prime example is an action in defamation; if the defendant pleads justification of his assertion that the plaintiff is a rapist, then evidence of a rape conviction of the plaintiff can be adduced by the defendant; as regards damages in defamation the general reputation of the plaintiff is in issue, to assess the injury done to it.

Where evidence of disposition is admissible as character evidence to show that a party has a propensity to a particular kind of misconduct, because it is sufficiently relevant to the facts in issue, that evidence is known as 'similar fact evidence' and is dealt with in Chapter 10 (in both civil and criminal proceedings).

b) *Witnesses in civil and criminal proceedings*

All witnesses, whether or not parties, may be cross-examined as to credibility. The answers of the witnesses to such questions in cross-examination are almost invariably final, ie evidence cannot be adduced to contradict the answers, as the issue is a collateral one. However, one major exception is where the witness denies the commission by him of a criminal offence, in which event the appropriate conviction can be proved by the cross-examiner. For example, in the case of *R* v *Edwards* [1991] NLJ 91, the Court of Appeal held that police officers could be cross-examined about relevant criminal offences or disciplinary charges found proved against them, but could not be questioned about any previous misbehaviour not yet adjudicated upon.

c) *The accused*

i) Good character

As a general rule at common law the accused may adduce evidence of his good character despite the general prohibition on the prosecution's adducing evidence of his bad character - but evidence of bad character may be given to rebut the accused's evidence of his good character (see below).

The evidential value of evidence of good character is unclear; in *R* v *Bryant* [1979] QB 108 it was held that such evidence goes not just to the credibility of the accused but also to his guilt or innocence. But in *R* v *Levy* [1987] Crim LR 48 it was held that where there are two co-accused, one of good character and one bad, the good character of one goes only to credibility not unlikelihood of offending - otherwise the bad character of the other would give rise to an inference that he was likely to have committed the offence, which would be unacceptable!

In the case of *R* v *Boyson* [1991] Crim LR 274, the Court of Appeal emphasised that the judge should make it clear that good character is more relevant to credibility. But in the case of *R* v *Marr* (1990) 90 Cr App R 154, the Court of Appeal suggested that telling the jury of its relevance to guilt is very important as well. The law is not clear. In *R* v *Bainbridge* (1991) The Times 25 January, it was merely said that a judge's direction to the jury about a defendant's good character must include its relevance to his credibility, but it was not obligatory for the judge to suggest its relevance to a defendant's guilt - in each case it was a matter for the judge's discretion.

ii) Bad character

At common law, evidence of the bad character of the accused may be given by the prosecution if it is admissible similar fact evidence (see Chapter 10); it may also be given to rebut evidence given by the defence of the accused's good character. Such rebutting evidence will usually be as to the general bad reputation of the accused, but evidence of previous convictions has been admitted under the common law: *R* v *Redd* [1923] 1 KB 104; *R* v *Winfield* [1939] 4 All ER 164.

Section 1 Criminal Evidence Act 1898 deals with cross-examination of the accused as to his bad character, and therefore *it applies only when the accused elects to testify for the defence*. Otherwise, the common law rules apply.

The 1898 Act made the accused competent for the first time, and the legislators compromised between treating the accused exactly the same as any other witness and making him immune from cross-examination; the result was to give the accused protection (often called a shield) from cross-examination as to character, but protection which may be lost in circumstances set out in the provisos to s1(f) of the Act. The provisions in s1(e) and (f) should be known *verbatim* by every Evidence student who hopes to do justice to examination questions on character.

iii) Relationship between s1(e) and s1(f)

Section 1(e) permits cross-examination of the accused even though it tends to incriminate him as to the offence charged, and in that context allows 'any question'. Section 1(f) prohibits questions in cross-examination which tend to show that the accused has committed or been convicted of any other offence. There is thus apparent conflict between s1(e) and (f), because a question tending to show the accused has committed or been convicted of some other offence may well also tend to incriminate him as to the offence charged - such a question is apparently allowed by s1(e) but prohibited by s1(f). After several conflicting decisions, the House of Lords ruled (by a bare majority) in *Jones* v *DPP* [1962] AC 635 that s1(e) must be read subject to s1(f). The majority also ruled that 'show' in s1(f) means reveal or disclose to the jury for the first time, so if the jury is already aware of the bad character of the accused, the prohibition in s1(f) does not apply. The ruling in *Jones* v *DPP* was used by the Court of Appeal in *R* v *Anderson* [1988] 2 All ER 549, but the principles were not merely followed but extended, to the disadvantage of the accused who testifies: see discussion in [1988] Crim LR 298.

iv) Exceptions to the s1(f) prohibition

- Section 1(f)(i) allows cross-examination of the accused on similar fact evidence which is admissible as proof of his guilt. However, only where the similar fact evidence shows the commission or conviction of an offence (not other misconduct or previous charges which did not result in convictions) is cross-examination under s1(f)(i) allowed as to the bad character of the accused.
- Section 1(f)(ii) contains two exceptions (the two 'limbs'). The first is where the defence has attempted to establish the good character of the

accused; the second where the defence involves imputations on the character of the prosecutor or prosecution witnesses.

Under the first limb, 'character' includes both general reputation *and* disposition: *R* v *Samuel* (1956) 40 Cr App R 8. Evidence of good character can go not merely to the credibility of the accused as a witness, but also to his innocence: *R* v *Bryant* supra. Yet the cross-examination under the first limb goes directly to credibility - any bearing on the guilt of the accused is the subject of controversy: *Maxwell* v *DPP* [1935] AC 309; cf *R* v *Samuel* supra. The better view would seem to be that the purpose of cross-examination is to discredit the accused as a witness, *not* to prove his guilt by disclosing prior convictions.

It is important that in this context the character of the accused is not divisible; if the accused puts any good aspect of his character forward then he may be cross-examined on his character, not just the aspect on which he relies: *R* v *Winfield* [1939] 4 All ER 164; *Stirland* v *DPP* [1944] AC 315.

Under the second limb of s1(f)(ii), the accused may be liable to cross-examination as to his bad character if imputations have been cast on the character of the prosecutor or prosecution witnesses. For the 'shield' to be lost under this limb, there must be something more than an emphatic denial of guilt - but it can be difficult to draw the line between a robust denial and an imputation on the character of a witness: compare, and reconcile *R* v *Nelson* (1978) 68 Cr App R 12 and *R* v *Tanner* (1977) 66 Cr App R 66. The second limb can be brought into play by implied, as well as express, imputations on the character of prosecution witnesses. (NB: it must be an imputation cast on the character of someone called as a witness for the prosecution; if the accused attacks the character of a person not called as a witness, the shield is not lost under the second limb: *R* v *Lee* [1976] 1 WLR 71.)

Even if casting imputations is necessary as a part of the defence case, nevertheless the shield is dropped: *Selvey* v *DPP* [1970] AC 304; *R* v *Bishop* [1975] QB 274. See also the case of *R* v *Lasseur* [1991] Crim LR 53 - the defendant suggested to an accomplice that he was only giving evidence against him so as to get a more lenient sentence. The Court of Appeal held that the shield had been dropped.

One very important point, made in *R* v *Turner* [1944] KB 463, and approved in *Selvey* v *DPP*, supra, is that where consent is in issue in a rape trial the accused can allege consent by the complainant (and even gross indecency on her part) without losing his shield, the reasoning being that a defence of consent is merely a denial that an element of the offence has been proved and thus is not an imputation. Evidence of the sexual activity of the complainant with the accused, and (with leave of the judge) with other males, again goes to the issue of consent and therefore will not result in s1(f)(ii) being activated (somewhat incongruously perhaps!)

- Under s1(f)(iii) an accused is liable to cross-examination as to bad character by a person charged in the same proceedings when he gives evidence against that person. It is not necessary that he attacks the person's character, only that he gives evidence that supports the prosecution's case against him.

  In *Murdoch* v *Taylor* [1965] AC 574, the House of Lords stated that the determinant is whether, objectively, the evidence undermines the other's defence or strengthens the case against him - regardless of whether this was intended. A denial of involvement by one accused, or evidence from him which appears to be in conflict with evidence given by the other, may, dependent on the particular facts, amount to evidence under s1(f)(iii): *R* v *Varley* (1982) 75 Cr App R 242.

  Under s1(f)(iii) the co-accused can cross-examine the accused who loses his shield as of right, ie leave of the judge is not required and the judge cannot restrict the scope of the cross-examination, the effect of which is to attack credibility, not to go to the issue of guilt.

v) Judicial discretion in cross-examination

The discretion of the judge to refuse the prosecution leave to cross-examine the accused as to his character was given the ultimate seal of approval in *Selvey* v *DPP* supra.

The judge must ensure a fair trial, and even where bad character of the accused goes to credibility rather than guilt, it would prejudice a fair trial if, for example, the accused had a bad record with many previous convictions, or one conviction for a very grave crime and the instant charge was relatively minor and/or the imputation on the prosecution witness was relatively slight. Alternatively, there may be a number of charges against the accused and an attack was made on the character of a prosecution witness to one charge only. Again, the greater the similarity of the previous convictions to the instant charge the greater the prejudice to the accused if they are all revealed. Finally, an allegation that a prosecution witness was mistaken may, objectively, amount to a necessary imputation of fabrication of evidence. Guidelines for the exercise of judicial discretion were laid down in *R* v *Britzmann & Hall* (1983) 76 Cr App R 134, and a detailed summary of the current law is given in the judgment of Neill LJ in the Court of Appeal in *R* v *Owen* (1986) 83 Cr App R 100.

9.3 Analysis of questions

The typical question on this topic is a problem question raising a number of the issues of detail under common law, and especially under the 1898 Act. Detailed knowledge of s1(f)(i) is rarely tested - this tends to appear in self-contained questions on similar fact evidence. Again, it is rare for problem questions to include character in civil cases. Occasionally essay questions are set on the subject of character, but these again tend to concentrate on criminal proceedings and particularly on permissible cross-examination of the accused under s1 of the 1898 Act. What is virtually certain is that evidence of character will appear in any examination paper; not so certain is that it will always be a question dealing *solely* with character!

9.4 Questions

Question 1

Hari, Kumar and Ranjit are charged with setting fire to a shop belonging to Hari, for the purpose of obtaining the insurance money on the shop.

Hari has two convictions for assault, Kumar has none. Both will give evidence on their own behalf, but Ranjit, who has four convictions for criminal damage, will not.

The Crown will lead evidence of PC Merrick that he identified Hari and Ranjit running away from the fire soon after the fire had started at about 10 pm. He is prepared to say that he could identify them, despite poor lighting, because he had previously arrested them at an anti-racist rally two months prior to the incident for causing damage to property. The Crown will also put in evidence a statement made on arrest by Ranjit, which exculpated himself but alleged that Hari and Kumar caused the fire.

Hari is prepared to say that Ranjit caused the fire and that Merrick had implicated him along with Ranjit because Merrick's wife, Daphne, had an affair with him. He is, however, prepared to admit that he was at the shop that night with Kumar but had left by himself around 9 pm, leaving Kumar in the shop. Kumar, it is understood, will say that he was away in Liverpool on the night in question. Hari also wants to call his bank manager, to say how sound his finances are.

Assume you are Hari's counsel and, in the context of the law of evidence:

a) evaluate your problems at the trial in conducting Hari's defence; and

b) assess the difficulties that Crown Counsel will encounter at the trial.

University of London LLB Examination
(for External Students) Evidence June 1984 Q7

Skeleton solution

- Losing shield under s1(f)(iii) - later under s1(f)(ii).
- Bank manager's evidence - relevance.
- Evidence of police officer.
- *Turnbull* direction on identification evidence.
- Previous conviction - similar fact evidence.

Suggested solution

The first problem is the evidence to be given by Hari that Ranjit had committed the offence. If he says this, he will leave himself open to cross-examination about his previous offences under s1(f)(iii) Criminal Evidence Act 1898. The evidence of Hari will be 'evidence against' Ranjit, because it is evidence making Ranjit's conviction more likely (see *Murdoch* v *Taylor* (1965) and *R* v *Varley* (1982)). This will give Ranjit the right to bring out evidence of Hari's two convictions for assault. The judge will be obliged to direct the jury that these convictions are not evidence of guilt, but merely evidence of Hari's character as a witness.

Hari, therefore, will have his character attacked by Ranjit. This will not, though, give Hari the right to attack Ranjit's character. Because Ranjit does not give evidence, his character and therefore, his convictions remain hidden from the jury unless he introduces it by calling character witnesses (see *R* v *Rowton* (1865)).

The attack on PC Merrick will also lead to the shield being lost, this time under s1(f)(ii). It would be an allegation that Merrick was perjuring himself in an act of revenge and clearly comes within the definition of casting imputations on a prosecution witness laid down in *Selvey* v *DPP* (1968), and *R* v *Britzman* (1983)). Of itself this will not affect Hari since his convictions will already have come in as of right under s1(f)(iii) and so the prosecution would have been free to ask him about them anyway because their questions would not 'tend to show' the convictions for the first time (see *Jones* v *DPP* (1962)).

The admission that Hari was in the shop will, of course, count against him, but if he wishes to say this, there is nothing to stop him. To say that Kumar was also in the shop when Kumar's defence is an alibi is, again, to give evidence against a co-defendant. This also will make no difference since the shield is already lost.

The evidence proposed to be given by Hari's bank manager will not be admissible as it is irrelevant. It does not prove anything. There are many precedents of wealthy men having committed offences for further financial gain and the manager will not be able to add anything of any substance to Hari's defence.

The problem that will arise in the course of the prosecution's case is the evidence of the officer that he had previously arrested Hari for criminal damage at an anti-racist rally. This could be highly prejudicial to Hari in that the jury could jump to the conclusion that if he had been arrested twice for similar offences he must be guilty. This matter will be discussed when considering the difficulties facing the prosecution.

The problems encountered by Crown Counsel start with the evidence of PC Merrick. He will give evidence of a fleeting identification. *R* v *Turnbull* (1976) and *R* v *Oakwell* (1978) hold that where the prosecution case rests substantially on a fleeting identification the judge must direct the jury to look for supporting evidence of that identification and should withdraw the case from the jury if there is nothing to support weak identification evidence. The Crown, following dicta in Turnbull, will want to show that the identification is not weak because the officer had previously encountered Hari and Ranjit at an anti-racist rally for criminal damage. This evidence will not be admissible for the prosecution. It is not permissible to give evidence of previous misconduct, including purported misconduct evidenced by an arrest, unless that misconduct comes within the similar fact rules. These rules allow evidence of previous misconduct where it is so probative with regard to the offence charged that its probative force out-weighs any prejudice there may be to the accused in the form of the jury jumping to the conclusion that because the accused has now been arrested twice for the same sort of offence that he must have committed the offence charged (see *Boardman* v *DPP* (1974)). Evidence that Hari had been arrested for some form of criminal damage two months before the fire at his shop does not prove one way or the other whether he committed the arson and so will not be admissible. This means that there will be little to support the identification evidence. It is not possible to say, without knowing all the other evidence available to the prosecution, whether the judge will withdraw the case from the jury, but it seems to be a possibility.

The similar fact rules also need to be considered in connection with Ranjit's previous convictions. We are told that he has four convictions for criminal damage. If there was some special hallmark to all the previous offences and that hallmark was present in the offences charged, then the prosecution will be allowed to lead evidence of the previous convictions as evidence that Ranjit committed the present offence (see, again, *Boardman* v *DPP*). We are told nothing that indicates that the previous conviction were for arson, let alone for arson of such a similar and unusual kind that they prove Ranjit's guilt on this occasion.

The Crown may wish to use Ranjit's statement on arrest as evidence that Hari and Kumar committed the arson. Although a statement made on arrest is always admissible to establish the reaction of the accused (see *R* v *Pearce* (1979)), it is not admissible under any exception to the hearsay rule unless it contains admissions. The statement therefore is not evidence that Ranjit is innocent, nor is it evidence that Hari and Kumar are guilty.

The prosecution will have to contend with an alibi defence being put up by Kumar. Kumar is obliged under s11 Criminal Justice Act 1967 to give notice to the prosecution not more than seven days after committal proceedings have ended. The Prosecution, therefore, will be in a position to research his alibi.

Question 2

Laura, Caroline and Frederique are charged with theft of sapphires from jewellery brought to their jewellery firm for repairs.

Laura and Caroline give evidence on their own behalf at the trial but Frederique does not. Laura says that she and Caroline handled the repair work of the firm but says the sapphires were probably stolen by Beatrice, who was sacked from the firm and who is not giving evidence for the Crown. Caroline says she had absolutely nothing to do with the repair work and that if there was any repair work it was done by Laura and Frederique.

At the main trial Inspector Julian gives evidence of confessions made to him by Caroline and Frederique. Caroline's counsel cross-examines Inspector Julian on the basis that he had threatened Caroline. Frederique's counsel cross-examines Julian on the basis that he was having an affair with Beatrice, who wanted to implicate Frederique and Laura. The trial judge permits Crown Counsel to cross-examine Caroline and Laura as to their previous convictions for a theft of an antique necklace, and permits the Crown to put in evidence Frederique's conviction for assault.

All three accused are convicted. Advise on grounds of appeal.

Adapted from University of London LLB Examination
(for External Students) Evidence June 1986 Q7

Skeleton solution

a) Laura - when cross-examination allowed - s1(f)(ii) - s1(f)(iii).

b) Caroline - s1(f)(iii) - cross-examination of Inspector Julian - s1(f)(ii) - judge's discretion.

c) Frederique - gave no evidence - *Boardman* - similar facts?

Suggested solution

a) *Laura*

Laura gave evidence that she and Caroline handled the firm's repair work and said that the sapphires were probably stolen by Beatrice, who did not give evidence. The trial judge allowed counsel for the Crown to cross-examine Laura as to her previous conviction. The judge would only have been correct in allowing that line of cross-examination if Laura had thrown away the shield given to her by s1(f) of the Criminal Evidence Act 1898, or if the conviction were admissible as similar fact evidence.

Beatrice was not a prosecution witness, nor, as far as we know, was she the prosecutor. Therefore, the allegation made about Beatrice's character is not within the type of conduct which gives rise to the loss of the shield under s1(f)(ii). Section 1(f)(ii) operates on a 'tit-for-tat' principle and, accordingly, unless either there was an attack on a prosecution witness or Laura put forward her own good character there is not scope for the Crown to let the jury know of Laura's bad character (*Selvey* v *DPP* (1968)).

Laura would lose her shield if she gave evidence against a co-accused (s1(f)(iii) Criminal Evidence Act 1898). In this case she has said that Caroline worked in the shop and handled the repair work, whereas Caroline has denied that she did any repairs. Whether Laura has given evidence against Caroline, on these facts, depends upon whether Laura has helped to undermine Caroline's defence. The Court of Appeal in *R* v *Varley* (1982) held that this matter is to be judged objectively and repeated the rule laid down by the House of Lords in *Murdoch* v *Taylor* (1965): 'it has to be objectively decided whether the evidence either supports the prosecution case in a material particular or undermines the defence.' Caroline's defence seems to be a complete denial that she had anything to do with the repair of jewellery, and Laura has given evidence which undermines this defence, although she has also said that the sapphires were probably stolen by Beatrice. In those circumstances the shield has not necessarily been lost. It must be asked, looking at the total effect of Laura's evidence, whether she has made Caroline's conviction more likely. It is not possible to say with any degree of accuracy what the answer to this question is, because we are not told what else, if anything, was said by Laura; but on the assumption that we are informed of all the relevant parts of Laura's evidence, it is submitted that the shield is likely to have been lost. Although Laura supports Caroline's denial that she was involved in a theft, she undermines her defence in so far as she gives evidence that Caroline did work on repairs, from which the jury could conclude that Caroline had the opportunity to steal the sapphires. When a defendant loses her shield by virtue of s1(f)(iii) the trial judge has no discretion to prevent counsel for the co-accused cross-examining her as to her previous conviction.

There is an automatic right in counsel for a co-accused to cross-examine a defendant as to her record where her shield was lost under s1(f)(iii), but the trial judge has a discretion to disallow cross-examination by the prosecution in those circumstances (*R* v *Varley*). This discretion must be exercised fairly so as to prevent the adduction of the defendant's record if it would be unfairly prejudicial to do so. The Court of Appeal has recently held that the general principle of 'tit-for-tat' should be paramount when the trial judge is exercising his discretion under s1(f)(ii) (*R* v *Britzman* (1983)), and there seems no reason in principle why that should not also apply to s1(f)(iii). The matter was within the discretion of the trial judge and provided that he directed the jury that the previous conviction was not evidence of guilt on the present charge, there was nothing wrong in allowing prosecuting counsel to cross-examine Laura.

The previous conviction would not be admissible as similar fact evidence because it is nothing other than evidence of disposition (*Boardman* v *DPP* (1974)).

b) *Caroline*

Caroline appears not to have given evidence against Laura because all she said was that Laura did repair work, which Laura had already admitted. In other words, Caroline had not undermined Laura's defence or given fresh evidence against her. We are not told whether any evidence had been given as to Frederique's position in the firm (we are not told the contents of the confession), but it will be assumed that evidence had already been given which showed that he had the opportunity to steal, otherwise he would have been entitled to have the case withdrawn from the jury at the close of the prosecution case (*R* v *Galbraith* (1981)). If this assumption is correct, then Caroline has not given evidence against Frederique either.

The cross-examination of Inspector Julian would lose Caroline her shield by virtue of s1(f)(ii) of the Criminal Evidence Act 1898 if it amounted to casting imputations on the character of a prosecution witness. We are told that Caroline's counsel cross-examined Julian about threats, to attempt to extract a confession. Because the challenge to the evidence of Julian is inconsistent with him having simply made a mistake in his testimony, so Caroline's shield will be lost (*R* v *Britzman*); the fact that the accusation may not be designed to challenge his credibility but merely to contradict the facts he attempts to establish does not prevent the shield being lost (*R* v *Britzman*, disapproving *R* v *Nelson* (1978)). The trial judge had the right to refuse to allow cross-examination on Caroline's record, but the most recent Court of Appeal decision on the exercise of this discretion makes clear that the Court will only interfere with the exercise of discretion in rare cases (*R* v *Powell* (1986), disapproving *R* v *Watts* (1983)).

Provided the trial judge directed the jury not to treat the previous conviction as evidence of guilt, there is no ground of appeal about the cross-examination on her record.

c) *Frederique*

Frederique did not give evidence, therefore her previous conviction could not be rendered admissible by the attack on Julian made by her counsel. The only way in which a conviction of an accused can be put in evidence where he has not given evidence is where it satisfies the stringent test for the admissibility of similar fact evidence (*Boardman* v *DPP*), which this conviction, of course, does not.

Question 3

'Decided cases in recent times reveal an unhealthy judicial antagonism to the Criminal Evidence Act 1898, so much so that when the accused needs its protection most he does not have it.'

Comment.

University of London LLB Examination
(for External Students) Evidence June 1988 Q8

Skeleton solution

- Criminal Evidence Act 1898 - rights given to defendant.
- Section 1(f)(i) - application to similar fact evidence - application to other uses of previous offences.
- Section 1(f)(ii) - two limbs described - first limb analysed - second limb analysed - assessment of interpretation of second limb.
- Section 1(f)(iii) - criteria for loss of shield.
- Discretion to disallow cross-examination - by co-defendant - by prosecution.

Suggested solution

Section 1 of the Criminal Evidence Act 1898 gave the defendant in a criminal case the right to give evidence for the first time. In doing so it provided certain protections for the defendant, but ensured that he could not refuse to answer questions directly relating to the offence alleged. The most important protections are that the accused should not be called as a witness otherwise than by the defence (s1(a) Criminal Evidence Act 1898), that his failure to give evidence shall not be commented on by the prosecution (s1(b) CEA 1898), and that he should not be asked questions tending to show that he has committed or been charged with, or convicted of, any other offence, or is of bad character (s1(f) CEA 1898). It is this third aspect of s1 of the Act which has been the subject of most judicial activity.

By s1(e) the defendant has no privilege against self-incrimination in relation to the offence charged. But s1(f) gives him such a privilege in relation to other offences. The terms of s1(f) go further than simply setting out a privilege against self-incrimination. The sub-section provides that the defendant may not be asked about other offences he has committed, been convicted of, or charged with, or about his bad character. The privilege which witnesses generally have against self-incrimination only allows them to refuse to answer questions where there is a real risk of prosecution if they answer truthfully (*R* v *Boyes* (1861)). The purpose of s1(f) is to go further and prevent the jury from hearing of the defendant's criminal record or of his previous acquittals because of the risk that they will judge him by his character rather than by the evidence. But the protection give to the accused (his shield) may be lost if any of the three provisos to s1(f) comes into play.

The first proviso (s1(f)(i) CEA 1898) allows evidence of the commission of, or conviction for, other offences to be given if that evidence is admissible evidence of guilt of the offence presently charged. This covers similar fact evidence. It also covers other obviously relevant matters; for example, if the defendant is charged with driving whilst disqualified, evidence may be given that he was disqualified following conviction for a motoring offence. There is little scope for judicial antagonism towards this proviso because it is a cardinal rule of long standing that evidence of one conviction is only admissible to prove another offence in relatively rare cases. The judge has an overriding discretion to prevent evidence being given even though admissible by virtue of s1(f)(i) if he is of the view that it is unduly prejudicial and that he will not be able to counteract that prejudice by a direction to the jury.

The second proviso (s1(f)(ii) CEA 1898) has two limbs. Firstly, the defendant will lose his shield if questions are asked by him or his counsel of prosecution witnesses with a view to establishing his good character, or the accused gives evidence of his good character. Secondly, it will be lost if the nature or conduct of the defence involves imputations against the character of prosecution witnesses.

The first limb has been construed favourably to the defendant. In *Malindi* v *R* (1967) the Privy Council held that the shield will only be lost by virtue of this limb if the purpose for which questions are asked of the prosecution witnesses is that the witnesses should put forward the defendant's good character. If the purpose is simply to elucidate the facts upon which the defence is based without separately inviting the jury to consider the defendant's good character, then the shield will not be lost. This is, it is submitted, an unavoidable construction because the proviso says the shield will be lost if questions are put 'with a view to establish' the defendant's good character.

In addition, the defendant will not be ruled to have given evidence of his own good character unless it is clear that that is what he has done (*Malindi* v *R*).

The second limb is more complex. There are two ways of determining whether the nature or conduct of the defence involves imputations on the character of the prosecutor or prosecution witnesses. On the one hand it could be said that the principle in *Malindi* v *R* should be followed, so that if all the defence does is put the defence case and invite the jury to find that the facts were as alleged by the defence and not as alleged by the prosecution, the shield will not be lost. On this basis, provided no express invitation is made to the jury to investigate the character of the prosecution witnesses, the shield will not be lost. This view of this limb was taken by the Court of Appeal in *R* v *Nelson* (1978).

The other view of the second limb is that the defence casts imputations on the character of prosecution witnesses if the conclusion which the jury is invited to draw necessarily involves the jury in deciding that the prosecution witnesses are deliberately lying. In *R* v *Britzman* (1983) the Court of Appeal followed *R* v *Tanner* (1977) and disapproved *Nelson* holding that it is not the form of the defence case but its substance which matters. If there is no scope for honest mistake, it is irrelevant that defence counsel may say to the jury that the prosecution witnesses are honestly mistaken. Where the defence case could be true only if the prosecution witnesses are lying, *Britzman* holds that the shield is lost.

It is clear that the wording of the second limb is different from the first and does not invite the court to investigate the motive behind the defence putting its case as it does. But the construction of this limb adopted in *Britzman* leaves a tactical difficulty for the defence. It is not always clear in advance of trial whether the judge will take the view that the defence can only be made out if the prosecution witnesses are deliberate lying. If there is doubt about this, defence counsel will have to decide whether to make direct challenges to the character of prosecution witnesses by, for example, asking them about their previous convictions. Once such questions are asked, the shield is undoubtedly lost. But if the questions are not asked, yet the judge decides that there is an implied attack on the character of prosecution witnesses, it will not be possible to recall the prosecution witnesses simply so that their convictions can be put to them. That difficulty for the defence is not present if the form rather than the substance of the defence case determines whether the shield is lost.

Britzman produces a further difficulty. The defence may present its case on the basis that the jury cannot be sure that the prosecution witnesses are accurate in what they say. The jury may entertain a doubt without thereby concluding that those witnesses are lying. There appears to be no scope for the defence to present its case in this way without falling foul of *Britzman*. The trial judge must ask whether the story told by the defence and the story told by the prosecution are at such variance that there is no scope for honest mistake. But, it is submitted, even though the stories may be wholly contradictory, the jury may not have to be sure that the prosecution witnesses are lying in order to acquit because they could simply say they cannot determine which version of events is true, and therefore acquit.

Section 1(f)(iii) provides that the shield is lost if the defendant 'has given evidence against' a co-accused. In *R* v *Varley* (1982) the Court of Appeal held that this subsection must be construed objectively so as to see whether the evidence of the defendant has supported the prosecution case in a material respect or has undermined the co-accused's defence. The intention with which the evidence is given is irrelevant. But there is a safeguard built in, because the conflict between one defendant's evidence and the case of the other must be clear; inconsistency is not enough.

There is no discretion to prevent one defendant from cross-examining another under s1(f)(iii) if the judge is satisfied that evidence has been given against that other. But there is a discretion to prevent the prosecution from cross-examining under any limb of s1(f) if the judge is of the view that the effect of bringing out the defendant's bad character would be unduly prejudicial (*Selvey* v *DPP* (1970)).

The recent case of *R* v *Powell* (1986) limits the power of the judge to exercise this discretion. It holds that normally a 'tit-for-tat' principle should be applied so that if the defendant casts imputations on the character of prosecution witnesses or gives evidence of his own good character, the prosecution should be free to cross-examine him as to his bad character. The only time when this should not be allowed is where the trial judge feels unable to counteract the prejudice to the defendant by a direction in his summing up. *R* v *Watts* (1983) suggested that the discretion should be exercised in the defendant's favour if his previous convictions were similar to the charge he now faced, but *Powell* disapproved that case, holding that the only effect of such similarity is that the judge should be particularly careful in his summing up to make it clear that the previous convictions are not proof of guilt but go to the defendant's credibility.

Particularly in cases falling within the rule in *Britzman*, the danger to the defence is great if the shield is lost and the defendant has similar convictions, because no matter how careful the summing up, it is a difficult task for untrained jurors to ignore drawing the inference that because the defendant committed a similar offence before, so he was more likely to do so at the time in question. It is submitted that it is in *Britzman*-type cases that the greatest flexibility is needed in order that the defence case can be put fairly and clearly, but the uncertainty about how the judge will view the presentation of the case may lead to tactical decisions being taken which turn out to have drastic consequences for the accused.

Question 4

Beater and Thwack, two school teachers, are jointly charged with severely beating a little girl Pettle, a six year old, who is at their school.

Consider the following questions:

a) What issues arise in the law of evidence if Pettle is to be called as a witness for the Crown?

b) If Pettle gives evidence in the case, what use could be made of a statement made by Pettle to her mother the day after the alleged beating that Pettle did not 'ever want to be in Mr Beater's or Mr Thwack's classes'?

Would it make a difference if Pettle had told her mother the day after the alleged assault that Beater and Thwack had assaulted her?

Would either of the above statements be admissible if Pettle does not give evidence?

c) If Beater and Thwack give evidence on their own behalf, what use could be made of Beater's previous convictions for assault and causing grievous bodily harm if he denies in evidence that he made a confession to the Police (which was permitted in evidence after a voire dire) which was allegedly made during the course of a one hour interrogation. He also says that Thwack and he had admonished Pettle for being naughty but that he had left the room leaving Thwack with Pettle; Thwack says he had never spoken to the child.

University of London LLB Examination
(for External Students) Evidence June 1989 Q4

General comment

With the enactment of the Criminal Justice Act 1988, it must have been expected that the question of evidence of children would appear. Other than in the context of an essay question on corroboration, competence etc, it was obvious that it would be one of several issues in a 'problem' question. The question raises quite a few issues, and the trap for the unwary candidate is to assume that the assault is a sexual assault - often the sort of offence specified when covering these issues - and thus to deal with some irrelevant material; a good example of the necessity to read questions with the utmost care.

Skeleton solution

- Competence of children of tender years; corroboration of evidence of children; special provision for their giving evidence.
- Circumstantial evidence; self-serving statements; recent complaints, inadmissible hearsay.
- Casting imputations on prosecution witnesses - s1(f)(ii) Criminal Evidence Act 1898.
- Giving evidence against co-accused - s1(f)(iii) Criminal Evidence Act 1898.

Suggested solution

At the outset it must be stressed that the specific charge which Beater and Thwack face is not stated - the question states 'severely beating'. If the dominant purpose of the beating were sexual gratification rather than (immoderate) chastisement, then the charges could include one of indecent assault, otherwise the charges would be of assaults contrary to the Offences Against the Person Act 1861, ss47, 20 and/or 18. Whether a sexual or non-sexual offence is charged is very relevant when dealing with part ii) in particular.

a) Pettle will be treated as a competent witness unless the contrary is shown, it seems, since the enactment of s52 of Criminal Justice Act 1991, which says all children under the age of 14 now automatically give unsworn evidence and s38(1) Children and Young Persons Act 1933 has been abolished. The case of *R* v *Wallwork* (1958) suggested that a child as young as five should not give evidence in criminal proceedings, but since s52. Pettle is assumed to be competent, and it will be up to the defence to produce evidence to the contrary and appeal to the judge's discretion to render her incompetent.

At Common Law the sworn evidence of a child of tender years required the judge to give a corroboration warning to the jury, ie there could be a conviction on that evidence alone provided the jury had been alerted to the dangers. In the case of unsworn evidence there could be no conviction unless the evidence was corroborated. These Common Law rules have been abrogated by s34 Criminal Justice Act 1988, so there is now no requirement for a warning nor for corroborative evidence merely because the witness is a child. (Corroboration is still as relevant as it ever was if it is not merely the age of the witness but also the nature of the offence etc which is a determinant - eg if Pettle is the complainant in a case of indecent assault, then the corroboration warning must be given, not now because of her tender years, but because the offence alleged is a sexual one). Section 34 refers only to trials on indictment, and in addition it merely states that a corroboration warning is no longer obligatory. As Pettle is only 6, the judge *may* consider it advisable to direct the jury to treat her evidence with some circumspection and in the absence of corroboration to convict only if sure of her credibility.

As Pettle is a witness to an assault charge, whether or not a sexual assault case, s32 Criminal Justice Act 1988 provides that, as she is under 14 (or under 17 if a sexual case), she may be allowed to give her evidence through a live television link if Beater and Thwack are tried on indictment. She may be able to give a video recording of an interview to replace her testimony at court (s32A Criminal Justice Act 1988, as inserted by the Criminal Justice Act 1991). However, she will still have to turn up to court to be cross-examined.

b) Pettle's mother's statement regarding Pettle's never wanting to be in Mr Beater's or Mr Thwack's classes could be excluded in that such testimony being given by the mother is hearsay and does not fall into any recognised category of exceptions to the general rule excluding hearsay in criminal trials. Arguably the statement by Pettle is not legally relevant in any case, so whether or not it is hearsay might not have to be decided (*Agassiz* v *London Tramway Co* (1872)). However, there is authority to support the proposition that a statement about the speaker's emotional state is admissible, when reported by another, if it is relevant to an issue before the court - its relevance is restricted to the emotional state of the speaker. Under this authority, Pettle's mother would be permitted to give evidence of the content of Pettle's first statement as circumstantial evidence (*R* v *Hagan* (1873); *R* v *Vincent* (1840); *Subramaniam* v *Public Prosecutor* (1956)).

Pettle's assertion to her mother that Beater and Thwack had assaulted her is a self-serving statement and therefore usually it would be inadmissible hearsay if the mother tried to relate it to the court (*R* v *Roberts* (1942)). If the defence alleged that Pettle's story was recently fabricated, then her assertion to her mother could be admitted to show consistency and thus tend to refute the allegation of fabrication, but in the absence of such a specific allegation the mother's evidence would not be admitted, and in any event it could never corroborate Pettle's evidence (*R* v *Baskerville* (1916); *R* v *Whitehead* (1929); *R* v *Oyesiku* (1971)). If the assault charged was a sexual assault, then the mother could report Pettle's statement, albeit not to corroborate Pettle's evidence but merely as evidence of a 'recent complaint' to show consistency (*R* v *Osborne* (1905)). There is some authority that such evidence of recent complaint is admissible in all cases involving violence whether of a sexual nature or not (*R* v *Wink* (1834)); however, the latest authority was in 1918 (*Jones* v *South Eastern Railway* (1918)), and the authorities seem to be strongly against admissibility of recent complaints except in criminal trials of sexual offences (*R* v *Whitehead*).

If Pettle does not give evidence in any form, then her assertion that Beater and Thwack had assaulted her could not be reported by her mother, as it would be a classic example of inadmissible hearsay (*R* v *Wallwork*). With regard to her other statement to the effect that she did not want to be in the teachers' classes, this circumstantial evidence would have little relevance (and little, if any, weight) if Pettle did not give evidence, and therefore would be ruled inadmissible, or if held to be technically admissible would be excluded by the judge in his discretion, as being more prejudicial than probative.

c) A denial by Beater that he made a confession is more than a mere denial of guilt, and in these circumstances goes beyond an assertion that the police officer(s) were genuinely mistaken - it amounts to an imputation on the character of prosecution witness(es), thus causing Beater's 'shield' to be dropped. Therefore, under the provision in s1(f)(ii) Criminal Evidence Act 1898, the prosecutor may, with leave of the judge, cross-examine Beater on his previous convictions (*R* v *Britzman & Hall* (1983)).

There has been some recent dispute over whether the judge should permit the prosecutor to cross-examine about offences similar to that of which the accused stands charged, as the purpose of revealing such bad character is not to prove guilt on the instant charge, but to indicate to the jury the credibility of the person casting the imputations on the character of prosecution witnesses (*R* v *Watts* (1983); *R* v *Bishop* (1975); *R* v *Burke* (1985); *R* v *Powell* (1985)).

The revealing of similar offences having been committed by the accused can be gravely prejudicial to the defence case, but this is a matter for the judge to take into consideration when exercising his discretion to allow unlimited, limited, or no cross-examination. The very close resemblance of the other offences (eg Beater's previous convictions for assault and gbh) to the offence charged does *not oblige* the judge to refuse the requested cross-examination (this is the view of Lord Lane, giving the judgment in *R* v *Powell* (above)). Only if the judge manifestly errs will the Court of Appeal interfere with his exercise of his discretion (per Ackner LJ in *R* v *Burke*).

Beater's evidence about he and Thwack admonishing and his leaving Thwack with Pettle, given that Thwack denies speaking to Pettle, is evidence given against Thwack, his co-accused. On the assumption that Thwack had already testified, or the defence Thwack was running was obvious, then Beater's evidence undermines Thwack's defence, therefore Beater loses his shield, and Thwack's counsel may cross-examine Beater as to his previous convictions as of right (s1(f)(iii) CEA 1898 and *R* v *Varley* (1982)). Leave of the judge is unnecessary, and therefore the considerations discussed above when dealing with the casting of imputations on the character of prosecution witnesses are irrelevant (*R* v *Burke*). Only if the prosecution seeks leave to cross-examine under s1(f)(iii) does the judge need to avert his mind to the relevant considerations before exercising his discretion (*Murdoch* v *Taylor* (1965)).

Question 5

Bill and Charles both have several convictions for theft and burglary, Charles also has a conviction for perjury and Bill for rape. They are both arrested by PC Nab and charged with burglary. Diane states that jewellery has been stolen from her bedroom and that she rang the police when she observed Bill and Charles inside the house as she was about to enter.

Bill and Charles are jointly charged with burglary (no jewellery was recovered). What will be the consequences if:

a) Bill testifies that his fingerprints were in the house because he had had an affair with Diane;

b) Charles testifies that Diane's identification of him is mistaken, and is the consequence of her having previously identified him in connection with theft from a shop where she was employed;

c) Charles further testifies that PC Nab was mistaken in attributing verbal admissions at the time of the arrest to him, Charles, and that the only person who said anything to PC Nab was Bill?

Written by editor

Skeleton solution

- General introduction, covering evidence of bad character of the accused.
- Section 1(f)(ii) Criminal Evidence Act 1898; imputations; loss of shield; relationship to s1(e).
- Section 1(f)(iii) Criminal Evidence Act 1898; when applicable.

Suggested solution

At common law, evidence of the bad character of the accused may be given by the prosecution in rebuttal of defence evidence of good character - this will usually, but not always, be evidence of general reputation of the accused. Prosecution evidence may also be adduced when the character of the accused is a fact in issue, eg the charge is driving a vehicle whilst disqualified. Character evidence may be adduced by the prosecution where it amounts to similar fact evidence and therefore tends to prove the guilt of the accused. In all these situations there is no requirement that the accused testifies, as the evidence can be given in chief by the prosecution and is not restricted to cross-examination of the accused.

Apart from these examples, there is provision in the Criminal Evidence Act 1898 for cross-examination of the accused as to character in certain circumstances; the 1898 Act only applies, therefore, when the accused elects to testify. In the case of Bill and Charles, the major question is whether their previous convictions may be put to them in cross-examination; of particular relevance is the second limb of s1(f)(ii), ie casting imputations on prosecution witnesses.

a) Bill's testifying as to the reason for his fingerprints being found in Diane's house goes beyond an emphatic denial of guilt, and could possibly be treated as an imputation. If casting imputations on prosecution witnesses is necessary to enable the accused to establish his defence, nevertheless the accused will thereby lose his shield and may be liable to cross-examination as to his previous convictions (*Selvey* v *DPP* (1970)). An assertion that a prosecution witness had a homosexual relationship with the accused has been held to amount to an imputation (*R* v *Bishop* (1975)), but an assertion that a prosecution witness was lying has been held to fall short of an imputation and amount merely to an emphatic denial of guilt (*R* v *Rouse* (1904)). But if the necessary inference from such an assertion is that the witness had fabricated evidence, then that will amount to an imputation (*R* v *Britzmann & Hall* (1983)). So if Diane has, either in her examination-in-chief, or under cross-examination by the defence, stated at length that she did not know Bill, had never seen him until the day of the burglary but had nevertheless identified him as the intruder etc, then Bill's allegation could be held to go beyond an emphatic denial to an allegation that Diane has committed perjury. If this is not the case, and Bill raises the alleged affair as a necessary part of his defence, then it is open to question as to whether an allegation of a heterosexual, as opposed to homosexual, relationship with a prosecution witness would be classed as an imputation on her character, whether or not the alleged relationship was or was not adulterous. If it should be held that Bill's allegation does amount to the casting of an imputation on Diane's character, then the prosecution may cross-examine Bill on his past record, but only with leave of the judge. If leave is given, the judge must direct the jury that the previous convictions do not have a bearing on the issue of Bill's guilt, but serve only to damage his credibility as a witness (*R* v *Jenkins* (1945)). It follows, therefore, that if knowledge of the previous convictions would obviously lead the jury to conclude that the accused had committed the instant offence, then the judge should exercise his discretion to prohibit the cross-examination (*R* v *Watts* (1983)). There is some conflict in the cases (*R* v *Powell* (1985); *R* v *Burke* (1986); *R* v *Watts*), but if the jury were to be informed of Bill's rape conviction, or of his convictions for burglary, it is difficult to conceive of his having a fair trial given the grave prejudicial effect such knowledge would have.

b) Whenever the accused testifies he 'may be asked any question in cross-examination notwithstanding that it would tend to criminate him as to the offence charged': s1(e) 1898 Act. This appears to conflict with the protection ('the shield') given to the accused by s1(f), that he shall not be asked 'any question tending to show' that he has been convicted of any other offence. The House of Lords ruled in *Jones* v *DPP* (1962) that 'tending to show' in s1(f) means revealing or disclosing to the jury for the first time. Therefore, since Charles has tried to explain away Diane's identification of him by revealing to the court her identification of him in respect of another theft, he may be cross-examined on that theft even though he has not lost his shield under s1(f). The case of *R* v *Khan* (1991) suggests the cross-examiner here should not go into the details of the previous conviction as this may get into the area of disposition rather than credibility. His assertion that Diane is mistaken, dependent on how it is worded, may in any case amount objectively to an imputation under s1(f)(ii) (*R* v *Britzman & Hall*). If it does not, relevant cross-examination about the other theft and Diane's identification will be permissible as it would not be in breach of s1(f) since questions put, and answers given, would not be tending to show the commission of, charge of, or conviction for that theft.

c) Charles is in danger of losing his shield under the second limb of s1(f)(ii) in that it can be most unwise for the accused to allege that a police officer was mistaken when he testified that a confession was made to him by the accused. The likely outcome, (though dependent to some extent on the amount of detail in the officer's evidence) is that Charles' assertion will amount to an implied imputation on the character of Nab, and with leave of the judge Charles will be cross-examined on his convictions. As such cross-examination goes to the credibility of Charles rather than guilt his conviction for perjury though prejudicial, is pertinent to such credibility (as opposed to Bill's conviction for rape which would be seriously prejudicial but have no bearing on credibility as a witness).

   If PC Nab does not testify for the prosecution, then Charles' allegation cannot, by definition, amount to an imputation on the character of a prosecution witness (*R* v *Westfall* (1912); *R* v *Lee* (1976)).

   By asserting that the only person who said anything to PC Nab was Bill and that Nab was mistaken in attributing verbal admissions to himself Charles falls foul of s1(f)(iii), in that by necessary implication he is attributing the admissions to Bill and thereby giving 'evidence against any other person charged in the same proceedings'. It is of no consequence that Charles did not intend to undermine Bill's defence or support the prosecution's case against Bill; all that is relevant is the effect of Charles' testimony on the jury (*Murdoch* v *Taylor* (1965)). It is a question of law for the judge as to whether Charles' evidence amounts to evidence against Bill. If the judge decides in the affirmative, then he cannot prevent Bill, or his counsel, cross-examining Charles on his convictions. Should the prosecution seek to cross-examine under s1(f)(iii) then the judge does have a discretion to prohibit that cross-examination (*Murdoch* v *Taylor*).

Finally, it has yet to be argued in an appellate court as to whether the discretion to exclude 'unfair evidence' given to the courts by s78 Police and Criminal Evidence Act 1984, now governs the prohibition against or restriction on cross-examination by the prosecution of an accused under the 1898 Act. It should certainly have some influence on the cases cited above regarding cross-examination under s1(f)(ii) (*R* v *Powell*; *R* v *Burke*; *R* v *Watts*).

10 SIMILAR FACT EVIDENCE

10.1 Introduction

10.2 Key points

10.3 Analysis of questions

10.4 Questions

10.1 Introduction

When evidence of the misconduct of the accused is admitted in the form of previous convictions, its relevance is generally to the credibility of the accused as a witness. This admissibility of convictions etc as evidence of bad character at common law and under the Criminal Evidence Act 1898 was dealt with in Chapter 9, where it was stated that evidence of bad character could sometimes be admitted as similar fact evidence - ie to prove the guilt of the accused on the instant charge. Usually it is not permissible for the prosecution to lead evidence of the propensity of the accused towards misconduct (whether or not criminal), or of specific misconduct by him, since this would be prejudicial and thus prevent a fair trial.

However, exceptionally, evidence of misconduct, for example the details of how the accused misbehaved, not purely the fact of conviction (there may not have been one) may be admissible as 'similar fact evidence', ie to tend to show that the accused, given the similar fact evidence, committed the crime with which he is charged. In the main the topic centres on this issue, but similar fact evidence is sometimes admissible in civil cases, and is occasionally admissible in criminal cases by statute when certain crimes are charged.

10.2 Key points

In *Makin* v *Attorney-General for New South Wales* [1894] AC 57, Lord Herschell LC made a pronouncement on similar fact evidence which has been referred to on innumerable occasions. In effect, he stated that, if evidence of other misconduct of the accused did no more than show a general disposition to commit crime or a particular crime, then such evidence is inadmissible; but if the evidence goes further than that, and is 'relevant to an issue before the jury', then it may be admissible. This relevance to an issue before the jury led to attempts being made to categorise circumstances where the evidence was admissible, eg to rebut a defence; to show design; to prove a system; to prove 'guilty relations'; as identification of the accused. This elaborate and complex systemisation did not help to clarify the law on similar fact evidence, and is to some extent responsible for the confusion which still prevails, despite the attempt by the House of Lords to move away from categories of relevance to degrees of relevance in *DPP* v *Boardman* [1975] AC 421. In other words, their lordships concentrated on the striking similarity between the conduct of the accused alleged in the instant case and that of which the prosecution seek to adduce similar fact evidence.

However, in the cases since *Boardman* there is evidence of some disquiet with the application of the test of 'striking similarity' to the exclusion of all other tests for admissibility; in *Boardman* itself it is considered that the standard of striking similarity was set somewhat low. Two Court of Appeal decisions soon after *Boardman* evinced the difficulties which the striking similarity test was to cause; on almost identical facts the court admitted evidence of similar facts to prove guilt in one case and rejected it in the other: *R* v *Johannsen* (1977) 65 Cr App R 101; *R* v *Novac* (1976) 65 Cr App R 107.

Recent, post-*Boardman*, cases have also confirmed that similar fact evidence is admissible not only if strikingly similar to the fact of the offence with which the accused is charged but also if strikingly similar to the circumstances in which the offence was committed, eg *R* v *Scarrott* [1978] QB 1016. Further, it has been held that such evidence of circumstances does not need to show the actual commission of the evidence, providing it goes beyond merely proving a propensity to commit that type of crime, or crime generally: *R* v *Barrington* [1981] 1 WLR 419; *R* v *Butler* (1987) 84 Cr App R 12; *R* v *Tricoglus* (1976) 65 Cr App R 16. But the problem still remains of the difficulty, to the point of impossibility, in formulating a test of striking similarity, and evidence has been admitted by apparently applying a standard lower than that in *Boardman* itself - see eg *R* v *Seaman* (1978) 67 Cr App R 234.

In the recent case of *R* v *Brookes* (1991) 92 Cr App R 36, the defendant was charged with sexual offences against three of his daughters. The Court of Appeal held that it was not enough for the facts to be similar, they must tell the court something useful. The court must enquire into what the evidence was being used to prove, and whether that evidence was then probative of that fact. In this case, the similarity alleged was the common coin of evidence in the case of father-daughter incest, and there was a real risk that the daughters had colluded. Therefore, separate trials were ordered.

Where, as in *Boardman*, the similar fact evidence consists of testimony by another witness or witnesses as to conduct of the accused on other occasions similar to that alleged by a prosecution witness or witnesses on the occasion giving rise to the charge, then the court must satisfy itself that there has been no collusion between the witnesses and therefore no question of concoction: *R* v *Barrington*, supra.

Similar fact evidence continues to be admitted post-*Boardman* to rebut a defence raised or which is reasonably open to the accused (this pre-emptive adducing of the evidence by the prosecution being permitted to avoid a successful defence submission of 'no case to answer'). In *R* v *Lunt* (1987) 85 Cr App R 241 evidence of other misconduct by the accused was admissible to rebut a defence of innocent association; in *R* v *Anderson* [1988] 2 All ER 549 evidence was admitted to prove how implausible was the defence which the accused raised. 'Striking similarity' was not the test applied, but rather the positive probative value of the evidence.

See now also the case of *R* v *Carrington* [1990] Crim LR 330, where the function of the similar fact evidence was to show the defendant's intent in relation to the charge of threatening to kill the victim, the similar fact evidence being a threat made in a similar (but not strikingly similar) way to the victim a few months before.

Consider also the important recent House of Lords' decision in *R* v *P* (1991) 93 Cr App R 267. Here the House of Lords held that it had been correct to admit evidence that the defendant (a father) had similarly abused children of the family other than the complainant, in the absence of collusion, despite the absence of 'striking similarities'. The essential feature, the House of Lords said, of the evidence which was to be admitted was that its probative force in support of the allegation that the defendant committed a crime was sufficiently great to make it correct to admit the evidence, notwithstanding that it was prejudicial to the defendant. Probative force can be achieved by striking similarity, but there are other means. Here, the evidence of the girls described a prolonged course of conduct by the accused, including threats, use of force, and payment for abortions. This, the court felt, gave strong probative force to the evidence of each of the girls. The important question here was not who had committed these crimes, but had they been committed at all. 'Striking similarity' is more concerned with identifying the assailant when the fact that the crime has taken place is not in issue.

The case of *R* v *McGranaghan* (1991) The Times 1 November makes the point that where a defendant is charged with two or more offences and similar fact evidence is adduced to support his identification in relation to the second, third or fourth offence, the jury should be directed to consider first whether they were sure the accused had committed the first offence. However, the jury should be told to consider the defendant's guilt as regards the first offence in isolation - ie without consideration of the other offences before his guilt as regards the first offence can be used as similar fact evidence with the other offences. Common sense? But what about the coincidence theory? - ie if the accused is said to have committed several different but similar offences by several independent witnesses, he must have committed the offences otherwise those witnesses would not have all told the same story against him.

It seems, therefore, that generally the prosecution may adduce similar fact evidence in chief if it shows some unique linking characteristic or is of sufficiently striking similarity to be positively probative of guilt. But, similar fact evidence would appear to be admissible despite lacking that degree of striking similarity, dependent on the particular facts in issue, for example to rebut a defence raised, to prove opportunity, identity etc where any of these is in issue, or where the probative force outweighs the prejudicial value.

Arguably, in the general run of cases, the judge has a discretion to exclude similar fact evidence if its prejudicial effect will outweigh its probative value; given these two factors should be weighed by the judge in deciding admissibility, it seems that there is no scope for discretionary exclusion - but the courts continue to recognise its existence. In *R* v *Butler*, supra, it was stated that where the similar fact evidence constitutes the commission by the accused of other offences there is greater prejudicial effect, which is relevant to the exercise of the judge's discretion.

Two important statutory provisions in criminal cases are:

a) s27(3) Theft Act 1968: allows the prosecution to prove mens rea on the part of the handler of stolen goods by evidence which shows a general propensity to dishonesty; judicial discretion to exclude this evidence in the interests of a fair trial of the accused is recognised without argument: *R* v *Perry* [1984] Crim LR 680

b) s1(2) Official Secrets Act 1911: allows evidence of disposition of the accused to prove that his purpose was prejudicial to the safety or interests of the State.

In civil proceedings, similar fact evidence is admitted more easily than in criminal proceedings, because the civil courts are not concerned with the fair trial of an accused and therefore prejudicial effect and probative value do not have to be weighed.

In *Mood Music Publishing Co Ltd* v *De Wolfe Publishing Ltd* [1976] 1 Ch 119, similar fact evidence was admitted even though some of it had been obtained by the plaintiff's setting a trap for the defendant; that was not considered oppressive or unfair to the defendant, who had had notice of the plaintiff's intention to adduce the evidence during the course of the pre-trial procedure.

10.3 Analysis of questions

Similar fact evidence in criminal proceedings is a favourite with examiners, either as a 'self-contained' essay question or as a problem question where it will almost invariably be accompanied by issues such as evidence of character under the Criminal Evidence Act 1898. The incidence of problems approximate that of essays, so it is advisable to be conversant with similar fact and character evidence.

10.4 Questions

Question 1

a) Adolf is charged with stealing a Roman vase from an antiques shop. Is evidence admissible that he was convicted of stealing another Roman vase one year ago from a different antiques shop? The two vases are regarded as being ten times more valuable as a pair in the antiques business than they are if sold individually.

b) Would your answer to (a) be different, if there is evidence that the vase stolen in the previous robbery has now been recovered by the police?

c) Would your answer to (a) be different if the vase stolen on the previous occasion did not form a pair with the vase which Adolf is now accused of stealing, but the Crown have additional evidence that Adolf has been involved in a number of thefts of antique ceramics?

University of London LLB Examination
(for External Students) Evidence June 1983 Q5

Skeleton solution

- Similar fact evidence - probative value test - striking similarity - link between pair.
- Similarities between cases themselves - but prejudicial effect?
- Previous convictions - need more details to decide if of sufficient probative value.

Suggested solution

In criminal cases similar fact evidence is admissible if its probative value in relation to the offence charged can be shown by the striking similarity between that evidence and the offence charged (*DPP* v *Boardman* (1975)). Such evidence is admissible because it tends to identify the defendant as the criminal or to rebut any defence raised by him. In *Makin* v *Attorney-General for New South Wales* (1894) Lord Herschell LC made clear that the evidence is not admissible merely for the purpose of leading to the conclusion that the accused is likely, from his criminal conduct or character, to have committed the offence in question. Although the test for the probative value of the evidence is in terms of 'striking similarity', it was made clear by Scarman LJ in *R* v *Scarrott* (1978) that the crucial factor is positive probative value and not mere similarity. See also *R* v *P* (1991). The mere repetition of similar facts does not per se provide the requisite probative value of 'underlying link'. Such a link may not be inferred from the similarity of facts so commonplace that they can provide no sure ground for pointing to the accused as the author of the offence charged.

In applying these principles of law to the facts of the instant case, we should heed the warning given in *R* v *Scarrott*, faced with the apparent contradiction of the decisions in *R* v *Novac* (1976) and *R* v *Johannsen* (1977), that each case must be decided on its own facts, the only rule of law on admissibility being the probative value of the similar fact evidence.

In this case, there clearly does not exist the striking similarity of, for example, *R* v *Smith* (1915), or *Makin* v *Attorney-General for New South Wales*. The elements of similarity in the instant case relate to the fact that both thefts were from an antique shop, in both a Roman vase was stolen, and the vases are vastly more valuable as a pair than as individuals. Theft is a common offence and the mere similarity of two offences of theft from two antique shops is unlikely to give rise to the underlying link necessary. In *DPP* v *Boardman*, Lord Hailsham gave some examples of what might suffice, the fact that a burglar left the same humorous limerick on the walls of the sitting room or an esoteric symbol, in lipstick, on the mirror, or the fact that a homosexual act was performed by someone wearing the ceremonial head-dress of a Red Indian Chief. It is clear that the underlying link can be forged from the distinctive modus operandi of the criminal or from distinctive features accompanying the commission of the offence. In this case, because of the dramatic increase in the value of the antiques as a pair it may be reasonably inferred that there are considerable similarities between the two pieces. They may be of similar size, shape, design, or colour; they may be the work of the same craftsman; they may actually constitute a matching pair. It is submitted that the similarity or link, coupled to the other more commonplace similarity, may provide the requisite probative value for the purpose of admissibility. The evidence tends to identify the defendant as the thief of the second vase. It is submitted that its admissibility does not depend on the nature of Adolf's defence. If the evidence is logically probative it is admissible irrespective of the defence raised (see *R* v *Sims* (1946) and *Harris* v *DPP* (1952)).

If, prior to the commission of the present offence, the former stolen vase had been recovered by the police the question becomes more problematical. Although the link based upon the increased value of the two pieces as a pair, would fall away, nonetheless there would remain the similarities, of which we are not given details, of the two pieces themselves. These may be numerous and striking, or few and commonplace. Even if the judge were to rule in his discretion to exclude it on the basis that its prejudicial effect outweighs its probative value, this discretion is part of the general discretion of the judge in any criminal trial to exclude evidence technically admissible but with a prejudicial impact out of proportion to its evidential value (Police and Criminal Evidence Act 1984 s82(3)).

If the first vase stolen did not constitute one of a pair, but there is evidence that Adolf has been 'involved' in a number of thefts of antique ceramics, it is submitted that such evidence would not be admissible as similar fact evidence. This is not on the basis that it is unclear whether Adolf was charged or convicted of the other thefts, because it is not a condition of the admissibility of similar fact evidence that the defendant was charged or convicted. The evidence in question may be the subject of dispute (*R* v *Rance & Herron* (1975)) or may be evidence of facts occurring subsequent to the offence charged (*R* v *Geering* (1849)). It is submitted rather, that on the bare facts given, there are no adequate distinctive characteristics or features in the offences concerned to render them of sufficiently probative value; they show merely that Adolf is likely to have committed the offence.

Question 2

Skinhead is to be charged with burglary of jewellery belonging to Agatha, an old woman, who lived on her own on a council estate, and of beating her face with a truncheon.

Agatha identified Skinhead some time after the event at a boys' club, in the presence of a police officer and Skinhead had said, 'The old biddy is mad.' The police have evidence that a week earlier another old woman, Martha, living on the same estate had jewellery stolen from her and she, too, had been beaten with a truncheon. A neighbour, Denis, had seen someone run out of Martha's house late at night and soon afterwards heard a voice exclaim, 'Skinhead, where the bleedin' hell are you running?' Neither Martha nor Denis has been able to identify Skinhead as the attacker.

The police have found some of the pieces of jewellery stolen from Agatha and Martha at the flat of Skinhead's girlfriend, Rachel. They had broken in without a warrant on that occasion. The police wish to charge Skinhead with both offences at the same trial so that evidence on one count can be admitted on the other count.

Agatha, in the meantime, has told the police she cannot be sure it was Skinhead she had identified at the club.

Advise the police as to admissibility of evidence available to date.

University of London LLB Examination
(for External Students) Evidence June 1985 Q8

Skeleton solution

- Introduction - defining the issues.
- Reaction of accused to allegation - *Pearce* - s1(f)(ii).
- Denis' evidence - hearsay - res gestae.
- Identification - *Osbourne & Virtue.*
- Illegal search - discretion to exclude evidence - effect of s78 1984 Act.
- Similar fact evidence - similar allegations - relevance.

Suggested solution

a) *Introduction*

There are five issues on which the prosecution must be advised. They are the admissibility of Skinhead's reaction on being accused by Agatha, Denis' repetition of what he hears, evidence of the identification of Skinhead by Agatha and the evidence obtained as a result of the illegal search. The fifth issue is the general question of whether the evidence on one count is admissible on the other. Each issue will be discussed in turn.

b) *Skinhead's reaction on being accused*

Agatha identified Skinhead as the man who burgled her home and assaulted her. His reaction was to say 'the old biddy is mad'. Of itself this reaction is not an admission. He did not accept the truth of the accusation in clear terms. The law recognises, however, that the true effect of words that are spoken depends not on what is said, but on how it is said, ie how it is phrased and the intonation of the speaker. For this reason the Court of Appeal has recently stated that the reaction of the accused on first being taxed with an allegation is always admissible in evidence (*R* v *Pearce* (1979)). The precise scope of this rule is not clear though. The court said that the reaction of the accused on first being accused of the offence by the police is always admissible (following *R* v *Storey* (1968)) and went on to say that this extends to the reaction of the accused when first 'taxed' by others than the police, provided this did not occur too long after the initial accusation was made. The reason for admitting such evidence was said to show the jury the accused's reaction, which was 'of vital relevance'.

How this principle applies to the facts here is not clear. The identification by Agatha occurred 'some time after the event'. It may be that this puts Skinhead's reaction outside the scope of the *Pearce* rule.

Older authorities indicate that the reaction of the accused to an allegation is only admissible if his reaction was to accept the truth of the allegation (*R* v *Norton* (1910); *R* v *Christie* (1914)). Such an approach begs the question, though: it makes the test of admissibility difficult in cases where the reaction of the accused was equivocal, where it could be interpreted as an acceptance of the allegation or it could be interpreted as a rejection. The approach in *Pearce* eliminates this problem. It allows the jury to hear the reaction of the accused and decide for themselves whether he accepted the allegation or not. It is probably the case that this creates a new hearsay exception in cases where the jury decides that the accused was rejecting the accusation and gives this rejection weight as evidence (contrary to the dicta in *Myers* v *DPP* (1965)). Nonetheless this does not detract from the common sense of the rule.

Therefore the prosecution is advised that the reaction of the accused to the allegation by Agatha will be admissible in evidence provided the identification did not take place so long after Skinhead was first accused that his reaction could be construed to be a considered reaction.

The admission of the statement 'the old biddy is mad' will not lose Skinhead his shield by virtue of s1(f)(ii), because it would not be the adduction of evidence by the accused so as to cast imputations on a prosecution witness, but rather a denial of guilt, in emphatic terminology.

c) *Denis*

Denis saw someone run out of Martha's house and heard a voice shout 'Skinhead where the bleedin' hell are you running?' The fact that he cannot identify Skinhead as the person who ran out of the house diminishes the relevance of what he has to say. The question with regard to Denis is whether he is allowed to repeat what he heard.

The relevance of what he would repeat is that it would be construed as an identification of Skinhead as being in the area at the time. It is by no means certain that the person identified by the unknown voice as Skinhead was the person running from the house, but this would be a legitimate inference in the circumstances. There has been much debate about whether the evidence of Denis would be caught by the hearsay rule. Cross pointed out that the definition of implied assertions as hearsay is difficult ('The Scope of the Rule against Hearsay' (1956) 72 LQR 91). Nonetheless, that the evidence of Denis would be hearsay is clear. The jury would draw the inference that Skinhead was present because Denis had repeated an assertion by someone else that Skinhead was present. 'Skinhead, where ... are you running?' can be written as '(i) I identify you as Skinhead; (ii) Where are you running?' In that form the repetition of part (i) of the statement would clearly infringe the hearsay rule. The fact that the speaker abbreviated his statement does not detract from the assertion he was making, that the person he was talking to was Skinhead. If Denis repeats that assertion the jury would be invited to rely on the assertion of someone who has not given evidence. That is hearsay.

Hearsay evidence is only admissible if it falls within one of the special inclusionary rules. The only one which could be relevant here is the so-called 'doctrine' of res gestae. This states that hearsay evidence is admissible if the statement repeated in court was made in circumstances so closely involved with the event concerned that the possibility of concoction can be disregarded (*Ratten* v *R* (1972)). In *R* v *Nye & Loan* (1977) the Court of Appeal held that such evidence would be admissible if the possibility of concoction or error could be excluded, thereby adding an additional qualification to the *Ratten* v *R* approach. More recently the Court of Appeal has again stressed that the essence of the res gestae exception to the hearsay rule is to allow hearsay where in the circumstances it is clearly reliable (*R* v *Turnbull* (1984); *R* v *Andrews* (1987)).

It is submitted that the evidence of Denis will not be admissible for the prosecution. In the circumstances - late at night, Denis could make no identification, no evidence could be given of the reliability of the person who did identify Skinhead - it must be doubted whether the identification was so reliable that its hearsay nature could be ignored.

d) *Identification by Agatha*

We are not told whether the identification of Skinhead by Agatha was made at an identification parade or was informal. If it was a parade then the Code of Practice issued under s66 Police and Criminal Evidence Act 1984 should have been complied with. Strictly speaking there is no sanction for failure to observe these rules, but the trial judge has a discretion to prevent use being made in court of the fact of identification (*R* v *John* (1973) and s78(1) Police and Criminal Evidence Act 1984), where it was made in improper circumstances. Given that the identification was made at a boys' club it will be assumed that it was an informal identification.

Agatha is unable to remember who she identified at the club. There is some authority to the effect that the prosecution may be allowed to call the policeman who was present to state who was identified. In *R* v *Osbourne & Virtue* (1973) the Court of Appeal laid down the rule that a police officer who had seen a witness make an identification at a parade was allowed to tell the court who was picked out, when the witness failed to make a positive identification in court. This rule was said to apply whether the witness remembered making an identification or not. The case has been subjected to considerable criticism on the ground that it ignores the hearsay rule and misinterprets earlier House of Lords dicta (see, for example, Murphy *A Practical Approach to the Law of Evidence* (3rd edition, 1988, p427). The status of *Osbourne & Virtue* as an authority is not strong; too little argument was addressed to the court on the hearsay aspects of the police officer's evidence in such a case for it to be given much credibility. The problem is that if the policeman says that Agatha identified Skinhead, the Court of Appeal said that repetition of the identification could be made because all the officer would be doing is repeating something he saw - repeating the fact that an identification was made. Clearly this is unsatisfactory. Skinhead would not be charged with having been identified by Agatha, he would be charged with having committed the offences against her. The mere fact that he was identified by her, therefore is irrelevant. The evidence of the officer would only be relevant because it would be treated by the jury as evidence in the following form: '(i) Agatha identified Skinhead; (ii) the purpose of the identification was to tell me who committed the offence; (iii) therefore Agatha told me that Skinhead committed the offence.' If the officer went into the witness box and simply said: 'Agatha told me that Skinhead committed the offence', such evidence would be inadmissible, being hearsay. It makes no difference that she told him that Skinhead was the offender in an indirect manner, by identifying him at the club, rather than in a direct manner. Therefore the evidence of the officer would be hearsay. The failure of *Osbourne & Virtue* to address itself to this hearsay argument makes it a very weak authority in support of admissibility.

The case of *McCay* (1990) causes problems as well. The Court of Appeal here held as admissible evidence given by a police officer as to the number chosen in an identification parade by the witness. The court appeared to believe that any identification carried out in accordance with Code D of Police and Criminal Evidence Act 1984 is admissible, whether hearsay or not; or it falls within the res gestae exception. But this clearly goes against most of the authorities.

Furthermore, no support for *Osbourne & Virtue* or *McCay* can be found in dicta in *Christie*. In that case the House of Lords was addressing itself to the question of whether the reaction of the accused to an accusation could be described to the court. Dicta to the effect that evidence can always be given of a previous identification are restricted to the case where the reaction of the accused to the identification is relevant. This has been dealt with in section (b) above, but is not relevant to the repetition of the identification in order to prove the identity of the offender.

Therefore, it is submitted that *Osbourne & Virtue* cannot be relied on by the prosecution to render admissible evidence of the officer as to the identification of Skinhead in order to prove the truth of the implied assertion by Agatha that he committed the offence. Perhaps a further point could be made in that *R* v *Osbourne & Virtue* involved the police officer describing the workings of an identification parade, whereas in this case there was no parade; this is a weak ground for distinguishing the cases though.

e) *Illegal search*

The admissibility of evidence obtained as a result of an illegal search is governed by s78 Police and Criminal Evidence Act 1984. This states that the trial judge may exclude it at his discretion if in his opinion it would have an adverse effect on the fairness of the proceedings. The section specifically mentions that one thing to be considered is the manner in which the evidence was obtained.

The reference in s78 to the fairness of the proceedings being the guiding factor does not sit easily with the requirement that the circumstances in which the evidence was obtained should be considered. The effect of any piece of evidence on the fairness of proceedings would be determined by whether it was more prejudicial than probative (*Kuruma* v *R* (1955)). If its prejudicial effect out-weighed its probative value then the judge would have no option but to exclude it because if it were left to the jury the accused would not receive a fair trial. The way in which evidence was obtained cannot possibly affect its probative force or its prejudicial effect. Therefore the reference to the circumstances in which it was obtained, in s78, must mean that 'fairness in the proceedings' should be given a wide interpretation covering not just the prejudicial effect of the evidence but also the fairness to an accused person of obtaining evidence in an underhand way. The common law on the subject of the discretionary exclusion of otherwise admissible evidence was left unclear by the House of Lords decision in *R* v *Sang* (1980). Some guidance was given as to the meaning of fairness to the accused. All five members of the House of Lords stated that the guiding principle in any definition of the discretion to exclude must be that of the overriding need to be fair to an accused person. Two elements of fairness were identified, the need to exclude unduly prejudicial evidence and the desirability of excluding evidence which has been obtained by a trick so that the accused was his own betrayer.

In *R* v *Mason* (1988) the Court of Appeal applied s78 to 'proceedings' in its wider interpretation, ie including police questioning of suspects before there is any question of 'proceedings' in the sense of a criminal trial.

In this problem question, the search undertaken was illegal but did not involve any sort of trick or inducement to the accused to give himself away. The judge nevertheless has a discretion to exclude this otherwise admissible evidence because of police impropriety and a breach of the Code of Practice.

f) *Similar fact evidence*

The prosecution wish to charge Skinhead with both offences so that evidence on one count will be admissible on the other. This can only be done if the evidence against him on one count can be treated as 'similar fact' evidence on the other count. The court in *McGranaghan* (1991) made it clear that the jury must be satisfied that he committed the first offence, without regarding the similar fact evidence. Only then can they use the first offence as similar fact evidence in relation to the second offence. But this causes problems for the 'coincidence' theory.

The House of Lords has recently made clear that the admissibility of evidence on two different counts is a question of relevance (*DPP* v *Boardman* (1975)). In other words whether the evidence of Agatha can be treated as evidence that he stole from and beat Martha depends on whether it helps to prove the commission by Skinhead of the 'Martha offences'. The meaning of 'relevance' in such cases as this has been obscured by the addition of qualifications such as that similar fact evidence must be 'strikingly similar' or 'positively probative' to be admissible. All that is meant by these phrases is that there is a natural tendency to reason along the lines that if an accused is said to have committed several different but similar offences by several independent witnesses he must have committed the offences otherwise those witnesses would not have all told the same story against him. In fact, when looked at logically, there is always a chance of coincidence. Therefore before 'similar allegation' evidence can be left to the jury the judge must be satisfied that the chance of coincidence is so small that the jury would in fact be justified in adopting the line of reasoning mentioned above. In most cases the chance of coincidence can only be excluded where the allegations made are so strange, so 'strikingly similar', that they must be true. Similarly, where the evidence to be put before the jury is not just of similar allegations, but is of circumstances which would make a jury think that both offences were committed by the same person. For example, in this case, jewellery found in Skinhead's girlfriend's flat came from both of the victims. Any reasonable juryman would think that there was a connection between the two offences for this to happen. He would think that the chance of the jewellery from two separate but similar burglaries being in possession of the same person without that person having some connection with the commission of the offence is so small that the fact that Agatha's jewellery was found in the flat is evidence that Skinhead or his girlfriend was a party to the burglary from Martha. The task of the trial judge is to consider whether such an inference by the jury is justified, or whether they would be jumping to the wrong, albeit understandable, conclusion.

So, is the evidence on each count here sufficiently relevant to be admissible on the other count? Both offences involved not just a burglary but also an assault. That, of itself, is not very unusual - any householder who interrupts a burglar runs the risk of injury. But the type of injury was the same in each case - a beating with a truncheon. In these circumstances it is submitted that the finding of the two lots of jewellery in the same place, added to the similarity of the offences, would justify an inference that they were both committed by the same person. The fact that Denis's evidence would not be admissible, therefore, would not be fatal for the prosecution because it may be that Agatha will be able to identify Skinhead in court after all - she would be entitled to refresh her memory out of court from any record there might be of the identification.

Question 3

'The admissibility of evidence of bad character of an accused under the rule in *Boardman* v *DPP* is simply another instance where evidence is admissible because its probative force greatly outweighs its prejudicial effect.'

University of London LLB Examination
(for External Students) Evidence June 1986 Q4

Skeleton solution

- General discretion of judge.
- Law before *Boardman* v *DPP* - categories or cases under similar fact evidence rule.
- *Boardman* - moving away from categories - striking similarity and probative force.
- Forbidden reasoning - prejudice of certain types of previous convictions.
- Law since *Boardman.*

Suggested solution

The rule is well established that the trial judge has a discretion to exclude evidence the prejudicial effect of which outweighs its probative force (see Pattenden, *The Judge, Discretion and the Criminal Trial* (1982)). It is somewhat inaccurate to say that the judge has a discretion, because once he has decided that the probative force of the evidence cannot be negatived then he has a duty to exclude it in order to ensure a fair trial (*R* v *List* (1965)), however, the judge's judgment must be used when considering whether he can counteract possible prejudice by a careful direction to the jury and to this extent the decision he makes is a matter for him and not for an appellate court, and so could be said to be a discretion.

Prior to the decision in *Boardman* v *DPP* (1974) the courts classified situations in which the prosecution may wish to use similar fact evidence, and laid down rules allowing it where a particular defence was put forward, or the offence charged was of a particular type. For example, in *R* v *Sims* (1946) the Court of Appeal held that whenever offences involving homosexual acts are alleged against an accused who is himself homosexual, then the jury may be told of his homosexuality. In *R* v *Bond* (1906) it was held that a defence of accident could be rebutted by evidence of the accused's propensity to commit acts of the type alleged. 'Accident' soon became a special category of defence such that whenever the defence was 'Yes, I did it, but it was an accident', so the prosecution could adduce evidence of disposition. Similarly the defence of ignorance became a category, so that in *Blake* v *Albion Life Assurance Society* (1874) a principal's plea that he was ignorant of his agent's fraudulent conduct was rebutted by evidence that on previous occasions the agent had acted fraudulently to the benefit of the principal. A third category was 'innocent association', which is a defence that, although the opportunity existed for the act alleged to have been done by the accused, that opportunity was not taken, for example in *R* v *King* (1967) a man was charged with having committed various indecent acts with boys who were staying at his house, in his defence he admitted that the boys were there but said that nothing indecent took place. The Court of Appeal held that evidence of the accused's homosexuality was admissible to rebut this defence. A fourth category was cases where the accused alleged that the wrong man had been arrested. For example, in *Thompson* v *R* (1918) the accused was identified by boys as the man who had previously made indecent advances to them; his defence that they had picked out the wrong man was rebutted by evidence of his homosexual propensity. The final category was a case where the prosecution wished to show various acts committed by the accused in order to show that he was engaged in systematic behaviour of the type alleged. In *R* v *Ollis* (1900) the accused faced several charges relating to the use of fraudulent cheques. Evidence was held to be admissible that on previous occasions he had acted fraudulently by use of false cheques.

These categories developed because of the large number of cases of their type which comes before the courts each year. If it were the case that all cases were essentially the same, then it would, indeed, make sense to have such categories so that at trial the allegation or the defence merely had to slot into the appropriate category in order for the judge to know whether similar fact evidence should be admitted. But, cases are not all the same, each revolves around its own facts and the use of strict categories may operate unfairly to the accused.

In *Boardman* v *DPP* the House of Lords held that the old categories should be discarded and each case looked at individually. In that case the House considered whether similar fact evidence was any different to other types of evidence, and made clear that in essence all evidence is the same - it is all adduced in order to assist the jury to reach its verdict. When evidence of the disposition of the accused towards a particular type of conduct is adduced there is always the risk that the jury will jump to the conclusion that because the accused is inclined to commit the type of conduct alleged, so he must have done so at the time alleged. Lord Hailsham referred to this as the 'forbidden reasoning'. Whether evidence is admissible depends simply upon whether it is relevant, in other words whether it assists the jury to reach a verdict. The fact that the accused is inclined to commit offences like the one charged will only be relevant where that disposition can be properly treated by the jury as evidence of guilt. For example, if the accused is charged with speeding, it does not really help the court one way or the other to show that he has been convicted of speeding on previous occasions; evidence of that disposition is almost wholly irrelevant. On the other hand, if the accused is charged with murder, the fact that he has murdered on previous occasions may be probative in as much as it shows that he is one of the relatively few people who could commit the offence alleged. Furthermore, if the accused is charged with having committed certain homosexual acts whilst wearing the headdress of a Red Indian Chief (see the example given by Lord Hailsham in *Boardman*'s case), evidence that he had done this on previous occasions is highly probative because it narrows down the group of suspects considerably. It can be seen from these three examples that evidence of the accused's disposition to commit the type of crime alleged may be probative or not depending on the nature of the allegation made.

Inevitably there is always only a certain number of people who could have committed the offence charged and anything which narrows down the group of suspects such that at the end of the trial the jury can say that the group has been reduced to one, the accused, will be of some assistance. It cannot be said that in the very wide categories which are mentioned above, the evidence of disposition will always assist the jury in its deliberations, any more than it would in other cases falling outside these categories, and this was expressly recognised in *Boardman* v *DPP* by the abolition of the categories.

The fact that evidence of disposition may lead the jury to jump to the conclusion that the accused committed the offence is no objection to the admission of that evidence if, in fact, the jury is right to jump to such a conclusion. But, there is the difficulty which Lord Hailsham recognised of the jury jumping to a false conclusion. For example, if the accused is charged with indecent assaults on children, the fact of his previous conviction for a similar offence may lead the jury to conclude that he must have done it this time, simply because of the feelings of horror and outrage which such offences excite. The jury may not be capable of bearing in mind the chance that the wrong man is in the dock and may give such weight to the previous conviction that other evidence in the accused's favour is not considered or is not properly weighed. To attempt to ensure that the jury does not give undue weight to such evidence, the trial judge must examine whether it really is as probative as the jury may think it is. If there is clear evidence that the accused has undergone treatment so that he no longer has the urge to commit such offences, then the trial judge may decide that justice is best done by omitting reference to the previous conviction.

In the recent case of *R* v *Brooks* (1991), an incest case, the court not only considered similarity but risk of collusion as well in deciding the probative force of the evidence. But it is submitted that the House of Lords' decision in *R* v *P* (1991) is superior in that the court goes away from 'striking similarity' as these cases are not about who committed the crimes but whether the crimes were committed at all. In other words, each case must be looked at individually, and what the evidence is to be used for is very important.

The balancing act between the probative force of the evidence and its prejudicial effect was said to be at the heart of the similar fact rules in *Boardman* v *DPP* so that the admissibility of similar fact evidence is simply a matter of relevance. In many cases the judge will feel himself able to reduce the prejudicial effect of the evidence of disposition and will allow it to go to the jury with an appropriate warning. It is not necessary for the probative value of the evidence to greatly outweigh its prejudicial effect, provided that it outweighs it sufficiently to lead to a fair trial. Indeed, where the evidence of previous misconduct is so probative that it proves that the accused must have committed the offence, then prejudicial effect is wholly irrelevant. For example, in *R* v *Straffen* (1952) the evidence of the previous strikingly similar murders was such overwhelming proof of guilt that it would have done no harm for the jury to ignore all other evidence and convict solely on the basis of the accused's most extraordinary disposition.

Since *Boardman* v *DPP* the Court of Appeal and House of Lords has dealt with similar fact cases on several occasions and, generally, has applied the balancing test between probative value and prejudicial effect. The only exception to this seems to be *R* v *Lewis* (1982) in which the old categories of admissibility made something of a comeback. Nevertheless, that case has been the subject of so much criticism that it is unlikely to have any long term effect on the way in which similar fact cases are dealt with.

Question 4

'Discretionary exclusion of evidence in criminal cases is to be preferred to rule-based automatic exclusion, but many evidential rules are so open-textured that the rule is not much more than discretion in disguise.'

Consider this quotation in the context of the rule on confessions and the rule in *Boardman* v *DPP* [1975].

Adapted from University of London LLB Examination
(for External Students) Evidence June 1988 Q7

Skeleton solution

- Confession - definition of- admissibility criteria in s76 - discretion in applying criteria - assessment of usefulness of discretion.
- Similar fact evidence - test of admissibility - discretion in applying test of admissibility.

Suggested solution

A confession may be given in evidence against a defendant as an exception to the rule against the admission of hearsay evidence. The admission of confessions is recognised at common law (*Customs & Excise Commissioners* v *Harz & Power* (1967)) but the applicable law is now found in s76 of the Police and Criminal Evidence Act 1984 (and s77 in the case of confessions made by the mentally handicapped).

But because a confession is often the most cogent evidence possible against an accused person, he is given certain protection. This takes the form of strict rules of admissibility. The prosecution must prove beyond reasonable doubt that the confession which it proposes to repeat in evidence was not obtained by either oppression or in consequence of anything said or done which was likely, in the circumstances existing at the time, to render unreliable any confession which might have been made by the accused in consequence thereof. Even if the judge is quite satisfied that the confession is true, in other words that the defendant did do the things he admitted doing, the confession may not be given in evidence unless the prosecution proves its admissibility.

There is a partial definition of oppression in s76(8), which includes torture, inhuman or degrading treatment and the use or threat of violence. In the case of conduct falling short of that, the definition given by Lord Lane CJ in *R* v *Fulling* (1987) will apply.

Section 78 gives the court a discretion to exclude evidence which would have an adverse effect on the fairness of the proceedings. The way in which evidence is obtained is one matter which is treated as affecting the fairness of the proceedings.

Prior to the enactment of s76, there were no statutory criteria to be fulfilled before a confession was admissible but the common law had its own test, known as the voluntariness requirement. This disallowed confessions unless the prosecution proved beyond reasonable doubt that they were not obtained by fear of prejudice or hope of advantage, excited or held out by a person in authority (*DPP* v *Ping Lin* (1976)). There was little scope for discretion because the voluntariness test relied on the proof by the prosecution of facts, and once the judge was satisfied as an exercise of judgment rather than discretion, that the confession was voluntary, he did not have a residual discretion to refuse to allow the prosecution to rely on it unless the exclusionary discretion recognised in *R* v *Sang* (1980) could operate, or, perhaps, there had been a breach of the Judges' Rules.

It is in relation to challenges to admissibility based on unreliability that there is scope for judicial discretion. It is a fine line between an exercise of discretion and an exercise of judgment in these cases, because the wording of s76(2)(b) is uncertain. It talks of the court disallowing a confession which was obtained by reason of anything said or done which was likely 'to render unreliable any confession which might be made by him (the defendant) in consequence thereof'. This test appears to require the judge to investigate not whether the confession made was unreliable, but whether in the abstract any confession made by the particular defendant was likely to be unreliable. In assessing this the judge must always employ a degree of guesswork about how the defendant might react to certain types of pressure applied to him. For example, in the case of *R* v *Barrett* (1991) the court distinguished between a weak and a strong personality as regards the applicability of s76(2)(b). To this extent there is an element of discretion.

Apart from the discretion just mentioned, the test in s76 for the admissibility of confessions does not depend on discretion. However, as already stated, the judge might feel that the behaviour of the police towards the defendant, perhaps by tricking him into making a wholly reliable confession, was so unfair that the confession should be excluded pursuant to s78. That section gives the judge a true discretion. Although there is authority that the trial judge may exclude evidence obtained by trick (*R* v *Mason* (1988)), it is also clear that he is not bound to do so if he is of the view that the evidence would have been obtained had the trick not been played (*R* v *Alladice* (1988)).

It is this last point which demonstrates the advantage of discretion over strict rules. In *R* v *Samuel* (1988) the Court of Appeal allowed an appeal against conviction on the ground that the refusal by the police to allow the defendant to see a solicitor was wrongful, because had a solicitor been allowed the defendant may not have made the confession which formed a major part of the prosecution case. But in *Alladice* a differently constituted Court of Appeal distinguished *Samuel* and stressed that there is no absolute rule that refusal to allow a suspect a solicitor renders any confession he may make inadmissible. The judge has a discretion and provided he takes into account all relevant matters and does not take into account any irrelevant matters, the appellate courts will not overturn his decision. Were there a firm rule that confessions are inadmissible unless the suspect had a solicitor of his choice present, much perfectly reliable evidence would be excluded. The protection of the accused lies in the power of the judge to prevent the prosecution acting unfairly, and the protection of the public lies in the prosecution being allowed to rely on evidence which is reliable even if there has been a breach of the Code of Practice by the police.

Boardman v *DPP* (1975) provides that similar fact evidence is inadmissible unless it reaches an appropriate standard of probity such that its prejudicial effect on the accused in the eyes of the jury is either justified by, or outweighed by, that probative force. In other words, evidence of similar wrongdoing to that alleged or evidence of similar allegations to those made against the defendant can be allowed. But there are two safeguards built in. Firstly, the judge must be satisfied that the evidence of similar facts really is probative of the defendant's guilt in the instant case. Secondly, the judge must be satisfied that the prejudice to the accused is not so great that the jury would convict because they are prejudiced rather than because they have sufficient evidence of guilt.

The probative force required of such evidence is not the same in every case because the issues before the court are not the same in every case. But what is essential is that the jury is not invited to hold evidence of similar facts against the defendant because it shows him to be a man of bad character. Rather, they should hold the evidence against the defendant because it shows his guilt independently of a general attack on character.

Inevitably there are some cases where the prejudice is overwhelming and the jury may not be able to ignore it, but the probative force of the evidence is so great that it is sufficient to warrant a conviction anyway, for example in *R* v *P* (1991) No injustice is done by the jury finding the defendant guilty because of his character if the evidence established guilt even of a man of unblemished character.

It is in the second safeguard mentioned above that there is scope for judicial discretion. At the end of the trial and immediately before the jury retires the judge sums up the case to them. In his summing up he is able to give directions about how the jury should approach certain pieces of evidence. If he is satisfied that in his summing up he can ensure that the jury look at the similar fact evidence for its true probative strength, and not for the way in which it blackens the defendant's character, his is entitled to allow the evidence to be admitted. But it is for the individual judge to decide whether he feels able to give the appropriate direction. The Court of Appeal may overturn him if it is of the view that the direction given was so defective that it could not achieve its purpose. But it is for the individual judge to decide whether he feels able to give the appropriate direction. The Court of Appeal may overturn him if it is of the view that the direction given was so defective that it could not achieve its purpose. But the judges of that court will always bear in mind that the trial judge was in a better position than them to assess the appropriate direction and only if he was clearly wrong will they overturn him.

The assessment of the probative force of evidence and the balancing of that against its prejudicial effect is a difficult exercise. No statutory test for the admissibility of similar fact evidence could possibly be devised which could remove from the trial judge the discretion which the common law gives him.

Question 5

Fence is charged with having received stolen goods, namely, a stolen television, video-tape recorder and video camera which have all been found in his garage. He denies knowing anything about the television and says that somebody else must have put it there without his knowledge. He admits having put the video-tape recorder in the garage but says he bought it from abroad as a present for the local old people's home. He also admits having put the video-camera in the garage and having bought it from Nicker in the local pub but says he did not realise it was stolen. The prosecution case is that all the items were bought by Fence from Nicker in the local pub, and that Fence knew they were stolen. It is not disputed by Fence that the television and video-camera were in fact stolen goods.

a) What use could be made of, and how should the judge deal with the following items of evidence:

Fence's conviction two years previously, for the theft of a television.

Fence's conviction six years previously, for handling a stolen video tape recorder and television which he had bought from Nicker in the local pub and then stored in his garage.

b) Suppose that Nicker is also charged in the same proceedings as Fence but Fence pleads guilty and gives evidence for the Crown. What issues in the law of evidence are likely to arise? What use could be made of a statement made by Fence to Blabbermouth, the barman at the local pub, that Fence had received the goods from Knave?

University of London LLB Examination
(for External Students) Evidence June 1989 Q2

General comment

Not a very difficult problem question, especially as, once the facts are given, a series of questions is put. However, candidates who have not got a fairly detailed knowledge of s27(3) Theft Act 1968 and of the definition of 'accomplice' given by Lord Simonds in the case of *Davies* v *DPP* could be deterred from attempting to answer this question even though they are competent to deal with admissible similar fact evidence and the operation of s1(f)(iii) Criminal Evidence Act 1898. Proof again that problem questions in Evidence examination papers tend to cover several issues, therefore 'question-spotting' is a dangerous practice!

Skeleton solution

Presumption re stolen goods; and similar fact evidence generally.

a)
- Section 27 Theft Act 1968.
- Similar fact evidence - modern approach.

b)
- Accomplice giving evidence for prosecution - corroboration warning.
- Evidence of character of witness - s1(f)(iii) and generally.
- General rule re inadmissible hearsay.

Suggested solution

There is an apparent contradiction in the question, which states initially that Fence denies knowledge of the presence of the television and says someone must have put it in his garage without his knowledge; later it is stated that Fence does not dispute that the television is stolen goods (whether this means he impliedly accepts that the television is stolen or merely does not attempt to refute the prosecution allegation is unclear). Whatever the interpretation put on this, any discussion would be futile, as will be seen later.

In proving Fence's guilt, which for the most part involves proof of his knowledge or belief that the goods were stolen (the mens rea for a s22 Theft Act 1968 offence) the prosecution will find it much easier to discharge their burden of proof if evidence of other, similar, misconduct by Fence can be adduced to prove his guilt on the instant charge. Additionally the prosecution is assisted by a presumption that the possessor of recently stolen goods has guilty knowledge, ie he knew or believed they were stolen. To rebut this presumption the possessor (Fence) must give an explanation of his possession consistent with innocence, or at least sufficiently convincing to leave the jury with a reasonable doubt as to guilty knowledge (*R* v *Hepworth & Fearnley* (1955)).

If Fence was found in possession of the stolen goods so soon after their theft that the only, or the unavoidable, inference is that *he* stole them, then on the charge of receiving Fence must be acquitted, and a conviction for theft cannot be substituted (*A-G of Hong Kong* v *Yip Kai-Foon* (1988)). However, there is nothing in the scenario to suggest such immediacy, nor is it stated that the goods were recently stolen therefore the prosecution may not be able to invoke the presumption.

a) Because of the difficulty of proving the means rea for receiving (knowledge or at least belief that the goods were stolen must be proved - suspicion, however strong, is insufficient) the task of the prosecution is reduced by s27(3) Theft Act 1968 which provides for the admissibility in evidence against an alleged handler of certain Theft Act convictions during the five years prior to the date of the offence charged, and of his possession of stolen goods from any theft which took place during the twelve months prior to the date of the offence charged.

   Applying s27(3) literally, Fence's conviction two years previously for the theft of a television should be admissible (the conviction can be proved under the provisions of s74 Police and Criminal Evidence Act 1984). All that could be admissible is the FACT of conviction, not the attendant circumstances (these could only be admissible, if at all, as similar fact evidence (*R* v *Fowler* (1988)). However, because the admission of such evidence is gravely prejudicial to the defence case, and thus can motivate against a fair trial, s27(3) has been construed strictly by the courts (*R* v *Bradley* (1980); *R* v *Wood* (1987)). Additionally, the judge can exercise his exclusionary discretion in respect of convictions under s27(3), and should do so where proof of previous conviction/possession would have prejudicial effect substantially outweighing any value in proving guilty knowledge or dishonest propensity, or would be of only 'minimal assistance to the jury' (*R* v *Perry* (1984)).

   Fence's theft conviction falls within the ambit of s27(3)(b) - 'evidence that he has within the five years preceding the date of the offence charged been convicted of theft or of handling stolen goods'. Since a description of the stolen goods (television) is not permissible (3), the crucial question for the judge is whether proof of a conviction for a theft would serve the interests of justice; as Fence denies knowledge of the television, but also does not dispute that it is stolen, it is difficult to reach any firm conclusion as to how the judge should deal with this previous conviction. On balance, and given it is for theft, not handling, he should exercise his exclusionary discretion.

With regard to Fence's conviction six years ago, this is outside the scope of s27(3)(a) and (b); if the prosecution are to use this it will not be the mere fact of conviction but the mode of misconduct leading to the conviction which may be admitted as similar fact evidence, to go to prove that, given the method used by Fence on the earlier occasion and the method allegedly used by him (and in part admitted by him) on this instant occasion, any defence of innocent reception and possession of the goods will tend to be rebutted. Such evidence of similar facts is highly prejudicial and therefore should not be admitted unless there is a sufficiently striking similarity between the two sets of Fence's activities. The more commonplace the unlawful misconduct, such as theft, handling etc, the more striking the similarity should be. Very frequently (stolen) goods are bought in pubs and storage of goods in a garage is commonplace, so unless there are some other very distinctive common features, evidence relating to the earlier handling should be inadmissible (*R* v *Inder* (1977)).

However, some of the cases since the House of Lords decision in *DPP* v *Boardman* (1975) are difficult to reconcile (*R* v *Novac* (1976); *R* v *Johannsen* (1977); *R* v *Tricoglus* (1976); *R* v *Barrington* (1981)). But the case of *R* v *P* (1991) makes it clear that 'striking similarity' is not always important. Each case must be looked at individually, and the judge must ask himself if there is material upon which the jury would be entitled to conclude that the evidence of one offence is so related to the evidence of another that it provides strong support for evidence against the defendant on the second offence. Relationships in time and circumstances may well provide important relationships even if not strikingly similar. But the vital question is what is the purpose of the evidence? If it is to prove identification (as here in Fence's case) then striking similarity is needed.

It appears to be accepted that where similar fact evidence is, strictly, admissible there is still a judicial discretion to exclude it if its probative value is outweighed by its prejudicial effect (*Noor Mohamed* v *R* (1949); *DPP* v *Boardman*). But given that probative value and prejudicial effect must be evaluated by the judge in deciding the admissibility of similar fact evidence, it is difficult to envisage situations where such a discretion could be exercised (however, note comment of Scarman LJ in *R* v *Scarrott* [1978] QB 1016, at 1028).

If Fence's previous misconduct is held to be admissible, then its purpose is to prove his guilt, not merely to affect his credibility as a witness for the defence. The admissibility would be decided by the judge (on a voir dire); if the prosecution are permitted to adduce the evidence, then they may give it in chief - ie there is no requirement that Fence testifies.

b) Where a witness is not disinterested, but may have 'an axe to grind', then the judge should tell the jury to treat that evidence with a degree of caution, explaining that they *may* convict on that evidence alone but only if satisfied of its reliability (*R* v *Beck* (1982); *R* v *Spencer*; *R* v *Smails* (1987); *R* v *Brown* (1991)).

However, as Fence is a handler of stolen goods giving evidence for the prosecution at the trial of Nicker, the alleged thief of those goods, Fence's testimony is much more 'tainted'; he falls within the definition of 'accomplice' given by Lord Simonds (*Davies* v *DPP* (1954)) and therefore in his case the judge should direct the jury that they should look for corroboration of Fence's testimony - ie independent evidence supporting Fence's and implicating Nicker in the theft. The judge must further direct the jury that in the absence of such corroboration they may nevertheless convict Nicker, but that it would be dangerous to do so because Fence may well have a purpose of his own to serve in giving evidence for the prosecution. This 'full' corroboration warning must be given, irrespective of whether Fence has already been convicted or sentenced; if the full warning is not given, then if the jury convict Nicker his conviction will be set aside on appeal, in that there will have been a material misdirection. Only if there were sufficient evidence other than Fence's to render the conviction safe and satisfactory would the Appeal Court apply the proviso and uphold the conviction despite the misdirection (*R* v *Stewart* (1986)).

Fence, in giving evidence for the Crown has 'given evidence against any other person charged in the same proceedings', per s1(f)(iii) Criminal Evidence Act 1898 (as amended by s1 Criminal Evidence Act 1979) and therefore Nicker's counsel has the right to cross-examine Fence as to both his previous convictions. The judge must direct the jury in that event that knowledge of those convictions must be used solely for the purpose of assessing the credibility of Fence's testimony (*R* v *Watts* (1983)).

With regard to Fence's statement to Blabbermouth, whether this could be used by the prosecution would depend on whether or not it is inadmissible hearsay. It may well have a bearing on the issue of whether the goods were stolen - which the prosecution must prove as a vital element of the offences charged - but could only be used for that purpose if Fence were making a statement of fact rather than one of his belief that Knave had stolen the goods (*R* v *Marshall* (1977)).

Alternatively the counsel for Nicker might well wish to call Blabbermouth to report Fence's statement in order to exonerate Nicker. However, there are problems! The House of Lords in *R* v *Blastland* (1986) recently decided that a statement made by another person which, if true, could lead to the conclusion that the accused was innocent, was inadmissible hearsay (*R* v *Blastland*). The statement which the Defence wanted to have reported to the court in that case was made by a person not charged with the offence. Nicker's counsel would have to argue that *R* v *Blastland* is distinguishable in that in the instant case the self-incriminatory statement was made by a co-accused who has given evidence for the Crown against Nicker and that the statement made to Blabbermouth contradicts Fence's earlier statement as to how he came by the goods, and must therefore be admitted *not* as evidence of its truth (and therefore *not* hearsay) but purely to show inconsistency on Fence's part, and thus to damage his credibility as a witness against Nicker. This line of argument for the reception of Blabbermouth's evidence as non-hearsay may succeed - the alternative is to ask the judge to give a ruling on admissibility which would be at odds with a decision of the House of Lords. Although the reasoning and decision in *R* v *Blastland* is open to a lot of criticism, it remains as a precedent until such time as the House of Lords should decide to depart from it.

Question 6

Charles and Douglas have been convicted of attempted burglary after their joint trial. Charles had four previous convictions for attempted burglary and Douglas a previous conviction for perjury.

The prosecution were allowed to lead evidence of the four previous convictions, where Charles had been arrested in the early hours of the morning on each occasion attempting to open a shop door with one of a bunch of keys. The prosecution's case was that on the instant occasion Charles and Douglas were trying keys in the keyhole of a shop door. Douglas testified that he was merely sheltering from the rain, saw no keys, and had he been aware of Charles' propensity to burgle shops he would not have acceded to Charles' suggestion that they shelter there. Douglas was cross-examined by the prosecutor on his previous conviction.

Charles' counsel accused the police of 'planting' the keys on him after his arrest. Charles' previous convictions were put to the jury by the prosecutor, who together with the judge commented on Charles' failure to testify.

Advise Charles and Douglas as to any grounds for appeal.

Written by editor

Skeleton solution

- Charles: similar fact evidence; admissibility and judicial discretion; rebutting defence raised or fairly attributable. Imputations cast, cross-examination; comment on silence of accused in court.
- Douglas: election to testify; evidence against co-accused - s1(f)(iii) Criminal Evidence Act 1898, cross-examination. Section 1(f)(ii) - imputations. Evidence of good character.

Suggested solution

The prosecution may have been allowed to lead evidence of the *circumstances* surrounding the four previous convictions of Charles for attempted burglary as similar fact evidence; but the mere fact of the convictions could not legitimately be revealed, as Charles has not given evidence directly or indirectly of his good character (thereby allowing evidence in rebuttal of bad character, including, on slender authority (*R* v *Wood & Parker* (1841)), evidence of disposition and previous misconduct, as opposed to merely evidence of bad reputation: *R* v *Rowton* (1865)). Also, Charles has not testified in his own defence, so no consideration is necessary of whether the previous convictions were put to him in cross-examination under the Criminal Evidence Act 1898. Therefore, if the judge allowed the *fact* of Charles' convictions to be put to the jury, whether in the guise of similar fact evidence or because Charles' counsel cast imputations on police witnesses, then this was improper and constitutes grounds for an appeal.

If the circumstances of the four previous occasions, leading to Charles' arrest each time, bore such a striking similarly to the circumstances forming the basis of the instant charge of attempted burglary, then the judge was right in allowing such probative evidence to be adduced by the prosecution in their evidence in chief, as tending to prove Charles' guilt (*DPP* v *Boardman* (1975)); ie if there were such a striking similarity that to withhold that evidence, albeit prejudicial, from the jury would amount to an affront to commonsense or given the way in which Charles misconducted himself on the other occasions it would be beyond the realms of coincidence if it were not his handiwork on the instant occasion (*DPP* v *Boardman*). Following *R* v *P* (1991), as the crime is in issue here, not identification, it should alternatively be argued that 'striking similarity' is not what is important, but the strength of the relationship between the previous and present offence - ie did Charles' previous commissions of burglary give him greater opportunity to commit the present offence? What happened to the keys?

Given Charles' defence that the police 'planted' the keys on him, the prosecution may be properly permitted to adduce evidence of his activities on the other occasions to rebut that defence (*R* v *Anderson* (1988)), and may reasonably anticipate, given his 'not guilty' plea despite his being found in the shop doorway, a defence of innocent association and therefore pre-empt it by rebutting evidence in chief, to prevent a successful defence plea of no case to answer (*R* v *Lunt* (1987)). Even though, in these specific situations the similar fact evidence does not need to have the same striking similarity, nevertheless it is not the fact of conviction for attempted burglaries which has relevance, but the attendant circumstances. In addition, the judge should have given consideration to the probative value and the prejudicial effect of this similar fact evidence, deliberating as to whether the former was outweighed by the latter, before deciding on its admissibility in law, or whether to exclude in his discretion if so admissible (*R* v *Butler* (1987); *R* v *Perry* (1984)).

If the judge allowed the previous convictions to be revealed to the jury because Charles' counsel cast imputations on the character of police witnesses for the prosecution by accusing them of fabricating evidence, then the judge was seriously in error, because Charles did not testify and therefore s1(f) Criminal Evidence Act 1898 did not apply. However serious and however numerous the imputations cast on witnesses for the prosecution, under the second limb of s1(f)(ii) the accused can, with leave, be cross-examined on his convictions - so by definition if he elects not to testify the cross-examination cannot take place, and the Act cannot be circumvented by the judge's allowing revelation of previous convictions by the prosecution when the accused does not give evidence. The silence of Charles cannot be the subject of any comment by the prosecution (s1(b) Criminal Evidence Act 1898 as amended by the Police and Criminal Evidence Act 1984), and any attempt by the prosecution to refer to Charles' election not to testify ought to have been thwarted by the judge. The judge may comment on the failure of an accused to testify, but the jury must be directed that the failure cannot amount to corroboration (*R* v *Jackson* (1953)), and although the comments of the judge depend on the facts of each case and the strength of the prosecution's case, the judge must preface his comment with a reminder that the silence of the accused has no evidential value and must not be equated with guilt (*R* v *Sparrow* (1973); *R* v *Mutch* (1973)). The judge's comment, therefore, depending on its content (or omissions) could amount to a mis-direction of the jury giving grounds for appeal.

The testimony of Douglas is to some extent favourable to Charles, ie his assertion that he saw no keys tends to support Douglas' defence of innocent association and his assertion that the keys were 'planted' on him after his arrest. This evidence of Douglas, the accomplice of Charles, would be 'tainted' because of their alleged complicity in the crime, and would have little evidential value without corroboration (*R* v *Prater* (1960)). But of much greater relevance is the fact that in the main Douglas' evidence tends to incriminate Charles, it tends to undermine Charles' defence and as such could be classed as evidence against a co-accused (s1(f)(iii) Criminal Evidence Act 1898; *Murdoch* v *Taylor* (1965)). If the judge rules that such evidence *is* evidence against a co-accused as opposed to, for example, a mere denial of guilt, then the co-accused has the right to cross-examine under s1(f)(iii) (*Murdoch* v *Taylor*). If, however, the prosecutor wishes to cross-examine under this proviso, this can only be with leave of the judge, and the judge will, exceptionally, grant such leave in his discretion (*R* v *Seighley* (1911)). The judge must weigh in the balance the prejudicial effect and probative value in deciding whether to permit such cross-examination by the prosecutor, and if he decides to permit the cross-examination must inform the jury that Douglas' conviction for perjury goes only to his credit, not to the issue of his guilt on the instant charge.

Douglas' assertion that he would not have acceded to Charles' request to shelter in the doorway is not by implication putting his character in issue; if it amounts to evidence of his general good character (which is dubious in this problem question) then rebutting evidence by the prosecutor should take the form of general bad reputation, not the disclosure to the jury (with or without leave of the judge) of one isolated conviction albeit for perjury.

11 OPINION EVIDENCE

11.1 Introduction

11.2 Key points

11.3 Analysis of questions

11.4 Questions

11.1 Introduction

Opinion evidence is perhaps the most straightforward topic in the laws of evidence, in that there is not a great deal of complexity or incongruity in the principles involved. There have been recent statutory changes in criminal proceedings which have made hearsay opinion evidence generally admissible. Judgments in previous proceedings are capable of being regarded as the opinion of that court, therefore will be covered in this chapter.

11.2 Key points

a) General rule is that opinion evidence, whether given as direct testimony or hearsay, is inadmissible as proof of the belief held - subject to three exceptions:

   i) General reputation

   Where direct evidence is unavailable on some matter of public concern, that matter may be proved by evidence of general reputation, eg pedigree or marriage (decreasing in importance as public records are more available and their content admissible as an exception to the hearsay rule) identifying a reference to a person, eg that a defamatory statement was accepted by the public in general as referring to the plaintiff; proving character, whether good or bad; evidence of reputation in these instances is admissible in civil cases by virtue of s9 Civil Evidence Act 1968, thus obviating the need for the notice procedure under the rules issued under s8. One final example of general reputation is the public's opinion on some matter, such as information from a survey admissible in cases involving trademarks, passing off etc: *Sodastream* v *Thorn Cascade* [1982] RPC 459.

   ii) Expert opinion evidence

   The court must be satisfied as to the competence of a witness to testify as an expert, whether by recognised qualification, and/or expertise gained by experience. Such a person's evidence is essential to assist the court not only to understand specialised facts but to form correct opinions and draw the correct inferences from those facts, or general facts. A medical orderly was held not to be an expert for the purposes of a prosecution against the defendant for assault occasioning actual bodily harm: *R* v *Inch* (1990) 91 Cr App R 51. A person who is competent as an expert witness is also compellable as such: *Harmony Shipping Co* v *Saudi Europe Line* [1979] 1 WLR 1380.

The expert evidence may be subjected to cross-examination, including cross-examination going to credit, and may be contradicted by other, usually expert, evidence, but otherwise the expert is regarded as an independent witness whose opinion evidence has substantial probative value: *R* v *Lanfear* [1968] 2 QB 77.

Expert opinion evidence is not admissible on subject matter of which the lay opinion of the court is just as valid: *R* v *Turner* [1975] QB 834, and also the case of *R* v *Weightman* (1991) Cr App R 291, where the Court of Appeal held that a psychiatrist's evidence was inadmissible where the purpose was to tell a jury how a person who was not suffering from mental disorder might react to the stresses and strains of life. The area which has given rise to most forensic and academic discussion is that of a person's state of mind. If the issue arises in relation to the reliability of the witness's evidence, then medical opinion evidence is admissible: *Toohey* v *MPC* [1965] AC 595. But if the issue is the state of mind of the accused at the time the offence was committed, then several cases highlight the difficulties the courts face. If there is no question of mental disorder, and the issue is purely the mens rea of the accused, then that is within the competence and experience of the court and therefore expert opinion evidence of a psychiatrist is not admissible because it is not necessary: *R* v *Chard* (1971) 56 Cr App R 268. However, where there is a question of mental disorder or similar conditions outside the usual experience of the court, then expert opinion evidence of psychiatrists is admissible because necessary, eg insanity, automatism, diminished responsibility. In *R* v *Smith* [1979] 1 WLR 1445, the opinion evidence of a psychiatrist was admitted to rebut a defence of automatism on a charge of murder; in *R* v *Turner* supra. In the recent case of *R* v *Toner* (1991) 93 Cr App R 382 medical evidence was admitted which related to hypoglycaemia and its possible effect upon intent (mens rea). The court could see no difference between this and medical evidence admitted as to the effect of a drug on intent. If no such medical evidence is allowed, the court said, the jury would be deprived of assistance in a field where their ordinary experience did not enable them to judge for themselves. In *R* v *Rimmer & Beech* [1983] Crim LR 250, expert opinion evidence relating to mental state was inadmissible because in effect it was tendered to prove the veracity of the statement made by the accused in his defence and thus would have tended to usurp the function of the court. These decisions are perhaps reconcilable with *Toohey* v *MPC* supra. But in *Lowery* v *R* [1974] AC 85, the opinion evidence of a psychiatrist as to the tendency of one of the two co-accused to murder for pleasure, the admissibility of which was naturally challenged by the other co-accused, was held to have been properly admitted to assist the jury to make a decision as to the veracity of the two co-accused! The decision in *Lowery* did not receive the approval of the Court of Appeal in *Turner*, but the former is a Privy Council decision, which should, and no doubt in due course will, be overruled by the House of Lords.

The common law rule prohibiting expert opinion evidence on the ultimate issue has been abrogated in civil trials by s3 Civil Evidence Act 1972 which provides for the admissibility of expert evidence on any 'relevant matter', stated in s3(3) to include 'an issue in the proceedings in question'. In criminal trials the issue of diminished responsibility on a charge of murder can be, and often is, the subject of expert opinion evidence - and often the expert will be asked the question: 'Do you think the accused was suffering from diminished responsibility?', despite the fact that that constitutes the ultimate issue in deciding guilt of murder or manslaughter. Lord Parker CJ gave this as an example of the inroads into the common law prohibition in criminal trials: see *DPP* v *A and BC Chewing Gum* [1968] 1 QB 159 at p164. It is generally accepted that the principle in s3 Civil Evidence Act 1972 now applies also in criminal cases subject to the discretion of the judge to exclude such evidence where the expert witness would be effectively usurping the function of the jury.

Where the expert bases his opinion on facts, he cannot thus make those facts evidence unless he has first-hand knowledge of them (*R* v *Abadom* [1983] 1 All ER 364) and in any situation where the expert is giving opinion evidence with an underlying factual basis, then those facts must be proved by admissible evidence of the expert himself as a witness of fact, or of some other competent witness.

Expert opinion hearsay evidence is admissible in civil cases under the Civil Evidence Act 1972. In criminal cases hearsay was restricted to statements of facts until s30 Criminal Justice Act 1988 provided for the admissibility of expert reports as hearsay, with leave of the court.

Disclosure of expert evidence pre-trial in criminal proceedings was provided for under s81 Police and Criminal Evidence Act 1984, under which Crown Courts Rules could be issued. Under the Act, the Crown Court (Advance Notice of Expert Evidence) Rules 1987 require that, following committal for trial, if either prosecution or defence proposes to adduce expert evidence of fact or opinion at the trial, then the other party must be furnished with that detailed expert evidence as soon as practicable. If a party fails to furnish details as required, then the expert evidence can only be adduced with leave of the court.

This requirement of disclosure has existed for some time in civil proceedings; RSC Ord 38, rules 36 to 44, issued under s2 Civil Evidence Act 1972, govern such pre-trial disclosure, whether the expert evidence be in the form of hearsay or direct testimony. Although the court may give leave to adduce despite non-compliance with the rules, Ord 38, r36 provides that expert evidence should not be adduced at the civil trial unless the party seeking to adduce has applied to the court to determine whether a direction should be given, and has complied with any such direction, or has complied with automatic directions under Ord 25, r8. Medical negligence cases are not, as was thought earlier, in any special category: *Naylor* v *Preston Area Health Authority* [1987] 1 WLR 958. Ord 38, r38 makes provision for the court to order a 'without prejudice' meeting of experts pre-trial to clarify the issues in dispute. Once an expert evidence report has been disclosed for the purpose of any contemplated civil proceedings, that report cannot be excluded from the evidence at the trial merely because the party originally seeking to adduce it has decided against using it or against calling the expert in question to testify (Ord 38, r42).

iii) Non-expert opinion evidence

Section 3(2) Civil Evidence Act 1972 provides for opinion evidence of non-expert witnesses to be admissible to convey to the civil court relevant facts perceived by them as evidence of what they perceived. It is considered that this sub-section restates the common law, and is therefore applicable also to criminal proceedings. Admissibility is confined to areas of general experience and competence of the lay person, for example evidence as to identity of a person or document etc; evidence as to physical or mental condition of a person, eg that a person had been drinking heavily, but *not* that he was so drunk as to be unfit to drive through drink: *R* v *Davies* [1962] 1 WLR 1111; evidence as to the speed of a motor vehicle (but see Chapter 5.2 as to corroboration), or as to age or value other than in relation to antiques when expert opinion evidence is essential. In the case of *R* v *Simbodyal* (1991) The Times 10 October the Court of Appeal made it clear that a judge would be vulnerable to proper criticism if he appeared to be acting as a handwriting expert by comparing the notes himself.

b) *Judgments in previous proceedings*

A judgment in any proceedings is in the nature of specialised opinion - ie the opinion of the court as to whether a party has discharged the general burden of proof to the appropriate standard.

At common law the rule in *Hollington* v *Hewthorn* [1943] KB 587 stipulated that a previous judgment was inadmissible in subsequent civil proceedings as evidence of the facts on which it was based. The rule has been held to apply in subsequent criminal proceedings: *R* v *Spinks* [1982] 1 All ER 587. As regards conviction in earlier criminal proceedings of the defendant in subsequent civil proceedings, s11 Civil Evidence Act 1968 not only makes the fact of the conviction admissible but renders it conclusive of the commission of that relevant offence unless the contrary is proved. It is the fact of conviction which is crucial, not the sentence, and therefore even if a pardon is given the conviction still subsists: *R* v *Foster* [1984]

3 WLR 401. The burden of proof on the civil defendant seeking to prove 'the contrary' when a conviction is proved against him is to the civil standard; ie proof on a balance of probabilities, which, given the standard of proof in his earlier prosecution, will be an uphill task: *Hunter* v *Chief Constable of the West Midlands* [1981] 3 All ER 727. A plaintiff in civil proceedings must include in his pleadings a statement of his intention to rely on s11 Civil Evidence Act 1968, together with the particulars of the conviction and the issue in the civil proceedings to which the conviction is relevant (RSC Ord 18, r7).

In s12 Civil Evidence Act 1968 there is a similar provision in relation to previous findings in matrimonial proceedings of adultery or paternity - the adultery or paternity shall be treated as conclusively proved unless the contrary is proved. (Again, the standard, as with s11 convictions, is the civil standard of balance of probabilities.)

In criminal proceedings, where proof of guilt of a person (including the accused) is admissible because relevant to an issue in those criminal proceedings, then the conviction of that person can be proved under s74 Police and Criminal Evidence Act 1984, and he shall then be taken to have committed the offence unless the contrary is proved. A relevant issue in criminal proceedings for handling is whether the goods were stolen, which may be shown by proof under s74 of conviction of the thief. The Court of Appeal has stated that s74 should be used sparingly, particularly in the case of joint trials for eg conspiracy, and should not be used where the evidence implicates the accused: *R* v *Robertson & Golder* [1987] 3 All ER 231. Problems arise under s74(1) and (2) where two or more defendants have been jointly charged, and one or more pleads guilty, leaving the other pleading not guilty. If it is alleged that the remaining defendant was very closely linked with what are now previous convictions of the other people, the jury is likely to infer that this defendant is guilty also. In such cases, the judge could exclude the convictions under s78 Police and Criminal Evidence Act 1984, if the prosecution counsel intended to rely on the convictions of the other(s) not merely to prevent mystification of the jury, but as evidence of the guilt of the appellant - *R* v *Kempster* (1990) 90 Cr App R 14; *R* v *Mattison* [1990] Crim LR 117. Where a person has a legal burden of disproving the commission of an offence by virtue of s74, the standard is the civil one only.

11.3 Analysis of questions

Opinion evidence tends to appear as part of an examination question, usually one issue of several in a problem question which will often deal also with hearsay statements of fact. Given the emergence of hypnosis, lie-detectors, truth drugs in forensic science, opinion is an area which could well expand, and become more complex and thus more 'exam-worthy'.

11.4 Questions

Question 1

Potbelly is charged with causing the death of Cleopatra by reckless driving.

The driver of the car which caused Cleopatra's death did not stop and Potbelly's defence is an alibi.

Advise on the admissibility of the following:

a) PC Bojak says he got to the scene to find Cleopatra lying on the road, and she said, 'It was a red Ferrari ... doing eighty.' She then died. Potbelly has a red Ferrari.

b) PC Bodie says he was at an identification parade when Doyle identified Potbelly as the driver but Doyle has now gone abroad.

c) Evidence of a psychiatrist, Quincy, who has examined Potbelly, that Potbelly is highly disturbed, an individual who is capable of behaving in a manner calculated to injure people around him.

d) A 'parking ticket' issued by a traffic warden to the owner of a Ferrari bearing the same number as Potbelly's car. The ticket had been found near the scene of the accident.

Adapted from University of London LLB Examination
(for External Students) Evidence June 1983 Q6

Skeleton solution

a)
- Hearsay - dying declaration - res gestae.
- Non-expert evidence as to speed.

b)
- Previous inconsistent statement - exception with identification.
- Hearsay rule - exception to rule.

c)
- Expert opinion evidence - admissibility - competence of jury to decide for itself.

d)
- Inadmissible hearsay - *Rice* versus *Lydon* - traffic warden as witness in court.

Suggested solution

a) In cases of murder or manslaughter, a dying declaration by the victim, under a settled and hopeless expectation of death, is admissible as to the cause and circumstances of the death (*R* v *Woodcock* (1789)). This exception to the rule against hearsay appears to be confined to the two offences mentioned (see *R* v *Hutchinson* (1822) and *R* v *Newton and Carpenter* (1859)) but arguably extends to cover all cases where the death is the subject of the charge and accordingly could apply in the instant case of causing death by reckless driving. Alternatively, it should be argued that Cleopatra's statement formed part of the res gestae. The judge must be satisfied that the statement was so clearly made in circumstances of spontaneity or involvement in the event that the possibility of concoction or fabrication can be disregarded (*Ratten* v *R* (1972); *R* v *Andrews* (1987)). If Cleopatra's statement is admissible, it is evidence of the truth of the facts contained in it. Part of her statement relates to the speed of the car. Non-expert opinion evidence as to speed is admissible being regarded as a matter within ordinary human experience, and in this case corroboration is not imperative, as the offence is not one of exceeding a speed limit.

b) At common law, former consistent statements are generally inadmissible. One recognised exception is evidence of prior identification admissible both by the identifying witness and by other witnesses who saw the identification being made (unless the evidence contradicts the evidence of the identifying witness). Thus in *R* v *Osbourne & Virtue* (1973) where the identifying witness was unable to remember having picked anyone out of the ID parade, the Court of Appeal held that a police officer, who saw the identification being made, could testify as to the person identified. The court held the same in the case of *R* v *McCay* (1990). On one view these cases should be confined to their facts. On a wider view it may be argued that since the evidence was not admitted as an exception to the rule on prior consistent statements (there was no evidence of identification in court with which the police officer's evidence could be consistent), it was admitted as an exception to the hearsay rule, ie to prove the truth of an out-of-court statement by conduct. Accepting this argument, PC Bodie may give evidence of Doyle's identification of Potbelly. However, in *Osbourne & Virtue*, the court made no reference to the hearsay problem, and the case has been much criticised on this basis. In *McCay*, the court seemed to believe it fell within the res gestae exception, but this goes against old authority. Furthermore, in *Sparks* v *R* (1964), Lord Morris held that there is no rule which permits the giving of hearsay evidence merely because it relates to identity, and that for hearsay to be admissible it must come within a recognised exception.

c) Expert opinion evidence is admissible on subjects demanding special knowledge and competence where in its absence the court would be unable to reach a proper conclusion (*Folkes* v *Chadd & Ors* (1782); also *R* v *Weightman* (1991)). However, such evidence is inadmissible if the lay opinion of the tribunal of fact is equally valid on the subject in question. Thus if Quincey's evidence is designed to show Potbelly intended the offence, and there is no question of mental illness, the matter is properly regarded to be within the competence of the jury (*R* v *Chard* (1971)). In *R* v *Toner* (1991) mental illness had been caused, it seems, by the hypoglycaemia, and so expert medical evidence was admissible as regards its effect on intent. By contrast, matters of insanity are regarded as proper subjects of expert opinion evidence. In the case of *Lowery* v *R* (1974) the Privy Council allowed one co-defendant to adduce psychiatric evidence to show that the other was of a character and disposition likely to have committed the offence. However, in that case, it was clear from all the circumstances that one or other or both of the co-defendants must have committed the offence. It is submitted that *Lowery* be confined to its own facts given the judgment in *R* v *Turner* (1975). In the instant, case, the evidence is not only inadmissible character evidence but also outside the boundaries of admissible expert opinion evidence.

d) The parking ticket is prima facie inadmissible hearsay, being a statement, in writing, made by a person outside court, and tendered for the purpose of proving the facts contained in it, ie that Potbelly's car was within the vicinity of the accident on the day in question (presumably). By analogy with *R* v *Rice* (1963), a much criticised case, it could be argued that the parking ticket, like the airline ticket bearing a traveller's name, is admissible evidence that a car with the same number as Potbelly's was within the vicinity of the accident. It is submitted that *Rice* should not be followed *R* v *Lydon* (1987). Although it was held in that case that the ticket did not speak its contents, the ticket was valueless as a piece of real evidence without regard to the truth of its contents. To allow a ticket in evidence so that an inference can be drawn as to the truth of its contents is, in effect, to do what is prohibited by the rule against hearsay. One practical solution, in the instant case, would be to call as a witness the traffic warden in question who could refresh his or her memory by reference to the parking ticket. It may be safely assumed that the statements in the ticket were made by the warden and were contemporaneous to the events to which they related.

Question 2

Caligula is charged with procuring Livilla, a severely subnormal woman, to have unlawful sexual intercourse with a number of men contrary to s9 of the Sexual Offences Act, knowing that she was severely subnormal. The Crown wish to put the following items of evidence at his trial:

a) A certificate of the Director of St Mary's Mental Health Institute that Livilla was an inmate of the Institute and that she was severely subnormal.

b) The evidence of her mother that Livilla was incapable of reading and writing and was subnormal.

c) The evidence of Phoebe, another subnormal girl, that she had been asked by Caligula to come to a party where she could 'earn lots of money from rich businessmen'.

Adapted from University of London LLB Examination
(for External Students) Evidence June 1984 Q5

Skeleton solution

a) Hearsay - documentary hearsay - s23 Criminal Justice Act 1988 - expert opinion.

b) Opinion evidence - outside experience of jury - subnormality - incompetence with reading and writing.

c) Competence - evidence of previous bad character of accused - probative value and prejudicial effect.

Suggested solution

a) It is for the prosecution to prove every element of the offence charged. In this case that includes proving that Livilla was subnormal. The certificate of the Director of St Mary's Mental Health Institute seems a sensible way of proving her subnormality, but since it is by no means certain that Caligula will accept the certificate the law requires the Director himself to give evidence in person. The hearsay rule will prima facie exclude the certificate but it could be admitted under the provisions of s23 Criminal Justice Act 1988, given that one of the requirements in s23(2) is satisfied, and the court gives leave, having considered the factors in s25. If the certificate contains elements of expert opinion as to severe subnormality, this is admissible as hearsay under s30, again with leave of the court, and subject to the conditions in s30(3).

b) Opinion evidence is only admissible in a criminal case if the jury is not in a position to decide an issue without hearing someone else's opinion - in other words if the matter on which opinion evidence is given is outside the normal experience and knowledge of the jury (see *R* v *Turner* (1975) and *R* v *Weightman* (1991), where the court would not allow in psychiatrist's evidence about a person's reaction to stress and strains of life, where there was no mental illness, although she may have an abnormal personality. But subnormality and abnormality are two different things).

The mother's opinion on the issue of subnormality is inadmissible. A lay witness is not allowed to give his or her opinion on an issue which is an issue for the jury. It is for the jury to decide whether Livilla is subnormal, not for her mother, and so her opinion on this matter is inadmissible. She is not an expert, as far as we know, and so her opinion is of no assistance and is inadmissible (*M'Naghten's Case* (1843)).

The mother's evidence of Livilla's inability to read and write would be admissible. This is not opinion evidence, but is evidence of facts perceived by the mother. We can assume that she had seen and knows her daughter well enough to know whether she can read and write and would not be giving an opinion, but would be stating a fact which she herself has seen. It is possible, though it seems unlikely, that the mother was only saying her daughter could not read and write because she was in the Institute and had not perceived these facts for herself. If that is the case, her evidence on the matter would be inadmissible.

The prosecution could try to rely on the case of *R* v *Davies* (1962) where the Courts Martial Appeal Court held that a witness to a motor accident could give evidence that in his opinion a driver had taken drink. Provided he also stated the grounds on which he comes to the conclusion, such a statement is quite proper. The Crown could argue that the mother could give evidence of what she perceived, using the term 'subnormal' to describe her daughter's behaviour. It is submitted though, that thc *Davies* case should not be stretched so as to allow such evidence, because the mother could give evidencc of what she saw of her daughter's condition without needing to use the word 'subnormal' to describe Livilla accurately and clearly.

c) The evidence of Phoebe will not be at all admissible unless the judge is satisfied that she is a competent witness. A person who is mentally ill may give evidence if the judge is satisfied that he or she understands the oath and is able to give evidence without the mental illness making it impossible for the witness to recall events (*R* v *Hill* (1851)). Even if Phoebe is competent, her evidence is unlikely to be ruled admissible. Evidence of previous misconduct of the accused is inadmissible as evidence of his guilt unless it is so probative of guilt that this probative value outweighs its prejudicial effect. This test, laid down in *Boardman* v *DPP* (1974), means that the evidence of Phoebe must prove Caligula's guilt on the charge with regard to Livilla, to such an extent that the jury will not be acting unfairly to the accused if they jump to the conclusion that because he made such an offer to Phoebe, so he must have done to Livilla.

   There seems to be nothing particularly strange about the offence charged which could be seen to make it strikingly similar to the offer made to Phoebe. Both 'victims' are mentally subnormal, but that of itself does not show such an underlying link or unity or system to make the evidence of Phoebe positively probative that the offence charged was committed. But following the case of *R* v *P* (1991) what matters more is what is in issue - identification, or the crime itself?

Question 3

Albert, Charles and Douglas are charged with armed robbery of a sub-post office and murder of the postmaster. Discuss the admissibility of the following:

a) medical evidence in the form of a psychiatrist's report in support of Albert's defence of diminished responsibility;

b) Charles having testified that he was unaware that Albert was armed, and had he known would not have been involved, psychiatric evidence that Charles is of a passive disposition and that psychopaths, such as Albert appears to be, are prone to violence and to lying;

c) evidence of Hinton, a priest, that Douglas is a regular churchgoer and a pillar of society who could not possibly commit any crime at all, let alone a grave crime of violence;

d) previous convictions of Charles and Douglas for armed robberies of sub-post offices.

Written by editor

Skeleton solution

- Expert opinion evidence; ultimate issue; hearsay - admissibility.
- Expert opinion; factual basis; pure hypothesis; competence of jury; s1(f)(iii) Criminal Evidence Act 1898.

- Character evidence - status of character witness - evidence of general reputation, and evidence in rebuttal at common law and under s1(f)(ii) Criminal Evidence Act 1898.
- Similar fact evidence.

Suggested solution

If Albert's plea is diminished responsibility, then he is admitting that he unlawfully killed the postmaster but running a defence which if successful will lead to his conviction for manslaughter rather than murder. The burden of proving diminished responsibility must be discharged by Albert - discharge of an evidential burden will not suffice (s2(2) Homicide Act 1957). As diminished responsibility bears on mental disorder of the accused, expert opinion evidence is admissible given that this is a matter not within the realm of the ordinary juryman's competence and experience (eg *R* v *Smith* (1979)). Given that the psychiatrist examined and questioned Albert and from that factual basis formed his opinion that Albert suffered from diminished responsibility, the evidence is admissible as expert opinion testimony of the psychiatrist (*R* v *Bradshaw* (1986)). Where the medical evidence with diminished responsibility is unequivocal and uncontradicted, the trial judge should direct the jury to accept it if there are no other circumstances to consider. Where, however, such other circumstances exist, the aforesaid medical evidence should be assessed in the light of those other circumstances - *R* v *Sanders* (1991) CA. If the underlying facts are not proved by admissible evidence - which can be percipient evidence of the psychiatrist or some other witness - then the opinion, formed on inadmissible hearsay rather than facts, would be inadmissible (*R* v *Bradshaw* and *R* v *Abadom* (1983)).

The Crown Court (Advance Notice of Expert Evidence) Rules 1987, issued under s81 Police and Criminal Evidence Act 1984, require reciprocal disclosure of expert evidence prior to a trial on indictment. Albert's counsel should therefore disclose to the prosecution, as soon as practicable after Albert's committal for trial (Rule 3), the expert evidence which the defence intend to adduce. Failure to comply is not fatal, but admissibility is then in the discretion of the trial judge (Rule 5). Given that Albert's counsel wishes to adduce a psychiatrist's report, although this is hearsay, it is now admissible subject to the Advance Notice Rules above, with leave of the court (s30 Criminal Justice Act 1988) if the psychiatrist is not to be called to give oral evidence. In deciding whether to grant leave to the report's being admitted in evidence without the psychiatrist attending as a witness, the court must have regard to factors such as the contents of the report and any unfairness to the accused (s30(3) CJA 1988).

On the facts of this murder trial, the diminished responsibility of Albert is going to be an 'ultimate issue'. The common law rule prohibiting opinion evidence on the ultimate issue has been repealed in civil cases (s3 Civil Evidence Act 1972), and it is considered that it no longer applies in criminal cases (*DPP* v *A & BC Chewing Gum* (1986)). Given the nature of the expert opinion evidence to be adduced, and its relevance to the ultimate issue, it is highly probable that the psychiatrist will have to attend and give oral testimony, being subjected to cross-examination. As he is a competent witness, he is compellable (*Harmony Shipping Co* v *Saudi Europe Line* (1979)).

The psychiatric evidence as to Charles's 'passive disposition' is of dubious admissibility, as such passivity (not bearing on mental disorder) is within the jury's sphere of competence and therefore expert evidence is unnecessary in helping them to form their own opinion (*R* v *Turner* (1975) and *R* v *Weightman* (1991). The opinion as to Albert's propensity to violence and mendacity appears to be pure hypothesis from the wording of the question - 'such as Albert appears to be' etc - and as such would be inadmissible. If there is factual evidence of Albert's psychopathy, then expert opinion evidence *may* be admissible as to the common traits of psychopaths, but contradictory opinion evidence could then be adduced on what in itself is, or should not be, an issue lending itself to expert opinion evidence. In *Lowery* v *R* (1974) opinion evidence of an expert was admitted apparently to tend to prove the veracity of one of two co-accused, but the decision was criticised in *Turner*, and the admissibility of the opinion of the psychiatrist in the case now under review appears to be less supportable than that in *Lowery*.

Charles's testimony would tend to undermine a defence by Albert of alibi or that he was unarmed etc, thereby causing Charles to lose his shield under s1(f)(iii) CEA 1898 and giving Albert's counsel the right to cross-examine Charles on his previous convictions (*Murdoch* v *Taylor* (1965)). But, given that Albert's defence is in essence that he was present, committed homicide with mens rea for murder but because of his arrested or retarded development etc ought to be convicted of manslaughter, Charles's testimony does not undermine that defence, is not favourable to the prosecution and is not therefore 'evidence against any other person charged in the same proceedings'. Therefore Charles's evidence should not result in his previous convictions being revealed in cross-examination.

Douglas's calling a character witness to state what Hinton said amounts to his adducing evidence of his good character, not just of general reputation but of specific acts and disposition. Such evidence is strictly inadmissible (*R* v *Rowton* (1865); *R* v *Redgrave* (1981)). However, if evidence of good character is adduced on behalf of the accused, then the prosecution may lead evidence of bad character in rebuttal but this must be merely evidence of bad reputation, not specific acts or convictions or disposition etc. However, if Douglas elects to testify after Hinton has given this evidence, then with leave of the judge the prosecutor may cross-examine Douglas on his previous convictions, not to prove his guilt but to attack his credibility (s1(f)(ii) Criminal Evidence Act 1898).

In the case of both Charles and Douglas, their previous armed robberies may bear such a striking similarity to the one which is the subject of the instant charge that the circumstances of those robberies (not purely the previous convictions) may be given in evidence by the prosecutor to prove their guilt, under the doctrine of similar fact evidence (*DPP* v *Boardman* (1975)). Whether there is such a similarity or any other kind of probative relationship is a question of law for the judge who must weigh the probative value against the prejudicial effect.

12 PUBLIC POLICY

12.1 Introduction

12.2 Key points

12.3 Analysis of questions

12.4 Questions

12.1 Introduction

There have been substantial developments in the past decade in this area of evidence, with the courts having to resolve the conflict between the public interest in the proper administration of justice and the public, or national, interest in safeguarding national security and related matters of state and the efficient functioning of the public service. Where the former interest prevails, then there will be full disclosure of all relevant evidence (eg at pre-trial discovery stage of civil litigation). Where the latter prevails, then the protected or sensitive information will be withheld from the court (ie excluded because of 'public interest immunity').

12.2 Key points

a) *Historical background and development*

In *Duncan* v *Cammell Laird* [1942] AC 624 the House of Lords held that the jury had no discretion to order disclosure of documents when a Minister certified that they should be withheld in the interests of national security or the efficient functioning of the public service. The decision was followed despite criticism of the rigidity of the rule and the fact that exclusion on the grounds of public interest immunity was in the hands of the Executive and could easily be abused. In *Conway* v *Rimmer* [1968] AC 910 the House of Lords reviewed its earlier decision and decided that where there is a claim of public interest immunity, the decision whether to exclude is ultimately that of the judiciary, not the executive. There were some reservations as to the position of 'class' documents, eg Cabinet papers, but in subsequent cases it was stated that, whatever the nature of the document, whatever the reason given for non-disclosure, the judges (if appropriate after private scrutiny of the documents) will decide whether public interest immunity shall obtain: *Burmah Oil* v *Bank of England* [1980] AC 1090; *Air Canada* v *Secretary of State for Trade (No 2)* [1983] 2 AC 394.

b) *Extent of public interest immunity*

The extent of non-disclosure on the grounds of public interest immunity was discussed at length, and with some conflicting opinions, in *D* v *NSPCC* [1978] AC 171, where their Lordships accepted that the list of categories of public interest is not closed - but its development will be by extending its ambit by reference to pre-existing, judicially recognised, public interests. In that case their Lordships, by reference to the long-established public interest in excluding the identity of police informers, extended the scope of public interest immunity to the NSPCC in regard to its efficient functioning being dependent, like the police, on information imparted in confidence.

i) Existing, recognised, categories

These can be summarised as:

- State security

  Duncan v *Cammell Laird* exemplifies this.

- International relations

  The public policy element figures strongly in sensitive areas of English foreign policy, such as territorial disputes with other countries: *Buttes Gas* v *Hammer (No 3)* [1981] 1 QB 223.

- Detection and prevention of crime

  The public interest in withholding evidence which would identify police informants has been recognised since, at the latest, 1794 (*R* v *Hardy*, 24 State Trials 199). (Consider the analogy in *D* v *NSPCC*.) The public interest is obviously not only in the detection of crime but also in its prevention, consequently it is not only the identity of informants which will be withheld but also methods used by police such as surveillance tactics and locations used, and sophisticated forensic methodology *R* v *Rankine* [1986] 2 All ER 566; *R* v *Brown and Daley* (1988) 87 Cr App R 52; *R* v *Johnson* [1989] 1 All ER 121. Where disclosure is requested by the defence to assist in establishing the innocence of the accused, then the judge must consider whether non-disclosure on this ground of public interest immunity will lead to injustice to the accused: cf *R* v *Brown and Daley* and *R* v *Johnson* supra. In the recent case of *R* v *Agar* (1990) 90 Cr App R 318, the defence counsel argued that the police informant had caused the defendant to arrive whilst they were searching the informant's house for drugs, and that the drugs were planted on the defendant by the police. On appeal, it was held that although there was a clear and well-established rule that the identity of police informants should be kept secret, there was even stronger public interest here in allowing the appellant to put forward a tenable case in its best light.

- Efficient functioning of public service

  This extends not just to government departments, but to the police, to local government and to other bodies (eg NSPCC - *D* v *NSPCC* above; Gaming Board - *Rogers* v *Secretary of State* [1973] AC 388). In the case of the police, in the recent case of *Sharples* v *Halford* (1991) The

Times 9 October, it was held that police disciplinary files were the subject of public interest immunity. The trend is to restrict this head of public interest immunity to bodies performing a statutory function, and to restrain a proliferation of agencies claiming the immunity merely on the grounds of confidentiality or candour: *Science Research Council* v *Nassé* [1980] AC 1028, per Lord Scarman at p1087.

- Confidentiality

Confidentiality of some communication or relationship is not in itself a reason for non-disclosure, but it is often a vital factor in a claim of public interest immunity. Often where confidentiality in respect of sources of information is an issue, there is a blurring of the distinction between public policy and private privilege (see chapter 13). In *British Steel Corporation* v *Granada TV* [1982] AC 1096 the House of Lords recognised that in deciding whether to order the disclosure of the identity of an informant and thus to induce a breach of confidentiality, the courts do have some discretion - but obviously it is very much the function of the person receiving the information which is the crucial factor, eg a police officer as opposed to a journalist.

In the recent case of *Brown* v *Matthews* [1990] 2 All ER 155, the Court of Appeal held that a court welfare report did not fall within that category of documents which in the public interest could not be disclosed except for the purposes for which it came into existence. Instead, the court may give leave for the report to be used in other proceedings if, after evaluating and balancing the confidentiality of the report against the need for the contents of the report to be put into evidence if there was to be a fair trial, the court decided that in this particular case, the interests of justice required the reports to be released. In other words, the Court Welfare Officer's report could be disclosed at the discretion of the court which had ordered the report.

It was also held in the case of *W* v *Edgell* [1990] 2 WLR 471, that a psychiatrist's report was not protected against disclosure.

Although a journalist who refuses to disclose his source of information is often said to be claiming journalistic, or media, privilege, the use of the word 'privilege' is almost as misleading as when public interest immunity was referred to as 'Crown privilege'. However, one distinction made between public policy and private privilege is that of waiver. If a matter is accepted as being the subject of public interest immunity, then it is not permissible for a witness to waive that 'right' to withhold evidence; but in the realm of privilege a witness may claim the privilege or may decide to waive the privilege and apprise the court of the evidence or the source of the information. In the case of journalistic privilege, s10 Contempt of Court Act 1981, governs the protection from disclosure of sources of information; on balance, this is an area of privilege rather than of public interest immunity, so will be dealt with in the next Chapter.

12.3 Analysis of questions

Questions on public policy reasons for non-disclosure, ie public interest immunity, do not appear with unfailing regularity; when they do appear they tend to be essay questions and quite often combined with private privilege, or occasionally some other area of evidence. The essay questions require a sound knowledge, plus, importantly, a critical awareness of the underlying principles and conflicts; but given that, they are often more 'self-contained' and give the knowledgeable student a better opportunity to achieve a good mark, than questions in many other more complex areas of Evidence.

12.4 Questions

Question 1

Examine critically the working of the exclusionary rule sometimes called 'Public Interest Privilege', and comment on why it was formerly called 'Crown Privilege'.

University of London LLB Examination
(for External Students) Evidence June 1983 Q8

Skeleton solution

- Crown privilege - definition - scope.
- Balance to be held by judge - Minister's certificate.
- Identity of informants - criminal cases - extension to other cases.

Suggested solution

Crown privilege may be defined as having been the absolute right of the Crown to object to producing documents in court on the ground that it would be against the public interest to do so. The claim, made in an affidavit by the Minister of the Crown, would prevent the court from looking at those documents - see *Duncan* v *Cammell Laird* (1942). Today, the phrase 'Crown Privilege' is regarded as a misleading misnomer (see Lord Simon in *R* v *Lewes JJ* (1973)) and although a Minister of the Crown is often the most appropriate person to assert the public interest, it is open to any interested person to raise the question, and the trial judge himself may raise it. Lord Simon, in *D* v *NSPCC* (1978) held that the 'state' could not be restricted to the Crown and the departments of central government, but included the whole organisation of the body politic for supreme civil rule and government. Formerly it was considered that only organs of central government could assert the privilege.

It is vital, if a party to litigation claims that certain documents are privileged from disclosure on the grounds of public policy, that the court hold the balance between that public interest and the public interest in the disclosure of the documents to ensure the proper administration of justice. This test was adopted in *Conway* v *Rimmer* (1968), the House of Lords rejecting their previous ruling in *Duncan* v *Cammell Laird* that the Minister's certificate was conclusive and binding on the court. Albeit that the Minister is more competent, compared to the court, in assessing the public interest, this represented a welcome reform, ending the possibility of ministerial misuse of power by requests for immunity in cases where the alleged public interest was barely discernible yet non-disclosure of the documents could have resulted in a partial or complete denial of justice to the parties (*Broome* v *Broome* (1955); *Gain* v *Gain* (1961); *Ellis* v *Home Office* (1953)). Thus the judge may now question ministerial assertions that documents be withheld and may balance against this the importance of the documents to the litigation and justice, and the importance of the litigation to the parties, provided that the party seeking disclosure has shown that the information is likely to help his own case or damage his adversary's in the sense that there is a reasonable probability, not a mere speculative belief, that it will do so (*Air Canada* v *Secretary of State for Trade (No 2)* (1983)). That this method of judging a claim of privilege on the grounds of public policy represents a fair balance between the competing public interests may be shown by contrasting *Burmah Oil* v *Bank of England* (1979) and *Williams* v *Home Office* (1981). In the former case, an inspection of documents relating to the formulation of government economic policy, it was held that they contained nothing of sufficient evidential value to order their disclosure. By contrast, in *Williams*, a case involving the rights of the citizen and the liberty of the subject, on inspection of the documents, disclosure was ordered. The public interest in justice prevailed over the fact that disclosure could lead to ill-informed criticism of the Home Office.

By contrast with the grounds of public policy privilege discussed above, there is a more inflexible rule in relation to information for the detection of crime. The rule, subject to few exceptions, is that in public prosecutions, and in civil proceedings arising from them, no questions may be asked and no evidence given, which would reveal the identity of an informant whose information led to the prosecution (*Marks* v *Beyfus* (1890)). The realistic and sensible basis for this rule is the danger that if disclosure were permitted, informants would be deterred from coming forward to help the police for fear of reprisal. This rule has been extended, by way of analogy, to persons supplying information to other bodies (*R* v *Lewes JJ*; *D* v *NSPCC*; *Alfred Crompton Amusement Machines Ltd* v *Customs and Excise Commissioners* (1974)). In each of these cases, the decision against disclosure was based upon the danger of the sources drying up (which would in turn lead to an impairment of the efficiency of those parts of the public service in question, ie, the Gaming Board, the NSPCC and the Inland Revenue). The fact that such information is given in confidence is not per se sufficient to create public interest immunity, but it is a material factor to be taken into account in deciding the privilege claim. It is for this reason that the above cases may be legitimately reconciled with the other confidentially cases (eg *Attorney-General* v *Mulholland* (1963); *Science Research Council* v *Nassé* (1979); *BSC* v *Granada Television Ltd* (1980)). In the case of *R* v *Agar* (1990) it was made clear, however, that the public interest in keeping the identity of an informant a secret had to be balanced against the public interest in seeing that a defendant is well able to defend his case in criminal proceedings. It has become forcefully argued that the immunity of the press from revealing its sources of information should be regarded as being in the public interest as much as, for example, the efficient functioning of the public service, and that the freedom of the press depends upon immunity. By analogy to *Marks* v *Beyfus* it is argued that disclosure would deter informants from providing journalists with the information necessary to a free press (see Lord Salmon, dissenting, in *BSC* v *Granada*).

Question 2

'Exclusion of evidence on the ground of public policy as a matter of law has only one thing in common with the exclusion of evidence which is illegally obtained as a matter of discretion: the absence of any coherent policy rationale underlying the case law.'

Discuss.

University of London LLB Examination
(for External Students) Evidence June 1987 Q3

Skeleton solution

- Categories of case covered by public policy - state secrets - minor state secrets, identity of police informants, identity of other informants.
- Exclusion of evidence under s78 Police and Criminal Evidence Act 1984 - disciplinary and reliability approach of courts.
- Public interest in protection of civil liberties.

Suggested solution

The exclusion of evidence on the ground of public policy is sometimes referred to as Crown privilege, public interest privilege or public interest immunity. Evidence will be excluded on grounds of public policy as a matter of law where it is deemed not to be in the public interest to allow it to be given. The privilege arises in relation to four different types or sources of information: (a) state secrets; (b) minor state interests; (c) identity of informants to the police; and (d) identity of other informants.

State secrets comprise, in general terms, matters involving the armed forces and the intelligence services. The courts have always been reluctant to allow any information to be given where the government has indicated that it should be kept secret. The policy behind this is that it is not for the courts but for government to take decisions about defence of the realm, which includes decisions about how much information should be made public of military and intelligence operations. The equation of the public interest with the interests of the government of the day is always criticised by the party of opposition, but once that party takes over in government it is quite content to use the equation in its own interest.

There are certain classes of document which the courts used to say are always privileged, for example cabinet minutes (*Conway* v *Rimmer* (1968)), but the tendency today is to examine each claim for immunity on its merits *Burmah Oil Co* v *Bank of England* (1980)). Where state secrets are involved the courts will not allow their repetition in court save in the most exceptional circumstances (*Burmah Oil Co* v *Bank of England*; *Air Canada* v *Secretary of State for Trade (No 2)* (1983)). The court will have received a certificate from a minister or senior civil servant setting out the reason why immunity is claimed and will hear the other party's outline reasons why the document should be disclosed and a balance must be struck. Either the nature of the information or its source will be a good enough reason for non-disclosure in a state-secrets case, or if the court is in some doubt about whether the information really is a secret then it may have a look at the document to see for itself, although it is reluctant to use this right.

The protection of minor state interests can be cited as a reason for withholding documents and these include matters of the internal operation of government departments. In such cases the court will rarely say that the information in the documents is of a type which should not be disclosed but may justify immunity by citing the type of document as being a type which should not be disclosed. It is usually where third parties have given the information in confidence that the court will uphold a claim to immunity (*Alfred Crompton Amusement Machines Ltd* v *Customs and Excise Commissioners* (1974)), but in the absence of involvement of innocent third parties there is no reluctance to order disclosure even where the government has said it is contrary to the public interest, provided that the nature of the document or of the information is such that the court is able to say that it cannot harm the nation's interests to order disclosure. There are cases which suggest that many internal government reports can be withheld (*Re Joseph Hargreaves* (1900); *Ellis* v *Home Office* (1953); *Broome* v *Broome* (1955)) but their authority is doubted by Cross, and since the court will now always balance the public interest in keeping them secret against the public interest in allowing a party full access to documents he needs in litigation (*Ellis* v *Home Office*), they cannot be treated as authoritative.

It is a cardinal rule that the police do not have to disclose the identity of informants. This rule has stood since well before *Marks* v *Beyfus* (1890) and cannot be challenged now, save in the most exceptional circumstances, for example in the case of *R* v *Agar* (1990). Recently the Court of Appeal has shown on a further three occasions that it is prepared to investigate whether the withholding of the informant's identity is in the public interest (*Neilson* v *Laugharne* (1981); *Hehir* v *Commissioner of Police for the Metropolis* (1982); *Peach* v *Commissioner of Police for the Metropolis* (1986)).

Two reasons have been given for this rule, firstly that sources of information may dry up and secondly that information given to the police is given in confidence and the confidence should be respected. There is, it seems, little evidence to support the first reason; but the second is persuasive. Today the court will attempt to balance the public interests cited above, but when deciding the strength of the public interest in keeping the information secret it will take into account the desirability of retaining confidence.

Informing public bodies other than the police of certain types of wrongdoing is likely to be done in confidence in the same way as information give to the police is given in confidence, but the rule appears to be that there can be no privilege arising out of confidentiality alone. Public interest immunity can arise where the recipient of the information has a statutory function to perform, but not otherwise (*D* v *NSPCC* (1978)). The apparent justification is that the scope of public interest immunity must be limited and that there can be no public interest in maintaining secrecy unless the purpose of giving the information is to start investigations.

It is clear that the courts will always try to balance the public interest in keeping matters secret against the public interest in allowing a litigant access to all information which he may need in litigation. The different types of information and the different sources from which it may come mean that different factors will be weighed when the balancing operation is done. In the recent case of ***Brown*** v *Matthews* (1990), the public interest in keeping a court welfare report secret was said to have to be weighed against the need for the contents of the report to be put into evidence if there was to be a fair trial. Nevertheless, it is also clear that until 1979 the balancing operation was not universally recognised and there are many cases giving different reasons for upholding or rejecting a claim of public interest immunity.

The exclusion of evidence obtained by illegal means is a matter for the discretion of the court under s78 of the Police and Criminal Evidence Act 1984. Prior to the enactment of that statutory discretion the courts had built up a complex body of law from which it was clear that a discretion existed in some circumstances but far from clear what those circumstances were. The rationale lying behind the exclusion of interest obtained by illegal means has never been clearly explained. In recent cases on the exclusionary discretion under s78, the accent has been on the 'unfairness' of admitting evidence improperly obtained, but the courts vacillate between a 'disciplinary' and 'reliability' approach (*R* v *Mason* (1987); *R* v *Alladice* (1987); *DPP* v *Marshall* (1988) and *R* v *Quinn* (1990)). Illegally, or improperly, obtained evidence (other than confessions) is admissible under English law; whether it will be excluded in any particular case depends on whether admissibility would result in unfairness, and/or whether the prejudicial effect of the evidence outweighs its probative value - but this is a matter of discretion rather than law.

One thing which is now clear about the exclusion of evidence obtained illegally is that the courts adopt the balancing operation applicable to claims of public interest immunity; they balance the public interest in using relevant probative evidence against the public interest in the protection of civil liberties (*R* v *Samuel* (1988)). Indeed it is important to note that once evidence has been obtained illegally, there is a discretion and not a duty to exclude it, and this, of course, differs from the position in true cases of public interest immunity where exclusion is a matter of law not discretion once the criteria for exclusion have been laid down.

Question 3

Annie was charged with neglecting her son, Tim, aged six, and ill-treating her daughter, Eliza, aged nine, contrary to s1 Children and Young Persons Act 1933. She has previous convictions for assaults on police, theft, forgery, and child neglect.

She alleged that the testimony of Snoopie, an NSPCC officer, contained fabrications, and testified that on the days he specified, she was in the house with her children, but her twin sister who was visiting came home late at night, and let herself in with the key Annie had lent her. She objected to the admissibility of statements made to the

NSPCC by unidentified informants, but the magistrates overruled her objection. She objected also to the evidence of Doogood, a social worker, that her children had been the subject of attention by many agencies and that in Doogood's opinion the condition of Tim and Eliza was caused by Annie's failure to exercise proper care. Annie demanded to see the file on herself and her family but this was not permitted. The chairman of the magistrates allowed cross-examination on all her previous convictions, and allowed without question both Tim and Eliza to give evidence for the prosecution.

Annie wishes to appeal against conviction and seeks your advice.

Advise her.

Written by editor

Skeleton solution

- Apparently many irregularities in the trial, but more details required.
- Admissibility of statements; hearsay and exceptions; public interest immunity.
- Doogood - evidence of fact; expert opinion evidence; hearsay; file contents - public policy.
- Evidence of character - s1(f)(ii) Criminal Evidence Act 1898.
- Competence of witnesses; children - testing; corroboration; s34 Criminal Justice Act 1988.

Suggested solution

Apparently there were irregularities at Annie's trial, but how serious and how many depends on facts which are not given. Annie has a right of appeal to the Crown Court from the decision in the Magistrates' Court - she obviously did not plead guilty - but the question is what chance of success does she have when there is a re-hearing (without a jury).

Snoopie gives direct testimony, being a percipient witness apparently alleging that he saw Annie on specified dates entering her house late at night. Given Annie's testimony there is a dispute over visual identification and the guidelines in *R* v *Turnbull* (1977), modified to suit summary trial, ought to have been followed; it is submitted that whether or not the case against Annie depends substantially on this identification evidence, and whether or not Snoopie knew Annie before, identification evidence must always be treated with some circumspection. Where it is disputed, then if it is in relation to an element of the offence, the prosecution must discharge the legal burden of proof to the criminal standard. More detail is required in Annie's case, to determine the relevance of this aspect of Snoopie's evidence, and sequentially to determine whether the court gave undue weight to it (or, conversely, insufficient attention to relevant, *Turnbull*, considerations and to Annie's contradiction).

Annie's testifying that Snoopie fabricated evidence (not that he mistook her sister for her, but that he lied) is without doubt an imputation cast on the character of a prosecution witness, therefore Annie lost her shield protecting her from disclosure to the court of her previous convictions (s1(f)(ii) Criminal Evidence Act 1898). Even if her allegation of fabrication was a necessary part of her defence, the shield is lost (*Selvey* v *DPP* (1970)). However, the prosecutor needs leave of the court to cross-examine Annie on her bad character, and any convictions revealed go to credit not to guilt. Although the magistrates perform the functions of both judge and jury, they must attempt to keep the two separate. If leave were not requested by the prosecutor, or if the magistrates gave 'carte blanche' without any consideration of the convictions, or if at any stage they alluded to the convictions as being evidence of Annie's guilt on the instant charges, then there is good evidence of irregularities and unfairness.

The statements of informants given in evidence amounts to hearsay, and inadmissible hearsay unless coming within a recognised category where the general exclusionary rule does not apply. Section 23 of the Criminal Justice Act 1988 provides for the admissibility of statements of fact as first-hand hearsay, provided direct oral evidence would have been admissible (s23(1) Criminal Justice Act 1988). However this admissibility is subject to one of the stipulated requirements such as death or incapacity of the maker of the statement (s23(2)(a)-(c) and s23(3) CJA 1988), and if so admissible, is subject to the discretion to exclude (s25(1) CJA 1988) which ought to be exercised if there is a likelihood of unfairness to the accused (s25(2)(d) CJA 1988). If the statements made by the informants are tendered by the prosecution, then the court's decision as to whether to admit them as hearsay is governed by the sections of the Criminal Justice Act 1988 just referred to, and if the requirements are not met the documentary hearsay is inadmissible; even if strictly admissible they may, and arguably *ought* to be excluded given the resultant unlikelihood of a fair trail. Had the information given in the statements led Snoopie to perceive facts of which he gave direct oral testimony, then although the *fact* of the statements *may* be referred to by him, the identities of the makers will not be disclosed, as they would be subject to public interest immunity (*D* v *NSPCC* (1978)), in that the overriding public interest is in the proper functioning of the NSPCC in performing its statutory duties rather than in 'open justice'. However a difficult situation arises where an accused insists on disclosure of material subject to public interest immunity in order to establish innocence (*R* v *Rankine* (1986); *R* v *Hennessey* (1978); *R* v *Hallett* (1986); *R* v *Agar* (1990)).

On appeal, the issue is going to be whether the magistrates averted their minds to the admissibility of this hearsay evidence, and if it was admissible whether they had regard to the relevant factors before deciding not to exercise their discretion to exclude.

Doogood's evidence as to the involvement of many agencies is very probably hearsay unless, (which is highly unlikely) Doogood is asserting that he was a percipient witness of facts perceived also by those agencies. Doogood may be an expert on child care, but it is debatable whether expert opinion evidence should have been admitted, given that from factual evidence as to the condition of Tim and Eliza and their being in the care of Annie throughout, the magistrates are competent to make the proper inferences by drawing on their own experience as lay persons (*R* v *Turner* (1975)). However, if the magistrates accept that the opinion evidence of an expert is necessary and therefore admissible, and they accept Doogood as an expert, then even though his opinion evidence is on the 'ultimate issue', it is nevertheless admissible (s3(1) Civil Evidence Act 1972). But the *facts* on which Doogood's opinion is based must be proved by admissible evidence, which may be evidence as to facts by Doogood personally or by other witnesses (*R* v *Abadom* (1983); *R* v *Mason* (1911)). If the magistrates allowed the factual basis to be established by inadmissible hearsay from Doogood, then the opinion based on that hearsay is pure hypothesis and thus inadmissible.

The file on Annie, if it were a case file kept by the Social Services Department of the local authority, is protected from disclosure on grounds of public interest immunity (*Gaskin* v *Liverpool City Council* (1980); *Re D (Infants)* (1970)) because the local authority performs a public function and public policy decrees that its proper functioning should not be impaired. If the case file is that of a voluntary agency, then there is a greater conflict between the proper administration of justice and the confidential nature of the file's contents. If Annie had a valid reason for information in the file to be disclosed to the court, this would open the issue of the development of the concept of public interest immunity, and whether the list of categories should be extended, given that a confidential relationship is not in itself a reason for non-disclosure (*D* v *NSPCC* (1978)).

Both Tim's and Eliza's competence to give evidence will now be assumed, it seems, until the contrary is shown, and both will automatically give unsworn evidence - s52 Criminal Justice Act 1991. Their evidence does not require corroboration - s34(2) Criminal Justice Act 1988.

Question 4

'Confidentiality is not a separate head of privilege, but it may be a very material consideration to bear in mind when privilege is claimed on the ground of public interest.' (Lord Cross in *Alfred Crompton Amusement Machines Ltd* v *Commissioners of Customs and Excise (No 2)).*

Discuss.

University of London LLB Examination
(for External Students) Evidence June 1990 Q2

Skeleton solution

- Balance of interests with public interest immunity.
- 'High' grade to 'low' grade documents - confidentiality less relevant.
- Confidentiality more relevant with public agencies, and police informants.
- Journalistic privilege - s10 Contempt of Court Act 1981.

Suggested solution

There are three main situations in which evidence can be withheld on grounds of privilege. Broadly, they are first, where by giving the evidence a witness exposes himself to the possibility of criminal proceedings (the privilege against self-incrimination), second, evidence of communications between party to proceedings and his lawyer or by a third party with either (legal professional privilege) and third, privilege arising on grounds of public interest (public interest immunity).

Confidentiality does not therefore of itself feature as a basis for exclusion. That said, it is true that confidentiality plays a substantial role in excluding evidence on grounds of public interest. This role will now examined.

Until comparatively recent times, establishing a claim to privilege on grounds of public interest was a relatively simple business. The minister or other political head of the organ of State claiming a privilege would submit a certificate and the courts regarded that certificate as final. This approach was approved by the House of Lords in *Duncan* v *Cammell Laird* (1942). The approach changed with the subsequent decision of the House of Lords in *Conway* v *Rimmer* (1968). That case established that the minister's view of the public interest was not conclusive and that the courts have a residual power to decide where that interest lies. It is in the evaluation that confidentiality plays a leading, though not necessarily explicit, part.

The approach adopted depends upon the type of document for which immunity is claimed. It has become the practice since *Duncan* v *Cammell Laird* for a claim of public interest privilege to be made on a contents or class basis. In the former case, the claim is that the particular document in question should not be disclosed in the public interest. It is clear from *Conway* v *Rimmer* that such a claim is very unlikely to be interfered with by the courts. Accordingly, the basis of the claim is unlikely to be investigated though it is readily apparent that the underlying reason for the claim for privilege and the reason for upholding it is the requirement of confidentiality for highly sensitive documents. For a class claim (where a claim is made on the basis that the document falls within a class of documents which should be withheld from production in the public interest) the role of confidentiality is even more evident. For class claims relative to 'high grade' documents such as Cabinet papers, privilege is very likely, subject to inspection of the relevant documents by the court, to be upheld and the usual basis is the sensitive nature of the material and the consequent need for confidentiality. This much is clear from *Conway* v *Rimmer* and subsequent authorities including *Burmah Oil* v *Bank of England* (1980) and *Air Canada* v *Secretary of State for Trade (No 2)* (1983). On the other hand, for lower grade documents or routine reports, a class claim based on confidentiality arising from the assertion that officials would feel inhibited from expressing their views if they thought that the information was to be disclosed (the 'candour' principle) is unlikely to be successful. The House of Lords in *Conway* v *Rimmer* made this clear and the courts have since rejected such claims consistently if based on this premise.

There are, however, circumstances where confidentiality in respect of routine information will found a successful claim for privilege in the public interest. These arise where disclosure might result in the drying up of information on which a public agency depends for undertaking work in the public interest. The *Alfred Crompton* case (1974) referred to in the question and *D* v *NSPCC* (1978) are examples. In the latter case, an order for disclosure of the identity of the individual who supplied information to the NSPCC about alleged cruelty to a child was refused. The information was routine but if disclosed people would be dissuaded from volunteering information to the NSPCC. If that happened, the work of the NSPCC in protecting children, manifestly in the public interest, would be seriously impeded. Similar principles can be seen in exclusion of evidence of the identity of police informers which can also be claimed under public interest privilege. *Marks* v *Beyfus* (1890) is authority for that proposition. The principle has been extended in *R* v *Rankine* (1986) to premises from which police conduct surveillance, although *R* v *Johnson* (1989) makes clear that the need for confidentiality must be made out on the evidence; such evidence should include the attitude of the occupier of the premises to be identified. Disclosure may also be ordered if it is necessary to establish an accused's innocence - *R* v *Agar* (1990).

The final area of public interest which requires comment arises in the context of the role of confidentiality in journalistic information. This is now subject to statutory intervention in the form of s10 of the Contempt of Court Act 1981. Under that section, journalistic sources are provided with protection in the public interest unless it is established to the satisfaction of the court that disclosure is necessary in the interests of justice, national security or the prevention of disorder or crime. The requirement for confidentiality in the public interest is nowhere stated in the section, but it is clear from the common law which preceded it and from *Secretary of State for Defence* v *Guardian Newspapers* (1984) that the protection of journalistic information by reason of confidentiality in the public interest forms its basis. Indeed, that is perhaps obvious because in the absence of such protection sources might well be reluctant to come forward to the media and the public would thereby be deprived of information which may be a matter of legitimate concern to them.

13 PRIVILEGE

13.1 Introduction

13.2 Key points

13.3 Analysis of questions

13.4 Questions

13.1 Introduction

As with public policy in the previous chapter, privilege is an area where relevant evidence is capable of admissibility but is excluded (or may be excluded) by some extrinsic rule which denies the court the benefit of that evidence. One bald distinction between public interest immunity and privilege is that in the case of the latter the person in whom the privilege vests may waive it and thus allow the court to hear the evidence, whereas in the case of the former the decision as to disclosure of the evidence is for the court, not the witness or party. Further, evidence which is privileged may nevertheless be put before the court in some circumstances in secondary as opposed to primary form, but if evidence is the subject of public interest immunity, then the immunity cannot be circumvented by adducing secondary evidence. In this area the law is continually developing, particularly in regard to journalistic, or media, privilege.

13.2 Key points

There are four main heads under which privilege falls to be considered, ie self-incrimination privilege; legal professional privilege; 'without prejudice' communications; journalistic privilege. This fourth head highlights the blurring of the distinction between privilege and public policy which often occurs when there is a claim for non-disclosure of evidence. In all cases of privilege, however, what must be borne in mind is that although a witness is both competent and compellable, to testify does not mean to answer every question put - privilege may be claimed, and if claimed successfully no inferences may be drawn from the refusal to answer questions.

a) *Self-incrimination privilege*

Any witness may refuse to answer a question (in examination in chief or in cross-examination) if the answer would tend to expose him to a criminal charge, penalty or, in criminal proceedings only, a forfeiture. It is for the court to decide whether there is a likelihood of any such consequence: *BSC* v *Granada TV* [1981] AC 1096. Self incrimination includes incrimination of one's spouse, but whether it includes incrimination of one's employer, principal etc has not been decided: *RTZ Corporation* v *Westinghouse Electric Corporation* [1978] AC 547. Without doubt an out-of-court admission by a servant etc is not capable of amounting at common law to an admission against the interest of the employer: *Burr* v *Ware RDC* [1939] 2 All ER 688, therefore it would seem to follow that until there is some statutory intervention a servant cannot claim a right not to answer a question tending to incriminate his employer, because such a question should not be put - but this reasoning cannot be employed to agents of principals, directors of companies etc.

If a witness is wrongly compelled to answer a question where the answer tends to expose him to criminal proceedings, then the answer is treated as an inadmissible confession. The privilege is not available to an accused in respect of the charge he faces, whether the question be put in cross-examination during the trial or on the *voir dire* - but the accused who testifies can refuse to answer questions where the answer would tend to expose him to other criminal proceedings.

b) *Legal professional privilege*

This covers both communications between lawyer and client regarding legal advice, and communications between client and/or lawyer and other persons where the 'dominant purpose' is to seek advice, opinion etc preparatory to contemplated or pending legal proceedings. In *Ventouris* v *Mountain* (1991) The Independent 4 March the Court of Appeal held that legal professional privilege could not attach to original documents which did not come into existence for the purposes of the litigation, but were already in existence before litigation was contemplated or commenced.

i) Lawyer-client communications

These are privileged (the privilege is in the client, who may therefore waive it) whether or not proceedings are pending, provided the purpose was to obtain, or give legal advice. Other communications made between lawyer and client, although not specifically seeking or giving legal advice, are similarly protected from disclosure, given they are part of the ongoing relationship: *Balabel* v *Air-India* [1988] 2 All ER 246. The lawyer need not be a solicitor or barrister, ie could be an unqualified employee, or in matters relating to conveyancing could be a licensed conveyancer: Administration of Justice Act 1985 s33.

The privilege does not attach to communications made to assist the client to commit crimes or to defraud, whether or not the lawyer is aware of the client's motive for seeking advice: *R* v *Cox and Railton* (1884) 14 QBD 153. But a distinction must be drawn between communications made to facilitate, or assist in, commission of crime or tort giving rise to the instant proceedings (no privilege) and those which relate to other wrongdoing even though relevant in the instant proceedings: *R* v *Crown Court at Snaresbrook, ex parte DPP* [1988] 1 All ER 315. Also, for the purpose of s10 of the Police and Criminal Evidence Act 1984, if items are held for the furtherance of some criminal purpose it is irrelevant whether the person holding the items is aware of the criminal purpose or not: *Francis & Francis* v *Central Criminal Court* [1988] 3 All ER 775. No privilege

No privilege here

attaches, per *Cox and Railton*, supra. The definition of 'furthering a criminal purpose' is restricted to some extent so that it does not extend to every unlawful scheme; for example, it does not apply to a conveyance carried out without consideration designed to defeat creditors - *Re Konigsberg* [1989] 3 All ER 289. In order to determine whether documents fall within s10(2) Police and Criminal Evidence Act 1984, the court has the power to inspect the documents - *R* v *Governor of Pentonville Prison, ex parte Osman* [1989] 3 All ER 701.

Legal professional privilege will not usually apply to communications, otherwise privileged, the production of which can assist in the defence of an accused person: *R* v *Barton* [1973] 1 WLR 115. But the court must consider the conflicting interests of respecting legal professional confidences and promoting the proper administration of justice: *R* v *Ataou* [1988] 2 All ER 321.

Where privilege attaches to a communication it attaches to the original only. If the communication falls into the hands of a third party who makes a copy, or if an oral communication is overheard, then a witness may give that secondary evidence of the communication: *Calcraft* v *Guest* [1898] 1 QB 759; *R* v *Tompkins* (1977) 67 Cr App R 181.

Where the party in whom the privilege vests is aware of the fact that the other party intends to adduce secondary evidence he may seek an injunction restraining the disclosure of the privileged information, and it is immaterial whether the other party obtained the material by some unfair means or fortuitously: *Lord Ashburton* v *Pape* [1913] 2 Ch 469. *Guinness Peat Properties* v *Fitzroy Robinson* [1987] 2 All ER 716. The recent case of *Webster* v *James Chapman* [1989] 3 All ER 939 said that where protection of confidential information was sought the court was required to exercise its discretion by balancing the legitimate interests of the plaintiff in seeking to keep the confidential information suppressed, and the legitimate interests of the defendant in seeking to make use of it. In carrying out that balancing exercise the circumstances in which the information came into the hands of the defendant, the issues in the action, the relevance of the document and whether the document would in one way or another have to be disclosed, were all highly relevant. In *Derby & Co Ltd* v *Weldon (No 8)* [1990] 3 All ER 762, the court held that where privileged documents came into the hands of the other side, inadvertently, and the other side must have realised a mistake had been made, the court had the power to intervene and order the other side to return all copies of the privileged documents and to grant an injunction to stop them using the information contained in or derived from documents. An injunction is an equitable remedy and therefore discretionary; it has been held that where privileged documents were filched in the courtroom they could not be used: *ITC Film Distributors* v *Video Exchange* [1982] Ch 431. It has also been held that no injunction will be granted to restrain the prosecution from adducing secondary evidence of privileged communications which have inadvertently fallen into their possession: *Butler* v *Board of Trade* [1971] Ch 680.

The person in whom the privilege vests, ie the client, may waive the privilege; an express waiver results in the lawyer having to answer any questions put to him about the communications in question. Alternatively, the client may, when testifying, impliedly waive the privilege by giving evidence about the content of such communications.

The client may also impliedly waive privilege by including a privileged document in the list exchanged between parties. If this has happened, the court should then conduct a balancing exercise to see whether or not the other side should be allowed to use this document (*Webster* v *James Chapman* (above)); but, if the other side must have realised the mistake, the court should order the return of the document and grant an injunction to stop the use of the information (*Derby & Co Ltd* v *Weldon (No 8)* (above)).

ii) Communications with third parties

Similar principles apply to those applicable to lawyer-client communications. However, for privilege to attach, communications with third parties must have been made in contemplation of litigation, eg seeking expert's opinion. There may be several purposes to be served by lawyer or client communicating with a third party, but if the communication is to be privileged under this head, the *dominant* purpose must be preparation for anticipated litigation: *Waugh* v *British Railways Board* [1981] 1 QB 736; cf *Peach* v *Commissioner of Police for the Metropolis* [1986] 2 All ER 129.

c) *Without prejudice communications*

Because one of the major objectives of civil procedure is settlement without resort to litigation, parties to a prospective or potential civil suit, and their lawyers, must be able to negotiate and make offers of settlement or compromise without the fear of such communications being admitted in evidence against them - as admissions of liability - if the attempts at settlement fail and litigation ensues. To remove such fear of disclosure in court if negotiations break down, privilege attaches to such 'without prejudice' communications.

This privilege is in many respects more valuable than legal professional privilege:

i) it is a *joint* privilege of both the parties, and their lawyers;

ii) waiver must be by *both* parties to be effective;

iii) the communication cannot be proved by secondary evidence.

Communications do not necessarily have to be headed 'without prejudice' for the privilege to attach; conversely the phrase 'without prejudice' on a communication does not automatically vest privilege in it - ultimately any dispute as to privilege will be resolved by the court: *South Shropshire District Council* v *Amos* [1987] 1 All ER 340; *Buckinghamshire County Council* v *Moran* [1989] 3 WLR 152.

A privilege similar to that attaching to such 'without prejudice' communications attaches (by analogy) to communications made in the course of attempts at matrimonial reconciliation. These may be communications between the spouses, or communications between spouse and conciliator. The conciliator may be someone such as a marriage guidance counsellor, probation officer, priest, doctor or any other individual who is invited to assist in reconciliation: *Theodoropoulas* v *Theodoropoulas* [1964] P 311; *Mole* v *Mole* [1951] P 21 and see Lord Simon's statement regarding the public policy underlying this privilege in *D* v *NSPCC* [1978] AC 171 at p236.

d) *Journalistic privilege*

Sometimes dealt with as part of public interest immunity, but it may be waived by the journalist who decides to disclose his sources, therefore, although to some extent 'straddling' public policy and private privilege, it seems to be correctly placed in the latter area of non-disclosure.

A journalist may decline to answer questions which would result in disclosure of his source of information contained in a publication - but this privilege is not without restriction. There are conflicting interests, viz:

i) freedom of the press, and the public's right to know;

ii) interests of administration of justice; prevention of crime;

iii) efficient functioning of the press if sources are open to disclosure and therefore may dry up (drawing an analogy with police and their sources).

Section 10 of the Contempt of Court Act 1981 recognises that sources of information may be privileged, *unless* disclosure is necessary 'in the interests of justice or national security or for the prevention of disorder or crime'.

Where disclosure is sought, the burden of proving that it is necessary for one of the four specified reasons is on the party seeking such disclosure: *Secretary of State for Defence* v *Guardian Newspapers* [1984] 3 All ER 601. As regards the definition of 'necessary in the interests of justice', in the case of *X Ltd* v *Morgan-Grampian Ltd* [1990] 2 WLR 1000 the House of Lords said it should not just mean administration of justice in legal proceedings. It should mean that persons should be enabled to exercise important legal rights and to protect themselves from serious legal wrongs whether or not court proceedings will be necessary to do this. As regards 'prevention of crime' as a reason for disclosure of the source of information, the party seeking disclosure does not need to specify any particular crime which will be prevented, but merely satisfy the court that disclosure is necessary to prevent criminal activity generally - which substantially erodes the privilege: *Re an Inquiry under the Company Securities (Insider Dealing) Act 1985* [1988] 1 All ER 203. However, there must be sufficient evidence to satisfy the court that disclosure is *necessary* for the prevention of crime: *X* v *Y* [1988] 2 All

ER 648, otherwise, if the burden of proof is not discharged by the party seeking disclosure, the privilege of the journalist prevails.

13.3 Analysis of questions

Privilege tends to arise quite regularly, often in conjunction with public interest immunity or with documentary evidence, especially documentary hearsay. Occasionally essay questions are set dealing with some area of privilege, eg self-incrimination privilege, therefore requiring knowledge of the right to silence and inadmissible confessions, but very often it is the blurred distinction between privilege and public interest immunity which is the pivotal point of essay questions in this area.

13.4 Questions

Question 1

a) What relationship do the rules as to privilege have with the concepts of admissibility and compellability?

b) Discuss, with reference to decided cases, to what extent the English courts have been prepared to exclude evidence on the ground of public policy where State interests are *not* involved.

University of London LLB Examination
(for External Students) Evidence June 1986 Q3

Skeleton solution

a)
- Definition of privilege, compellability and admissibility.
- Reliance and admissibility.
- Different types of privilege - relation to admissibility.
- Compellability - waiver of privilege.

b)
- Privilege against self-incrimination - risk of criminal charges - risk of civil suit.
- Legal professional privilege - two types - definition.
- 'Without prejudice' communications.

Suggested solution

a) *Privilege, admissibility and compellability*

Evidence is privileged if it is prevented from being given for reasons of policy. Admissibility is the concept which allows a court to hear certain evidence, no evidence is allowed to be given which is inadmissible. A witness is compellable if he can be forced to give evidence. Compellability only arises in relation to witnesses, not in relation to other evidence.

The basic test for admissibility is that of relevance. If evidence helps or may help the case of a party to a trial, then it is prima facie admissible. There are few

English cases which have specifically decided the degree of relevance required in order that evidence be admissible, and this can be explained by the unwillingness of the Court of Appeal to offer an opinion on a matter which is primarily for the trial judge. All that can be said with conviction is that evidence may not be given which wastes the court's time by discussing issues which do not further the case of either party. Indeed, perhaps the most common exclusion of evidence on the ground of irrelevance arises where the proposed evidence is merely a repetition of previous evidence without anything new being added.

Relevance is a condition of admissibility, in that irrelevant evidence is always inadmissible (*Noor Mohamed* v *R* (1949)). But, it is not enough that evidence be relevant, because it will still be excluded if it falls foul of an exclusionary rule. The rules about privilege prevent relevant evidence being adduced if it is felt that public policy is better served by its exclusion. Privilege can be a public or a private matter. Private privilege allows a party to refuse to answer a relevant question, or refuse to supply a document or other relevant real evidence, where he would incriminate himself by so doing, or where any document concerned was expressed to be 'without prejudice' or was a communication from him to his legal advisers or from a third party to those legal advisers where the dominant purpose of the communication was to further current or contemplated litigation. The rules of private privilege are restricted in their scope, because it is only in rare instances that public policy would place the need to protect confidentiality above the need to allow relevant evidence to be adduced; after all, a privileged document could contain the vital evidence without which one party is unable to prove his case, and where that is so the effect of upholding a claim to privilege would be drastic. Public privilege (sometimes called public interest privilege, Crown privilege or public interest immunity) prevents evidence being called where the public interest in requiring confidentiality outweighs the public interest in requiring that a party to litigation should be able to call upon all relevant evidence in support of his case. The public interest most commonly requires confidentiality to be upheld where the evidence concerns either state secrets or the identity of informants.

Although there are various differences between private and public privilege, in relation to admissibility they have the same effect - a successful claim of privilege prevents otherwise admissible evidence being admitted.

Most witnesses who are competent are compellable. In other words, most witnesses who are allowed to give evidence if they wish to may also be forced to give evidence even if they do not wish to. There are some instances where a witness may give evidence if he or she wishes to, but cannot be forced so to do. For example, the wife or husband of the accused is competent to give evidence against him or her (s80(1)(a) Police and Criminal Evidence Act 1984, overturning the common law rule in *R* v *Deacon* (1973)), but she or he can only be forced to give that evidence in the limited circumstances set out in s80 of the Police and Criminal Evidence Act 1984. The position of a witness who is competent but not compellable is comparable to that of a person who is entitled to claim a private privilege. In both cases it is the decision of the witness himself, or herself, which determines whether the evidence will be given, because the competence of the witness means that he or she may testify and the fact that a claim to privilege may be successful does not mean that the claim must be made, the witness is always allowed to waive a private privilege (*Great Atlantic Insurance Co* v *Home Insurance Co* (1981)).

In the realm of public privilege, however, it is generally thought that no waiver of that privilege may be made because the privilege is not personal to either party in the case or to any one else (see *Cross on Evidence* (7th edition, 1990, p457). There are some dicta which would give limited scope for waiver of public privilege, but they do not go so far as to say that all public privileges may be waived (*Air Canada* v *Secretary of State for Trade (No 2)* (1983)). It is unlikely that the courts would hold that public privilege may be waived if that point ever needed to be specifically decided. The balancing act which must be undertaken between the public interest in maintaining secrecy and the public interest in allowing a party to use all available relevant evidence (*Burmah Oil* v *Bank of England* (1980)) could take into account that, say, a government department whose internal memorandum could be useful to a party does not object to the disclosure of that memorandum. But if this matter is considered relevant to the balancing exercise, the result would be that the memorandum would not be privileged, not that it is privileged but the privilege is waived. To this extent, admissibility and public privilege can be seen to be co-extensive, once evidence is covered by public privilege it is rendered inadmissible. The position in relation to public privilege, therefore, is comparable to that of a witness who is incompetent because the law prescribes inadmissibility to be the result of the privilege or incompetence, regardless of the wishes of the parties concerned.

b) *Private privilege*

It is in connection with public privilege that we talk most often of public policy having effect, but the decision to allow certain personal interests to be so important that evidence may be excluded in protection of them is itself a policy decision. The policy does not require the courts to decide whether the public interest is in having the particular item of evidence used in court; rather the policy lays down that in certain circumstances the party or witness concerned may decide that he does not wish his own position to be jeopardised by giving evidence. We have already noted that the courts recognise a claim to private privilege where the party or witness concerned is in danger of incriminating himself, or of disclosing matters which passed between a party to the litigation and his legal advisers (*Wheeler* v *Le Marchant* (1881)), or of disclosing matters which passed between a third party and the legal advisers of a party to the action where the dominant purpose of that communication was to further current or contemplated litigation (*Waugh* v *British Railways Board* (1980)).

The privilege against self-incrimination manifests itself in many ways, not all of which are usually stated to be examples of privilege. The defendant in a criminal case does not have a privilege against self-incrimination as regards the charges which he is currently facing (s1(e) Criminal Evidence Act 1898), so if he gives evidence he will be required to answer a question which suggests his guilt; but the accused always has the choice of not giving evidence at all - he cannot be forced to give evidence if, for example, he knows that he would have to admit his guilt in order not to commit perjury (s1(a) Criminal Evidence Act 1898 makes the accused competent in his own favour, but nothing makes him compellable). In this way public policy allows the accused to protect himself from the danger of self-incrimination. Any other witness may always refuse to answer a question which would tend to leave him open to a reasonable possibility of facing criminal charges (*Rio Tinto Zinc* v *Westinghouse Electric Corporation* (1978)) or (if he is a witness in a criminal case) to forfeiture (this no longer applies in civil cases, since the enactment of the Civil Evidence Act 1968 ss14 and 16). This privilege does not extend to cases where the witness would leave himself open to a civil action if he answered the question; in such cases he must answer and hope that the civil proceedings are not taken (Witnesses Act 1806 - his admission would be admissible against him in subsequent civil proceedings, by virtue of s9 of the Civil Evidence Act 1968). Again, it is not enough that there is a chance of criminal proceedings being taken, those proceedings must be a reasonable possibility. For example in *R* v *Boyes* (1861) a witness who had been granted a pardon following his conviction unsuccessfully claimed privilege in relation to the offence for which he had been pardoned. He argued that he was still open to impeachment, but it was held that this was such a remote possibility that it did not justify his refusal to answer the question. The privilege against self-incrimination is personal to the witness and may be waived by him. It should be noted that it is the practice for judges to warn a witness that he is in danger of self-incrimination so that the decision whether to answer the question, and thereby waive the privilege, can be made in an informed way.

The two branches of legal professional privilege noted above, revolve around the policy that confidential communications with legal advisers should remain confidential. This is not a policy which must be investigated in every case, there is no balancing exercise whereby the court must look at whether confidentiality should or should not be upheld in the case before it (unless a privileged document inadvertently falls into the hands of the other side - *Webster* v *Chapman* (1989). Rather it is a 'blanket' rule or policy that confidential communications between client and legal adviser are always privileged and communications between those legal advisers and persons other than the client are always privileged where the dominant purpose of the communication was the furtherance of current or contemplated litigation (*Waugh* v *British Railways Board*). The privilege does not extend to other confidential relationships, such as priest and penitent (*Normanshaw* v *Normanshaw* (1894)) or doctor and patient (*D* v *NSPCC* (1978)) or psychiatrist and patient (*W* v *Edgell* (1990)); and is designed to allow advice concerning litigation to be given on the basis of full disclosure from client to legal adviser. It would be a virtually impossible task for the trial judge to have to decide whether in every case before him a claim to legal professional privilege should be upheld, so the privilege is a 'blanket' privilege, covering all cases which fulfil the criteria mentioned above.

A communication between the parties which is said to be, or is clearly understood to be (*Paddock* v *Forrester* (1842)), 'without prejudice' may not be given in evidence unless both parties consent (*Stotesbury* v *Turner* (1943)). This is a hybrid privilege carrying some of the characteristics of the privilege against self-incrimination and some of the characteristics of legal professional privilege. Such communications often contain statements which could be considered to be admissions by the maker, and if such admissions could be used against him, then it is clearly arguable that he would not make them and therefore that attempts to settle a case without recourse to the courts would be fewer than they are today. Policy dictates that it is better if the parties can settle matters privately rather than spending time and money in courts, therefore attempts to make such a settlement can be made without danger of anything said being used against a party later in the event that the attempt fails.

Question 2

'The law relating to privilege is in need of substantial reform.'

Discuss.

University of London LLB Examination
(for External Students) Evidence June 1989 Q7

Skeleton solution

- Private privilege generally, and distinctive nature of public interest immunity.
- Exclusion of evidence under three main heads: self-incrimination privilege; legal professional privilege; 'without prejudice' communications.
- Arguments for reform of the law.

Suggested solution

For evidence to be admissible it must firstly be legally relevant to the issue before the court and, given that high degree of relevance, it must not infringe any of the exclusionary rules which, for varying reasons, forbid the admission of evidence or permit a party or witness to refuse to give evidence on some issue. Evidence which is relevant may be excluded by the laws of evidence where public policy so dictates - ie the concept of 'public interest immunity' - or, alternatively, a party or a witness may be permitted to claim a privilege whereby he is not compelled to give evidence despite its relevance and reliability because there are recognised extrinsic factors which outweigh the public interest in the court's being apprised of all relevant facts in order to reach the proper conclusion.

The basic difference between 'public interest immunity' and 'privilege' is that in the case of the former the courts decide as a matter of law (and policy) whether the evidence, albeit relevant, must be excluded, in the case of the latter the party or witness may claim the privilege (in which case the court will decide on the issue of exclusion) or may waive any potential privilege, thus relieving the court of the duty to deliberate and to adjudicate on disclosure.

The successful claiming of privilege means that the court must decide the issue before it without the benefit of all the relevant facts; this, however, is fairly commonplace in the adversarial or accusatorial system in English courts where a number of exclusionary rules deprive the court of the entirety of relevant material (the hearsay rule in criminal cases is a prime example).

One general, but important, point to bear in mind is that where a person whether witness or party claims privilege, no inferences adverse to that person can be drawn (*Wentworth* v *Lloyd* (1864)).

There are three main heads of privilege:

a) *Self-incrimination privilege*

This is based on the law's encouragement of witnesses to testify without fear of being forced to choose between incriminating themselves and committing perjury and, more importantly perhaps, on the unwillingness of the law to force any person (whether a witness or a party in civil or criminal proceedings) to give evidence which will be self-incriminatory (*Blunt* v *Park Lane Hotel* (1942)). It is for the judge to decide whether there is a real as opposed to fanciful risk of criminal proceedings if the question is answered by the witness (*R* v *Boyes* (1861)). If the evidence against the witness is already so strong that proceedings will be taken whether or not the witness answers the question, then any claim of privilege will fail (*RTZ Corpn* v *Westinghouse* (1978)).

If a witness is wrongly denied the self-incrimination privilege and thus compelled to answer the question, his response, in any subsequent criminal proceedings against him, is on the same footing as an inadmissible confession and therefore cannot be used (*R* v *Garbett* (1847)). This, however, is not a great safeguard since the response will be an admission of guilt of that crime. Therefore, although that response cannot be used in subsequent proceedings, it alerts the police to the fact that the witness committed that offence and a subsequent interview could well elicit an admissible confession which could be used without any reference to the earlier proceedings or the denial of the self-incrimination privilege. Apart from that weakness, value judgments must be made when the privilege is claimed, ie is there a *real* likelihood of subsequent criminal proceedings? Are those proceedings, should they be instituted, for an offence the triviality of which is outweighed by the need to have the relevant evidence put before the court in the instant case? Given the wide margin for error by the judge, either the repugnance of enforced self-incrimination or the proper administration of justice by the admission of relevant evidence should be the one determinant. Additionally there is alarming uncertainty as to whether the privilege can be claimed by directors, agents or employees of a corporate body on behalf of the corporate body (*RTZ Corpn* v *Westinghouse*).

Finally, the privilege can be claimed in respect of the witness' spouse, but perhaps incongruously in 1989, not in respect of a co-habitant or 'common law' spouse.

b) *Legal professional privilege*

This privilege covers two sorts of communications: (i) communications between client and legal adviser for the purpose of obtaining or giving legal advice; and (ii) those between client or lawyer and third parties (eg experts) where the dominant purpose is preparing for contemplated or imminent legal proceedings. The rationale of this privilege is said to be that the lawyer-client relationship would be unworkable if communications were liable to compulsory disclosure by the courts (*Waugh* v *British Railways Board* (1980)).

As regards lawyer-client communications under (i) above they are privileged from disclosure even though there was no prospect of litigation, provided the purpose was requesting or giving legal advice. Provided there was no question of the advice being sought or given to facilitate fraud (*R* v *Cox & Railton* (1884) but see *R* v *Crown Court at Snaresbrook, ex parte DPP* (1988)), the communication will not be disclosed in court unless the client waives the privilege. But the privilege will be overriden by the public interest in avoiding the conviction of an innocent accused person. In *R* v *Barton* (1973) it was held that no privilege attached to lawyer-client communications where their production in court could help the defence of an accused person. Obviously there is in this situation a degree of conjecture on the part of the judge in resolving the conflict between legal professional privilege and public policy regarding the administration of justice. The problem of resolution of these conflicting interests is highlighted in the case of *R* v *Ataou* (1988) (where the judge did not even avert his mind to the competing interest!).

As distinct from matters of public interest immunity or 'without prejudice' communications (infra), when legal professional privilege attaches to original documents or conversations, then these communications may be proved by secondary evidence (*Calcraft* v *Guest* (1898)). Therefore, overheard privileged conversations, duplicates of privileged documents etc may be admitted in court whether this secondary evidence has been obtained fortuitously or by some wrongful act. Where the possession of the secondary evidence becomes known to the party in whom the privilege vests, then an injunction may be obtained to prevent its disclosure, but an injunction is discretionary (*Lord Ashburton* v *Pape* (1913); *Calcraft* v *Guest*) and whatever the circumstances is not retroactive (*ITC* v *Video Exchange* (1982)). The case of *Derby & Co Ltd* v *Weldon (No 8)* (1990) suggests that where a privileged document falls into the hands of the other side by mistake, and that side must have realised the mistake, the court should exercise its discretion to prevent the information being used by that side.

An illogical distinction has been made between privileged documents stolen inside the court and those stolen elsewhere - secondary evidence of the former is not admissible; secondary evidence of the latter is admissible, subject to a speedy application for an injunction (*ITC* v *Video Exchange*).

A further illogicality is the distinction made in *Butler* v *Board of Trade* (1971) where it was held that in the case of a prosecution there can be no question of an injunction prohibiting the adducing of secondary evidence of privileged material. It was stated that public policy dictated that decision but it has since been quite strongly criticised (in *Goddard* v *Nationwide Building Society* (1986)).

Again, therefore, in the realm of legal professional privilege there abound incongruities and anomalies. Reform is long overdue to clarify the extent to which legal professional privilege attaches to primary and secondary communications in both civil and criminal proceedings. So much uncertainty and irreconcilability has been created by appellate court decisions that it may require the intervention of Parliament to clarify the law.

c) *'Without prejudice' communications*

Where attempts are being made by parties to settle their differences without litigation, then public policy dictates that there should be joint privilege attaching to such negotiations, ie they cannot be disclosed in subsequent litigation unless *both* parties agree (*La Roche* v *Armstrong* (1922); *Rush & Tompkins* v *GLC* (1988)). Unlike the illogicality in legal professional privilege, secondary evidence of the communication is not admissible because the rationale of the privilege is to encourage uninhibited negotiation, settlement, and avoidance of litigation.

The fact that the phrase 'without prejudice' is not specifically used is immaterial provided a genuine attempt was being made to settle a dispute (*Chocoladefabriken Lindt* v *The Nestlé Co Ltd* (1978)). Conversely, merely heading a document or communication 'without privilege' does not *ipso facto* render it privileged; it is for the court to determine whether it amounted to a genuine attempt to resolve a dispute without resort to litigation (*South Shropshire District Council* v *Amos* (1987)).

In this area of attempted settlements which also covers genuine attempts at matrimonial reconciliation (see *D* v *NSPCC* (1978)) the content of communications may be protected from disclosure, for sound reasons of public policy in civil law where one of the major objectives is the settlement of disputes without recourse to litigation. In this area also there is less need for reform of the law than in the other two areas of privilege discussed.

Question 3

Archie was employed as a technician at the Government's laser weapon laboratories, and has brought an action alleging that he has suffered brain damage as a result of exposure to high energy lasers.

His solicitors have requested disclosure of reports showing the level of laser activity in Archie's work sector, but the Ministry of Defence have refused disclosure on the ground of national security.

The goggles worn by Archie during exposure to a laser are the same as those used by US workers in Chicago and there is a report by a team of Chicago scientists that the goggles have proved ineffective as protection in a number of tests conducted by them with lasers. Archie's solicitors have not been able to obtain a copy of the report but a summary has been published in a British scientific journal. Archie's friends in the laboratory have also obtained a copy of a memorandum indicating that high energy laser activity was too high in the laboratory. The signature of the scientist at the bottom of the memorandum is smudged so as to be illegible.

It is understood that at the trial the Crown will lead evidence as to breaches of applicable safety and security regulations by Archie, which the Crown will contend contributed to Archie's injuries. Such breaches attract criminal sanctions under the relevant statute.

What evidential issues arise and how would you resolve them?

University of London LLB Examination
(for External Students) Evidence June 1985 Q6

Skeleton solution

- Introduction - defining issues.
- Ministry records - public interest immunity - balance of conflicting interests.
- Chicago study - relevance - first or second hand hearsay - Civil Evidence Act 1968.
- Memorandum - Civil Evidence Act 1968 - notice - discretion - public interest immunity.
- Safety regulations - contributory negligence - standard of proof of criminal allegation.

Suggested solution

a) *Introduction*

This question involves four evidential issues, with several sub-issues. The four main issues are the admissibility of the Ministry of Defence reports, the summary of the Chicago study, and of the memorandum, and the burden and standard of proof relating to the alleged breaches of security regulations.

Archie's action will be in negligence (we are not given sufficient information to be able to say whether he should sue for breach of, say, Factories Act Regulations). The general burden will be on Archie to prove, on balance of probabilities, that he was owed a duty of care by the Ministry, that that duty was breached and that the breach caused the brain damage. There will be no problem establishing the duty. The question revolves around proof of breach and damage.

b) *Ministry reports*

We are told that Archie has requested the disclosure of reports on the level of laser activity at his place of work. There is a general principle in English civil procedure that each party should disclose to all other parties relevant evidence in his possession. The rule is not limited to requiring the party to disclose the evidence which he plans to use - he must disclose all relevant evidence on request. The Ministry would be entitled to refuse to disclose the reports by relying on the doctrine of public interest immunity (sometimes called public policy privilege or

Crown Privilege). This doctrine allows certain evidence to remain undisclosed if it is in the public interest to prevent disclosure. It used to be the case that whenever a Ministry certified that a document should remain secret on the ground of privilege the courts would be bound by that decision (*Duncan* v *Cammell Laird* (1942)). That rule has not been applicable since 1968. In that year the House of Lords laid down the present rule that the courts are to determine questions of privilege by balancing the public interest in maintaining secrecy against the public interest in enabling a litigant access to relevant evidence (*Conway* v *Rimmer* (1968)). The House has restated the principle on several occasions (*Rogers* v *Home Secretary* (1973); *Alfred Crompton Amusement Machines Ltd* v *Customs & Excise Commissioners (No 2)* (1974); *D* v *NSPCC* (1978); *SRC* v *Nasse* (1979); *BSC* v *Granada* (1981); *Home Office* v *Harman* (1982); *Secretary of State for Defence* v *Guardian Newspapers* (1984)). It has been argued (in *Phipson on Evidence* (14th edition, 1990, paras 19-27) that there is no authoritative support for the proposition that the balancing process must be undertaken in every case, but the list of authorities where it has been applied is too long for such an argument to have much force (see Phipson, ibid).

The burden of proof on the issue of public interest immunity has never been made clear, but dicta from Lord Cross of Chelsea in *Alfred Crompton Amusement Machines Ltd* v *Customs and Excise Commissioners (No 2)* indicate that the burden will be on Archie to establish that the claim for privilege is not well founded. This approach goes against the normal rule that he who asserts privilege must prove privilege, but is justified by the nature of public interest immunity. A degree of trust in the judgment of government departments is both reasonable and inevitable; if their judgment in refusing to disclose a document is being questioned, then there is nothing unreasonable in requiring the party who wishes to use the document to prove his right to do so. Therefore, Archie will have to prove that the claim of public interest immunity is not well founded.

It has been stated many times in the courts that the public interest in doing justice to a litigant is of great importance (see generally *D* v *NSPCC*. On the facts given, there is only limited evidence of a public interest in maintaining secrecy. There seem to be two points involved, firstly the public interest in preventing disclosure of details of a weapons system and secondly, public interest in preventing the government being embarrassed. Clearly the former point is strongly in favour of upholding the department's claim to immunity, the latter point has no force at all. Therefore, if the disputed document would disclose defence secrets then the claim to privilege would, it is submitted, be upheld. If, though, the Ministry objects to disclosure simply because this would show breaches of safety regulations then Archie will be entitled to see and use the reports.

c) *Chicago study*

Two points arise when considering the admissibility of the summary of the Chicago study. Firstly it must be asked whether the evidence is relevant, secondly one must consider whether the summary is admissible as hearsay evidence under the Civil Evidence Act 1968.

It is an absolute rule that only relevant evidence is admissible. That is, only evidence which helps a party prove his case may be put before the court. Questions of relevance have been studied many times, but it is always difficult to say with any confidence what degree of probative force is required for evidence to be sufficiently relevant to be admissible. The guiding principle appears to be that evidence of dubious relevance will be allowed if it does not raise side issues, but will be inadmissible if it leads to the court spending more time considering its weight and reliability than is reasonable in the circumstances (*Cross on Evidence* (7th edition, 1990, pp51-52)). We are told that the goggles used in the Chicago research were the same as those worn by Archie and that they were subjected to laser light. In order for this evidence to help Archie, though, it would have to be proved that the goggles were the same, that the intensity of the lasers used was the same as that at Archie's place of work, that the time of exposure was similar to that suffered by Archie, that the research was statistically significant and so on. It is submitted that too many side issues would be raised for the Chicago study to be sufficiently relevant to be admissible. The question may be asked why such research was not conducted on the very goggles used by Archie. Therefore, it is submitted that the research evidence from America will not be admissible. Nonetheless the question of admissibility under the 1968 Act will be considered.

The Act draws a distinction between first-hand and second-hand hearsay evidence (s2 Civil Evidence Act 1968). Put in general terms the difference is that first-hand hearsay only passes through one pair of hands (or one mind) on its passage from the person with knowledge to the court; whereas second-hand goes through more than one intermediate stage. First-hand hearsay is generally admissible in civil cases, second-hand is only allowed if the requirements of s4 are met. Section 4 allows second-hand hearsay contained in documentary records compiled by a person acting under a duty. The High Court has considered the definition of 'documentary record' twice in recent years. In both cases it was held that a documentary record is a record which a respectable historian would consider to be an original source of the information cited (*H* v *Schering Chemicals* (1983); *Savings & Investment Bank* v *Gasco* (1984)). In the *Schering Chemicals* case Bingham J refused to allow a party to rely on summaries of research into the effect of drugs which had been published in a medical journal. It is submitted that the present case is indistinguishable from that decision. The original source of the information is the report compiled by the Chicago researchers; any summary suffers from the potential problem of distortion and so is inadmissible under s4.

Therefore for both reasons the summary cannot be relied on by Archie.

d) *The memorandum*

The memorandum also raises two issues - admissibility under the 1968 Act and public interest immunity. It would appear that the memo is first-hand hearsay evidence. It contains a statement by a scientist who had personal knowledge of the truth of the fact stated. Nonetheless, despite the general admissibility of first-hand hearsay by virtue of s2, there are obstacles in the way of the adduction of this memo. In order to be able to use first-hand hearsay the party wishing to adduce it must serve notice on all other parties (s8 Civil Evidence Act 1968; RSC Ord 38 r21). The notice must state the circumstances in which the memorandum was made, including the name of the maker and the person to whom it was addressed (RSC Ord 38 r22(10(b)). We are told that the name of the maker is illegible. Therefore the notice requirement cannot be adhered to strictly by Archie. If he wishes to use the memo, then he must request the trial judge to exercise his discretion. RSC Ord 38 r29 contains two principles which could help Archie. Firstly there is the general discretion to allow a party to adduce hearsay despite the proper notice not having been given. The courts will only exercise this discretion if it is just to do so (RSC Ord 38 r29(1)). One of the guiding principles to the question of the use of this discretion is that it will only be exercised where the party requesting it has acted fairly (*Ford* v *Lewis* (1971); *Morris* v *Stratford-on-Avon RDC* (1973)). On the facts given here Archie is best advised to serve a notice complying with RSC Ord 38 r22, but explaining why the name of the maker cannot be given. The second principle in r29 which could help Archie is contained in Ord 38 r29(2), which directs the court that a party should

be allowed to rely on hearsay evidence if the effect of requiring him to call the maker of the statement would be to force him to call an employee of the opposite party. If Archie could trace the scientist, this case would fall squarely within Ord 38 r29(2). Therefore, it would appear that Archie is entitled to put in the memo as first-hand hearsay evidence.

For reasons given in para (b), above, any claim to public interest immunity in respect of the memorandum will fail. The only interest in keeping it secret would be to prevent embarrassment among those responsible for the running of the laboratory. This is not a public interest which can be set against the public interest in allowing Archie to use relevant evidence. Therefore Archie will, it is submitted, be allowed to rely on the memo under s2 Civil Evidence Act 1968 (the memorandum is not a 'record' and therefore s4 of the 1968 Act is not applicable).

c) *Safety regulations*

If it could be established that Archie breached safety and security regulations, then the Ministry will be able to rely on the Law Reform (Contributory Negligence) Act 1945 which has the effect of allowing a reduction in damages to allow for the plaintiff's own fault. This is a matter which goes to causation - even if there is negligence the Ministry is only liable in damages to the extent that it was at fault. If Archie's carelessness added to his injuries then he must bear responsibility for that himself.

If the Ministry alleges contributory negligence then it is for the Ministry to prove that Archie was at fault (*Nance* v *British Columbia Electric Railway Co* (1951)). Contributory negligence does not rely on normal tortious principles of duty, breach of duty and non-remote damage, it rests on simple carelessness (*Jones* v

Livox Quarries (1952)). But, it must be stressed that the Ministry would have to prove not just that Archie was careless, but that his carelessness contributed to his injuries (*Stapley* v *Gypsum Mines Ltd* (1953)). The burden of proof, then is on the Ministry. The standard of proof on any issue is determined by the nature of the proceedings and the party who bears the burden. This case being a civil action the civil standard applies (for a recent affirmation of this point see *R* v *Hampshire CC, ex parte Ellerton* (1985)). The fact that the allegations made by the Ministry are of the commission of criminal offences makes no difference to the standard of proof (*Hornal* v *Neuberger* (1957)). There is no estoppel requiring a criminal court to find Archie guilty if the civil court in this case holds that he committed the alleged breaches of regulations, therefore there is no need to apply the criminal standard of proof. However, the recent case of *Halford* v *Brookes* (1991) suggests that where the allegations are very serious, the criminal standard should be used despite it being a civil trial. However, in that case the allegations were of murder. Not so serious here. Therefore, the Ministry will have to prove the allegations on balance of probabilities.

Question 4

Mrs Windfall is suing the Rest in Peace Hospital Company (RIPH) for negligently causing the death of her husband, during an operation in which the drug Happydreams had been administered by Dr Corpsemaker, one of the hospital's doctors, to Mr Windfall. Consider the issues in the law of evidence relating to the following items of evidence:

a) A research paper by Dr Ironlegs, in which he warns of the danger of administering Happydreams where a patient's heart rate is above a particular level. The paper is published in the medical journal 'Bones and Skeletons'. Dr Ironlegs is unavailable to give evidence in the case.

b) Two computerised documents produced by advanced computers at St Lucifer's hospital and St Juda's hospital recording the effects of administering Happydreams to two patients during an operation. The computer had controlled the administration of the drug during each operation according to a programme fed into it by research scientists. In each case the computer recorded the amount of the drug fed into the patient and the resultant change in heart rate.

c) The record of a disciplinary enquiry against Dr Corpsemaker in which the hospital's Board had found him guilty of negligence. The report had been forwarded to RIPH's internal lawyers in the event that the hospital was sued or prosecuted, and the hospital have refused to give discovery of the document.

d) The conviction of Corpsemaker for recklessly causing death on a previous occasion at another hospital.

Adapted from University of London LLB Examination
(for External Students) Evidence June 1987 Q6

Skeleton solution

a) • Relevance of article - documentary hearsay - s2 Civil Evidence Act 1968 - notice procedure.

b) • Relevance - admissibility under s5 Civil Evidence Act 1968 - conditions.

c) • Legal professional privilege - dominant purpose test.

d) • Relevance - similar fact evidence.

• Relevance to vicarious liability of hospital,

Suggested solution

It is not known on what basis the Rest in Peace Hospital is being sued in negligence. It is most likely that the claim depends upon proof of the negligence of Dr Corpsemaker, for which the hospital is vicariously liable, although part (iv) indicates that there may be a claim that the hospital was primarily liable for employing Dr Corpsemaker at all.

a) *The research paper*

The research paper could be of relevance in one of two ways, either because Dr Corpsemaker did not read it and therefore acted negligently or because he did not act according to its advice. In either case it would be necessary to prove that what it said was correct. If it is alleged that Dr Corpsemaker was negligent in not reading it then the question arises whether that caused any damage because if, in fact, the article was nonsense and would properly have been ignored then his failure to read it would not have caused any damage. If, on the other hand, the allegation is that Dr Corpsemaker, although having read it, should have followed the advice of the article then the question arises whether he acted with due care by not checking Mr Windfall's blood pressure first.

In civil proceedings documentary hearsay evidence is admissible if either it is first hand hearsay or it is second hand hearsay contained in a documentary record. In addition notice should have been served of Mrs Windfall's intention to adduce it.

It is submitted that the research paper contains first hand hearsay evidence of the truth of its contents. The maker of the assertions contained within it was Dr Ironlegs and although it would have passed through the hands of the printers they would not be making a separate statement themselves. Therefore the article as published would still have been Dr Ironlegs's statement and would be admissible under s2(1) of the Civil Evidence Act 1968. Necessarily the article would contain elements of opinion but these would be admissible because s1 Civil Evidence Act 1972 extends the 1968 Act so as to allow hearsay evidence of opinion as well as of statements of fact.

To an extent the article may contain restatements of research of people other than Dr Ironlegs. If it did then statements in it about that other research would be inadmissible because Dr Ironlegs would not be able to give direct oral evidence of their truth (*The Ymnos* (1981)).

Before the article could be used, however, it would be necessary for Mrs Windfall to give notice to the hospital in compliance with RSC O38 rr21 and 22. In outline, this requires her to give notice of her intention to use the hearsay evidence, attaching a copy of it to the notice. We are told that Dr Ironlegs is unavailable to give evidence, but not the reason for his unavailability. If it is because he is dead, overseas, unfit or cannot be found then such a reason should be given for his proposed non attendance.

b) *The computer print-outs*

There is a question of the relevance of the evidence of what happened to two other patients. It is not necessarily the case that what happened to them would always happen to a patient to whom Happydreams is administered. In the absence of any further information on the matter it will be assumed that this evidence is relevant.

Computer print-outs in civil cases are only admissible if they fall within the strict rules of admissibility contained in s5 of the 1968 Act. Section 5 requires, firstly, that the statement produced by the computer is one of which direct oral evidence would be admissible. The statement upon which Mrs Windfall will wish to rely is the statement about the change in heart rate occurring after the administration of Happydreams. This is something about which direct oral evidence would be admissible if there were anyone with direct knowledge of it. Therefore, provided the appropriate notice is served (RSC Ord 38 rr21 and 24) and the strict conditions relating to use of the computer are complied with (s5 Civil Evidence Act 1968) the print-out would be admissible as evidence of what happened to those other patients. The trial judge would be entitled to draw any reasonable inference from the print-outs, for example the need to check assiduously the patient's heart rate (s6 Civil Evidence Act 1968).

c) *The disciplinary report*

The hospital would be entitled to refuse to disclose the report if the dominant purpose of compiling it was for the furtherance of pending or contemplated litigation (*Waugh* v *British Railways Board* (1980)). It appears that this was not so, and that the dominant purpose was for disciplinary purposes within the hospital itself. A party cannot protect a report simply by passing it to his lawyers, it is the purpose for which it is compiled which counts for the purposes of privilege and not the purpose to which it is put after it is compiled (*Neilson* v *Laugharne* (1981); *Guinness Peat* v *Fitzroy Robinson* (1987); *Ventouris* v *Mountain* (1991)).

d) *Dr Corpsemaker's conviction*

Unless the conviction of Dr Corpsemaker for causing death at the other hospital shows that he acted negligently on this occasion it would not be admissible. The admissibility of similar fact evidence in civil cases is more easily achieved than in criminal cases, but it is still necessary for it to be probative of the issue on which it is adduced (*Mood Music* v *De Wolfe* (1976)). As far as can be gathered from the information given, there is nothing about the conviction which proves negligence in relation to Mr Windfall.

Evidence of the conviction could be relevant not in relation to whether Dr Corpsemaker was negligent in treating Mr Windfall, but in relation to whether the hospital was negligent in employing Dr Corpsemaker in the first place. The liability of the hospital in such a claim would be primary not vicarious. In the absence of any information about the way in which Dr Corpsemaker killed the other patient it cannot be said whether the hospital was negligent in employing him to administer Happydreams to Mr Windfall.

14 PROOF WITHOUT EVIDENCE

14.1 Introduction

14.2 Key points

14.3 Analysis of questions

14.4 Questions

14.1 Introduction

In some circumstances a court may be satisfied that facts are established without requiring them to be proved by relevant evidence. In some cases the facts may be established with virtually no evidence, eg the facts are formally admitted or judicially noticed; in others the facts are presumed in favour of the party alleging them and therefore may be established by less evidence than would otherwise be required. These three exceptional areas, therefore, are formal admissions, judicial notice, and presumptions.

14.2 Key points

a) *Formal admissions*

Where a fact is formally admitted for the purpose of the proceedings, then no proof is necessary as that fact is no longer in issue between the parties.

In civil cases, formal admissions may be made at various pre-trial stages or at trial. Such formal admissions bind those making them only for the purpose of those proceedings, but in those proceedings are conclusive of the facts which are admitted.

In criminal cases, provision is made for formal admissions by s10 Criminal Justice Act 1967. If such admissions are made otherwise than in court they must comply with thc requirements of s10(2) as to their form. Formal admissions in court may be made orally by counsel: *R* v *Lewis* [1989] Crim LR 61. Formal admissions may be withdrawn, but only with leave of the court: s10(4).

Whether in civil or criminal proceedings, formal admissions, which are conclusive, must be distinguished from informal admissions and confessions which are by no means conclusive but rather may be rejected as inadmissible after the party against whom they are tendered has adduced rebutting evidence - or in the case of confessions, the criminal court of its own motion may put the prosecution to proof of admissibility.

b) *Judicial notice*

In both civil and criminal cases the court will acknowledge the truth of some facts without any need for proof. This creates no problems in civil cases, but in criminal cases there is the problem, when the judge takes judicial notice of a fact, as to how the jury ought to be directed; it appears to be accepted that although in the jury's realm of fact rather than the judge's realm of law, the judge must nevertheless direct the jury to take the fact as proved: *R* v *Simpson* [1983] 1 WLR 1494; cf *Gibson* v *Wales* [1983] 1 WLR 393.

Judicial notice may be taken of notorious facts, or may be taken after reference.

i) Notoriety

Where the fact is a matter of common knowledge (universally, or in the case of magistrates it may be locally) which is so notorious as not to be open to any serious dispute, then judicial notice will be taken of it without reference to any source. Classic examples of a miriad of such facts include a fortnight being too short a period for human gestation, criminals leading unhappy lives, postcards being correspondence which may be read by anyone.

ii) Notice after reference

The party seeking such judicial notice of a fact must provide any required source of reference. Most of these cases of judicial notice relate to political matters, such as the existence of a state of war; the meaning of the classification 'secret' on a government document; the extent of territorial sovereignty (and therefore jurisdiction of English courts). Others have involved professional practice, eg that of the Ordnance Survey (in interpreting map references), and readily demonstrable public facts, eg the meaning of words in common usage, or geographical facts, where reference may be made to dictionaries, maps etc.

Problems arise where judicial notice is taken after receiving evidence, and where personal knowledge of the judge is involved. In the classic case of *McQuaker* v *Goddard* [1940] 1 KB 687, the judge consulted books and heard evidence on the issue before taking judicial notice of the fact that a camel was a domestic animal. This is on the borderline of judicial notice/proof by evidence, but can be justified as being the former given that it is confined to constant facts which are therefore not determined by the special facts of any case. The problem of the extent to which a judge can utilise his personal knowledge has spawned a lot of case law, yet the basic distinction is between the judge's properly applying his general knowledge of the subject matter to his understanding, and evaluation, of the evidence which has been adduced, and his improperly using his personal knowledge in place of evidence adduced. But in this latter situation a distinction must be drawn between judges and on the other hand magistrates and jurors whose local knowledge may be of something so notorious in the locality that judicial notice may be taken rather than evidence: *Ingram* v *Percival* [1969] 1 QB 548.

c) *Presumptions*

When a presumption operates, then the court either must, or may, come to the conclusion which the presumption points to, unless there is evidence (or sufficient evidence) to the contrary. All true presumptions are rebuttable by evidence to the contrary; there are two so-called 'irrebuttable presumptions', ie that a child under ten cannot commit an offence, and that a boy under 14 is incapable of any offence which involves proof of his commission of sexual intercourse. These are not presumptions, but rules of substantive law. In addition there are presumptions which do not depend on proof of a basic fact, but are rather rules governing the incidence of the evidential and legal burdens of proof, and to some extent the standard in criminal cases; for example the presumption of sanity and of innocence - the former dictates that the defence has a legal burden of proving a defence of insanity or insane automatism and the latter dictates that the prosecution must prove beyond reasonable doubt every element of the offence charged and any other fact in issue such as the admissibility of a confession.

Further presumptions of fact need not detain the student of Evidence for long - they are merely commonly recurring examples of circumstantial evidence, ie illustrations of evidence relevant to the facts in issue. For example, if a party destroys or conceals evidence the court may infer that the evidence was unfavourable to his case; or the 'presumption of continuance', to the effect that any proven state of affairs may be assumed to have continued for some time, the duration depending on all the circumstances (examples being the question of the speed of a vehicle at a specific time and the continued existence of a person proved to be alive at some earlier time than that in question); and the inference which the court *may* draw as to whether the natural and probable consequences of an act of the accused were intended or foreseen by him.

All the above are often classed as not being 'true presumptions', in that rules of substantive law, rules governing the incidence of the burdens of proof, and pieces of circumstantial evidence, do not amount to presumptions in the true sense. 'True' presumptions are said to be rebuttable presumptions of law, ie on proof of a basic fact the presumption arises, and in the absence of sufficient evidence in rebuttal the prescribed conclusion *must* be drawn by the court. How much evidence is required in rebuttal determines whether the presumption is persuasive or evidential; conversely, whether the rebuttable presumption of law is persuasive or evidential dictates whether the party seeking to rebut must discharge a legal burden of proof or merely an evidential burden. If the appropriate burden is not discharged the court *must* draw the prescribed conclusion; if the burden is discharged the presumption is rebutted and the issue must be proved by admissible evidence without the aid, or hindrance, of the presumption.

The most frequently recurring, and therefore examinable, rebuttable presumptions of law are marriage, legitimacy, death, regularity, *res ipsa loquitur*.

i) Presumption of marriage

On proof of a marriage ceremony, the law presumes the formal validity of the marriage: *Piers* v *Piers* (1849) 2 HL Cas 331. The presumption is persuasive in civil cases, but only evidential in criminal cases when the prosecution bears the legal burden of proving validity. The law will also assume the essential validity of the marriage - ie that the parties had the capacity to marry (16 years old and not already validly married). This presumption of essential validity appears to be persuasive in civil cases, but the standard of proof in rebuttal, albeit the civil standard, is lower than that imposed in respect of rebuttal of the presumption of formal validity: *Re Peete, Peete* v *Crompton* [1952] 2 All ER 599. On proof of cohabitation, a presumption arises that the couple were living together as lawful spouses. In civil proceedings this presumption of marriage is persuasive: *Re Taylor* [1961] 1 WLR 9, but when relied on by the prosecution, proof of cohabitation does not even raise an evidentiary presumption unless coupled with production of a marriage certificate: *R* v *Birtles* (1911) 6 Cr App R 177.

ii) Presumption of legitimacy

On proof of the basic fact that a child was born, or conceived, in wedlock, it is presumed that he is the legitimate issue of the spouses. In civil proceedings, the presumption is persuasive - to the civil standard of proof: s26 Family Law Reform Act 1969. In criminal proceedings, eg a charge of incest by the accused with a child born to or conceived by his wife during the subsistence of their marriage, the presumption can only be evidential. On general criminal law principles, the accused merely has to raise a reasonable doubt as to an element of the offence to ensure an acquittal, therefore evidence sufficient to raise such a doubt as to the legitimacy of the daughter must suffice, as opposed to proving illegitimacy in a civil dispute over paternity, custody, access, maintenance, etc.

iii) Presumption of death

The rebuttable presumption of death arises on proof of basic facts which were stipulated in *Chard* v *Chard* [1956] P 259, ie there were persons likely to have heard of the person whose death is an issue, but they have not heard of him for at least seven years immediately preceding the proceedings and all due, appropriate, enquiries have been made, then the person will be presumed to have died at some time within the seven year period of silence and absence. The presumption is evidential only. There is conflict, however, as to whether, without evidence in rebuttal, death will be assumed to have occurred at some time during the seven years immediately preceding the hearing, or whether death can be assumed at the end of the seven year period of continuous silence and absence and at all times thereafter. Whichever view prevails, if a specific date of death must be established (for purposes of succession etc), then evidence must be adduced to prove the actual time of death.

iv) Presumption of regularity

On proof of the basic fact that some person acted as the holder of a public office (eg judge, magistrate, police constable) it is presumed that he was duly appointed. It is presumed that devices which are usually efficient (eg speedometers of police vehicles, intoximeters, radar speed meters, radar guns) were working properly at the relevant time. On proof of necessary business transactions being carried out, it is presumed that they were carried out in the correct sequence. The presumption is evidential only, but in criminal proceedings the defence *must* adduce evidence to discharge the evidential burden borne by them on proof of the basic fact; it is not enough merely to challenge the regularity: see *Hill* v *Baxter* [1958] 1 QB 277 re discharge of evidential burden by defence.

v) Res ipsa loquitur

On proof by the plaintiff in a negligence action that the accident which caused his injuries is one which in the normal course of events would not occur without negligence on the part of the person in control of the relevant operation, and that he, the plaintiff, cannot prove it was caused by the defendant's negligence, then the plaintiff may seek assistance from the principle *res ipsa loquitur*, ie 'the thing speaks for itself'. Given that, in the circumstances of the accident, the sole control by the defendant or his employees, and the ignorance of the plaintiff as to the defendant's conduct is proved, then it may be presumed that the accident was caused by the defendant's negligence (primary or vicarious). But whether the presumption is merely one of fact, or whether it is an evidential, or a persuasive, presumption of law is open to debate as the law is far from clear. If a presumption of fact, then in the absence of evidence from the defendant, the court *may* reach the conclusion prescribed by the presumption but does not have to. If the presumption is an evidential presumption of law, then it is rebutted if the defendant adduces evidence consistent equally with negligence and pure accident. If the presumption is persuasive, the defendant must disprove negligence. There are authorities in support of all three contentions, but this could be the result of the wide variance in the basic facts which give rise to the presumption in the reported cases.

vi) Conflicting presumptions

Where there are two presumptions in conflict in the proceedings, then if they are of equal effect (eg both are persuasive presumptions) the court may decide that they cancel each other and the parties must discharge their burdens of proof by admissible evidence only: *Monckton* v *Tarr* (1930) 23 BWCC 504. Alternatively, the court may take account of public policy considerations in determining which presumption prevails: *Taylor* v *Taylor* [1965] 1 All ER 872. The classic case of *R* v *Willshire* (1881) 6 QBD 366 on conflicting presumptions can be interpreted as being purely a case of deciding which party had to discharge a legal, as opposed to evidential, burden of proof; but where presumptions arise they will have a bearing by their nature, on the incidence of the legal and/or evidential burden.

14.3 Analysis of questions

Once the student has mastered the classification of 'true' presumptions, then the rules are not very complex. Given an understanding of the burdens of proof, a student is then well equipped to deal with questions in this area, where, perhaps above all, essay questions are 'self-contained'. Judicial notice and formal admissions rarely appear, even as part of a question.

14.4 Questions

Question 1

Monica and Clint were married in California in 1960.

In 1965 Clint goes off to Vietnam with the Marines. In 1966 Monica hears that he was reported missing. In 1975 she gives up waiting for him to return and comes to England where she meets and marries Ogilvy in 1977. One of Clint's old Vietnam friends, Matt, turns up in London, visits Monica and Ogilvy and he says that he could swear he saw Clint in a village in Vietnam in 1971, where he was living with a Vietnamese girl.

In 1983 Monica sues Ogilvy for divorce and Ogilvy's defence is that their marriage is a nullity because in 1977 Monica was still married to Clint. Matt is a mercenary in Africa and can no longer be traced. Monica has some evidence that Clint might have been married previously to Jane in 1955 and that Jane is still alive.

Advise Monica.

University of London LLB Examination
(for External Students) Evidence June 1983 Q3

Skeleton solution

- Presumption of validity of marriage - standard of proof needed with evidence in rebuttal.
- 1960 marriage validity - 1977 marriage validity - presumption of death.
- Where two presumptions apply - ordinary rules of burden and standard of proof.

Suggested solution

Beginning with the marriage of M and C in California in 1960, it will be presumed that they were validly married and that they had the necessary capacity to marry on proof of the primary fact that they went through a ceremony of marriage. The presumption of marriage is a very strong presumption, rebuttable only by strong evidence. Lord Cottenham LC in *Piers* v *Piers* (1849) held that the presumption is not lightly to be repelled and required evidence, going beyond a mere balance of probability, which is strong, distinct, satisfactory and conclusive. In *Mahadervan* v

Mahadervan (1964), it was held that the court must be satisfied beyond reasonable doubt in order for the presumption to be rebutted. However, later in *Blyth* v *Blyth* (1966), the House of Lords seem to suggest that the standard of proof in matrimonial matters is the ordinary civil standard. Whatever the true position, it is submitted that the evidence in rebuttal is required to be cogent. Evidence of a valid prior marriage may suffice (*Gatty & Gatty* v *Attorney-General* (1951)) unless that marriage itself cannot be shown conclusively to have been valid (*Taylor* v *Taylor* (1967)). Accordingly M may here argue that the persuasive presumption of validity of the marriage of 1960 is rebutted by evidence of a valid prior marriage, that between C and J in 1955. The conclusion would be that her marriage to O in 1977 is valid. However, the weak link in this argument is the doubt that surrounds the alleged marriage of 1955. It is submitted that M will fail to show conclusively the validity of the 1955 marriage and will therefore fail to rebut the presumption of validity in relation to the marriage of 1960. Nor may she argue that the presumption is inapplicable to a foreign marriage (that of 1960) in order to prevent the invalidation of the subsequent English marriage (that of 1977). In *Mahadervan* v *Mahadervan* it was held that a presumption in favour of validity carried as much weight in relation to a foreign marriage as to an English one. In this respect the nationality of the marriages in question is irrelevant.

If the above reasoning is correct, the 1960 marriage will be held to be valid, the subsequent marriage of 1977 invalid. However, M may argue the validity of the 1977 marriage on the basis that at that time C was dead. If there is no acceptable affirmative evidence that a person was alive at some time during a continuous period of seven years or more and if it can be proved (a) that there are persons who would be likely to have heard of him over that period, (b) that those persons have not heard of him, and (c) that all due enquiries have been made appropriate to the circumstances, that person may be presumed to have died at some time within that period (*Chard* v *Chard* (1956)). It is no bar to M employing the presumption that she wishes to show that C was dead at the date of her marriage to O (1977) as opposed to the date of the present trial. In *Chipchase* v *Chipchase* (1939) it was assumed that the presumption could apply retrospectively, ie at some date prior to the date of the trial. However, even assuming that M satisfied the first and the third conditions, of *Chard* v *Chard* (supra), there is evidence here that C was heard of in 1971, by M. This would interrupt the continuous period of seven years, which must have begun in 1966 when C was reported missing, after only five years. Does evidence of the alleged sighting of C in 1971 suffice to rebut the presumption? It seems clear from *Prudential Assurance Co* v *Edmonds* (1877) that the presumption of death is evidential, ie it casts a burden of adducing evidence on the party against whom it operates (in our case, O). If O gives evidence of the sighting of C in 1971, this may rebut the presumption. However, whether this evidence is reliable is a question for the judge as trier of fact. One important factor concerning reliability is that M is unavailable to give evidence or to have his evidence challenged in cross-examination. Even assuming that M were to succeed in showing that C died at some stage between 1966 and 1977, in reliance on the presumption of death, and that the 1977 marriage was therefore valid, this conclusion would conflict with that based on the presumption of the validity of the marriage of 1960. In this situation, where two presumptions apply but produce different conclusions, the ordinary rules for burden and standard of proof apply without resort to any presumptions (*R* v *Wiltshire CCR* (1881)) ie the presumptions cancel each other out. On this basis it is submitted that the weight of the evidence suggests that the marriage of 1960 was valid, that C was alive in 1977 and that the marriage of that date was accordingly invalid.

Question 2

'Every writer of sufficient intelligence to appreciate the difficulties of the subject matter has approached the topic of presumptions with a sense of hopelessness and left it with a feeling of despair.' (Morgan)

Why are presumptions so difficult to analyse and classify?

University of London LLB Examination
(for External Students) Evidence June 1985 Q3

Skeleton solution

- Introduction - different effects of presumptions - scope of discussion.
- The general context - definition of terms - stages of a trial.
- Traditional classification, introduction - irrebuttable presumptions of law.
- Rebuttable presumptions of law - two types - new names - Lord Denning and Lord Bridge - two types .
- Presumptions of fact - definition - Lord Denning and Lord Bridge - distinction between evidential and factual presumptions - permissive presumptions.
- Criminal cases - burden placed on accused.
- Conclusion - reasons for confusion.

Suggested solution

a) *Introduction*

The area of presumptions has given rise to a great deal of division of terminology and of conceptual thinking. These differences among many eminent academic and practising lawyers has come about because of the three-part role of presumptions in English law. Presumptions sometimes alter the normal rules on burden of proof, for policy reasons; at other times they allow the proof of fact 'A' to be the result of proving fact 'B'; at other times they act simply to direct the mind of the trier of fact towards possible inferences which may be drawn from the evidence adduced. Indeed at time a presumption may do all three of these things. This complex role can only be understood if the rules on burden of proof are borne in mind, together with the procedure at each stage of a trial. These will be discussed in section (b) below.

There are many different presumptions and many policy reasons behind those presumptions. As conceptions of public policy change, so the effect of presumptions will change; this makes the task of classification all the more difficult. It is proposed to deal with the traditional, or orthodox, classification and to show how each old category has been altered in terminology by recent commentators. The following discussion will be in relation to civil cases only, when covering basic principles; the rules applicable to criminal cases will be dealt with separately.

b) *The general context*

Although there is a considerable variation in terminology in the area of burdens of proof, this answer will use that favoured by Cross (*Cross on Evidence* (7th edition, 1990, pp120-124)). In other words the burden of proving an issue will be referred to as the legal burden of proof; the onus of raising an issue not already raised will be called the evidential burden; the risk of not calling evidence on an issue which one's opponent has already raised is the tactical burden; and the overall burden of persuading the court to find in one's favour will be called the ultimate burden.

It must be remembered that burdens and standards of proof are irrelevant unless the trier of fact or law actually has to make a decision. Throughout the calling of evidence it is naive to assume that the trier of fact takes each piece of evidence in turn and considers whether the case has been proved - that decision is only taken at the end of the case, when all the evidence has been called, so that everything can be seen in context. There are only three stages of a trial at which burdens are important. The first is at the end of the plaintiff's case, when the judge has to decide whether the evidential burden on the plaintiff has been discharged, in other words whether he has called evidence from which a reasonable jury could find for him (the rare case where the defendant has the right to begin works on the same principle). The second is when all evidence has been called and the judge has to consider whether sufficient evidence has been called on each issue for that issue to need to be decided. The third stage comes immediately after the second and is when the trier of fact (usually the judge in a civil case) has to decide whether the ultimate burden has been satisfied. At the first two stages questions of the discharge of evidential burdens arise, at the final stage it is the legal burden on each issue which is important.

c) *The traditional classification - introduction*

The traditional classification on presumptions is into three categories, ie irrebuttable presumptions of law, rebuttable presumptions of law and presumptions of fact. Irrebuttable presumptions of law are not true presumptions at all (this is one of the few statements on this topic with which all commentators agree!). Rather they are rules of law put into presumptive form. For example s50 Children and Young Persons Act 1933 (as amended by s16(1) Children and Young Persons Act 1963) states that 'it shall be conclusively presumed that no child under the age of ten years can be guilty of any offence'. This could be amended by the omission of the first six words so as to be the same rule, but not in presumptive form: 'no child under the age of ten years can be guilty of an offence'.

Clearly nothing is added, or lost, by stating the rule in terms of a presumption, but it is not really a presumption at all. Therefore irrebuttable presumptions of law will not be discussed further.

d) *Rebuttable presumptions of law*

Rebuttable presumptions of law all follow the same logical form. On proof of fact 'A', fact 'B' is presumed to be true. The traditional classification of presumptions does not further divide these presumptions, but as has been pointed out many times there are two types of rebuttable presumption of law. The first type is the presumption which says that on proof of fact 'A' fact 'B' shall be taken to be true unless it is proved that fact 'B' is not true. The other type is the presumption which says that on proof of fact 'A' fact 'B' shall be taken to be true unless sufficient evidence is raised to throw doubt on whether fact 'B' really is true. The distinction can be illustrated by the following example:

A child is born to Mrs X while she is married to Mr X.

Mr X leaves Mrs X and refuses to pay any maintenance for the child, because he claims he is not the father.

Mrs X sues for maintenance.

There is a presumption that a child born in wedlock is the child of the mother's husband (*Banbury Peerage Case* (1811)). Theoretically this presumption could be rebutted by Mr X (the defendant) proving that he was not the father, or by him adducing evidence which showed a 50-50 chance of him not being the father. Since the burden of proving the right to maintenance will be on Mrs X (the plaintiff), so if Mr X could show an equal chance of him not being the father then he would have prevented Mrs X proving on balance of probabilities that she was entitled to maintenance money from him. So the presumption could require proof to the contrary or it could require the defendant merely to prevent the plaintiff proving her case, without proving his case himself. In fact the presumption of legitimacy places a legal burden on the party rebutting the presumption (see now s26 Family Law Reform Act 1969). But the theoretical position of rebuttable presumption is clear - they are of two types.

This failure of the traditional classification to distinguish between the two types of rebuttable presumption of law led to various attempts to adopt a two-part classification.

Lord Denning called the presumptions which put a legal burden on the rebutter 'compelling presumptions' ((1945) 61 MLR 379; see also Carter, *Cases and Statutes on Evidence* (2nd edition, 1990, pp78-79) though the more common terminology is 'persuasive presumptions' (*Cross on Evidence* (7th edition, 1990, pp126-129); Heydon, *Evidence Cases and Statutes* (2nd edition, 1984, p43)). This new title is useful in that it distinguishes such presumptions from those which impose a lesser burden on the rebutter. But it has not gone without criticism. Lord Bridge ((1949) 12 MLR 272) has argued that the classification of such rules as presumptions is all wrong. He pointed out that these compelling or persuasive presumptions are rules of law which determine that a certain result must follow from the proof of certain facts. In the example given above, on proof by Mrs X of birth in wedlock the law stipulates that legitimacy must be found unless there is proof to the contrary. Lord Bridge's argument was that this is not a presumption at all, it is a rule of law dressed up as a presumption. It is certainly true that there is little difference between a common law rule that says the burden of proving illegitimacy is on the defendant once the plaintiff has proved birth in wedlock. Each of the rules is really in the same form - on the happening of a certain event, certain consequences follow; on the happening of the start of the case the ultimate burden is on the plaintiff, on the happening of proof of birth in wedlock the legal burden of proving illegitimacy is on the defendant. Each rule can be put into the same pattern. Therefore the question arises whether it is right to classify 'compelling' or 'persuasive' presumptions as presumptions. Lord Bridge argued that one should bear in mind the stages of the trial at which the issue of legitimacy will arise. The plaintiff must produce evidence on which a reasonable jury could find birth in wedlock; then the defendant has to prove illegitimacy. No question of presumption arises, he argued; there are two distinct issues - has the plaintiff prove birth in wedlock, has the defendant proved illegitimacy? It is submitted that Lord Bridge's approach does not properly explain the concept of the persuasive presumption. It is certainly true that the effect of the 'presumptions' is to state a rule of law, that the defendant bears the burden of proving illegitimacy; but that burden only arises once the basis for it has been established by the plaintiff. If the plaintiff calls no evidence relating to birth in wedlock, then her case would be rejected on the defendant making a submission of no case. It is artificial to separate the cases where a presumption places a legal burden of proof on the rebutter and those where only an evidential burden is placed on him, by arguing that the former category is not a presumption but is a rule of law. Both are presumptions and both presumptions arise because the law says they arise. In both cases the trier of fact must draw a certain conclusion unless some evidence is called to the contrary. The only difference between the two is the amount of evidence required to rebut the presumption.

The classification of the second type of rebuttable presumption of law is not subject to the same difficulties. This second category - the presumption that on proof of fact 'A', the trier of fact must conclude fact 'B' unless the other party can balance the probability of 'B' being true and being not true - has been defined by Cross as the 'evidential presumption' (*Cross on Evidence* (7th edition, 1990, pp126-129)) but Lord Bridge simply called these 'presumptions'; this being the result of his basic thesis that there is only one sort of presumption, all other things which are called presumptions being defined using other terminology (12 MLR 272, 279).

The effect of an evidential presumption, as mentioned above, is to place a burden on the rebutter to adduce sufficient evidence to prevent the proponent from proving his case. In other words a tactical burden is placed on the rebutter.

Evidential presumptions may be of two types. The first type reflects common sense by requiring fact 'B' to be presumed on the proof of fact 'A' even though as a matter of common sense the natural conclusion is that fact 'B' is true; the second type gives additional weight to fact 'A that common sense would always indicate. For example, the common law presumption of regularity states that if a person acts in an office for which certain formal qualifications are needed it is to be presumed that he has those qualifications (*Berryman* v *Wise* (1791)). As a matter of common sense proof that a man sat as a judge at the Old Bailey would be clear proof that he was qualified to do so; after all, if he were not qualified then he would have been found out. In such a case there is no need for there to be any legal presumption, the trier of fact would draw the required conclusion anyway. But, it could be that the use of a church for a wedding ceremony would not, necessarily, be construed by a reasonable man to be proof that it was properly licensed for weddings; nonetheless the presumption of regularity applies so that the trier of fact must find that it was licensed unless the opponent on the issue can show that there was an equal chance of the church not being licensed (*R* v *Cresswell* (1876)). Despite these two types of evidential presumptions, there seems to be no need to divide them into separate categories of presumptions because they both work in the same way. They both place a tactical burden on the opponent of the issue once the proponent has proved the basic facts.

There has, though, been some difference of terminology in that Lord Denning did not give evidential presumptions a separate name, but classed them together with presumptions of fact, as 'provisional' presumptions. This analysis will be discussed below, when dealing with presumptions of fact.

e) *Presumptions of fact*

The traditional presumption of fact has two aspects. The first is that there are some inferences which a trier of fact will draw because common sense tells him to. For example, if evidence is given that a man walking alongside a golf course was hit by a golf ball the trier of fact will conclude, in the absence of other evidence, that the ball came from the golf course. The second aspect of presumptions of fact is that there are certain issues of fact which arise regularly in trials and the courts have stated that the jury is entitled to draw certain conclusions in those cases. For example, there is a presumption of continuance of life, which states that a life is presumed to continue for a reasonable time. This is a commonsense inference from proof of the fact that someone is alive and well, but arises so frequently that the appellate courts have from time to time identified it as a presumption (*R* v *Lumley* (1869)). It is interesting to note that it has been said that presumptions of fact only arise in this second sense of the commonly recurring fact. The argument here seems to be that some presumptions of fact are recognised by the appellate courts so often that it would be an error of law by the trial judge if he failed to make a direction that the presumption can be made.

Furthermore, it must be noted that Lord Denning called presumptions of fact 'provisional' presumptions, on the basis that they put a tactical burden on the opponent of the issue, and this tactical burden can be satisfied by calling evidence which throws doubt on the truth of the presumed fact. In other words, the presumption will only be drawn when the proponent's evidence is called and may be displaced before the final decision has to be made; it is provisional not permanent. He seemed to group evidential presumptions (presumptions of law placing a tactical burden on the rebutter) and presumptions of fact together in that they both place a tactical burden only on the rebutter. But, as Lord Bridge pointed out, evidential presumptions must be drawn as a matter of law, whereas factual presumptions are permissive only, they may be drawn (12 MLR 272, 278-279). It is submitted, with respect, that Lord Denning failed to appreciate the true effect of the evidential and factual presumptions. Both presumptions only arise at the end of the case; they help the discharge of the legal burden on an issue, by allowing the trier of fact to draw an inference from the evidence presented. But what if no evidence is given by the defendant, must he necessarily fail? Is there a difference between the evidential and factual presumptions? It is submitted that there is a difference. In order to appreciate the difference it is necessary to go back to basics and consider the essence of a presumption.

All presumptions can be written in the same form: on proof of fact 'A' fact 'B' is proved. There are two elements - the proof of fact 'A'; and the proof of fact 'B'. In the case of a conclusive or irrebuttable presumption of law it is not possible to call evidence disproving fact 'B', once fact 'A' has been established. For example, it is not possible to prove that a 13 year old boy committed rape (*R* v *Waite* (1892)). But it is possible to call evidence that the boy in question was over 13 at the time of the alleged rape. In other words, although the presumption cannot be rebutted, it is possible to prevent the presumption arising in the first place.

Applying that principle to evidential and factual presumptions, the trier of fact could always conclude that the evidence called is not strong enough to prove that a certain man sat as a judge at the Old Bailey. If the trier of fact is not satisfied that he sat, then no presumption as to his qualifications must be drawn. Similarly, if the judge is asked to presume that a 35 year old man was likely to live for a further ten years, the judge may find on the evidence presented that the man was not 35 at the time alleged. In both cases the failure to prove the basic fact means that the presumed fact is not proved. But the converse case shows the difference between evidential and factual presumption. Say the judge is satisfied that the man in the first case sat at the Old Bailey, or that the man in the second case was aged 35 at the relevant time; in the first case if the party who wishes to dispute the man's qualifications calls no evidence then, as a matter of law, the trial judge would have to find that the man in question was qualified to sit. In other words once the basic fact is established the presumed fact *must* be found to be true. In the second case, though, even if the trial judge is satisfied that the man in question was 35 and in good health at the relevant time he would still be free to find that he would not be expected to live for a further ten years if, for example, there was a war on and the man was likely to be conscripted for dangerous duties. The second case illustrates that the trier of fact *may* draw a presumption once the basic facts are proved, but does not have to as a matter of law; whereas when dealing with evidential presumptions the presumed fact must be found to be true in the absence of rebutting evidence, once the basic fact is established. Therefore, it is submitted, Lord Denning was wrong to argue that there is no difference between evidential presumptions and presumptions of fact.

There is a further difficulty in the area of presumptions of fact, in that certain rules of law state that the trier of fact may draw a certain conclusion on the proof of certain basic facts. These instances are different from evidential presumptions in that the trier of fact is not bound to find the presumed fact once the basic fact is true and they are different from presumptions of fact in that the law stipulates that the conclusion may be drawn from the basic fact, rather than that being the result of applying commonsense. For example, if an employer has issued an employee with a timetable which directs him to drive from one place to another in an unreasonably short time, then by virtue of s78A Road Traffic Regulations Act 1967, the timetable 'may be produced as prima facie evidence' of incitement to commit a speeding offence. There is no requirement that the jury must find the employer guilty in the absence of proof or evidence to the contrary. The effect of this sort of statutory provision is clear if the stages of the trial mentioned in section (b) above are remembered. The prosecution must make out a prima facie case, fit to be left to the jury. If they cannot do so then the accused may make a submission of no case, which would lead to his acquittal. Section 78A provides that the evidential burden on the prosecution will be satisfied by the timetable being adduced. In other words, the trier of law must draw the presumption that there is a case to answer, even though the trier of fact would be free to reject the timetable as being insufficient evidence to found a conviction.

Such a statutory presumption is not classified by most writers. Lord Denning did not mention them, nor Lord Bridge, nor Cross, nor Heydon, nor Nokes. Carter has labelled them 'permissive' presumptions because the trier of fact is permitted but not obliged, to conclude that there was incitement once the timetable has been adduced (*Cases and Statutes* (2nd edition, 1990, p77)).

f) *Criminal cases*

Although the occasional criminal example has been given above, the general rules stated are only applicable to civil cases. This point is not always appreciated. The reason for it is simple. In a civil case there is no conceptual difficulty in placing a legal burden of proof on the defendant once the plaintiff has adduced some evidence on an issue (nor on the plaintiff if the defendant raises the issue). But in a criminal case the accused only bears a legal burden in two instances - if he wishes to prove insanity (*M'Naghten's Case* (1843)) and where a statute requires him to prove his defence (*R* v *Carr-Briant* (1943); *R* v *Edwards* (1975)). In all other cases the burden on him can be evidential only. Therefore if the prosecution wishes to rely on a presumption, the accused never has to disprove the presumed fact.

g) *Conclusion*

It can be seen from the above discussion that presumptions cover many areas of the law and have been subject to many differences in analysis. It is submitted that the difficulty of analysis and classification is caused by six main factors. Firstly, the failure to distinguish between criminal and civil cases has caused confusion to those who have attempted to set out rules of presumption applicable across the board. Secondly the use of the word presumption can cause a reaction, as with Lord Bridge, that a presumption is a conclusion drawn from the proof of basic facts and anything which does not fit into that model must be called something else - even if it has been called a presumption by other writers for many years. Thirdly, it is not always fully appreciated that some presumptions place a legal burden on the party rebutting and sometimes merely a tactical burden. In this area more than any other the terminology of writers tends to confuse. Williams talked of evidential presumptions because of his definition of the evidential burden; others define that burden as the tactical burden, but retain the term 'evidential presumption', the potential for confusion then is clear. Fourthly, the place of presumptions of fact is changing. The so-called doctrine of recent possession (someone found in possession of stolen goods shortly after they were stolen may be presumed to have come by them dishonestly) has been classified as a presumption of law (*R* v *Hepworth & Fearnley* (1955)) but the Court of Appeal has recently made it clear that it is a presumption of fact only (*R* v *Ball* (1983)). Similar confusion has been caused with the presumption that a man intends the natural and probable consequences of his acts; this started out as a presumption of fact (*R* v *Steane* (1947)), was turned into a presumption of law (*DPP* v *Smith* (1961)) and is now a presumption of fact again (s8 Criminal Justice Act 1967). This sort of change makes the use of older definitions of presumptions dangerous. Fifthly, presumptions of law are random rules affecting the way cases are proved and the way burdens of proof are distributed. The lack of any system of policy behind the presumptions misleads some commentators to attempt to over-simplify the categories. It is submitted that Lord Denning's classification of certain presumptions as 'provisional' falls within this point. Sixthly, the use by the judges of the term 'shifting of the burden of proof' is so widespread, and in many instances so misconceived, that one is tempted to look for a presumption to justify the supposed shift. For example, the 'doctrine' of res ipsa loquitur is treated as a presumption of fact in all parts of the world, where it is recognised that if the only logical inference to draw from the facts proved is that there was negligence then that conclusion must be drawn. But nowhere other than this country has consistently held that the doctrine creates a persuasive presumption placing a legal burden of proof on the rebutter. The confusion has been caused by inexact use of burden of proof terminology.

It is interesting to note that of all the major works on evidence only Carter has pointed out the true effect of what he calls 'permissive' presumptions - rules of law which allow the trier of law no right to reject a piece of evidence as insufficiently probative to be left to the trier of fact. But, even he does not make the point that such a presumption is useless by itself. To use the example given above, s78A Road Traffic Regulations Act 1967 allows the prosecution of an employer for incitement to exceed the speed limit, to use a timetable issued by the employer as evidence against him. This prevents the trial judge withdrawing the case from the jury for lack of evidence on the issue of incitement, but if the case is one where the judge would be minded to withdraw the case for lack of evidence and the jury convicts, then surely the convicted employer would have a ground for appeal in the same way that any appeal should be allowed where the evidence against the accused should, at common law, have been ruled to be insufficient. This new category of presumption, therefore, also has its problems. It only need be relied on if there is no other evidence against the employer, but in that case any conviction could well be perverse. By dressing-up s78A as a presumption there is every possibility that it will be given more significance than it deserves.

Finally, it cannot be stated that the existence of so many classifications and names of presumptions is of any real use unless and until the courts start to put one terminology or another into practice. Although Lord Denning introduced his own terminology and analysis in several cases (eg *Emmanuel* v *Emmanuel* (1946); *Huyton-with-Roby UDC* v *Hunter* (1955)) such usage has not been uniform. The source of confusion in the absence of judicial guidance is clear once the many sources of the word 'presumption' have been seen.

Question 3

a) What place has judicial notice in the context of our trial system?

b) How much use may a judge or magistrate make of his or her personal knowledge?

University of London LLB Examination
(for External Students) Evidence June 1985 Q4

Skeleton solution

- The place of judicial notice, introduction - defining the problem.
- Judicial notice of facts - notice without inquiry - notice after inquiry.
- Judicial notice of law - scope of rule - rationale.
- Theory of judicial notice - two principles - policy - function of judge place of judicial notice.
- Personal knowledge, introduction - definition of the problem.
- Knowledge of the law - tacit notice.
- Knowledge of fact - introduction.
- Judge's personal knowledge of fact - limited scope of use - practical considerations.
- Magistrates' personal knowledge - knowledge of local matters - expert knowledge - difference in treatment of judge and justices.

Suggested solution

a) *The place of judicial notice*

i) Introduction

The principle that questions of fact are for the jury and questions of law for the judge is so well established that no authority need be cited in its support. There is, though, a significant area where the judge decides questions of fact and directs the jury to reach a decision in accordance with his direction. This is the area of judicial notice. In this answer the place of judicial notice will be examined from three angles. Firstly will be considered the extent to which a judge in a criminal case may decide issues of fact. The second perspective will involve discussion of the way matters of law are proved. Thirdly will be examined whether there is any consistent theory as to the proper place for judicial notice.

ii) Judicial notice of facts

There are some facts of such common knowledge that it is thought improper to leave the jury any scope for diversion from accepted wisdom. (This discussion will assume that there is a judge and jury, for the sake of convenience.) For example, the Court of Common Pleas once held that it was right for a judge to direct a jury that rain falls (*Fay* v *Prentice* (1845)). To allow the jury the possibility of disagreeing in such a case may be harmless in that it could be said with some confidence that no jury would disagree. Nonetheless, just to be sure, no evidence is allowed to go to the jury to give them cause for doubt.

Clearly this is a usurpation of the function of the jury by the trial judge. He directs them that an issue of fact must be decided in a certain way. As has already been mentioned, there is no harm in this in such an obvious case. But the right of the judge to direct the jury on questions of fact goes beyond cases where the fact is obvious to anyone. There are some facts of which judicial notice will be taken even though the trial judge may not have been able to state the fact without help from a work of reference. In such cases he is said to take notice after inquiry (*Cross on Evidence* (7th edition, 1990, pp64-67)). For example in *Duff Development Co* v *Government of Kelantan* (1924) the House of Lords held that judicial notice should be taken of the fact that Kelantan was a sovereign state once the Secretary of State for the Colonies had certified that this was so. There is a clear policy element to such a decision, namely that the courts should not reach decisions which might upset the comity of nations. Notice after inquiry is not limited to such cases, though, it applies also to questions of fact which arise frequently and so should be decided in a consistent manner by the courts. To leave such questions to juries may lead to embarrassing conflicts of decisions. For example, in *Davey* v *Harrow Corporation* (1958) the Court of Appeal stated that judicial notice could be taken of the practice of the Ordnance

Survey, primarily to prevent different juries reaching different decisions where similar points of the interpretation of maps arise.

iii) Judicial notice of law

It is no usurpation of the function of the jury for a trial judge to direct them on the law, because that is his exclusive province. It is frequently said that everyone is presumed to know the law (the closes thing we have to be an authority on this is *Bilbie* v *Lumley* (1802)). To expect every trial judge to know the full contents of every statute and precedent is, obviously, quite unreasonable, though. Therefore the judge is allowed to 'refresh his memory' by references to statutes, precedents and works of authority. The formal rules of admissibility of evidence do not apply to legal argument, because the judge does not hear 'evidence'. Rather he refers to various authorities in order to remind himself of what he is seemed to know already.

Judicial notice is taken of English law, but not of other jurisdictions, except in certain special circumstances (for which see Nokes, 'The Limits of Judicial Notice' (1958) 74 LQR 59, 61-62). Judicial notice is also taken of the contents of statutes (s3 Interpretation Act 1978 and s4(2) European Communities Act 1972 for the taking of judicial notice of the contents of the Community Treaties) and of general customs (*Brandao* v *Barnett* (1846)). In some instances even local customs have been the proper subject of judicial notice; for example the local custom that markets in the City of London are market overt for the sale of goods, but not for their purchase by the shopkeeper (*Hargreave* v *Spink* (1892)).

The rationale behind all these cases seems to be that the judge must decide questions of law in a way which allows for accuracy of decision and consistency from case to case (see Carter, *Cases and Statutes on Evidence* (2nd edition, 1990, pp123-125)). To impose rules of evidence on the adduction of law reports, for example, would exclude them as hearsay (subject to civil cases where the statutory exceptions, ss2 and 4 Civil Evidence Act 1968, apply). Such a result would be absurdly inconvenient, so by making questions of law the subject of judicial notice this inconvenience can be circumvented.

iv) Theory of judicial notice

It will be seen from the above discussion that there are three common areas within which the rules of judicial notice apply. Firstly to questions of fact which are known to all; secondly to questions of fact which need to be decided uniformly from case to case, but which need inquiry to be established; and thirdly questions of law which are within the judge's exclusive domain. The question arises whether there is a consistent policy behind all three areas.

It is often asserted that the underlying principle of the rules of judicial notice is that 'notorious' matters should not be the subject of dispute, instead they should be recognised as notorious and applied the same in every case (see, for example, *Phipson on Evidence* (14th edition, 1990, paras 2-21)). This theory is supported to an extent by the history of judicial notice (Nokes, 74 LQR 59, 63-70), but there are, in fact, two distinct principles which are applied. The first is that for reasons of policy certain facts should not be challenged by evidence. An example is given above in the *Duff Development Co* case and this principle also explains such cases as *Fay* v *Prentice*. The other principle, which applies to the taking of judicial notice of questions of law, is that the function of the judge to decide questions of law should not be hampered by technical arguments over the admissibility of reference works.

The place of judicial notice in the trial system, therefore, is to provide a degree of consistency of decision to everyday questions of fact and to allow judges to reach decisions on questions of law in the most effective way. Judicial notice can thus be seen as a set of rules providing for the saving of time and the increase of efficiency in the courts.

b) *Personal knowledge of judge or magistrate*

i) Introduction

The above discussion of judicial notice divides the subject into two parts - notice of fact and notice of law. This distinction is maintained in the rules relating to the use which may be made of personal knowledge by a judge or magistrate.

ii) Personal knowledge of law

If a judge has to decide a question of law he will not always need to be referred to statutes or authorities. Some areas of the law will be well known to him and his memory of these will not need to be refreshed. Clearly it would be unsatisfactory for a judge to have to be referred to statutes and authorities every time, therefore he is allowed to rely on his personal knowledge of the law. Cross has pointed out that some reliance on personal knowledge is inevitable in the decision by a judge or jury of any issue (*Cross on Evidence* (7th edition, 1990, p70)). For example, if a judge has to decide whether a particular house is covered by the Rent and Housing Acts provisions which give tenants statutory rights against their landlord, he would not have to be referred to a dictionary in order to know what 'dwelling' means because he will already know what it means. In every case where a legal point arises it will be discussed in English, the judge relies on his personal knowledge of the English language in order to understand the argument. This is what Cross called a 'tacit' application of judicial notice.

iii) Personal knowledge of fact

The decision of questions of fact by a judge raises different principles, though. In criminal cases it is, of course, the function of the jury to consider questions of fact, subject to directions of fact of which judicial notice has been taken. In civil cases the virtual extinction of the jury means that the judge has to decide both law and fact. The judge when deciding questions of fact is in essentially the same position as a jury or a bench of magistrates. It is not yet clear whether judges and magistrates are in the same position when it comes to the use of personal knowledge in the reaching of a decision of fact.

iv) Judge's knowledge of fact

It is clear that a judge may rely on his personal knowledge of matters of general, or common, knowledge. The problem arises when he had to deal with an issue on which he has local knowledge. Is he allowed to rely on that local knowledge?

The start of the discussion must be the normal rule that questions of fact must be decided according to the evidence called, the trier of fact being entitled to draw any legitimate logical inference from that evidence. If, for example, the question arises whether the defendant trespassed on the plaintiff's land and the plaintiff calls evidence that the defendant was seen entered the land by climbing over a particular gate, and the defendant calls no evidence in rebuttal; then it would appear that the judge would have no option but to find for the plaintiff.

The position is made difficult if the judge knows that the gate is twenty feet high and covered from top to bottom in barbed wire. Is he allowed to rely on this knowledge and use it as the basis of rejecting the evidence called by the plaintiff? The old position was that the trier of fact, whether judge or jury, was not allowed to rely on personal local knowledge (*R* v *Sutton* (1816)). But this was altered gradually, so that in 1841 the trier of fact was allowed to make limited reference to his personal knowledge, and over 100 years later the general rule was stated that personal knowledge of notorious local matters could be relied on provided it was properly used and reasonably applied (*Reynolds* v *Llanelly Associated Tinplate* (1948)). The rule laid down is very wide and vague, indeed this was accepted by the judge who decided the *Reynolds* case. The position of the trained judge does not appear to have altered since 1948. Therefore it can be said, albeit tentatively, that a judge may rely on his personal knowledge of notorious local facts when it is proper and reasonable so to do. The test of when it is proper and reasonable is, necessarily, wide because much would depend on the availability of cogent evidence to prove the point and on whether time and expense would be saved by the judge relying on his knowledge rather than hearing such evidence. In the example give above, therefore, the trial judge would only be allowed to rely on his personal knowledge of the state of the gate if it was a matter which was notorious in the locality.

It may be useful to add that many County Court actions are heard by local judges who, it seems, must from time to time rely on their personal knowledge of the area. But the judges in such cases will not usually give detailed judgments, so the reliance on personal knowledge may be greater in practice than the Court of Appeal has ever had the opportunity to appreciate.

Certainly in principle, there is little to commend any distinction between a professional judge acting as a trier of fact and any other tribunal; nonetheless, such a distinction is drawn, as will now be shown.

v) Magistrates' knowledge of fact

It has been stated above that magistrates are treated differently to professional judges in the respect that they may rely on personal knowledge to a greater extent. Two recent Divisional Court decisions uphold a distinction between magistrates and judges.

In *Ingram* v *Percival* (1969) it was held that local magistrates were entitled to rely on their own knowledge of the tidal limits of local waters. In *Wetherall* v *Harrison* (1976) the Divisional Court held that a magistrate was allowed to rely on his professional knowledge as a doctor when considering a medical defence put forward by the accused. The reasoning in both cases was similar and was that magistrates are local justices untrained in the law; as such their local expertise should be used to the advantage of the administration of justice, as should any other specialist knowledge which they have to offer. In *Wetherall* v *Harrison* the position of the professional judge and the lay magistrate was said to be different because the professional judge is trained to put certain matters out of his mind, whereas the layman was not. Manchester (42 MLR 22, 28) has argued that there was no authority to support this distinction between the use by the different tribunals of personal knowledge. Perhaps it is not fair to counter this with the trite argument that there is never an authority for any proposition until the first authority is created. His point is that the Divisional Court when drawing this distinction assumed that it should be drawn, without sufficiently citing reasons why it should be drawn.

The position of magistrates, therefore, can be summarised in two propositions. Firstly, they may rely on their knowledge of local matters and are not limited, as are judges, to local matters which are 'notorious' (note: there is a signal failure in the authorities to define 'notorious', see 74 LQR 59, 59-70). Secondly they may rely on their professional knowledge in assessing the weight to give evidence called. The first principle has been criticised on the ground that no adequate reason has been given why the distinction should be drawn. Indeed it is hard to see why one trier of fact should be in any different position to any other. Perhaps the rule does not apply very often in practice, though. If evidence is called as to the circumstances of the case then there will be little scope for the justices to rely on their local knowledge. In *Ingram* v *Percival* they only relied on their own knowledge because no evidence had been called on the extent of the tidal waters. It may be that such a position will only rarely arise, usually evidence would be called. The trained judge, unlike the lay magistrates, would be able to direct the parties towards the lack of evidence if he feels that there is a relevant matter which requires to be proved. Perhaps this is the true reason behind the distinction - ability of the trier of fact to determine whether the case is better proved by relying on personal knowledge or by requiring evidence to be called.

The second principle may, in fact, reflect less of a difference in treatment between justices and judges than Manchester suggests. He argues that *Wetherall* v *Harrison* allows justices to rely on professional knowledge to a greater extent than judges (42 MLR 22, 28). It is arguable that this is not so. A professional judge is allowed to rely on his professional instincts and experience when assessing the credibility of a witness. He would have seen and heard more witnesses in his career than any magistrate. Inevitably he would have developed a 'feel' for when a witness is honest or untruthful. There has never been any suggestion that he cannot rely on that experience. Is this any different to the position of the lay justice who is a doctor who does not believe a witness because professional experience tells him that the story told is untrue? It is submitted that there is no difference.

Question 4

What is the relationship between the burden of proof and presumptions? It is possible to classify presumptions by reference to their impact on the burden of proof? Give reasons.

University of London LLB Examination
(for External Students) Evidence June 1986 Q2

Skeleton solution

- Burden of proof - two types - definition.
- Standard rule on burden of proof in civil and criminal cases - exceptions.
- Presumptions - definition - examples - effect on burden of proof.
- Challenge of basic facts or challenge of conclusion.
- Classifying presumptions according to their effect on burden of proof.

Suggested solution

The burden of proof in any trial, civil or criminal, involves two elements, namely, the evidential burden and the legal burden. Indeed, these two burdens arise on each issue in the trial, as well as on the overall issue of which party is to win the case. The evidential burden lies on the party who has to adduce sufficient evidence to make an issue a live issue (*Cross on Evidence* (7th edition, 1990, p113)). In other words it is the burden of raising sufficient evidence such that the issue involved could be decided in his favour. The legal burden is the burden of raising sufficient evidence to prove the issue, in other words sufficient evidence to satisfy the trier of fact that the issue in question should be decided in his favour (*Cross on Evidence* (7th edition, 1990, p112)).

The normal rule in both civil and criminal trials is that the party who first raises an issue should prove it (*Abrath* v *North East Railway Co* (1886)); *Woolmington* v *DPP* (1935)). So, for example, if a prosecution is brought accusing a man of rape, it is for the prosecution to adduce sufficient evidence on all the elements of the offence which could satisfy a reasonable jury of the accused's guilt and it is also for the prosecution to prove guilt before it will win its case. Similarly the plaintiff in a negligence case must adduce sufficient evidence upon which a reasonable trier of fact could be satisfied that a duty of care was owed, that that duty was broken and that the damage incurred was non-remote, and must also satisfy the judge that all three elements were present.

Sometimes this normal rule is altered, however. On occasion it is for the defendant to raise an issue before the prosecution must disprove it - here the defendant bears an evidential burden and the prosecution the legal burden once that evidential burden has been satisfied. At other times the defendant bears a legal burden once the prosecution has raised an issue. At other times, still, the defendant bears both evidential and legal burdens on an issue; the most important examples of this later case are where the defendant argues insanity (*McNaghten's Case* (1843)) and where he seeks to rely in his defence upon some exception, exemption, proviso, excuse or qualification to a statutory offence tried in the magistrates court (s101 Magistrates' Courts Act 1980 and see *R* v *Edwards* (1975)).

In civil cases it is more difficult to be precise about the incidents of the legal and evidential burdens, because, in almost all cases, the whole matter will be tried by judge alone and there is limited scope for a submission of no case to answer. The submission of no case is the stage of the criminal trial at which the prosecution has to satisfy the judge that it has adduced evidence upon which a reasonable jury could convict the accused (*R* v *Galbraith* (1981)). In civil trials the defendant's election to make a submission of no case is tantamount to a decision not to call evidence (*Alexander* v *Rayson* (1936)) and is, therefore, only rarely employed; in criminal trials, however, the submission is made in the absence of the trier of fact (the jury) and there is no bar on calling evidence afterwards in the event that the submission fails.

There is another burden which is of great practical importance, but does not form part of the strict theory of the law of evidence. Whenever one party has seen his opponent put forward evidence which could persuade a reasonable trier of fact that an issue should be decided in his (the opponent's) favour, the party has a choice, he could sit back and call no evidence, hoping that in fact the trier of fact will not be persuaded, or he could put forward evidence himself so as to counteract the effect of the evidence already adduced. When the evidence against him is strong he knows that he is almost certain to lose unless he calls evidence, and it is not uncommon for it to be said that in such circumstances he bears a tactical burden - he does not have to prove anything and the issue has already been raised, but if he does not call evidence to rebut the evidence already called then his tactics will have failed because he will lose his case (*Cross on Evidence* (7th edition, 1990, p117)).

A presumption is a device by which one party may be aided in the task of satisfying a burden. The basic position is that the judge or jury approaches each issue with an open mind and in the absence of evidence which would satisfy a reasonable man that the issue concerned is made out, that mind will not be swayed to decide in favour of the party bearing the burden. But, presumptions come to the assistance of the party bearing the burden by allowing, or requiring, the judge or jury to decide that the burden is satisfied once certain prescribed evidence has been adduced, even though that evidence may not satisfy the judge or jury in the absence of the presumption. For example, once it has been proved that a person has not been heard of for seven years by those who would normally be expected to hear from him and reasonable enquiries have been made to ascertain his whereabouts, it will be presumed that he is dead (*Chard* v *Chard* (1956)). Of course it is by no means the case that such a person will be dead, he may just have disappeared from circulation, and therefore it may be that left alone a judge or jury may not be satisfied of his death, but the law prescribes as being conclusions which are drawn after the proof of certain basic facts. If we use the example already adverted to and assume that one party wants to prove that Mr A is dead; he could prove this by direct evidence, say, that his corpse was identified, and this will be direct proof of death; alternatively when proving the issue of death it is possible to prove the absence for seven years etc and from proof of those basic facts the conclusion will be drawn that Mr A is dead.

Generally, the nature of a presumption is that it prescribes a conclusion which could or should be drawn once the basic facts are proved, but it can be rebutted, either by proving that the basic facts are not made out or by direct evidence to contradict the conclusion which would otherwise be drawn from those basic facts. The rebuttal of presumptions may arise in one of two ways. Firstly it may be that once a presumption has been drawn it must be disproved in order to be rebutted, on the other hand it may be enough to rebut a presumption that it is shown that there was an equal chance of the conclusion drawn being untrue as there is of it being true. These are normally explained by saying that in the first type a legal burden is placed on the rebutter, whereas in the second an evidential burden only is imposed, but this explanation does not tell the full story. The true position is that sometimes a presumption must be drawn once the primary facts are proved, for example the presumption of death mentioned above - in such cases the only way in which the conclusion reached can be challenged is by challenging the basic facts. For example, if it is desired to rebut the presumption of death it will be necessary to show that the person in question is still alive, but once that has been shown the presumption simply never arises. It is not the case that the plaintiff can satisfy the judge that the three elements of the presumption are made out and then it is for the defendant to challenge that result, because the presumption can only ever be drawn after all the evidence has been heard, for plaintiff and defence. On the other hand some presumptions can be rebutted by leaving the basic facts intact and challenging the conclusion. For example, there is a presumption that a child born in wedlock is legitimate provided the husband had access to the wife at the likely time of conception (*Banbury Peerage Case* (1811)). It is quite possible for the husband to challenge the wife's evidence about access, but it is equally possible for the husband to accept the basic facts and rebut the presumption by more direct evidence of illegitimacy, for example blood group evidence which shows that he is definitely not the father. In such a case the presumption arises once the wife has called evidence on the basic facts and that evidence is not challenged, but the husband can still rebut the presumption.

Therefore, the position is that some presumptions arise only after all the relevant evidence on the fact in issue has been adduced, whereas others arise once the basic facts are proved and it is then open to rebuttal on the ground that despite the basic facts being proved the conclusion should not follow. It is in the context of this latter type of presumption that the different burdens on the rebutter arise. If it is proposed to challenge the basic facts of a presumption then all that the rebutter has to do is show that the basic facts are not proved, in other words he must show it equally likely that the basic facts are not true as that they are true. If, though, it is proposed to challenge the conclusion without challenging the basic facts, then it must be asked what is the standard of challenge required; sometimes the rebutter will have to prove that the conclusion is not merited on the facts of the case, at other times he will successfully rebut the presumption by showing that the conclusion is equally likely to be untrue as it is to be true.

Presumptions rarely have the effect of deciding the overall outcome of a trial, it is more likely that they will assist in the decision on one or more issues. But, in some cases, the only issue at trial is the very one on which the presumption assists.

It can be seen from what has been said above that a presumption may have one of five effects. A presumption may allow one party to satisfy his evidential burden on a particular issue without affecting his legal burden; or it may allow him to satisfy his legal burden on that issue and place a legal burden of disproof on his opponent; or it may allow him to satisfy his legal burden on that issue and place a burden on his opponent to show that the conclusion drawn is equally likely to be false as true; or it may allow him to satisfy his evidential burden on an issue on which he bears no legal burden; or it may allow him to satisfy his legal burden on an issue on which his opponent bears an evidential burden. There is no presumption which determines the whole outcome of a case except in cases where one issue is paramount and a presumption assists in the determination of that issue.

Following what has been said above, it becomes possible to classify presumptions according to their effect on the burden of proof. If a presumption helps a party to meet his evidential burden then it is 'permissive', though of the leading writers only Carter specifically covers this type of presumption (*Cases and Statutes on Evidence* (2nd edition, 1990, pp77-78)). No distinction is drawn between permissive presumptions where the party using the presumption bears the legal burden on the issue and where his opponent bears that burden once the presumption is drawn. If it allows a legal burden to be satisfied in the absence of proof to the contrary then a presumption may be called 'persuasive' (*Cross on Evidence* (7th edition, 1990, pp126-129)) or, as Lord Denning prefers 'compelling' ((1945) 61 LQR 379). If it allows a legal burden to be satisfied but can be rebutted by evidence that the conclusion is equally likely to be false as true then it is an 'evidential' presumption (*Cross on Evidence* (7th edition, 1990, p126); Carter, *Cases and Statutes on Evidence* (2nd edition, 1990, p78)). Lord Bridge wrote of such presumptions that they should be known simply as 'presumptions' because if a legal burden is imposed on the rebutter then we are not concerned with a presumption but with a rule of law which determines that a certain result must follow the proof of certain basic fact ((1949) 12

MLR 272). Lord Bridge's classification, it is submitted, is artificial because almost all presumptions involve rules of law which give special weight to the proof of basic facts. In some cases the conclusion which is drawn on proof of the basic facts is one which common sense would dictate in any event, but in many more cases the conclusion is only drawn because the law requires it; and, in such cases, whether a legal burden of disproof is placed on the rebutter or just a burden to balance the probabilities makes no difference in as much as a rule of law is involved which gives artificial weight to the basic facts.

Question 5

Consider whether the presumptions of legitimacy, death and marriage serve any practical purpose in the law in relation to:

a) facilitating proof of the presumed fact;

b) their impact on the burden of proof.

University of London LLB Examination
(for External Students) Evidence June 1987 Q4

Skeleton solution

Definition of the three types of presumption:

a) *Presumptions of legitimacy* - other methods of proving legitimacy - effect on burden of proof - civil and criminal cases.

b) *Presumption of death* - alternative methods of proving that the person is alive - effect on burden of proof - evidential only.

c) *Presumption of marriage* - practical effect of presumption - relatively easy alternative proof - effect on burden of proof.

Suggested solution

The three presumptions mentioned in the question provide means of proving certain facts for the purpose of legal proceedings without having to call evidence which actually proves them to be true. In outline the three presumptions operate as follows. The presumption of legitimacy provides that once it is proved that a child was born to a woman who was married either at the time of conception or at the time of birth then it will be presumed that it is her husband's child (*Banbury Peerage Case* (1811)). The presumption of death provides that once it is proved that someone has been unheard of for seven years by those who are most likely to have heard of him, then he will be presumed to be dead (*Chard* v *Chard* (1956)). The presumption of marriage is more complicated since it can operate in two ways. Firstly, it will be presumed that a couple are married if it is proved that they have gone through a ceremony of marriage and that they have cohabited as man and wife (*Piers* v *Piers* (1849)). Secondly, it will be presumed that a couple are married if they cohabit as man and wife and are reputed to be married (*Sastry Velaider Aronegary* v *Sambecutty Vailalie* (1881)). Indeed the first of the two aspects of the presumption of marriage itself has two aspects in that it will be presumed that the ceremony itself was effective and that the parties had the capacity to marry.

a) *The presumption of legitimacy*

The presumption of legitimacy as outlined above operated to allow proof of paternity without the need to call medical evidence to establish that the husband could be the father. Indeed there is little evidence that can ever be used to prove that a particular man is the father of a child. Blood group evidence can prove that he is not and can prove that someone with the same blood type is the father, but it cannot go any further than that. Other more technical medical evidence could be called to establish paternity (for example so-called 'genetic fingerprint' evidence) whether the case is criminal or civil.

The effect of the presumption on the burden of proof differs according to whether the case is criminal or civil. In criminal cases where the prosecution wishes to rebut the presumption it will always bear a legal burden of proof and if the defence wishes to rebut it then an evidential burden only must be satisfied. There appears to be no authority directly to point but this results from the normal common law rules of burden and standard of proof, namely that the defence only bears a legal burden where the defence is insanity or where statute imposes such a burden.

In civil cases the presumption places a legal burden of proof on the party seeking to rebut it, whether that be plaintiff or defendant. The standard of proof in civil cases is the balance of probabilities. There is a question whether the presumption itself carries any weight, in other words whether the judge should consider the presumption itself to be evidence which points towards legitimacy, but it is thought that it does not and that its only effect is to place the burden of proof on the rebutter. If the presumption were intended to have weight as evidence then its effect would be not just to dictate who bears the burden of proof but also to increase the standard of proof required from the rebutter, yet the standard is the balance of probabilities only by virtue of s26 of the Family Law Reform Act 1969.

b) *The presumption of death*

Of the three presumptions discussed the presumption of death probably has the most widespread application in practice. It is also the most effective of the three in terms of assisting the court to reach a conclusion on a matter on which there is likely to be no evidence. A person (X) will be presumed to be dead if it can be proved: (1) that there are persons who could be expected to have heard of him; (2) that those persons have not heard of him for seven years; and (3) that reasonable steps have been taken to ascertain whether he is still alive. On proof of these three basic facts the judge must conclude that X is dead unless there is direct evidence that he is not dead. The presumption of death operates to allow for death to be presumed in many cases where it simply cannot be proved one way or the other whether X is in fact dead.

It is, of course, quite possible that X will still be alive but the possibility of this is reduced by the need to prove the first of the three basic facts outlined above. Unless it can be proved that someone is likely to have heard of him then the presumption cannot arise. If X goes abroad, declaring that he wants no further contact with his family or friends and is not heard of for seven years by them then the presumption would not arise, because as a matter of common sense as much as anything else, it is not a compelling conclusion that the reason for not hearing of him is that he is dead.

The need to prove seven years' absence does not give rise to a presumption that X died seven years from the time he was last heard of. The presumption, according to *Re Phene's Trusts* (1870) operates only to establish that X is dead at the time of the legal proceedings. There is some authority to the contrary, notably *Chipchase* v *Chipchase* (1939), but the proper view of such cases is that there was some evidence to show the time of death.

The presumption of death places an evidential burden only on the rebutting party, not a legal burden. To this extent it differs in its operation from the presumption of legitimacy. This difference also means that the effect of the presumption is the same no matter which party it operates against and no matter whether the proceedings are civil or criminal. The presumption will not, of course, be rebutted simply because some evidence is called which shows that one of the basic facts may not be made out. If that evidence is sufficiently cogent then the presumption will not arise at all because the basic fact would not be proved by the party trying to establish death, but once the judge is satisfied on all the evidence that the basic facts are proved then it is only direct evidence that X is alive which can rebut it.

In addition to the formal presumption of death which must arise on the proof of the three basic facts outlined above, the court is always entitled to presume that someone is dead as a matter of inference from other facts. For example, if someone falls from a ship into the middle of the Atlantic ocean and despite attempts to find him he is declared lost, the possibility of him still being alive a year later when nothing has been heard to suggest that he had been picked up by another vessel is remote. The court would be entitled to draw the inference that he is dead from the circumstances of his disappearance. This is not a question of a formal presumption of law being applied, but is a purely factual exercise.

c) *The presumption of marriage*

Whether two people are married can have consequences in both criminal and civil cases. Today the compulsory registration of marriages allows little scope for the presumption to arise, save in cases where there is a question over the legitimacy of the ceremony. Whether the presumption arises on proof of a ceremony and cohabitation or on proof of cohabitation and repute the effect is the same - marriage is presumed unless there is strong evidence that the parties are not legitimately married.

The proof of a ceremony of marriage gives rise to two presumptions which together form the presumption of marriage. The first is the presumption that the ceremony was conducted by an authorised person and in an authorised place. The second is that the parties had the capacity to marry, in other words that they were over 16 years of age, had any parental consent that may have been necessary and were not already married. The practical effect of the presumption is to allow the court to consider a couple to be properly married. The practical effect of the presumption is to allow the court to consider a couple to be properly married without having to investigate all sorts of matters upon which evidence may not be available. For example where a couple underwent a ceremony of marriage 40 years prior to the court proceedings it is highly unlikely that it could be discovered whether the person who married them was properly authorised, so the presumption operates to allow a common sense conclusion to be drawn by the court.

To presume marriage from cohabitation and repute, in other words to presume marriage from evidence that the couple lived together and were reputed to be married, raises rather different issues. In such cases there may be no evidence before the court that any ceremony was entered into, but the presumption still allows a common sense conclusion to be drawn from the proof of the basic facts. In practical terms cases are rare where cohabitation and repute need to be relied upon because of the registration of marriages, but such cases can still arise for example where the parties originally came from a country where there is no such registration.

It is arguable that the presumption of marriage adds little to the right of a court to draw an inference from facts which are proved to it. Perhaps the only effect of it is to prevent the court from refusing to draw the inference of marriage where evidence of the basic facts is proved on balance of probabilities but not to any higher standard.

The presumption of marriage which arises from proof of a ceremony and cohabitation operates somewhat differently to the other presumptions discussed above. This is because the presumption itself is not really concerned with marriage but with the validity of appointment and certification of places and people. The presumption is that: (1) the place in which some ceremony was carried out was licensed; (2) the person conducting it was authorised to do so; (3) the parties concerned were over 16; (4) neither party was already married; and (5) the parties had obtained any parental or other consent which was required. It is these formal matters which are presumed and once they are presumed it then follows that the ceremony was valid. There is no presumption applied directly to the marriage itself.

The effect of this presumption on the burden of proof is also somewhat difficult to state. It is often said that the party who wishes to show that the parties are not married bears a legal burden of proof. But this burden is usually a burden of proving that the basic facts are not established rather than a burden that the presumed fact is not established from the basic facts. The challenge may be made, for example, on the ground that the official who married the parties was not properly authorised or that one of the parties was already married. But that challenge goes to proof of the basic facts not of the presumed fact. In other words it prevents the basic facts being established. To put it another way, where a party to an action wishes to argue that the basic facts are not established then it is for him to prove it. The standard required is the balance of probabilities (*Blyth* v *Blyth* (1966)), but of course, the more unusual the argument being put forward the less probable it is that that argument is correct. For example if it is alleged that a ceremony carried out in a church was not valid because the church was not a proper place for the celebration of marriage then the burden will be very heavy because of the inherent unlikelihood of the allegation.

Once the basic facts of this presumption are established then the only way of rebutting the presumption of marriage is by proving that the marriage has been dissolved.

The presumption which arises out of proof of cohabitation and repute probably places a legal burden of disproof on the rebutter in civil cases. The scope for rebuttal of this presumption is greater because the basic facts can be established without having to prove any ceremony at all. Therefore the rebutter may successfully challenge the presumption by proving that the ceremony which was undergone was not valid. The effect of the cohabitation and repute presumption in many cases is to add to the other presumption of marriage. There are cases, like *R* v *Shepherd* (1904), where a ceremony has been proved and cohabitation and repute have also been proved, and the judge has held that the challenge to the validity of the ceremony had failed because the evidence of cohabitation and repute is strong.

In criminal cases, as shown above in the case of the presumption of legitimacy, nothing more than an evidential burden can be placed on the accused and nothing less than a legal burden on the prosecution, although the prosecution's task may be made easier in bigamy cases because evidence of cohabitation and repute could be an admission by the defendant(s) that they are married.

15 UNIVERSITY OF LONDON LLB (EXTERNAL) 1991 QUESTIONS AND SUGGESTED SOLUTIONS

UNIVERSITY OF LONDON
LLB EXAMINATION
PARTS I AND II
for External Students

EVIDENCE

Thursday, 6 June 1991: 2.00 to 5.30 pm

Answer *FOUR* of the following eight questions, including at least *ONE* from Part A and *ONE* from Part B.

PART A

1. 'Whether the courts should refuse to entertain evidence because it has been obtained by the party tendering it in an illegal or improper manner is a question principally of policy, to which no answer is to be found in the law of evidence.' (Murphy).

   Discuss.

2. 'When Parliament by the Act of 1898 effected a change in the general law and made the prisoner in every case a competent witness, it was in an evident difficulty, and it pursued the familiar English system of compromise.' (The House of Lords in *Maxwell* v *DPP*).

   Discuss in relation to s1(f) of the Criminal Evidence Act 1898.

   What changes, in your view, would be desirable?

3. 'The concern of the law of evidence is not always the truth. Other values constantly intrude, sometimes overriding the value of truth.'

   Discuss in relation to public interest immunity.

4. 'It is not only the adduction of *prima facie* evidence by the proponent which results in an evidential burden being cast on the opponent. The same effect may result from the operation of a presumption.' (Phipson and Elliot).

Discuss. To what extent do you agree that the operation of presumptions is based more on considerations of public policy than of logic?

PART B

5. A is suing B Jewellers Ltd for the loss of two rubies from a ring which A handed in to them for restyling. B Jewellers Ltd are relying on an exemption clause contained in the contract exempting them from accidental loss. A possesses a written valuation of the ring from X Valuers Ltd, dated ten years earlier, in which it is stated that the ring is worth £10,000. Unfortunately, X Valuers Ltd since went into liquidation and the valuer cannot be traced. A has also obtained a photocopy of an internal memorandum at B Jewellers Ltd which implicates C, an employee, in the theft of precious stones from jewellery handed in by customers. This memorandum had been forwarded to the company's solicitors who have refused to release it. A has further obtained a copy of an entry in the books of D Pawnbrokers Ltd which shows that C had pledged two rubies as security for a loan. The entries show that the carat weight and the refractive index of the rubies as determined by the firm's computer tally with the weight and index of A's jewels.

   Advise A on the admissibility of these items as evidence and the standard of proof applicable to the assertion that C stole the rubies.

6. E and F are charged with indecent assault on G, aged 10. The assault is alleged to have taken place in a park near G's home. After the alleged incident G ran home crying and with her clothes torn. When questioned by her mother, H, G said that she had been attacked by two men. She described one man as tall with a black moustache and the other as thin with a mole on his chin. At a subsequent identification parade she picked out E, who is tall with a blonde moustache, and F, who is thin with a large mole on his cheek, as the men who attacked her. When challenged by Inspector L to account for themselves E claimed to have been at work at the time and F refused to say anything.

   At the trial, G gives unsworn testimony describing the assault, but she is unable to identify her assailants. H gives evidence about G's statement and her physical condition at the time. Inspector L testifies that G picked out the defendants at an identification parade, and he describes their responses to his questions. F does not give evidence. E testifies that he is innocent but admits in cross-examination that he was not at work on the day in question.

   Advise E and F.

7. M is charged with the murder of N, the lover of M's wife O, by running him down in the street. M has stated to the police that N unexpectedly stepped off the pavement into the path of his car and that a collision was unavoidable. Four days before his death, N wrote in his diary that he was afraid because M had become enraged about the affair with O and that he intended to 'watch over his shoulder' from now on. On the day N died, P, a passer-by, heard an unidentified woman at the scene of the accident say, pointing to M, 'That man went straight for him; he gave him no chance.' O has stated that M told her later on the same day that N had been

involved in an accident, adding that 'he got what he deserved'. M proposes not to testify himself at his trial but seeks to adduce psychiatric evidence that P is schizophrenic and that he, M, has a timid personality and is unlikely to behave aggressively.

Advise the prosecution on any evidential issues arising.

8. Q is charged with burglary and R with handling stolen goods. The prosecution allege that Q induced S to let him into S's house by stating falsely that his car had broken down, and that once inside he stole S's jewellery when her back was turned. The jewellery was later found on sale in R's shop. Q and R make statements to the police. Q claims that his car had broken down and he denies taking the jewellery. R claims that he bought the jewellery in good faith from a stranger and says that he will call witnesses who will testify to his integrity. The prosecution seek to adduce the following evidence:

   a) Seven years earlier Q was convicted of theft of money from a householder to whom he had stated falsely that he had come to read the gas meter.

   b) During a search of Q's flat after P reported her loss, the police found a set of skeleton keys and a letter to Q from the receiver of stolen goods, now dead, advising on how to dispose of stolen jewellery.

   c) R has twice been dismissed from employment in jewellers' shops after rumours that he was buying stolen jewellery. His neighbour is prepared to testify that he would not trust R an inch.

Advise the prosecution.

Question 1

'Whether the courts should refuse to entertain evidence because it has been obtained by the party tendering it in an illegal or improper manner is a question principally of policy, to which no answer is to be found in the law of evidence.' (Murphy).

Discuss.

University of London LLB Examination
(for External Students) Evidence June 1991 Q1

General comment

This question requires the candidate to discuss the principles governing the exercise of discretion, thereby demonstrating the legal (as opposed to policy) basis on which such evidence is excluded. It primarily concerns criminal trials.

Skeleton solution

- Admissibility of illegally or improperly obtained evidence as a matter of law in criminal and civil trials.
- Role of discretion at common law - *R* v *Sang*; s78 of the Police and Criminal Evidence Act 1984.
- Present status of agent provocateur evidence (*R* v *Harwood*; *R* v *Gill*).
- Interpretation of s78 (*R* v *Mason*; *R* v *Samuel*; *R* v *Alladice*; *R* v *Keenan*).

Suggested solution

It is fair to say that the principles on which illegally or improperly obtained evidence is excluded are less than clear, particularly in criminal cases. There are, nevertheless, some established ground rules which demonstrate that exclusion of such evidence depends primarily on the exercise of judicial discretion. The manner in which the discretion is exercised is not, however, based simply on policy questions, but rather on rules which form part of the law of evidence.

In order to explore the quotation in the question, it is necessary to examine the way in which the courts have approached the question of excluding such evidence. By that means, it becomes more easy to establish the rules by which courts make decisions.

One proposition is well established, and is authority for limiting the discussion to discretion. The fact that evidence has been illegally or improperly obtained makes no difference to its admissibility as a matter of law in a criminal case - it remains admissible: *Kuruma* v *R* (1955). This is also true for civil cases, and, according to Lord Denning in *Helliwell* v *Piggott-Sims* (1980), no discretion even exists to exclude it.

In criminal cases, the governing authority for the exercise of discretion at common law is *R* v *Sang* (1980). The common law now lies alongside a statutory discretion in s78 of the Police and Criminal Evidence Act 1984 and is preserved by s82(3) of that Act. Under the *Sang* principles:

a) the fact that evidence has been obtained as a result of the activities of an agent provocateur is no reason to exclude such evidence;

b) apart from admissions and confessions and other evidence obtained from the accused after the commission of an offence, there is no discretion to exclude evidence by reason of the manner in which it was obtained; but

c) the court always has a discretion to exclude evidence where necessary to ensure a fair trial.

The common law discretion to exclude improperly obtained evidence where it is not either a confession (which is governed by special rules - now s76 of the Police and Criminal Evidence Act 1984) or unduly prejudicial compared with its probative value, is, however, extremely rarely exercised. One of the few authorities is the driving case of *R* v *Payne* (1963) in which a motorist was duped into providing evidence against himself by false representations as to the purpose of medical examination.

It is therefore apparent that the exercise of discretion to exclude improperly or illegally obtained evidence at common law is governed by ground rules laid down by the law of evidence as developed by case law. It may be said that policy considerations have affected the way the rules have developed but it is the rules which govern admissibility.

The other basis for excluding this sort of evidence is s78 of the Police and Criminal Evidence Act. A discretion arises where, in all the circumstances, including the circumstances in which evidence is obtained, its admission would adversely affect the fairness of the proceedings. Taking this section at face value, it confers a very broad discretion on a judge and, as was made clear in *R* v *Mason* (1987), it is not to be taken as a recitation of the common law.

That said, it is as yet unclear how far the discretion to exclude will be applied in practice. There are conflicting indications in *R* v *Gill* (1963) and *R* v *Harwood* (1989) on the question of whether evidence obtained through the activities of an agent provocateur might be excluded under s78. Likewise, it is unclear how far the circumstances of the obtaining (other than by the agent provocateur) will result in a trigger for exclusion under s78. *R* v *Mason* in which exclusion under s78 arose when the police deliberately misled an accused and his solicitor into thinking there was evidence against the accused, is an example of a deliberate deception which might have been sufficient to trigger the common law discretion comparable with what happened in *R* v *Payne*. In *Kinsella* v *Marshall* (1988), a refusal to exercise the s78 discretion where plain clothes policemen made a test purchase to see if a shopkeeper was selling alcohol unlawfully was explained on the basis that it was not a 'clear deception'. Perhaps rather, it was a recognition of the fact that evidence in such cases would be difficult to secure by any other means.

Cases involving exclusion of confessional evidence have been a rich source of case law under s78, which is not excluded by the operation of s76 - *R* v *Mason*. It is possible to distil some general principles from them. Failure to afford access to legal advice, being a fundamental right under the Police and Criminal Evidence Act, will be a good ground for exclusion: *R* v *Samuel* (1988). Bad faith on the part of the police will, according to the Lord Chief Justice in *R* v *Alladice* (1988), mean that courts will have little difficulty in excluding evidence thereby obtained. This principle was applied in case of a failure to give access to legal advice, but indications are that it is a principle capable of application more broadly.

The code on detention and questioning issued under s66 of the 1984 Act is to be taken into account (s67) in deciding whether to exclude under s78. According to *R* v *Keenan* (1990) the requirement is that the breach of the code's provisions is significant and substantial. Failure to give access to legal advice is such a breach, but there are, of course, many others related to the questioning process which can be so described.

Again, what can be said from the above analysis is that whilst the judicial approach to s78 is still developing, it is not simply a matter of policy. The judge is restrained by the terms of s78, the principles developed by the case law and guidance in the Codes of Practice. A judge is not entitled to apply his discretion simply on policy grounds. It is a fair assumption that policy considerations have played their part in developing the principles by which discretion is to be decided and undoubtedly, played a role in the formulation by Parliament of the statutory provision in s78. Such considerations will, no doubt, affect future developments. This is, however, no different from the other areas of the law of evidence. What, however, the courts have to be concerned with in any given case is the way the principles which have emerged are to be applied, and it is that rather than the underlying policy concerns which determine the exercise of discretion to exclude evidence.

Question 2

'When Parliament by the Act of 1898 effected a change in the general law and made the prisoner in every case a competent witness, it was in an evident difficulty, and it pursued the familiar English system of compromise.' (The House of Lords in *Maxwell* v *DPP*).

Discuss in relation to s1(f) of the Criminal Evidence Act 1898.

What changes, in your view, would be desirable?

University of London LLB Examination
(for External Students) Evidence June 1991 Q2

General comment

A question requiring critical discussion of the interpretation of s1(f) of the Criminal Evidence Act 1898, coupled with an appreciation of the circumstances in which character evidence may be given at common law. A knowledge of the law before 1898, other than the surviving principles, is not required.

Skeleton solution

- The common law governing the adduction of character evidence against the accused - the *R* v *Rowton* principle; *R* v *Redd*; the 'similar fact' rules.
- Requirements and interpretation of s1(f)(i) - comparison with common law (*Jones* v *DPP* and *R* v *Anderson*); s1(f)(ii) first and second limbs; comparison with common

law noting in particular the extension offered by the second limb; efficacy of the case law; the role of discretion. Section 1(f)(iii) - comparison of requirement with common law on cross examination of opponents and witnesses: *R* v *Murdoch & Taylor*; the potential unfairness of *R* v *Varley*.

- Desirable changes - the interpretation of 'tending to show'; achieving consistency in evidential effect and reversal of *R* v *Powell*; reforming of the rule in *R* v *Varley*; clarification of use by prosecution of s1(f)(iii) and by co-accused of s1(f)(ii).

Suggested solution

In making the accused competent to testify, Parliament had to address the extent to which an accused exercising the new right should be protected from hostile cross-examination designed to show him to be a dog with a bad name.

The practice of juries in inferring guilt from bad character was then, as now, a well recognised problem, and even before the 1898 Act, there were restrictions on the circumstances in which the prosecution could adduce such evidence. These remain today. Accordingly, only where the defence first gives evidence of the accused's good character can the prosecution retaliate with evidence of adverse general reputation or prior convictions: *R* v *Rowton* (1865); *R* v *Redd* (1923). The prosecution is also allowed to adduce evidence of the accused's misconduct on other occasions where that conduct is specially relevant to the issues in the case under the 'similar fact' principle laid down in *Makin* v *Attorney-General of New South Wales* (1894) and subsequent cases. Evidence under both heads go to the accused's guilt as well as his credibility.

The 1898 Act recognises the existing common law allowances for bringing evidence of the accused's past misdeeds, but provides a self-contained code within which cross-examination of the accused on character may take place.

Section 1(f) provides that no question in cross examination shall be asked tending to show the accused has committed, been convicted of or charged with any offence, other than one subject of the proceedings, or is of bad character unless (1(f)(i)) the prosecution would be allowed to give evidence in chief; (1(f)(ii)) the accused (or his witnesses) have given evidence of good character, or imputations have been cast on the prosecutor or prosecution witnesses; or (1(f)(iii)) the accused has given evidence against a co-accused in the same proceedings.

Section 1(f)(i) is wholly consistent with the similar fact principles at common law. Where the prosecution is allowed to adduce character evidence in chief, it is only reasonable that the accused should be amenable to cross examination. The jury has already properly heard the evidence and the protection which 1(f) is intended to afford does not arise for consideration. In fact, as a result of the decision in *Jones* v *DPP* (1962) and more recently, in *R* v *Anderson* (1988), where character evidence is properly made known to the jury before cross-examination occurs, there is no need to rely on s1(f)(i) because 'tending to show' in s1(f) has the meaning 'made known to the jury for the first time'. It is clear from the terms of s1(f)(i) and the common law rules that when evidence is adduced under 1(f)(i) it goes to guilt as well as to credit of the accused as a witness.

The subsection is, therefore, a recognition of the common law and does not seek to extend it. It is a sensible compromise between allowing cross examination and protecting the accused's legitimate interests.

The first limb of s1(f)(ii) is relatively straightforward and reflects the common law *Rowton* rule. An accused who gives evidence of his own good character can be cross-examined by the prosecution. If the prosecution can lead evidence, the matter is before the jury, and no purpose is served by disallowing cross-examination. But there are some differences in approach, although it is far from clear that they were intended by Parliament. Good character is not confined to evidence of general reputation as at common law, but extends to evidence of particular acts: *R* v *Dunkley* (1927). In this sense, the ability to cross examine has been liberalised. Second, what may amount to good character under s1(f)(ii) is generously interpreted in the prosecution's favour as argument in *R* v *Coulman* (1927) (in which the accused's statement that he was a family man and had employment was regarded by the court as an allegation of good character) demonstrates.

The second limb of s1(f)(ii) provides recognition of the fact that an accused who questions the integrity of prosecution witnesses should not, as the common law supposed (*R* v *Butterwasser* (1948)) leave the prosecution powerless to retaliate. The requirement of the casting of imputations was the chosen mechanism to effect the compromise between the common law and this recognition. The provision has received considerable judicial attention. The interpretation of 'tending to show' in the case of Jones and more recently Anderson demonstrate that the protection does not apply where an aspect of the accused's bad character has been indicated to the jury before the cross examination occurs. In the early cases, there was a certain degree of reluctance to find that an imputation had been made. For example, in *R* v *Rouse* (1904) an accusation that a witness was a liar was held not to be imputation. But more recently, with the formal recognition in *Selvey* v *DPP* (1970) of a discretion to disallow cross-examination, this reluctance has tended to evaporate so that in *R* v *Lasseur* (1991) such a contention was held as capable of being an imputation as a matter of law. In addition to establishing the judicial discretion in s1(f)(ii), Selvey laid down other principles which are helpful in deciding the question of what amounts to an imputation. These are however, rules of case law. There is nothing to indicate that Parliament had such results in mind. Likewise, with the role of discretion in disallowing cross-examination, the guidance to be derived from *R* v *Britzman and Hall* (1983) for police interviews can hardly be distilled from the wording of 1(f)(ii). The compromise here is perhaps that Parliament decided to set out a new rule as a framework provision, thus leaving the common law to develop in a way best suited to the general objectives the section is intended to meet. It must, however, be questionable how far such an expectation has been fulfilled through the case law.

Nothing is said in the section about the evidential effect of either part of s1(f)(ii). If that was intended as a compromise with the common law by allowing the latter to take its course, it is doubtful whether the results are satisfactory. Predictably, both parts of s1(f)(ii) have been treated as going to credit rather than guilt of the accused (*Maxwell* v *DPP* (1935); *R* v *Vickers* (1972)). But according to *R* v *Powell* (1986) (not following the earlier case of *R* v *Watts* (1983)) the danger that a jury may be inclined to treat a conviction as going to guilt because they are similar in nature is no reason to disallow the cross examination in the exercise of judicial discretion. The danger is to be dealt with by directions from the judge. It must be doubtful how effective such directions are in practice.

Section 1(f)(iii) allows cross examination where an accused has given evidence against a co-accused. This provision was evidently designed as a compromise between the common law which would allow the testifying co-accused to be treated in the same way as any other opposing witness, allowing the cross examining co-accused to ask character questions and about prior convictions, and prove them on denial, and the undue prejudice which might be caused to accuseds if such cross examination were allowed unfettered. 'Evidence against' is normally interpreted in accordance with authorities of *R* v *Murdoch and Taylor* (1965) and *R* v *Varley* (1982). The co-accused is at risk of cross examination if his evidence advances the prosecution's case or damages his co-accused's or if his defence necessarily means that if he did not do it, then his co-accused did. But the problem of such an approach is that co-accuseds with a criminal past may in effect be hamstrung. It is common for one co-accused to blame the other (a 'cut-throat defence'). This will, according to *Varley*, put him on risk of cross examination and the exposing of his past to the jury. That is likely to put a co-accused without a criminal past, whose colleague with a criminal past seeks to shift the blame, in a strong position to secure an acquittal.

The following changes are desirable. The meaning of the phrase 'tending to show' should be redefined so that revealing to the jury for the first time merely by indicating some unrelated aspect of prior misbehaviour before the cross-examination does not make an accused susceptible to cross-examination on prior convictions. In other words, this is to reverse the trend apparent in *Anderson*. The evidential effect of good character and retaliation evidence of bad character should be rationalised so that there is consistency between evidence adduced under the *R* v *Rowton* principle at common law, and under the first limb of s1(f)(ii). Under the second limb of s1(f)(ii), it would be very desirable to enable the judge to exclude cross examination where the jury are likely to infer guilt on account of the similarity of the prior misconduct; in other words, to restore the law as decided under Watts; and if greater reliance is to be placed on the role of discretion by interpreting what amounts to an imputation more restrictively, then further ground rules on the way it is to be exercised are desirable.

With s1(f)(iii) perhaps the major point is the potential harshness of the rule in *Varley* for an accused with a criminal past who is running a cut-throat defence, especially since cross-examination under 1(f)(iii) is of right and not subject to exclusionary judicial discretion.

A final point which has not hitherto surfaced much in the case law but which would benefit from clarification is the extent to which a co-accused can utilise cross-examination under 1(f)(ii) or the prosecution cross-examination under 1(f)(iii). The rules as they have developed assume cross-examination by the prosecution under 1(f)(ii) and a co-accused under 1(f)(iii). There is a case for making this a formal requirement if only to ensure a greater certainty in the ground rules for the future, because it is desirable that an accused's legal advisers should be as clear as possible as to what the circumstances in which he will be susceptible to cross-examination are.

Question 3

'The concern of the law of evidence is not always the truth. Other values constantly intrude, sometimes overriding the value of truth.'

Discuss in relation to public interest immunity.

University of London LLB Examination
(for External Students) Evidence June 1991 Q3

General comment

This question requires a discussion of the principles by which relevant evidence can be excluded in the public interest. Since the court is thereby denied information which would otherwise form part of the consideration in determining the outcome of the case, the proposition advanced in the question can then be shown to be supported.

Skeleton solution

- Development of exclusionary criteria - *Duncan* v *Cammell Laird*; modification under *Conway* v *Rimmer*; scope of the rule as presently interpreted.
- Situations in which the immunity is upheld, although *Conway* v *Rimmer* approach indicates otherwise - agencies depending on the free flow of voluntary information - *D* v *NSPCC*; police informers - *Marks* v *Beyfus*; journalistic information - s10 of the Contempt of Court Act 1981.

Suggested solution

Public interest immunity is a principle of the law of evidence which enables relevant evidence to be excluded. The exclusion of such evidence means, of course, that the tribunal of fact is less able to make an informed decision about the case before it. The justification in the case of public interest immunity is that the interests of justice in the case are outweighed by the public interest in withholding the information. To the extent that relevant facts withheld may result in a different complexion being put on the facts adduced, the truth is obscured.

With public interest immunity, this withholding process and thus, deploying the reasoning above, the obscuring of the truth, is carried out in accordance with criteria which are not always easy to apply.

The analysis of the way in which these criteria affect the decision to exclude is best started by considering *Duncan* v *Cammell Laird* (1942) and *Conway* v *Rimmer* (1968). The former case is the basis for the principle that a claim for public interest immunity should proceed on the consideration of whether it is a contents or class claim. The first type of claim is reserved for most sensitive documents whose contents, if disclosed, would in the opinion of the Minister or other head of the organisation claiming it, be gravely prejudicial to the interests of the State. A class claim is appropriate where the document is not itself highly sensitive, but is the sort of communication which the

Minister or other head considers ought not be disclosed, normally because such a practice would inhibit frank discussion by the authors of such documents.

Duncan v *Cammell Laird* decided that a Ministerial certificate on either type of claim was conclusive, and that the courts had no power to look into the claim. *Conway* v *Rimmer* is noteworthy in having found that the courts do have a residual discretion to consider the claim of public interest immunity (so the certificate is not conclusive), and that for class claims on routine documents, the 'candour' argument for applying the immunity should not in future prevail.

In general for contents claims, the principle being applied continues to be that confidentiality should be upheld at the suit of the applicant Minister in the public interest without question. For class claims, the court will be prepared to investigate the merits of the contention, although it must first be established that the disclosure really is necessary for disposing fairly of the case. The court will therefore be prepared to inspect and decide on a balance between the competing interests of disclosure and non disclosure. Candour will not be influential as a reason for resisting disclosure. There are different degrees of sensitivity in the 'class' description, and Lord Reid in *Conway* v *Rimmer* indicated that certain high grade documents such as Cabinet minutes should never be disclosed. Lord Keith in *Burmah Oil* v *Bank of England* (1980) said, however, that this went too far, a sentiment echoed in *Air Canada* v *Secretary of State for Trade and Industry* (1983).

But the criterion of confidentiality for routine documents is still upheld in certain areas, where the judgment is that a greater public good is served by withholding information. First, there are organisations working for the public interest which depend on information from the public to do their work and where information would dry up if disclosure arose; second, there are police informers for whom confidentiality is a prerequisite for their operation; third, there is the protection of journalistic information, recognising the value which is put on the ability of journalists to expose misdeeds or scandal without having to name sources, thus facilitating flow of information from people who might otherwise be uncommunicative.

D v *NSPCC* (1978) provides a leading example of the first situation. The court refused to compel disclosure of the identity of a complainant to the NSPCC, sought by the aggrieved parent against whom the complaint had been made, on the basis that if such disclosure were allowed, the sources of information on which the NSPCC relied would dry up. The leading case in the second category is *Marks* v *Beyfus* (1890). The police were, it was held, entitled to withhold the identity of a police informer on the basis that such an informer would only operate if confidence were maintained. This demonstrates the importance placed on the availability of informer evidence in criminal trials. The interests of justice in disclosure can outweigh it - where the information is necessary for an accused to present his defence properly (a recent case in point being *R* v *Agar* (1990)), but this requirement is strictly applied. Indeed, the immunity shows signs of extension - for example, in *R* v *Rankine* (1986) to prevent disclosure of premises from which police observations had been made, on the basis that people would tend not to allow the police to use premises if their identity were disclosed, thus risking retribution.

The last category - journalistic information - is now governed by s10 of the Contempt of Court 1981. Under the section, disclosure may be resisted unless disclosure is necessary in the interests of justice, on grounds of national security or the prevention of disorder or crime.

So far as the interests of justice are concerned, the assessment must take into account whether the general public really have an interest in ensuring confidentiality, or whether the requirement is only to protect the personal interest of certain individuals, a point emphasised in *Re Goodwin* (1989). But, where journalistic 'privilege' is applied under s10, a prospective plaintiff can find himself denied a remedy if he cannot otherwise establish the identity of the informant against whom he wishes to initiate civil proceedings.

The conclusion to be drawn from the analysis of the way in which public immunity interest operates is that the decision on withholding relevant evidence does not proceed on the basis of the supremacy of ascertaining the true facts. It is true that the reassessment of 'class' claims indicates recognition of the importance of putting all relevant information before the Court, as the above discussion shows. The final arbiter is, however, the public interest in withholding information in recognition of the fact that this interest must outweigh the interests of litigants where the occasion demands.

Question 4

'It is not only the adduction of *prima facie* evidence by the proponent which results in an evidential burden being cast on the opponent. The same effect may result from the operation of a presumption.' (Phipson and Elliot).

Discuss. To what extent do you agree that the operation of presumptions is based more on considerations of public policy than of logic?

University of London LLB Examination
(for External Students) Evidence June 1991 Q4

General comment

This rather long question requires a treatment in outline of the role of evidential burden under the general law and (as the main part of the answer) the effects of common law presumptions on the burden. The latter is best dealt with by reference to the principal rebuttable presumptions of law.

Skeleton solution

- Role of the evidential burden under the general law with particular reference to common law defences; distinction of tactical or provisional burden.
- Effect of presumptions - res ipsa loquitur; death; legitimacy; marriage. The relationship in criminal trials with the *Woolmington* principle; the diffuseness of the language used to describe the evidential effects of presumptions and the variations of approach in the case law.

Suggested solution

A party wishing to establish his case to the requisite standard of proof in civil or criminal proceedings has two hurdles to surmount. He must first ensure that the tribunal of fact considers his story. He must then ensure that the jury act on it in his favour. The second is the discharge of the burden of proof on the party. The first is the discharge of the evidential burden - sufficient evidence to make the party's case a live issue. Sufficient in other words, for the tribunal of fact to consider his story at all.

Clearly, if a party has to discharge the burden of proof, he must get his contentions considered by the tribunal of fact in the first place. The party having the legal burden also generally has the evidential burden. To this extent, therefore, the evidential burden is of little consequence. There are, however, cases where the evidential burden can be critical. Common law defences are a case in point. The prosecution have the legal burden to establish an accused's guilt, but before a jury is entitled to consider an accused's defence of provocation (*Mancini* v *DPP* (1942)), duress (*R* v *Gill* (1963)), self-defence (*R* v *Lobell* (1957)) and, probably, accident (*Bratty* v *Attorney General for Northern Ireland* (1963)) and alibi (*R* v *Johnson* (1961)). The evidential burden must be discharged by the accused before the jury will be entitled to consider the defence. Indeed, it would appear that any defence which is more than the denial of an essential element of the prosecution's case is subject to such a burden.

But the fact that one party puts up a case which, in the absence of contradictory evidence, he may win does not result in an evidential burden being placed on that party, unless the term is being used as a description of the need by that opponent to produce factual controverting evidence, or to neutralise the evidence by cross-examination, or lose the case. It is submitted that this is not the meaning properly ascribed to the term evidential burden in its technical sense. The requirement for an opponent to meet unfavourable evidence is sometimes called a 'tactical' or 'provisional' burden and this is a source of confusion. It is not an evidential burden.

The field of presumptions does however provide examples for which the quotation in the question is apt. These presumptions have the effect of establishing certain facts ('the presumed facts') once other facts ('the basic facts') are proved. For the purposes of discussion, the presumptions of res ipsa loquitur, death, legitimacy and marriage will be examined.

Res ipsa loquitur applies only to civil proceedings. If a state of affairs is under control of a party and an accident occurs which would not in the ordinary course of events happen in the absence of negligence, then negligence will be presumed. The evidential effect is not entirely settled, and there are cases indicating that it is really no more than a label for circumstantial evidence - or a presumption of fact (*Langham* v *Governors of Wellingborough School* (1932)). *The Kite* (1933) indicates that it is a rebuttable presumption of law casting an evidential burden on the opposing party. On the other hand, the presumption casts the legal burden on the party against whom it operates, according to *Barkway* v *South Wales Transport Executive* (1949). The most recent pronouncement from the Privy Council in *Ng Chun Pui* v *Lee Chuen Tat* (1988) follows the proposition that the maxim casts an evidential burden on the opposing party.

Under the presumption of death, the fact of death is presumed on proof of an absence of seven years or more, nothing having been heard of the absentee by persons who might have heard of him, due enquiries having been made. It is apparent from the decision of the House of Lords in *Prudential* v *Edmonds* (1877) that this presumption operates to cast an evidential burden on the party against whom it operates.

The presumption of legitimacy is less straightforward in that it is overlaid by statute, and also reveals the need to consider the position in civil and criminal cases separately.

At common law, the presumed fact - legitimacy - was established by proof of the basic facts of birth or conception in lawful wedlock. The effect of the presumption according to *Morris* v *Davies* (1837) was to place the legal burden (and not just an evidential burden) on the opposing party. Clearly, the former requirement is the important one, since to discharge the legal burden, the party must discharge the evidential burden on that issue.

But in criminal trials, the placing of the legal burden on an accused would appear to conflict with the *Woolmington* (1935) principle. The exceptions under that rule (insanity raised by defence and statutory exceptions) clearly exclude presumptions. Thus, it might be that the presumption of legitimacy if deployed by the prosecution has the maximum effect of placing an evidential burden on the accused.

Finally, with the presumption of marriage, there are three different situations to consider, formal validity, essential validity and presumption of marriage by cohabitation and repute. A marriage proved to have complied with the necessary formalities of local law is presumed to be formally valid. Likewise, the parties are presumed to have had the capacity to enter into the marriage. *Piers* v *Piers* (1849) applied *Morris* v *Davies* from which it is apparent that the evidential effect was to put the legal burden on the party against whom the presumption operated in civil trials. Essential validity is more ambiguous. *Tweny* v *Tweny* (1946) indicates that the effect is to place evidential burden on the party against whom the presumption operates, though it hardly seems very sensible to invest in two related aspects of the same presumption with different evidential effects.

On the third aspect of the presumption, a cohabiting couple reputed in the community to have been married are taken at common law to have been through a valid marriage ceremony at some time in the past. *Sastry* v *Sambecutty* (1881) is authority for the view that this places the legal burden on the opposing party, although, as with the other aspects of the presumption, the language is less than clear. This aspect, together with formal validity, must be subject to the proviso that in criminal trials, the maximum effect of the presumption when relied on by the prosecution is to place an evidential burden on the accused, for the *Woolmington* principle is otherwise infringed.

There is little doubt that public policy has played a significant part in development of presumptions. The sanctity of marriage and the stigma of illegitimacy were influential in establishing their evidential effects. It is also true that notwithstanding efforts to provide a coherent strategy for analysis of those evidential effects, satisfactory classification of them is still elusive. This is apparent from the above discussion, demonstrating, for example, seemingly different evidential effects for different aspects of the same presumption, and divergence in judicial views of the effects of the same presumption.

One explanation for this elusiveness is that they were developed to satisfy policy concerns rather than legal principle. If that is the case, establishing a coherent legal framework for the operation of presumptions may not be capable of achievement.

Question 5

A is suing B Jewellers Ltd for the loss of two rubies from a ring which A handed in to them for restyling. B Jewellers Ltd are relying on an exemption clause contained in the contract exempting them from accidental loss. A possesses a written valuation of the ring from X Valuers Ltd, dated ten years earlier, in which it is stated that the ring is worth £10,000. Unfortunately, X Valuers Ltd since went into liquidation and the valuer cannot be traced. A has also obtained a photocopy of an internal memorandum at B Jewellers Ltd which implicates C, an employee, in the theft of precious stones from jewellery handed in by customers. This memorandum had been forwarded to the company's solicitors who have refused to release it. A has further obtained a copy of an entry in the books of D Pawnbrokers Ltd which shows that C had pledged two rubies as security for a loan. The entries show that the carat weight and the refractive index of the rubies as determined by the firm's computer tally with the weight and index of A's jewels.

Advise A on the admissibility of these items as evidence and the standard of proof applicable to the assertion that C stole the rubies.

University of London LLB Examination
(for External Students) Evidence June 1991 Q5

General comment

The question requires a knowledge of the Civil Evidence Acts 1968 and 1972 and also character evidence, legal professional privilege and standard of proof. The points to be addressed are however fairly well compartmented and provide a framework for answering the question.

Skeleton solution

- Status of opinion evidence - application of the Civil Evidence Act 1968 by the Act of 1972.
- Notice procedure.
- Admissibility of evidence under s9 of the 1968 Act.
- Evidence of character.
- Legal professional privilege - lawyer/client/third party.
- Use of copies of privileged document - *Calcraft* v *Guest* and subsequent cases.
- Discretion to exclude evidence in civil trials.
- Admissibility of hearsay and non hearsay computer evidence, the principle in *Hornal* v *Neuberger Products.*

Suggested solution

Issues bearing on the admissibility of the evidence are dealt with in the order in which they arise in the question.

The valuation

The fact that it is 10 years old goes to the weight to be attached to it, and not to its admissibility. It is however produced as evidence of the opinion stated on it. As it is not being given by the valuer in court, it is hearsay and to be admitted must satisfy the Civil Evidence Act 1968, applied to statements of opinion by the Civil Evidence Act 1972. It must also be established to the court's satisfaction that the valuer can properly give evidence of opinion, that is, he is an expert. This is assumed to be the case from the facts given. Assuming the valuation is not agreed, s2 or s4 of the 1968 Act must be satisfied. As the written statement is of the valuer who could give first hand evidence of it in court, it is a first hand hearsay statement, and s2 applies. Before it is admitted the notice procedure must however be complied with. This is somewhat different for experts as compared with ordinary witnesses and requires directions from a judge for which A should apply. The judge is entitled to impose the conditions applicable to ordinary witnesses - ie that in the absence of agreement the valuation may not be adduced as of right unless one of the statutory grounds exists. The valuer cannot be traced, which fits the ground 'cannot be found' in s8 and reflected in RSC O.38, r25.

One further point remains, which is proof of the valuation as a document. If its authenticity is contended, A must establish it, which can be done in any manner authorised by the court under s6 of the 1968 Act.

The internal memorandum

The value of this to A is to establish B Jewellers' culpability through the employee. Its production will therefore be subject to the hearsay rule and its admissibility governed by the Civil Evidence Act 1968.

Since the statement is self incriminatory, A can take advantage of s9 of the 1968 Act which preserves certain common law exceptions to the hearsay rule, one of which is admissions. The notice provisions of s8/RSC O.38 do not apply to s9, and admissions such as this are therefore admissible as of right.

It is possible however that A will face arguments that s9 is not applicable, because it is not self incriminating of B Jewellers, having been made (presumably) by an employee about another employee. This raises a difficult question on vicarious admissions. An answer cannot be given from the facts given, but if A is unsuccessful in contending admissibility under s9, an alternative approach is for him to use s2 or s4 of the 1968 Act. It is not clear that the statement is first hand hearsay (that is, the writer has personal knowledge). If it is not, A should pass over s2 in favour of s4, and contend that the memorandum is a record (an original source as in *H* v *Schering Chemicals* (1983)) compiled by a person acting under a duty (the employee who can be said to be under a duty to report such things) from information of which he had personal knowledge or indirectly from others acting under a duty who transmitted it to him, the originator, having first hand knowledge. Assuming these conditions are met, A must also issue a notice (RSC O.38 r21) and if B Jewellers issues a counter notice, (RSC O.38 r26), A must establish one of the statutory reasons for not calling the valuer. However, since calling the witness will require evidence to be given by an employee of B Jewellers, ie the defendant, A can claim the statement should be admitted in the exercise of judicial discretion even if the rules are not complied with (RSC O.38 r29).

Two further points arise. B Jewellers may contend that as the memorandum discloses a disposition to criminal conduct by an employee, imputed to them, it amounts to general *character* evidence and is therefore inadmissible. A's counter to this allegation should be that the evidence has probative value which brings it within the 'similar fact' rule, allowing such evidence to be admitted at common law. A should contend that prejudicial effect is outweighed by its probative value on the basis of the improbability of coincidence. The striking similarity test of *DPP* v *Boardman* (1975) is only a label and it is positive probative value that the law requires (*R* v *Scarrott* (1978); *R* v *P* (1991)).

The third aspect which A will have to meet is that of legal professional privilege. On the basis that the internal memorandum can be taken as a communication of B Jewellers with their solicitors, the privilege will apply, since a legal relationship evidently existed between them and the purpose of sending the information was presumably relative to the securing of legal advice. On the other hand, it is possible for A to argue that the memorandum was a pre-existing document which has not become privileged simply because it was subsequently sent to the solicitors (*Ventouris* v *Mountain* (1991)). Further, A can contend that unless written by a very senior officer of the jewellers, it is a communication between lawyer, client and third party as to which privilege will only apply if the dominant purpose of the production of the memorandum was submission to lawyers in connection with actual or contemplated litigation; *Waugh* v *British Railways Board* (1980). If for whatever reason, legal professional privilege applies, A can nevertheless use the copy in his possession, under the principle in *Calcraft* v *Guest* (1898). He must establish authenticity if contended by B. B will also, however, be entitled to seek a pre-trial injunction: *Ashburton* v *Pape* (1913). But the injunctive relief can be resisted if A neither came by the copy by underhand means, nor received it as a result of an obvious mistake by B Jewellers or their advisers: *Goddard* v *Nationwide* (1986); *Guinness Peat* v *Fitzroy Robinson* (1987).

The admissibility of the copy entry in the books of D Pawnbrokers will not depend on the way A obtained it, even if that was improperly. The courts have no discretion to exclude evidence in civil trials on the basis of the way it was obtained: *Helliwell* v *Piggot-Sims* (1980). The entry is useful to A in showing disposal by an employee of rubies, and it is an implied assertion of that fact. Assuming, as is probable, that it is an implied assertion to which the hearsay rule applies, A will need to invoke s4 of the Civil Evidence Act 1968 (it is not clear whether the entry was made by the person who handled the transaction so s2 which requires first hand hearsay evidence may not be satisfied). The same comments as made for the memorandum (above) apply here.

It is not clear whether the entry as to carat weight and refractive index is produced directly, or copied from a computer printout. No hearsay point attaches to the fact that the calculations are not subject to oral evidence. They were prepared automatically as in *The Statue of Liberty* (1968). But in either case, the details are in essence 'a statement and document produced by a computer' and there is a need to satisfy s5 of the Civil Evidence Act 1968. The provisions are complicated, but essentially they require that the computer was doing its normal type of work, that it was in proper working order and was being used properly. This information can be supplied by certificate. Section 5 is silent on the requirement for personal knowledge on the part of the person supplying the information to a computer, but the fact that s4 is expressed to be 'without prejudice to section 5' whereas s2 is not, raises an assumption that if the information produced by the computer is dependent on what information the operator puts in (as opposed to a wholly automatic process not subject to the hearsay rule), then s2 will also apply and its provisions will need satisfying.

The authenticity of the copy must also be established. Under s6 of the 1968 Act, this can be done in any way approved by the court.

Finally, there is the question of the burden of proof. It now seems established that where a crime is alleged in civil proceedings, the standard of proof applicable is the civil standard of a balance of probabilities, that is, the allegation with regard to C is more probable than not: *Hornal* v *Neuberger Products* (1957). It has sometimes been suggested that there is a third or different standard applicable to serious allegations in civil trials (as here), but such suggestions are best treated on the basis that in deciding whether the scales have been tipped to satisfy the civil standard, the court has regard to the seriousness of the allegations.

Question 6

E and F are charged with indecent assault on G, aged 10. The assault is alleged to have taken place in a park near G's home. After the alleged incident G ran home crying and with her clothes torn. When questioned by her mother, H, G said that she had been attacked by two men. She described one man as tall with a black moustache and the other as thin with a mole on his chin. At a subsequent identification parade she picked out E, who is tall with a blonde moustache, and F, who is thin with a large mole on his cheek, as the men who attacked her. When challenged by Inspector L to account for themselves E claimed to have been at work at the time and F refused to say anything.

At the trial, G gives unsworn testimony describing the assault, but she is unable to identify her assailants. H gives evidence about G's statement and her physical condition at the time. Inspector L testifies that G picked out the defendants at an identification parade, and he describes their responses to his questions. F does not give evidence. E testifies that he is innocent but admits in cross-examination that he was not at work on the day in question.

Advise E and F.

University of London LLB Examination
(for External Students) Evidence June 1991 Q6

General comment

This requires a knowledge of the law of corroboration and various aspects of the law relating to the testimony of child witnesses and victims of sexual crimes. The general law of hearsay and its exceptions also call for discussion.

Skeleton solution

- Unsworn evidence under s38 of the Children and Young Persons Act 1933.
- Section 34 of the Criminal Justice Act 1988.
- The *Baskerville* criteria of corroboration.
- Complaints in sexual cases - *R* v *Osborne*.
- Lies as corroboration under *R* v *Lucas.*
- Application of hearsay to implied assertions.
- The exception of *R* v *Osbourne and Virtue.*
- Statements made to the police admissible under the *R* v *Storey*/*R* v *Tooke* principle.

Suggested solution

G gives unsworn testimony which he is entitled to do under s38(1) of the Children and Young Persons Act 1933. (Under provisions to be enacted in the Criminal Justice Act 1991, all children under 14 will give their evidence this way). Section 34 of the Criminal Justice Act 1988 abolished the mandatory requirement for corroboration in respect of such evidence, but because this is a sexual case, a mandatory corroboration warning (a warning by the judge to the jury that it is dangerous for them to convict in the absence of corroboration) will be necessary in respect of G's testimony. If E's defence amounts to his conceding that the offence occurred, but that he was not the perpetrator, then under the rule in *R* v *Chance* (1988) a *Turnbull* (1977) type warning referred to further below will be sufficient. It is, however, not clear from the facts given whether he makes this concession, and so this is not assumed.

As to the items of evidence which might corroborate G's evidence, in satisfying the *Baskerville* (1916) criteria, ie independent of but supporting G's testimony and implicating the accused, evidence of her distressed condition and torn clothes are unlikely to be corroborative. Distressed condition can exceptionally be corroborative (*R* v *Redpath* (1962)) but in this case, there is nothing to connect the evidence with the accused, unless the witness can give testimony of G's condition in the park and associate the accused with the location at the relevant time. Such association might be obtained by adding different items of evidence together, following the principle in *R* v *Hills* (1988), but on the facts, this does not seem possible.

The evidence of H as to what G said may be admissible, *R* v *Lillyman* (1896), provided it was not obtained from G by prompting (this is not clear from the facts) and that G made the statement at the first opportunity which reasonably presented itself (which seems to be the case) - *R* v *Osborne* (1905). But evidence will only go to G's consistency and will not be corroborative because it is not independent. The evidence may alternatively be received as part of the res gestae (see below), but if so, will likewise lack independence and will not therefore be corroborative. This is also true (assuming it is admissible - see below) of L's testimony as regards G. L's testimony as regards E does not support it, and so it is not corroborative, and nor is S's failure to say anything because he has a right to silence at common law (*R* v *Jackson* (1953)). E's testimony can, however, be treated as corroborative of what is said provided the lie he has told concerning L's whereabouts satisfies the test in *R* v *Lucas* (1981). The lie must be shown to be deliberate, relate to a material issue, be prompted by the acknowledgement of guilt by the accused, and be shown to be a lie by other evidence. There is insufficient information to decide on these points finally, though the facts given point to their being satisfied.

Apart from showing consistency, H's testimony can be received as evidence of the facts stated if there is an applicable exception to the hearsay rule. The rule will otherwise exclude it since H does not have personal knowledge of the facts. It may be within the res gestae criteria of *Ratten* v *R* (1972) and *R* v *Andrews* (1987). The satisfaction of these criteria depends primarily on whether G's mind was dominated by the event at the time the statement was made. Clearly, the time interval between them and the commission is relevant, and so is the fact that G's statement was the result of H's overtures.

L's testimony is open to objection because G's act in picking out E and F is assertive conduct which, as such, is subject to the hearsay rule (*Chandrasekera* v *R* (1937)). The prosecution will seek to rely on the implicit hearsay exception indicated by *R* v *Osbourne and Virtue* (1973). The limits and legitimacy of the case are not free from doubt, but if G gives evidence that an identification parade took place, the case is authority for the proposition that H could give evidence of the identification of E and F, if he was there at the time. Alternatively, if G stated who he was identifying at the time (for example, by reference to a number or letter held by each member of the parade), it would be possible to argue admissibility on the basis of res gestae - a statement accompanying a relevant act: *R* v *McCay* (1990).

The evidence of what E said, even though self-serving at the time, made it admissible under the *R* v *Storey* (1968) principle recently reaffirmed in *R* v *Tooke* (1989), being a statement made to police when taxed with incriminating facts. The evidential value is not entirely clear, but seems to be based on the inference which might be drawn from the accused's reaction, rather than as a straight exception to the hearsay rule. F's refusal to say anything is no evidence against him, although silence in the fact of an accusation can be subject to an adverse inference. In order for that to arise, however, the parties must be on even terms: *R* v *Mitchell* (1892). Since L is a police officer, this requirement is not met.

Question 7

M is charged with the murder of N, the lover of M's wife O, by running him down in the street. M has stated to the police that N unexpectedly stepped off the pavement into the path of his car and that a collision was unavoidable. Four days before his death, N wrote in his diary that he was afraid because M had become enraged about the affair with O and that he intended to 'watch over his shoulder' from now on. On the day N died, P, a passer-by, heard an unidentified woman at the scene of the accident say, pointing to M, 'That man went straight for him; he gave him no chance.' O has stated that M told her later on the same day that N had been involved in an accident, adding that 'he got what he deserved'. M proposes not to testify himself at his trial but seeks to adduce psychiatric evidence that P is schizophrenic and that he, M, has a timid personality and is unlikely to behave aggressively.

Advise the prosecution on any evidential issues arising.

University of London LLB Examination
(for External Students) Evidence June 1991 Q7

General comment

This question raises a number of issues relating to the application of the hearsay rule and its exceptions. Predominantly they concern res gestae. The admissibility of opinion evidence also features, and there is also a point on silence.

Skeleton solution

- Admissibility of evidence as an exception to the hearsay rule under res gestae as a contemporaneous state of mind. Scope of the exception; possible use of the Criminal Justice Act 1988 s23. Res gestae exception to the hearsay rule exemplified by *Ratten* v *R* and *R* v *Andrews* - scope of the exception.
- Application of the hearsay rule to implied insertions; illustrative case law. Comparison of hearsay and original evidence and relevance of the latter to the facts in question. Evidential value of silence.
- Admissibility of expert opinion evidence in state of mind cases; exemplification by reference to *R* v *Chard* and subsequent cases, and *Lowery* v *R*.

Suggested solution

The diary entry must first be proved as a document if it is to be produced. This can be achieved by the production of the original document and the calling of evidence identifying the handwriting of N. The original is available and so poses no difficulty. As long as the prosecution have a witness who knows N's handwriting (or there is material to compare and on which a handwriting expert can give evidence under the Criminal Procedure Act 1865 s8), the second requirement should present no difficulty either.

As to the uses to which the entry can be put, N's statement that he was afraid and intended to watch over his shoulder is receivable as evidence of that fact as an exception to the hearsay rule which would otherwise be infringed, since M is not giving evidence. The exception is that of res gestae - showing a contemporaneous mental state four days before the event. The jury is entitled to find that state of mind continued to the time of the event, its being circumstantial evidence of N's state of mind then. The res gestae exception does not however extend to the cause of the state of mind, even if it explains it. The evidence of the affair with O, and M's rage, will not be receivable under this head. The evidence is, however, relevant as it goes to motive. It is possible for the prosecution to argue that M's reaction is receivable under s23 Criminal Justice Act, being a first hand hearsay statement in a document, the writer, now dead, having personal knowledge of that reaction. Such reception is subject to a discretion to exclude in the interests of justice under s25 of the Criminal Justice Act 1988, though the fact that M might have to counter the allegation by giving evidence himself will not necessarily mean that the statement is excluded (*R* v *Cole* (1990)). The evidence as to the reason (the affair) would be receivable as original evidence explaining M's reactions.

P's testimony that a woman pointed and said M went straight for him is hearsay because P does not have personal knowledge of the facts stated, and the pointing is an implied assertion within the rule, *Chandrasekera* v *R* (1937). It will therefore be inadmissible unless an exception to the hearsay rule applies. The prosecution can argue that the res gestae exception is applicable. Statements made in circumstances of such spontaneity or involvement in the events concerned, that the possibility of concoction or distortion can be disregarded, are admissible (Lord Wilberforce in *Ratten* v *R* (1972)), an approach upheld by the House of Lords in *R* v *Andrews* (1987). In this case, the woman was at the scene of the crime, and on the assumption she was an eyewitness who made her statement at or shortly after the event, when it was still dominating her mind, the test appears satisfied. It is submitted that there are no 'special features' within *R* v *Andrews* having a bearing on admissibility, although the circumstances of the identification by P of M as the person pointed out by the woman will be relevant to the weight to be attached to the evidence by the jury and may be a case in which judge gives them a *Turnbull* (1977) type warning in respect of its potential weakness, inviting them to consider carefully the circumstances in which it was made. The defence could counter that this evidence amounts to a 'special feature' relative to the issue of error which goes to admissibility rather than weight, and may draw on support from certain passages in *Andrews* to support this claim.

The prosecution will not be able to use the evidence that the woman said N was given no chance. This is evidence of opinion and as such inadmissible because at common law witnesses must give evidence only of fact. There are some exceptions to this rule, most notably evidence given by experts, but none seems applicable here.

O's evidence.

As evidence implicating N by both suggesting his presence at the scene of crime and that he may have been responsible for it, the prosecution's case is assisted. Taken as an implied assertion of those facts, it is likely that the defence will argue that it is hearsay (not being O's personal knowledge) and therefore inadmissible.

The prosecution can answer this in three alternative ways. First, they can contend that M's statement is an implied assertion outside the hearsay rule. Cases such as *Woodhouse* v *Hall* (1980), and more recently *R* v *Harry* (1988), can be taken as supporting the view that statements not intended to be assertive of the facts they are tendered to prove to fall outside the rule. But this is an uncertain area and the prospects for success on this line cannot be guaranteed.

The second available contention is that even if O's testimony is hearsay, it is nevertheless admissible because an exception to the rule applies by reason of s76 of the Police and Criminal Evidence Act 1984. Clearly, M's statement is against his interest and therefore a confession within the definition in s82 and, subject to s76(2), admissible under s76(1).

The grounds for exclusion under s76(2) (a confession obtained by oppression or in consequence of anything said or done which in the circumstances existing at the time was likely to render any confession unreliable) do not arise because M clearly made this statement voluntarily to O.

The third argument is that M's statement is produced to show M's knowledge rather than the truth of the facts stated, and as such is receivable as original evidence. On this basis, no hearsay problem arises. It is, however, doubtful whether the prosecution will succeed in this submission. In *R* v *Blastland* (1986) such an argument was rejected on the basis that the real purpose was to rely inferentially on the facts stated by the witness, and that the hearsay rule therefore applied.

Finally, the prosecution should bear in mind that O is M's wife. She is a competent witness for the prosecution under s80(1) of the Police and Criminal Evidence Act, but because M's offence does not fall within those described in s80(3), she is not compellable for the prosecution. If, therefore, O refuses to testify, the prosecution cannot oblige her to.

M's failure to testify cannot be used against him by the prosecution, and the judge's direction to the jury must not infer guilt from that failure: *R* v *Bathurst* (1968); *R* v *Sparrow* (1973). M is entitled to impugn the credibility of an opposing witness at common law, and this may be used as the reason for bringing medical evidence that the witness suffers from a condition which undermines his reliability: *Toohey* v *MPC* (1965).

The prosecution can however challenge M's right to bring psychiatric evidence about his own mental state. The cases are not easy to reconcile and there have been instances, notably *Lowery* v *R* (1974), where such evidence has been admitted. The balance of the authorities supported by *R* v *Chard* (1971), *R* v *Masih* (1986) and *R* v *Reynolds* (1989) leans heavily towards the view that to be admissible, the evidence must be tendered to establish mental illness, rather than a mere personality trait. The underlying principle being deployed is that expert opinion evidence is received on the basis that the matter is outside the experience of the average jury. The jury is able to assess the contentions about personality falling short of mental illness. The prosecution are therefore in a strong position to contend admissibility because the evidence adduced about M does not seek to establish mental illness or a condition which the jury could not establish for themselves.

Question 8

Q is charged with burglary and R with handling stolen goods. The prosecution allege that Q induced S to let him into S's house by stating falsely that his car had broken down, and that once inside he stole S's jewellery when her back was turned. The jewellery was later found on sale in R's shop. Q and R make statements to the police. Q claims that his car had broken down and he denies taking the jewellery. R claims that he bought the jewellery in good faith from a stranger and says that he will call witnesses who will testify to his integrity. The prosecution seek to adduce the following evidence:

a) Seven years earlier Q was convicted of theft of money from a householder to whom he had stated falsely that he had come to read the gas meter.

b) During a search of Q's flat after P reported her loss, the police found a set of skeleton keys and a letter to Q from the receiver of stolen goods, now dead, advising on how to dispose of stolen jewellery.

c) R has twice been dismissed from employment in jewellers' shops after rumours that he was buying stolen jewellery. His neighbour is prepared to testify that he would not trust R an inch.

Advise the prosecution.

University of London LLB Examination
(for External Students) Evidence June 1991 Q8

General comment

The predominant issue in this question concerns the admissibility of character evidence. A fairly detailed knowledge of the similar fact principles is required, although part (c) of the question essentially concerns the common law exemplified by *R* v *Rowton.*

Skeleton solution

a) The common law prohibition of reception of character evidence and the similar fact exception; tests for establishing application of the exception - striking similarity and positive prohibitive value.

b) Availability of the exception referable to surrounding circumstances of an offence as opposed to the mode of its commission. Hearsay evidence and applicable exception under s23 of the Criminal Justice Act 1988. Original evidence.

c) Common law principle exemplified by *R* v *Rowton*; extent of the rule with particular reference to limitation to general reputation applicable to both defence and prosecution.

Suggested solution

a) There is a general common law prohibition on the reception of character evidence to show guilt on a subsequent charge. An exception to this prohibition is the similar fact principle. Under this principle, character evidence is admissible to show guilt as to the crime charged when legally relevant, that is positively probative - *Makin* v *Attorney-General for New South Wales* (1894); *R* v *Scarrott* (1978). In a case such as this, deciding on positive probative value rests on whether the previous offence is strikingly similar to the one under investigation - *DPP* v *Boardman* (1975). It appears that similarity can be assessed from similarity of surrounding circumstances as well as the 'basic facts' of the offence - *R* v *Johannsen* (1977); *R* v *Barrington*

(1981), distinguishing *R* v *Novac* (1976) - but even so, the similarity in the circumstances must be 'striking'. It is questionable whether this is so here. In addition, there is a question of whether it is proper to refer to conviction as much as seven years old. This will depend on the sentence imposed for the theft. Although the Rehabilitation of Offenders Act 1974 does not apply to criminal proceedings, it is a rule of practice that a 'spent' conviction will not be referred to in front of the jury.

b) As from the facts given, there is nothing to connect the material with the instant case; it amounts to character evidence and is caught by the general common law rule against the prosecution's giving such evidence. The prosecution can however argue that the evidence can be adduced under the exception to the rule provided by the 'similar fact' principle.

The items found by the police do not establish the actual commission of an offence on a prior occasion. There have been cases, such as *R* v *Tricoglus* (1976), indicating that this is required for admission under the 'similar fact' principle. The alternative view, which the prosecution should contend, is represented by *R* v *Barrington* to the effect that misconduct is sufficient to allow reception under the principle.

This is not a similarity situation, and so establishing the requisite positive probative value for admission will not be undertaken on the basis of the striking similarity test. Instead, the basis will be the improbability of coincidence. The prosecution should contend that it is too much of a coincidence the man they allege to have committed this theft is a man who happens to have items at his home consistent with the commission of such a crime.

It is, however, far from certain that the prosecution submission will succeed, because although the letter refers to jewellery, and jewellery is allegedly stolen by Q, commission of the present crime did not involve skeleton keys, and disposal of stolen goods will be of interest to any thief. Thefts are widespread, and in the absence of any greater nexus between the items found and the offence charged, the defence may successfully contend that the improbability of coincidence is not that great for so common a crime.

It is not suggested that the reference to the jewellery is the jewellery subject of the present proceedings, and is assumed not to be. The fact that the writer is dead will not make the letter inadmissible as hearsay. The purpose of the prosecution's adducing the letter is to show that Q has an interest in information about disposing of stolen goods, and is thus a thief, and not to establish the truth of what was said by the writer. It is original evidence. If it were suggested that the jewellery referred to was the jewellery subject of the present proceedings, the statement in the letter could be treated as an implied assertion that Q was the thief, and it may well be that the hearsay rule would be found to apply. The scope of the hearsay rule to implied assertions is unclear. If it were taken to be within the rule, then the letter would be inadmissible as evidence of the facts inferred, subject to any available exception to the rule. Section 23 of the Criminal Justice Act 1988 (first hand documentary hearsay) may be a possibility, but more information is needed before the prosecution can be advised fully on this point.

c) The evidence of R's character, like Q's, is inadmissible by reason of the common law prohibition unless an exception applies. Here the prosecution can argue an exception applies because R intends to call witnesses establishing his integrity. On the assumption that this will be received as general reputation it will be admissible under the *R* v *Rowton* (1865) principle. The prosecution will then be able to counter-attack with evidence of R's bad character, though this must, likewise, be evidence of general reputation and not specific acts or opinions of character. The prosecution's evidence is not in this form, and as such will not be admissible. The prosecution should instead seek to adduce evidence of R's general reputation, either from the neighbour if he is able to give it in that form, or from another witness if available.

ORDER FORM

LLB PUBLICATIONS	TEXTBOOKS		CASEBOOKS		REVISION WORKBOOKS		SUG. SOL. 1985/90		SUG. SOL. 1991	
	Cost £	£	Cost £	£	Cost £	£	Cost £	£	Cost £	£
Administrative Law	17.95		18.95				9.95		3.00	
Commercial Law Vol I	18.95		18.95		9.95		9.95		3.00	
Commercial Law Vol II	17.95		18.95							
Company Law	18.95		18.95		9.95		9.95		3.00	
Conflict of Laws	16.95		17.95							
Constitutional Law	14.95		16.95		9.95		9.95		3.00	
Contract Law	14.95		16.95		9.95		9.95		3.00	
Conveyancing	17.95		16.95							
Criminal Law	14.95		17.95		9.95		9.95		3.00	
Criminology	16.95						+3.00		3.00	
English Legal System	14.95		12.95				*7.95		3.00	
Equity and Trusts	14.95		16.95		9.95		9.95		3.00	
European Community Law	17.95		18.95		9.95		+3.00		3.00	
Evidence	17.95		17.95		9.95		9.95		3.00	
Family Law	17.95		18.95		9.95		9.95		3.00	
Jurisprudence	14.95				9.95		9.95		3.00	
Labour Law	15.95									
Land Law	14.95		16.95		9.95		9.95		3.00	
Public International Law	18.95		17.95		9.95		9.95		3.00	
Revenue Law	17.95		18.95		9.95		9.95		3.00	
Roman Law	14.95									
Succession	17.95		17.95		9.95		9.95		3.00	
Tort	14.95		16.95		9.95		9.95		3.00	

BAR PUBLICATIONS										
Conflict of Laws	16.95		17.95				†7.95		3.95	
European Community Law & Human Rights	17.95		18.95				†7.95		3.95	
Evidence	17.95		17.95				14.95		3.95	
Family Law	17.95		18.95				14.95		3.95	
General Paper I	19.95		16.95				14.95		3.95	
General Paper II	19.95		16.95				14.95		3.95	
Law of International Trade	17.95		16.95				14.95		3.95	
Practical Conveyancing	17.95		16.95				14.95		3.95	
Procedure	19.95		16.95				14.95		3.95	
Revenue Law	17.95		18.95				14.95		3.95	
Sale of Goods and Credit	17.95		17.95				14.95		3.95	

* 1987–1990 papers only
† 1988–1990 papers only
+ 1990 paper only

HLT PUBLICATIONS

All HLT Publications have two important qualities. First, they are written by specialists, all of whom have direct practical experience of teaching the syllabus. Second, all Textbooks are reviewed and updated each year to reflect new developments and changing trends. They are used widely by students at polytechnics and colleges throughout the United Kingdom and overseas.

A comprehensive range of titles is covered by the following classifications.

- **TEXTBOOKS**
- **CASEBOOKS**
- **SUGGESTED SOLUTIONS**
- **REVISION WORKBOOKS**

The books listed above should be available from your local bookshop. In case of difficulty, however, they can be obtained direct from the publisher using this order form. Telephone, Fax or Telex orders will also be accepted. Quote your Access, Visa or American Express card numbers for priority orders. To order direct from publisher please enter cost of titles you require, fill in despatch details overleaf and send it with your remittance to The HLT Group Ltd.

cut along dotted line

DETAILS FOR DESPATCH OF PUBLICATIONS

Please insert your full name below

Please insert below the style in which you would like the correspondence from the Publisher addressed to you

TITLE Mr, Miss etc.	INITIALS	SURNAME/FAMILY NAME

Address to which study material is to be sent (please ensure someone will be present to accept delivery of your Publications).

POSTAGE & PACKING
You are welcome to purchase study material from the Publisher at 200 Greyhound Road, London W14 9RY, during normal working hours.

If you wish to order by post this may be done direct from the Publisher. Postal charges are as follows:

UK - Orders over £30: no charge. Orders below £30: £2.50. Single paper (last exam only): 50p
OVERSEAS - See table below

The Publisher cannot accept responsibility in respect of postal delays or losses in the postal systems.

DESPATCH All cheques must be cleared before material is despatched.

SUMMARY OF ORDER

Date of order:

				£
			Cost of publications ordered:	
			UNITED KINGDOM:	
OVERSEAS:	TEXTS		Suggested Solutions (Last exam only)	
	One	Each Extra		
Eire	£4.00	£0.60	£1.00	
European Community	£9.00	£1.00	£1.00	
East Europe & North America	£10.50	£1.00	£1.00	
South East Asia	£12.00	£2.00	£1.50	
Australia/New Zealand	£13.50	£4.00	£1.50	
Other Countries (Africa, India etc)	£13.00	£3.00	£1.50	
			Total cost of order:	

Please ensure that you enclose a cheque or draft payable to THE HLT GROUP LTD for the above amount, or charge to ❑ Access ❑ Visa ❑ American Express

Card Number

Expiry Date .... Signature ....